The EARTH-BOUND BOUND COOK

The EARTH-BOUND COOK

250 Recipes for Delicious Food *and* A Healthy Planet

BY MYRA GOODMAN

WITH PAMELA McKINSTRY, SARAH LaCASSE, AND RONNI SWEET

Recipe photography by Miki Duisterhof and Patrick Tregenza

WORKMAN PUBLISHING • NEW YORK

Library of Congress Cataloging-in-Publication Data is available.
ISBN 978-0-7611-5634-5 (pb); ISBN 978-0-7611-5920-9 (hc)

Cover and book design by Janet Vicario
Front cover photograph by Scott Campbell (author) and Greig Cranna (farm)
Back cover photographs by Miki Duisterhof (recipes) and Alli Pura (Farm Stand)
Recipe photographs by Miki Duisterhof and Patrick Tregenza
Additional photography credits on page 460.

Workman books are available at special discounts when purchased in bulk for premiums
and sales promotions as well as for fund-raising or educational use. Special editions or book
excerpts can also be created to specification. For details, contact the Special Sales Director at
the address below or send an e-mail to specialmarkets@workman.com.

WORKMAN PUBLISHING COMPANY, INC.
225 Varick Street
New York, NY 10014-4381

Printed in the U.S.A.
The Earthbound Cook is printed on recycled paper with soy-based inks.
First printing, July 2010
10 9 8 7 6 5 4 3 2 1

Dedication

For Jeffrey, Marea, and Drew

And to Laura and Joe,
on the occasion of their marriage

Acknowledgments

This book is the result of a collaboration between me and two wonderful chefs, Pamela McKinstry and Sarah LaCasse, and Ronni Sweet, a gifted and insightful writer. Pam and Sarah each contributed signature recipes they had developed over decades of cooking, and they helped create new dishes with me just for this book. Ronni researched the majority of the eco-facts, and she helped immeasurably in putting my ideas and stories into words. This book wouldn't have been possible without their creativity, dedication, patience, and hard work, and I am extremely grateful for such a wonderful team.

I am incredibly thankful to my wonderful family for their support, good humor, and enthusiasm for this project—I can't imagine having done this without them. My husband, Drew, is gifted with an amazing palate that can detect even the most subtle spices and flavors, and he made countless essential suggestions during months of almost daily trials that helped perfect our recipes. He also supported me tremendously by reading every single word in this book and making dozens of helpful suggestions on everything from recipe directions to eco-sidebars. He has my deep admiration and gratitude. This project would have been overwhelming without our teenage son, Jeffrey, and his athlete's appetite, which was much appreciated with so much food around all the time. And our daughter, Marea, a huge food enthusiast, who spent her summer weeks at home from college tasting, testing, and fine-tuning many recipes with me.

Thanks to Suzanne Rafer, my wise and wonderful editor. The chance to work with her again was one of the reasons I wanted to write a second book. And thank you to the brilliant and bold Peter Workman, who honored me, yet again, by having his company publish this book. My appreciation also goes to my agent, Angela Miller, and to the great team at Workman, who put their time and talent into this book: Janet Vicario, art director; Amy Trombat, layout designer; Anne Kerman, photography director; and Danielle Hark in the photography department. I also want to thank Kathie Ness, Carol White, Erin Klabunde, and Barbara Peragine, for their help in getting the book in editorial shape, as well as Selina Meere and Ron Longe, my publicists, and the people in the sales department, who make sure the book gets out into the world.

Thanks to the fabulous photographers who contributed to this book: Miki Duisterhof, Patrick Tregenza, Scott Campbell, Tom O'Neal, Greig Cranna, and Alli Pura; and to the gifted food and prop stylists, Jamie Kimm and Sara Abalan, and Diane Gsell and Janna Williams. I need to especially acknowledge Janna and Alli (both Earthbound Farm employees), who spent many months photographing people, food, and our farms throughout the seasons, putting their hearts and time into making this book as wonderful as possible. Thanks to Teresa Basham for always being there for me when I needed my makeup done, and to Hillary

Fish and Angelynn Odom for all their assistance.

Thanks to Chad Smith, our very smart and committed eco expert (Earthbound Farm's manager of green initiatives) for all his fact-gathering and fact-checking, and to his friends who spent time helping us get our facts right: Forrest Melton from NASA and Steven Davis, Jim Sweeney, and Matt Rothe of the Climate Conservancy. I am grateful to Sheila Bowman from the fabulous Monterey Bay Aquarium, who was so generous with her time and knowledge as we navigated the complicated issues of sustainable seafood; Jonathan Kaplan and the Natural Resources Defense Council (NRDC) for many important facts and figures; Kimberle Herring and Jeff Lindenthal of the Monterey Regional Waste Management District for their help with research about the recycling industry; and April Sheldon, a gifted designer, who helped us create the Green Kitchen Design section. Many thanks to Samantha Cabaluna for her constant assistance fact-finding and editing, and to Darryle Pollack, a brilliant writer and great friend, who so generously helped improve a lot of essential copy.

We were fortunate to have three great local chefs contribute their recipes to this book: Cal Stamenov from Bernardus Lodge, Craig von Foerster from Sierra Mar, and Jon Magnusson from Bistro 211. Thanks to everyone who contributed recipes: Hendrik Bowens, Pete Johnson, Samantha Cabaluna, Bonnie Sweat, Kathy Goodman, and Jill Goodman (for helping us perfect Nan's Tomato Rice Soup and the Goodman Family Meatloaf). I greatly appreciate and treasure all the time my amazing mom, Edith Rubin, spent helping us learn to make (and then to photograph) her wonderful stuffed cabbage, as well as sharing her Hungarian Goulash recipe and her many stories that helped shape me and this book. I feel incredibly blessed to be her daughter.

A lot of work went into getting these recipes just right. I want to thank the many employees at Earthbound Farm's Carmel office and Farm Stand who tasted dish after dish, often filling out evaluation surveys between bites. Thanks to Pam's husband, David Sullivan, for all his help shopping and tasting, and to Mary Murphy, whom I credit with igniting my passion for cooking with cast-iron.

I want to express my appreciation to all of Earthbound Farm's dedicated employees and farmers. I am grateful to our grower partners Otto Kramm, Stan Pura, Mike Hitchcock, John Romans, and the Tanimura and Antle families, who have converted tens of thousands of acres to organic production, and who grow the beautiful and healthy organic produce that inspires my cooking every day. Special thanks to our partner and CEO, Charles Sweat, for his support of this cookbook and all of Earthbound Farm's green initiatives, and to our newest partners, Andrew Rosen, John Muse, and the folks in Dallas.

Thanks to my sister, Ruth Rubin, and her husband, Steve Harmer, for tasting many recipes, and also for their help in consuming the tremendous amounts of food we were testing so that almost none went to waste. And thanks to their daughter Nina Harmer for her excitement about a second cookbook. And I thank all my treasured friends for their love and encouragement.

Finally, I wish to thank the many people who told me how much they loved my first cookbook. Their appreciation and enthusiasm motivated me to continue to share my recipes for delicious food and a healthy planet in this book.

Contents

Earthbound Farm Health Salad (page 48)

CHAPTER 9

Desserts

Decadent, pleasurable, sweet endings make any meal special, especially when you select one of the 30 or so in this chapter. Chocolate Pecan Cake. Lemon Macaroon Pie. Roasted Banana Cream. Raspberry Yogurt Panna Cotta. Chunky Cherry-Nut Bark. Choosing isn't easy! Plus:

AND MORE ON ECO-MINDED LIVING.

CHAPTER 10

Breakfast and Brunch

Whether you have plenty of morning time for a relaxing meal or hardly any time at all, there's something here to enjoy: Whole Wheat Pecan Pancakes with Pecan Maple Syrup, Buttermilk Blueberry Muffins, Warm Citrus Compote, and Orange Cream Lassi. Plus:

AND MORE ON ECO-MINDED LIVING.

CHAPTER 11

Pantry Basics

The recipes for stocks, pie crusts, salsas, and other ingredients and condiments that taste so much better and fresher when made from scratch. Plus:

AND MORE ON ECO-MINDED LIVING.

APPENDIX

Some eco-friendly ideas for greening up your kitchen.

Pineapple Mint, Raspberry, and Mango Lassis (page 395)

Becoming an Earthbound Cook

Food can be a very powerful force. Even at this point in my life, I continue to discover the extent of this far-reaching truth. Family values are often shaped around the dinner table, and the way we grow food as a nation is influenced significantly by what we choose to eat ... one family at a time.

Since writing my first cookbook, *Food to Live By,* I've been inspired by the many people who told me about their experiences after reading it: They found a new favorite dish, or regularly eat a vegetable they discovered in a recipe, or have a renewed confidence to cook healthier, better-tasting meals from scratch. This book, *The Earthbound Cook,* was born from my desire to share more delicious recipes, but also to connect our kitchens to everyday actions we can all do to protect the environment. I wanted to combine the *pleasures* of food with the *power* of food.

My hope is to offer you three resources at once. First of all, this is a comprehensive *cookbook* with more than 250 recipes for exceptional main dishes, side dishes, soups, salads, breakfasts, desserts, and more. Second, it's a helpful *reference* book full of easy-to-follow tips, cooking primers, and detailed ingredient information. And third, it's a *guide* to help you make your kitchen more eco-friendly.

Woven around all these great recipes and cooking information are many interesting and relevant essays and tips to help you learn more about how your food choices and preparation habits affect the environment. I want you to feel empowered when you think about environmental issues, not overwhelmed, so I've included tips and suggestions that are easy, effective, and doable on a daily basis. I purposefully drew a circle around the kitchen for the ecological information in this book. Even within that seemingly limited boundary, you'll be amazed at how many issues there are to cover, and also at how much our actions in the kitchen can affect the planet.

Cooking from scratch with sustainably produced ingredients is one of the most beneficial things you

Serving up a freshly made salad. What could be better?

can do for the environment. I hope the recipes in this book will inspire you to cook fresh and delicious foods in your home as often as possible. A conscientious cook who cherishes the endless variety of food produced on this planet while striving to protect it for present as well as future generations is what I call an Earthbound Cook.

How I Became an Earthbound Cook

I have always felt an instinctive need to be close to growing things—a deep hunger for a connection with nature. During high school I lived in Manhattan, and because of (or maybe in spite of) the stark contrast between city and country life, I longed for fresh air and greenery. This feeling wasn't something I could clearly describe—I was just conscious of a profound longing to be close to things rooted in the earth.

My chance came in 1984 when I moved to a house on a 2½-acre plot of heirloom raspberry vines and fruit trees in Carmel Valley, California, with my future husband, Drew. We'd just graduated from college, and this was to be an adventure before we moved ahead with our serious goals of graduate school and careers. We had no farming experience, and we didn't intend to become "real" farmers. But as New York City innocents, we were ripe for nature's "miracle show"— heirloom raspberry vines flowered

white, then produced the sweetest red berries; seeds germinated in rich coastal soil and became delicate baby lettuces, vegetables, and herbs; juicy fruit from our own trees ripened for the picking. We were simply seduced by the land—its natural rhythms, rich flavors, and complex wisdom—and we opened a small roadside stand.

As novice farmers we educated ourselves about organic methods and discovered surprising rewards. Selling the produce we grew in our backyard gave us an immediate and intimate knowledge of the earth, plus the deep satisfaction of producing delicious, healthy food both for ourselves and all the people who stopped by our farm stand to buy raspberries and fresh-baked raspberry muffins. Many of our first customers are still friends today, decades later. Our connection with the land inspired the name we gave our little organic farm and roadside stand: Earthbound Farm. To us, the word *earthbound* succinctly and powerfully conveyed both the amazing bounty to be appreciated and enjoyed, as well as the undeniable truth that our very sustenance comes from resources that must be nurtured and protected.

I fell in love with cooking and organic farming at the same time, and to me they are completely intertwined. My cooking was inspired by what we grew on our little farm. Drew and I started growing beautifully colored baby lettuces nurtured by sunshine and just the right amount

of coastal fog. We had bumper crops of fruit and vegetables that came in waves, challenging my ability to use everything before it spoiled. At my fingertips were the perfect raw ingredients to create recipes and try out new techniques. I was inspired by the sheer wonder of it all, and I've been experimenting with the flavors of fresh-picked organic produce ever since.

The Delicious Pleasures of a Green Kitchen

The kitchen is the heart of the home—a perfect place to connect with our enjoyment of food, with each other, and with the very real ecological challenges facing our planet. The kitchen is the center of our food preparation, requiring us to use a lot of energy, water, and cleaning products, and, in turn, generating a lot of waste. Making more mindful decisions about what we eat can have an enormous beneficial impact on the environment. Recent studies have shown that your food choices affect the planet even more than the kind of car you drive.

When Drew and I first started tending our crops, we had no preconceived ideas about the "best" or "correct" way to farm. The berries we inherited had always been grown conventionally, but because almost all farming techniques were new to us, we followed our instincts and looked at everything we did with fresh eyes. As

we inspected the cans and bottles of pesticides and chemical fertilizers left in the old shed on the property, we just couldn't bring ourselves to use them. Instinctively, we didn't want to touch the pesticides or other chemicals. We didn't want them on our food. We also couldn't imagine worrying about chemicals in the air, on our clothes, or tracked into the house on our shoes. We chose to farm organically because we were acutely aware that whatever we did in the field literally followed us into our home.

Ironically, we were not as scrupulous about the chemicals we used *inside* our home. As conscientious as we were about toxic pesticides and synthetic fertilizers on our crops, we still used chemical cleansers in our home because that's all we knew. Maybe if we had worked in a factory that made cleansers and had seen firsthand what went into them, we would have had a reaction similar to the one we felt when we came into contact with conventional agricultural chemicals.

But in 1984, neither of us had much of a sense of the environmental impacts of many of our actions beyond farming. I didn't think twice about using plenty of aluminum foil, paper towels, and plastic wrap. We didn't worry about whether our oceans were being overfished, or the environmental impact of how our meat was produced. We weren't particularly aware of the real need to conserve water or energy. And I don't remember if we'd even heard of global warming or greenhouse gases. But now that I have learned so much more about these issues, I've gradually changed many of the things I do in my own kitchen.

My first book, *Food to Live By: The Earthbound Farm Organic Cookbook,* focused on the many benefits of eating delicious organic foods. Since writing it, I've wanted to share more great-tasting recipes and also some of the things I now do in addition to cooking with organic ingredients to make my kitchen more Earth-friendly. I've learned a lot about environmental issues and solutions by helping to run Earthbound Farm, which has grown from a backyard garden to the largest grower of organic produce in the country—a little salad-packing line in our living room that grew to produce millions of servings of organic salad every week. The company uses substantial amounts of resources—fuel, electricity, packaging, and water—and we work very hard to find ways to lessen our environmental impact.

There is a lot of environmental information packed into this book, which I've organized into five different formats: bite-size *Living Green* tips; *Your Green Kitchen* and *The Basics* boxes, which are fairly short and contain easily accessible facts and tips; essays, which go into more depth about a certain topic; and personal mini essays recounting how I've put certain eco-friendly actions to work in my own kitchen. You'll find everything from the importance of organic farming, to handy shortcuts for minimizing plastic wrap use, to an essay about water conservation, which includes my mom's stories of her life in pre–World War II Hungary, where every drop of water she used came from a well more than a mile from her home.

In one of my favorite essays, I talk about how cooking with cast-iron is an example of an eco-choice that reaps huge rewards. It's also a metaphor for the way I look at cooking and the environment. In cast-iron cookware I see the perfect marriage of great-tasting food and an old-fashioned environmental hero that lasts for generations— with no chemical coatings or throw-away mentality behind its manufacture. Cooking with cast-iron is much like farming organically. I feel a "relationship" with my cast-iron as I inspect it to see what it needs after every use, and care for it like an old friend. And like organic soil, my cast-iron gets better over time with proper use and care.

Me with my son Jeffrey, daughter Marea, and husband Drew.

Fresh Strawberry Jam (page 424)

Reawakening to the Joys of Cooking

The connection with the food we eat and how it is produced is an intrinsic part of our sense of home and who we are. When I take time to really pay attention to the food I'm eating, I'm still awed to taste the hot summer sun on the skin of a just-picked ripe tomato or the rich soil that sweetens a stalk of broccoli. Eating good food is a pleasure; we should revel in it! Need I mention that homemade usually tastes so much better? It's also almost always the best way to make sure that ingredients are fresh, healthful, and eco-friendly. Sometimes we get so used to buying prepared foods that we forget it wasn't so long ago that our grandmothers or great-grandmothers used to make these dishes from scratch as a matter of course.

When we moved to the farm, Drew and I enjoyed creating all sorts of foods we'd previously only bought in stores. These early experiments are still part of our regular routines, and many of the recipes are included here: our bagels, whole wheat bread, pies and jam, just to name a few. I hope you'll try some of these recipes yourself. Even if you make something only once, your sense of accomplishment can last a lifetime, plus you'll appreciate it far more each time you buy it in a store.

Learning more about what we eat has many delicious rewards, but it's also important to realize that the choices we make as consumers affect the way food is produced in this country. I witnessed firsthand how the growth of the organic food movement was truly a consumer revolution. When consumers change what they buy, they are truly changing the world.

Creating Lasting Food Memories

As my children grow into adulthood, I'm thinking more generationally. Unlike their city-bred parents, our son and daughter have been surrounded since birth by growing things in a rich stew of cooking experiments and eco-friendly philosophy. I know this heritage will nurture them as they go out in the world, but I also wonder how the flavors of the food they remember from home will follow them.

Now that my daughter, Marea, is in college and cooking for herself in her own first kitchen, I sent her off with one of my beloved, well-seasoned cast-iron pans and some other start-up utensils for her college apartment. What special recipes will she take with her to cook there? Maybe the recipe for the apple pie we made together last Thanksgiving (page 326), weaving an intricate lattice-top crust only to undo it because we forgot to put the pats of butter on top of the filling. Afterward, the crust didn't look perfect, but the pie tasted delicious, and the laughter and cosmetic imperfections made it an experience we'll never forget.

Maybe she'll also take the recipe for the Winter Vegetable Soup (page 26), inspired by the season and my desire to make a special gift for a friend who was convalescing after surgery. I left the recipe on the kitchen counter to use later that evening, only to discover when I came home from work that Marea had made it for our family dinner. I'm not sure who was more thrilled—Marea, who felt a great deal of accomplishment bringing the recipe to life, or me, who was so grateful that a delicious bowl of soup had magically appeared at the end of a long, exhausting day.

I will always remember the day Drew served our son, Jeffrey, his first bowl of Nan's Tomato Rice Soup (page 4)—a childhood favorite Drew used to eat at his grandmother's house more than forty years ago, now re-created for this cookbook. As Jeffrey's face lit up when he tasted the rich broth, the two of them shared an experience that spanned three generations. It makes me smile to imagine Jeffrey's children enjoying that same soup some day in the future.

It's never too late or too early in life to learn more about how to enjoy delicious food in ways that help preserve and protect our environment—the bountiful and beautiful planet we have merely borrowed from future generations. Earthbound cooking includes small yet powerful actions that anyone can easily bring to their own kitchen and successfully put into practice one delicious bite at a time. I hope you enjoy these recipes, stories, and eco-tips as much as I enjoyed writing them. Dig in and discover your own inner Earthbound Cook!

Myra

Myra Goodman
Carmel Valley, California

Turn baby spinach leaves into a side dish with garlic and lemon (page 219), a salad with sesame vinaigrette (page 51) and so much more.

SOUP

Soups That Satisfy

I LOVE THE AROMA OF SOUP AS IT SIMMERS ON THE STOVE AND THE appreciative smiles when it's served up hot by the bowlful. Delicious and versatile, soup stretches to feed a crowd of family and guests. It's also a healthy, satisfying meal to quickly reheat on days when there's no time to cook. And if you're looking for ways to cut down on your family's meat consumption, soup makes the most out of smaller amounts, without anyone feeling deprived.

Most soup recipes are forgiving, too: More often than not, you can safely play around with spices, ingredients, and proportions. I like the novelty of a batch of soup turning out a bit different each time I make it. The pot of soup I have simmering in my kitchen usually contains vegetables in season and the thrifty serendipity of ingredients I have on hand and need to use up.

Serving soup is also an easy way to work in a generous amount of healthy vegetables. When my teenage son comes home from sports practice, he has often eaten something not-so-healthy with his teammates or friends. He's not hungry for a big meal, but he usually has enough appetite to eat a bowl of soup. He eats my Winter Vegetable Soup because it's delicious, warming . . . and insistently offered by his mom. Just the sheer concentration of ten different vegetables with a rainbow of colors and nutrients is enough to make that soup a superstar in my kitchen.

This chapter offers an eclectic variety of soup recipes. Try making an American classic like Chef Pam McKinstry's New England Clam Chowder—a recipe she developed for her Nantucket Island restaurant, with signature touches of dill, thyme, white wine, and bacon. Go a bit exotic with the unusual and delicious ingredient combinations in our Zanzibar Chicken Soup, inspired by the tastes of Africa: curry, coconut, and bananas in a light, flavorful stock. Nourish yourself with our rich Red Lentil and Coconut Soup, with its lovely Asian high notes of lime, lemongrass, and basil in a creamy base of lentils and coconut milk. Or make a big batch of Nan's Tomato Rice Soup, a satisfying family favorite that my husband's grandmother used to make. Falling somewhere between the consistency

A young red cabbage plant.

of her usual chicken soup and the heartiness of a beef stew, Nan's soup is a delicious tangy tomato broth infused with the flavors of short ribs and rice. This is the kind of soup that just gets better every time you reheat it. In our family, it's also a lasting link to the generations— a special "flavor memory" my husband, Drew, now shares with *our* children.

Over the years, as I've grown to love cooking and have moved away from the prepared foods of my childhood, I hardly ever have soup from a can. Homemade soup just tastes so much better, and the initial investment of time is more than repaid in the special flavor right out of the pot.

I also love the convenience of reheating soup for a meal later in the week when I'm feeling time-deprived and frazzled. Tasting the freshness of the ingredients and knowing where each one came from truly nurtures body and soul.

Zanzibar Chicken Soup (page 11)

Nan's Tomato Rice Soup

D REW AND HIS SISTER JILL SAY that when they were young, their grandma Charlotte (whom they always called "Nan") made this soup for them as an extra-special treat, and to this day it remains one of their favorite family recipes. The secret to the richness of this tomato-rice soup is the short ribs that simmer for hours, infusing the tomato juice with an intense meaty flavor, making beef stock unnecessary. Although composed of only a handful of simple ingredients, its hearty, satisfying flavor comes from long, slow cooking. I've specified beef short ribs, but you can substitute stew meat supplemented with a soup bone or two to achieve the same depth of flavor. I advise keeping the rice separate and adding some to each bowl at serving time; otherwise it will absorb all of the liquid in the soup. ⟶ *Serves 6 to 8*

3 pounds beef short ribs on the bone, untrimmed

2 large yellow onions, cut in half through the stem end

4 ribs celery, including leaves

2 large cans (64 ounces each) tomato juice

1 cup long-grain white rice

Salt and freshly ground black pepper

1. Combine the short ribs, onions, celery, and tomato juice in a large stockpot. Place the pot over medium-high heat, cover, and bring to the start of a simmer. Reduce the heat to medium-low and simmer until the meat is so tender that it falls off the bones, about 4 hours. Then let the soup cool for 30 minutes.

2. While the soup is cooling, combine the rice and 2 cups water in a medium-size saucepan, cover, and bring to the start of a boil over high heat. Reduce the heat to low and

cook until all the water has been absorbed and the rice is just tender, about 15 minutes. Remove the lid and let the rice cool.

3. Strain the soup through a colander set over a clean saucepan. Skim off any fat that has risen to the surface, and discard it. (Alternatively, you can refrigerate the soup until it is chilled, and then remove the layer of congealed fat that rests on the surface.) When the bones and vegetables are cool enough to handle, remove the meat from the bones and add it to the liquid. Discard the bones, onions, and celery.

4. Reheat the soup, covered, over low heat. Season with salt and pepper to taste. (Depending on the brand of tomato juice you use, the soup may have enough salt without adding

Nan's Tomato Rice Soup

more.) Divide the rice among the soup bowls, ladle in the soup and serve hot.

Note: If you are not planning to serve the soup immediately, see the reheating sidebar on page 4.

Chicken Parmesan Soup

WHEN MY FAMILY CRAVES THE WARMTH OF SOUP on a wintry day, chicken soup is always high on the list. What makes this version unusually delicious is the combination of homemade stocks: Parmesan and rich chicken. At the sky-high price of Parmigiano-Reggiano cheese, don't throw out the rinds. Wrap them tightly and freeze them until you have enough to whip up a batch of Parmesan Stock. It's easy to make, and you'll find that the stock is very handy for making pasta dishes as well as soups. Although we like to start with uncooked chicken and cook it in the stock, this soup is also a great way to utilize leftover cooked chicken (see Note, facing page). For a more substantial meal and an easy way to stretch the soup, add cooked pasta or rice at Step 4. ⟶ *Serves 6*

1 tablespoon olive oil

About 2 cups diced yellow onion
  (¼-inch dice)

2 medium carrots, peeled, halved lengthwise
  and sliced ¼-inch thick (about 1 cup)

2 celery ribs, thinly sliced

1 tablespoon minced garlic

5 cups Parmesan Stock (page 408)

3 cups Chicken Wing Stock (page 403),
  Quick Chicken Stock (facing page), or
  store-bought low-sodium chicken broth

1 can (28 ounces) diced tomatoes,
  with their juices

1 tablespoon dried oregano

1 whole skinless, boneless chicken breast
  (about 12 ounces), cut into ½-inch
  cubes (see Note)

¼ cup fresh basil leaves, coarsely chopped

¼ cup chopped fresh parsley

Salt and freshly ground black pepper

Freshly grated Parmesan cheese, for
  garnish (optional)

1. Heat the oil in a large, heavy pot over medium-high heat. Add the onion, carrots, and celery and cook, stirring frequently, until the vegetables begin to soften, about 8 minutes.

2. Add the garlic and cook, stirring constantly, until fragrant, about 1 minute.

3. Add the Parmesan and chicken stocks, tomatoes, and oregano. Bring the soup to the start of a boil, and then reduce the heat to low. Simmer, uncovered, until the vegetables are just tender, about 15 minutes.

4. Add the chicken, basil, and parsley and simmer until the meat is cooked, 6 to 8 minutes. Season the soup with salt and pepper to taste, and serve it hot, garnished with Parmesan cheese if desired. For reheating instructions, see the sidebar on page 4.

Note: If you wish to substitute cooked chicken, add 2½ cups shredded cooked chicken at Step 4, and simmer the soup until the chicken is heated through, 3 to 5 minutes.

Celery, ready to pick.

Quick Chicken Stock (Save the Bones!)

Rather than let food go to waste, save leftovers from a rotisserie or roast chicken. With a few basic ingredients you can make a flavorful stock that is far superior to anything you can buy.

Makes about 4 cups

Carcass of 1 cooked chicken
1 small yellow onion, unpeeled, halved
1 carrot, cut into 2-inch pieces
1 celery rib, with leaves if any, cut into 2-inch lengths
½ dried bay leaf
8 whole black peppercorns

1. Place the chicken carcass in a stockpot or Dutch oven. Add all the remaining ingredients and enough cool water to cover (about 10 cups). Bring to the start of a simmer over medium-high heat. Then reduce the heat to a slow simmer, and cook uncovered for 2 hours. (Do not allow the stock to boil, or it will be cloudy.)

2. Pass the stock through a fine-mesh sieve into a large bowl, and discard the solids. If you will be using it immediately, let the strained stock stand until the fat rises to the surface, about 5 minutes; then skim off and discard the fat. If you're not using it right away, cool it completely using the quick cooling method (page 405), and then refrigerate it, covered, for up to 5 days; remove and discard any congealed fat before using. The stock can be frozen for up to 6 months.

indful about water conservation

–World War II
ys been fascinated by
here. For example, every
ater her family needed was carried in buckets
from the town well, which was about a mile from her
house. And if someone needed hot water for washing
dishes or bathing, it had to be heated on a wood or
coal stove. Household chores got done, children and
adults bathed regularly, but there was a different
consciousness about water. It wasn't taken for granted
or wasted. And the extra fuel and effort needed for
heating water was clearly visible. All water—but
especially hot water—was precious, and people used
every drop as efficiently as possible.

Fresh running water is something most of us take
for granted in this country. We turn on the tap, and it
simply appears. If we want hot water, we just twist a faucet
handle. We seldom think about life without access to clean
drinking water or enough water to grow our food, maintain
proper sanitation, and manufacture goods, yet an estimated
36 states anticipate water shortages by 2013.

There are few things we depend on more for our
survival than water, and I've come to realize that even
though my water flows freely from a faucet instead
of arriving in a bucket, there is a web of costs and
ecological burdens attached to it. I find that the image
of hauling buckets from a well makes me more mindful
of how I use water and motivates me to conserve.

Here are some facts about water usage and why it's
important to consume this precious resource wisely:

We're using more water than ever before.

Population growth is putting a strain on water supplies,
but in this country, we're actually using *more* water per
person than we used to. Environmental Protection
Agency (EPA) reports show that between 1950 and 2000,
the U.S. population nearly doubled; water demand during
that same period, however, more than tripled.

Providing clean water uses a lot of energy.

The energy needed to heat water in our homes and to
power water treatment plants, costs money, depletes
natural resources, and adds emissions to the atmosphere.
Many people feel that they don't need to conserve
because water is abundant in their area, but this leaves
energy costs and emissions out of the equation. Letting
your faucet run for 5 minutes uses about as much
energy as letting a 60-watt light bulb run for 14 hours.
American public water supply and treatment facilities
consume about 56 billion kilowatt-hours per year—the
same amount of yearly electricity needed to power more

A leaking faucet or showerhead over time adds up to a tremendous waste of water.

than 5 million homes. In addition, the Natural Resources Defense Council calculates that the energy consumed for the collection, distribution, and treatment of drinking water and wastewater nationwide releases approximately 116 billion pounds of CO_2 per year—the equivalent to the global-warming pollution of 10 million cars.

A lot of our water literally goes down the drain. If your water is in a bucket, you see exactly how much you're using, but what if you get water from a modern-day sink? How much goes down the drain? Water from a typical kitchen faucet runs at a rate of 2 gallons a minute. That means that if you leave the water running the whole time you're doing dishes, you use 30 gallons of water in just 15 minutes. A leaky faucet can waste between 10 and 100 gallons of water a day.

There are many easy ways to reduce our water use See below for our favorite tips.

YOUR GREEN KITCHEN

Being More Water-Wise in the Kitchen

The first step in conserving water is simply to be mindful of this precious resource. Awareness alone can make finding creative ways to cut water use almost second nature. But there are some not-so-obvious water-use facts you may not be aware of.

A full dishwasher uses less water than hand washing. The amount of water used to wash dishes by hand varies according to how long you run the faucet (remember, you're using approximately 2 gallons every minute), but experts agree that washing dishes by hand uses more water than washing a full load in your dishwasher. As of 2009, Energy Star–qualified dishwashers are required to use no more than 5.8 gallons of water per cycle. If you bought your dishwasher before 1994, it probably uses around 13.8 gallons per cycle. According to Energy Star, washing dishes in an Energy Star–qualified dishwasher can net a yearly savings of 5,000 gallons of water over hand washing, plus $40 in energy costs and 230 hours of your time.

Be sure to wait until your dishwasher is full before running it, and rather than rinsing under running water, scrape or sponge off dishes before loading them if you are going to run your dishwasher soon. And when you need to hand-wash dishes, don't leave the water running the whole time. Fill one of the dirty pots or bowls with sudsy water instead of filling the sink basin, turn off the tap while you're scrubbing, and try to rinse dishes all simultaneously rather than one at a time.

Avoid using the garbage disposal. Since food scraps that wind up in the landfill decompose anaerobically and produce the destructive greenhouse gas methane, some people have argued that using a garbage disposal is better than throwing out food waste. But a garbage disposal uses some electricity and a lot of water. Your ground-up food then winds up in a water treatment plant or septic system to be processed with sewage, requiring even more water and energy to clean up the wastewater. The best alternative is to compost your food waste to create rich fertilizer for your garden or yard (see page 247). If you can't compost your scraps, most experts agree that it's better just to throw them in the garbage rather than use a garbage disposal.

Install low-flow faucet aerators. Inexpensive and easy-to-install aerators mix air into your faucet's water stream to limit the amount of water that slips away, and most do it without any noticeable difference in water pressure. In one study, installing low-flow aerators on all household faucets resulted in a 13 percent annual reduction in water consumption for each household member.

Zanzibar Chicken Soup

Coconut Rice

Coconut rice has a slight sweetness and a subtle nutty taste that adds interest and flavor to white rice. It's delicious spooned into Zanzibar Chicken Soup, and we like it served as a side dish with Coconut-Crusted Salmon (page 134). It's a great accompaniment to any dish where coconut is a complementary flavor.

Serves 4

1 can (14 ounces) light coconut milk, shaken well
water
oon peanut or canola oil
salt
ain white rice, such as jasmine

conut milk, water, oil, and dium-size saucepan. Cover l bring to the start of a boil n-high heat. Add the rice, uce the heat to low. Cover simmer for 20 minutes, f the heat. Fluff the rice with r the pan, and let the rice 10 minutes. Serve hot.

ools/Print

http://allrecipes.com/Recipe-Tools/Print/Recipe.aspx?Recip

Page 1 of 2

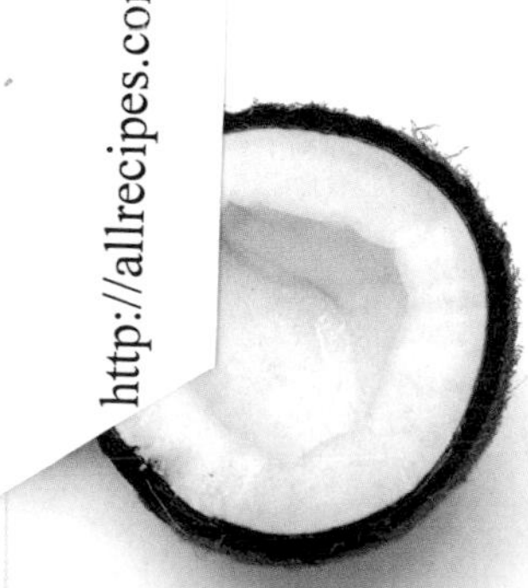

Overnight Asparagus Mushroom Strata

allrecipes.com

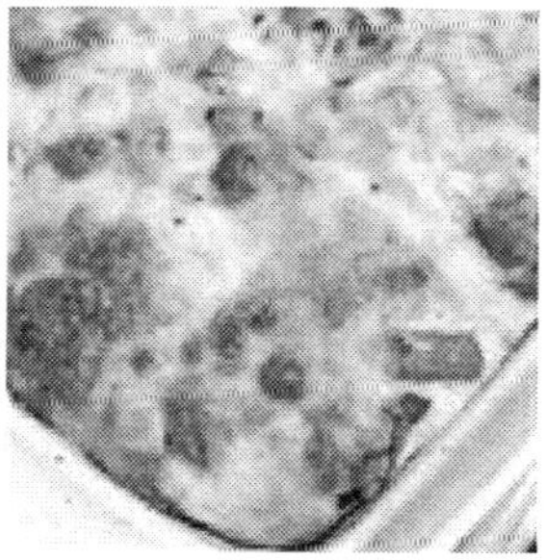

Rated: ★★★★★
Submitted By: Shandeen
Photo By: Olive and

Prep Time: 25 Minutes
Cook Time: 45 Minutes
Ready In: 9 Hours 15 Minutes
Servings: 8

"Perfect for a special breakfast or brunch, this make-ahead eggy casserole combines toasted English muffins with layers of cheese, mushrooms, and asparagus. Refrigerate overnight, bake the next day, and keep your morning clear for celebrating instead of cooking."

INGREDIENTS:

- 2 teaspoons butter, or as needed
- 1 3/4 cups sliced crimini mushrooms
- 5 English muffins, split and toasted
- 1 cup shredded Colby-Monterey Jack cheese
- 1 pound fresh asparagus, trimmed and
- 1/2 onion, finely chopped
- 8 eggs
- 2 cups milk
- 1 teaspoon salt
- 1 teaspoon dry mustard powder
- 1/4 teaspoon ground black pepper

Country Apple Dumplings

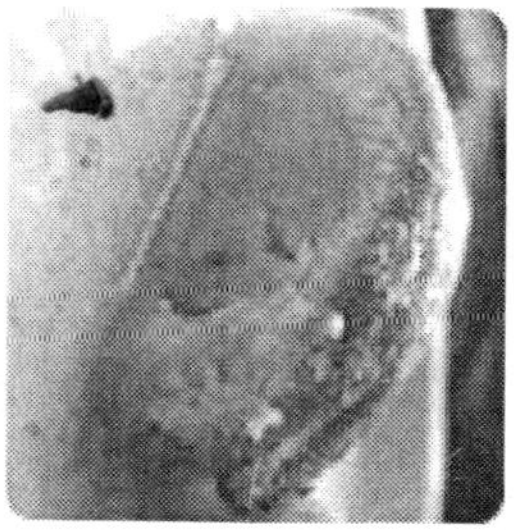

★★★★★
Rate/Review
Read Reviews (665)
19,256 people have saved this
24 custom versions

"Oh my Goodness!! Who knew that fresh apples,

Southwestern Turkey Soup

Jalapeño Heat

Judging the heat of jalapeño peppers by sight alone is a challenge. Every pepper, even those of the same size, has a different level of heat, depending on the amount of capsaicin it contains. (Capsaicin is a potent compound responsible for the fiery intensity of some chiles.) The only way to accurately gauge a pepper's nature is to sample a small piece. To lessen the kick, remove some or all of the white ribs and seeds, which is where the capsaicin is concentrated. The flesh of the pepper has only a fraction of the heat of its interior components.

THIS FLAVORFUL AND NUTRITIOUS SOUTH-OF-THE-BORDER SOUP has a bit of everything—aromatic vegetables, a hint of jalapeño, sweet corn, and protein-rich black beans. The foundation of any delicious soup is a great-tasting stock, so if you have leftover bones from your holiday turkey, use them to create a Quick Turkey Stock (see facing page). For a lighter soup with the same great southwestern flavor, chicken stock will work just fine. And speaking of leftovers, if you have cooked turkey on hand, you can add 4 cups cubed meat to the soup at Step 3 instead of starting with raw turkey. ⬥⬥⬥ **Serves 6 to 8**

3 tablespoons olive oil

About 1 cup diced yellow onion (¼-inch dice)

½ cup diced carrot (¼-inch dice)

½ cup chopped celery

1 tablespoon finely minced jalapeño pepper, with or without seeds, or to taste (see sidebar, this page)

1 tablespoon minced garlic

¾ teaspoon ground cumin

1 teaspoon chili powder

¾ teaspoon dried oregano

6 cups Quick Turkey Stock (recipe follows), Chicken Wing Stock (page 403), or store-bought low-sodium chicken broth

1½ pounds raw turkey breast, cut into ½-inch cubes (about 4 cups)

2 medium tomatoes, cored and cut into ¼-inch dice (about 1½ cups)

1 cup fresh or frozen corn kernels (no need to thaw)

1 can (15 ounces) black beans, rinsed and drained

Salt

½ cup chopped fresh cilantro

1. Heat the oil in a large, heavy pot over medium heat. Add the onion, carrot, and celery and cook, stirring frequently, until the vegetables soften, 5 to 8 minutes. Add the jalapeño, garlic, cumin, chili powder, and oregano and cook, stirring frequently, until fragrant, about 2 minutes.

2. Add the stock, raise the heat to high, cover the pot, and bring the soup to a boil. Then reduce the heat to low and let simmer until the flavors meld, about 10 minutes. Add the turkey and cook, covered, for 5 minutes.

3. Stir in the tomatoes, corn, and black beans and simmer, uncovered, until the vegetables and meat are cooked, about 10 minutes. Season the soup with salt to taste. Serve hot, garnished with the cilantro. For reheating instructions, see the sidebar on page 4.

Quick Turkey Stock ~~~ *Makes about 6 cups*

Carcass of 1 cooked turkey,
    including any leftover meat
2 yellow onions, halved
3 large carrots, cut into chunks
2 celery ribs, including any leaves,
    cut into 2-inch lengths
12 fresh parsley stems or whole sprigs
10 whole black peppercorns
1 dried bay leaf

1. Place the turkey carcass and any meat in a large stockpot and add enough cool water to cover completely (about 12 cups). Add all the remaining ingredients and bring to a simmer over medium-high heat. Then reduce the heat to maintain a gentle simmer and cook, uncovered, for 3 hours.

2. Pour the stock through a fine-mesh sieve into a large bowl, discarding the solids. If you will be using the stock immediately, let it stand until the fat rises to the surface, about 5 minutes; then skim off and discard the fat. If you are not using it right away, cool it completely using the quick cooling method (see page 405), and then cover and refrigerate it for up to 5 days; remove the congealed fat from the surface of the stock before using. The stock can be frozen for up to 6 months.

LIVING GREEN
Cover your pot when boiling liquids. Confining heat in the pot with a lid keeps the energy from your stove on the job cooking your food instead of escaping into the air.

YOUR GREEN KITCHEN

What's the Best Packaging for Store-Bought Broth?

Certainly making your own broth is more eco-friendly than purchasing packaged broth, and it's decidedly more delicious. But the reality is that we don't always have the time to make our own. If you do use store-bought broth, you have a choice of packaging: cans or pliable aseptic boxes known as Tetra Paks. Although opinions vary on which is the better choice for the environment, when I buy broth, I almost always buy it in Tetra Paks.

Generally, Tetra Paks are comprised largely of paper (70 percent), much of which is made from sustainably grown pine trees. They are lighter and require less energy than steel cans to manufacture, fill, and ship. They are also commonly available in a large, reclosable 32-ounce size. Tetra Paks are not as widely recycled as steel cans, but this is rapidly changing: As of 2008, 20 percent of U.S. residents (and growing) have access to carton recycling. On a human health note, unlike most steel cans, Tetra Paks do not contain bisphenol A (BPA) liners. BPA acts like estrogen in the body and has been linked to health concerns.

Even though homemade broth has no packaging at all, like many people, I'm much more likely to make homemade soup if I have boxes of broth on hand. Homemade soup is fresher and more flavorful than anything I could buy, and if I bought that same amount of prepared soup, whether it was in cans or Tetra Paks, I would generate maybe three or four times the packaging waste of the broth containers.

THE BASICS

Shrimp or Prawns

A shrimp is a shrimp is a prawn. Although they are actually two different species, they are very similar in appearance. In the United States, jumbo and colossal shrimp (15 or fewer per pound) are often marketed as prawns.

Just-picked corn, kernels plump and juicy.

Shrimp and Corn Chowder

SHRIMP AND SWEET CORN COMBINE FOR A MATCH MADE IN heaven, and when simmered in a light stock made from the shrimp shells, the result is rich, flavorful, and satisfying. This elegant chowder makes a wonderful first course or a satisfying meal when served with hot crusty bread and a generous green salad. —ww— *Serves 4 to 6*

12 ounces raw, unpeeled shrimp, preferably small (31 to 35 per pound)

4 tablespoons (½ stick) unsalted butter

3 tablespoons unbleached all-purpose flour

¼ cup dry sherry or Marsala

1 cup whole milk

3 cups Shrimp Stock (page 409) or bottled clam juice

1 tablespoon tomato paste

About 8 ounces red new potatoes, peeled or unpeeled, cut into ¼-inch dice (1½ cups)

2 cups corn kernels, fresh or frozen (no need to thaw)

¼ teaspoon cayenne pepper

Salt

3 tablespoons fresh parsley, for garnish

1. Peel and devein the shrimp, removing the tail pieces as well. Reserve the shells for making Shrimp Stock, if desired. If your shrimp are large, cut them in half or in smaller pieces. Cover and refrigerate.

2. Melt the butter in a stockpot over medium heat. Add the flour and cook, stirring continuously, for 2 minutes to cook off the raw flour taste. Add the sherry and milk and cook, stirring frequently, until the mixture is smooth and has thickened, about 4 minutes.

3. Stir in the Shrimp Stock and tomato paste, and cook over medium-high heat until the liquid begins to simmer. Reduce the heat to medium and cook for 5 minutes to concentrate the flavors. Add the potatoes, cover the pot, and simmer until they are tender, 10 to 12 minutes.

4. Add the corn and the shrimp, and simmer until the shrimp are cooked through, about 4 minutes.

5. Season the chowder with the cayenne pepper and salt to taste. Garnish with the parsley and serve hot. For reheating instructions, see the sidebar on page 4.

Shrimp and Corn Chowder

Dungeness Crab Bisque

DUNGENESS CRABS ARE ABOUT AS FRESH AND LOCAL as you can get in our neighborhood, because they're pulled right out of nearby Monterey Bay. The Pacific Coast Dungeness crab fishery is considered the most sustainable crab fishery in the world. Dungeness crabs are found along the entire coast from California to Alaska, with a season ranging from November through July. They tend to be large, often running 3 pounds each, so it's quite easy to extract the meat from these dinner-plate-size crabs.

Most of the flavor in this bisque comes from the shells of the crustaceans, so you must begin with whole hard-shell crabs, whether they come from the Pacific or Atlantic coast. Have your fishmonger crack the crab for you. It will make picking out the crabmeat much easier. Use the body meat for this soup, and save the large pieces of claw and leg meat for another dish, such as Cal Stamenov's Dungeness Crab Salad with Persimmon "Carpaccio" (page 146). At the price of fresh crab, you definitely want to use every morsel, and this recipe is a great way to capitalize on the flavor of the shells, which are usually discarded. Instead, you turn those shells into a tasty stock which in turn creates a rich and elegant soup. Serve the bisque as a first course for a special-occasion meal, or pair it with a hearty salad for a light luncheon. ⁓⁓ *Serves 6*

Dungeness crabs, ready to crack and eat.

1 cooked Dungeness crab, fresh or thawed
    (3 pounds; see Note)
Crab Stock (recipe follows)
5 tablespoons unsalted butter
1 cup diced yellow onion (¼-inch dice)
1 cup thinly sliced leek (white and light
    green parts)
½ cup thinly sliced celery
⅓ cup Cognac or brandy
¼ cup unbleached all-purpose flour
1 tablespoon tomato paste
2 cups heavy (whipping) cream
Salt and freshly ground white pepper
3 tablespoons snipped fresh chives,
    for garnish

1. Remove the meat from the crab, and set aside about 3 cups of crabmeat for the bisque. (Reserve the remaining crabmeat for another use.) Use the shells to prepare the Crab Stock. Set the stock aside.

2. Melt 2 tablespoons of the butter in a medium-size skillet over medium heat. Add the onion, leek, and celery and cook, stirring frequently, until the vegetables are tender but not browned, 5 to 8 minutes. Add the Cognac and cook until the liquid has almost completely evaporated, about 5 minutes. Set aside.

3. Melt the remaining 3 tablespoons butter in a large saucepan over medium heat, and stir in the flour. Cook the roux, stirring constantly, for 2 minutes to cook off the raw flour taste. Add the Crab Stock and whisk to blend. Bring the mixture to a simmer, and stir in the tomato paste and cream.

4. Add the onion-leek mixture and simmer the soup, uncovered, for 30 minutes to allow the flavors to marry.

5. Strain the soup through a fine-mesh sieve set over a clean saucepan. Discard the solids. Place the pan over low heat and add the 3 cups of crabmeat. Cook gently until the crabmeat is warmed through, about 3 minutes. Season with salt and white pepper to taste. Divide the bisque among four warmed bowls, and garnish each serving with a sprinkling of chives.

Note: If you are not planning to serve the bisque immediately, let it cool to room temperature after straining it; then cover and refrigerate it for up to 3 days. When you are ready to serve it, reheat the soup over low heat or in the microwave, add the crabmeat, and cook until the soup is hot. Season with salt and white pepper, and garnish with the chives.

Crab Stock

Before those crab shells go into the garbage, consider making crab stock. You'll maximize your purchase by utilizing every part of the pricey crustaceans, and at the same time you'll extract every last ounce of flavor. Making shellfish stock is really very simple: Sauté the shells with some vegetables and then simmer in water to infuse the flavors. Use whatever vegetables and aromatics you have on hand, or try our version below. You'll be happy to have crab stock on hand in your freezer to add depth of flavor to bisque, chowders, pasta dishes, and risottos. —*** *Makes about 4 cups*

2 tablespoons olive oil

Shells from 1 cooked Dungeness crab (3 pounds)

2 leeks, white and light green parts only, rinsed and thinly sliced

1 small fennel bulb, sliced

1 medium carrot, chopped

3 celery ribs with leaves, chopped

10 whole black peppercorns

12 fresh parsley stems

1 strip lemon peel

2 cups dry white wine

4 cups cold water

1. Heat the oil in a large stockpot over medium-high heat. Add the shells and cook, stirring frequently, until they are hot and fragrant, about 5 minutes. Add the leeks, fennel, carrot, and celery and reduce the heat to medium. Cook, stirring frequently, until the vegetables soften, 7 to 10 minutes.

2. Add the peppercorns, parsley, lemon peel, wine, and water. Raise the heat to high and bring the mixture to the start of a boil. Reduce the heat to maintain a simmer, skimming off any foam that rises to the top. Simmer, uncovered, for 45 minutes or until the liquid reduces by about a quarter.

3. Strain the stock through a fine-mesh sieve and cool. Store for up to 2 days in the refrigerator, or freeze for up to 3 months.

New England Clam Chowder

O N THE COAST OF NEW ENGLAND, where clams are a staple, chowder features prominently on most menus. Chef Pam McKinstry created this award-winning version for her Nantucket Island restaurants many years ago, and she says fans have told her that this is the best chowder they've ever eaten. Subtle hints of bacon and dill enhance, but don't overwhelm, the fresh, briny flavor of the shellfish. Creamy, rich, and full of clams, this chowder is sure to please! ⁓⁓ *Serves 8*

6 ounces (about 6 slices) thick-sliced bacon, cut into ¼-inch dice

About 2 cups diced yellow onion (¼-inch dice)

¾ cup diced celery (¼-inch dice)

1 large carrot, peeled and finely grated (about ¾ cup)

1 tablespoon dried dill

2 teaspoons dried thyme

½ teaspoon freshly ground white pepper

⅓ to ½ cup unbleached all-purpose flour

3 cups bottled clam juice

½ cup dry white wine

2 dried bay leaves

3 cans (6.5 ounces each) chopped clams, with their juices

1 cup half-and-half

3 cups diced cooked potatoes (¼-inch dice; any variety will work)

Salt and freshly ground black pepper

1. Cook the bacon in a large stockpot over medium heat, stirring occasionally, until it is crisp, 15 to 20 minutes. Add the onion, celery, carrot, dill, thyme, and white pepper to the pot, and cook, stirring frequently, until the vegetables are soft, 10 to 15 minutes.

2. Add ⅓ cup of the flour and cook, stirring constantly, over medium-low heat to make a thick roux. Cook for 3 to 4 minutes to eliminate the raw flour taste. If the roux is oily, add more of the flour and continue cooking for 2 more minutes. (The exact quantity of flour needed will depend upon the amount of bacon fat in your pot.)

3. Add the clam juice, wine, and bay leaves, and raise the heat to medium.

Cook, uncovered, stirring occasionally, until the mixture is hot and has thickened, 10 to 15 minutes. Add the chopped clams with their juices, the half-and-half, and the potatoes, and cook gently until the soup is hot. Season the chowder with salt and pepper to taste.

Note: The chowder can be refrigerated, covered, for up to 4 days. For reheating instructions, see the sidebar on page 4.

Red Lentil and Coconut Soup

MAKING SOUP IS THE BEST KIND OF KITCHEN ALCHEMY. This pureed soup boasts a remarkably silky texture, thanks to the coconut milk. A squeeze of fresh lime juice brightens the lentils and spices, and basil contributes an essential herbal component. Notes of ginger and lemongrass linger in the background, adding to the rich complexity of flavors that subtly meld into a nuanced, well-balanced, beautiful soup. If you want to turn up the heat, add the optional chile pepper. ⎯⎯ *Serves 4*

2 tablespoons olive oil

About 2 cups diced yellow onion (¼-inch dice)

1 tablespoon grated peeled fresh ginger

1 lemongrass stalk, trimmed and finely minced (see sidebar)

1 teaspoon ground cumin

½ teaspoon ground star anise

½ teaspoon ground coriander

4 large garlic cloves, peeled and minced

3½ cups Vegetable Stock (page 410) or store-bought low-sodium vegetable broth

1 cup red lentils, rinsed

½ small jalapeño or serrano chile, finely minced (optional)

1 cup coconut milk, preferably light

3 tablespoons chopped fresh basil

2 tablespoons fresh lime juice

Salt, to taste

1. Heat the oil in a large saucepan over medium heat. Add the onion and cook until it is soft and translucent, 5 to 8 minutes. Stir in the ginger, lemongrass, cumin, star anise,

THE BASICS

Working with Lemongrass

Lemongrass is a staple of Asian cuisines, used like an herb to add a subtle, aromatic, lemonlike flavor without the bite of citrus. Sold in individual stalks that are long, pale green, and reedlike, it is generally available in most well-stocked supermarkets and in specialty food stores and Asian markets. Only the inner core of the lower 5 inches of the stalk is usable. To prepare lemongrass, cut off and discard the root end and the reedy top, leaving about 5 inches of usable stalk. Peel and discard the outer three layers of leaves, or as many as required until you reach the pale, soft inner core. Finely slice the lemongrass, crush it with the side of a cleaver, or chop it.

coriander, and garlic. Cook, stirring constantly, until the mixture is fragrant, about 2 minutes.

2. Add the vegetable stock, lentils, and chile (if using). Cover the pan and bring the mixture to the start of a simmer. Reduce the heat to medium-low and simmer until the lentils are tender, 15 to 20 minutes.

3. Transfer the mixture to a food processor and puree until the mixture is smooth. If necessary, do this in

batches. (Or, let the soup cool slightly and then puree it with an immersion blender right in the saucepan.)

4. Place a fine-mesh sieve over a clean saucepan and strain the soup into it. Discard the solids.

5. Reheat the soup over medium heat, and add the coconut milk. Just before serving, stir in the basil and lime juice, and season with salt to taste. For reheating instructions, see the sidebar on page 4.

YOUR GREEN KITCHEN

Eco-Choices: Frozen vs. Canned

When fresh produce isn't available, what's the best choice: frozen or canned? Unfortunately, the answer isn't always clear, but here are some of the trade-offs to consider.

Energy Use, Carbon Footprint, and Recyclability

Frozen produce is usually packed in a plastic bag, which is far lighter and requires less energy to create and transport than metal cans. But once you freeze the product, you have to keep it frozen, and that requires a lot more energy (and therefore more emissions from whatever power source is used) than a can that sits unrefrigerated on a shelf for a long time. Also, metal cans are much more widely recycled than are plastic bags.

Nutrition and Other Health Concerns

Many people argue that frozen is more nutrient-rich than canned, and that the higher nutrient return justifies the additional energy required to freeze something and keep it frozen. Up to half of some of the vitamins are lost in the typical canned item that sits on the shelf for months, whereas frozen fruits and vegetables are harvested and flash-frozen shortly after harvesting.

Most metal cans also involve a potential health risk factor: They contain a plastic liner that in nearly all cases is made with bisphenol A (BPA), a compound that has been associated with health problems. Metal cans may leach trace amounts of BPA into the

product, a problem that is made worse because canned items tend to sit on the shelf for a while, extending the food's exposure time to BPA. If you are purchasing canned items, also consider that acidic products, such as tomatoes and citrus, may promote more leaching of BPA than alkaline products, such as spinach, pumpkin, peas, and garlic.

Personally, when I can't get a fruit or vegetable fresh, I usually choose frozen over canned. In addition to the better nutrition, I like the taste better, and I don't worry about exposure to BPA. There's also a bit more variety available in frozen produce, and it usually doesn't contain sugar, preservatives, or other additives.

Curried Garnet Yam Soup

THIS SILKY-SMOOTH SOUP is so rich-tasting that you'll be amazed to learn it's actually very low in fat and calories. The conjunction of vitamin-rich, naturally sweet yams and the subtle, nuanced flavors of curry and garam masala yields a light but full-bodied soup that's very satisfying. The curry flavor is subtle, but you can boost it by adding more of the spice. Topping each bowl with a dollop of yogurt and a sprinkling of chopped Savory Nut Mix makes it unique and delicious. ⎯⎯ *Serves 4 to 6*

LIVING GREEN
Use the microwave to reheat. It's quicker and more energy efficient to reheat a bowl of soup in the microwave rather than on the stovetop.

1 tablespoon olive oil

About 1½ cups diced yellow onion
  (¼-inch dice)

⅓ cup chopped carrot

1 tablespoon minced garlic

2 teaspoons good-quality curry powder

1 teaspoon Garam Masala (page 432)

2 pounds Garnet or Jewel yams (sweet
  potatoes), peeled and cut into ½-inch dice

4 to 5 cups Vegetable Stock (page 410),
  Chicken Wing Stock (page 403), or
  store-bought low-sodium chicken or
  vegetable broth

Salt and freshly ground black pepper

¼ cup plain yogurt (optional)

⅓ cup chopped Savory Nut Mix
  (page 431, optional)

1. Heat the olive oil in a large, heavy pot over medium heat. Add the onion and carrot and cook, stirring frequently, until the vegetables soften, 5 to 8 minutes. Add the garlic, curry powder, and Garam Masala and cook, stirring frequently, until fragrant, about 2 minutes.

2. Add the yams and 4 cups of the stock, cover the pot, and raise the heat to high. Bring the soup to a boil. Then reduce the heat to medium and cook until the yams are soft, 20 to 30 minutes.

3. Using an immersion blender, puree the soup in the pot. (Or let the soup cool slightly; then puree it in a blender or food processor and return it to the pot.) Season the soup with salt and pepper to taste, and add more stock as needed to achieve the desired consistency. Gently reheat the soup over medium-low heat.

4. To serve, divide the soup among warmed bowls. If you like, add a dollop of yogurt to each serving and sprinkle some of the nuts around the edges of the bowls. For reheating instructions, see the sidebar on page 4.

Note: If you are not planning to serve the soup immediately, let it cool to room temperature; then cover and refrigerate it for up to 5 days. Reheat over low heat to serve.

Mushroom Bisque

CREAMY MUSHROOM BISQUE, with its rich, earthy flavor and woodsy aroma, is a perennial favorite. We've combined three kinds of mushrooms for an incredible depth of flavor, mellowed with just a touch of cream. For a vegetarian version of this soup, substitute Vegetable Stock, preferably homemade (page 410). ⎯⎯ *Serves 4 to 6*

2 tablespoons (¼ stick) butter

About 1 cup diced yellow onion (¼-inch dice)

½ cup thinly sliced leeks (white and pale green parts)

4 cups (about 10 ounces) thinly sliced white mushrooms

2 cups (about 6 ounces) thinly sliced brown (cremini) mushrooms

½ cup (2½ ounces) thinly sliced shiitake mushroom caps

1 teaspoon dried thyme

5 to 6 cups Chicken Wing Stock (page 403) or good-quality store-bought low-sodium chicken broth

½ cup heavy (whipping) cream

Salt and freshly ground black pepper

1. Melt the butter in a large saucepan over medium heat. Add the onion and leeks and cook, stirring frequently, until soft, 5 to 8 minutes.

2. Add all the mushrooms and the thyme, and raise the heat to medium. Cook, stirring frequently, until the mushrooms give off liquid and begin to soften, about 5 minutes.

3. Add 5 cups of the chicken stock, cover the pan, and bring to a simmer. Then reduce the heat to medium-low and cook until the mushrooms are very tender, 40 to 50 minutes. Remove the pan from the heat and let the soup sit, covered, for 10 minutes.

4. Transfer the soup to a food processor, add the cream, and process to a coarse puree, with small bits of mushroom still discernible. Return the soup to a clean saucepan and reheat it gently over low heat until hot. Season with salt and pepper to taste.

Note: If you are not planning to serve the soup immediately, let it cool to room temperature; then cover and refrigerate it for up to 3 days. Reheat over low heat to serve.

Mushroom Barley Soup

MOST DELIS IN NEW YORK serve mushroom barley soup, and I grew up eating it regularly. Barley is chewy, moist, slightly sweet, and it goes with just about anything, but I especially love it paired with mushrooms. The natural starch in this grain acts as a thickener and gives the soup a lovely sheen. Three different varieties of mushrooms add earthy flavor, with the porcinis contributing an intriguing hint of smokiness. Although this recipe specifies the use of hulled barley, it can also be made with the hull-less form, with no sacrifice of nutrients. Barley is a thirsty grain that soaks up whatever cooking liquid it encounters; if you choose to use the pearled (hull-less) form, you will need less stock as it does not absorb as much liquid during cooking or storage. For a vegetarian version of this soup, simply substitute Vegetable Stock (page 410) for the beef stock. ⎯⎯ **_Serves 8_**

3 tablespoons olive oil

About 1 cup diced yellow onion (¼-inch dice)

½ cup thinly sliced leek (white and light
    green parts)

2 small celery ribs, thinly sliced
    (about ½ cup)

1 medium carrot, peeled and cut into
    ¼-inch dice (½ cup)

¾ ounce (about ½ cup) dried porcini
    mushrooms (see sidebar)

1 cup boiling water

4 cups (1 pound) thinly sliced shiitake
    mushroom caps

2 cups (about 6 ounces) thinly sliced brown
    (cremini) mushrooms

1½ teaspoons dried thyme

8 cups Basic Beef Stock (page 402)
    or store-bought low-sodium beef broth,
    or more if needed

1 cup hulled barley
    (also called barley groats)

Salt and freshly ground black pepper

1. Heat the oil in a large stockpot over medium heat. Add the onion, leek, celery, and carrot and cook, stirring frequently, until the vegetables soften, 5 to 8 minutes.

2. Meanwhile, place the dried porcini mushrooms in a small bowl and cover with the boiling water. Let sit for 10 minutes.

3. Add the shiitake mushrooms, cremini mushrooms, and thyme to the stockpot. Raise the heat to medium. Cook, stirring frequently, until the mushrooms give off liquid and begin to soften, about 5 minutes.

4. Using a slotted spoon, remove the porcini mushrooms from their soaking liquid and add them to the soup. Pour in the soaking liquid, taking care to leave behind any grit

THE BASICS

Dried Porcini Mushrooms

Fresh porcini mushrooms, also called cèpes, are one of the world's most delectable wild mushrooms. Characterized by their earthy, woodsy flavor and meaty texture, they are highly prized by chefs. Fresh porcini are rarely found outside of specialty shops in major metropolitan areas, but fortunately the mushrooms are widely available in their dried form. Choose dried porcini that are tan to pale brown in color, and look for large pieces, not crumbles.

Dried porcini need to be softened in hot water for about 10 minutes before using. The soaking liquid is extremely flavorful, so make sure you add it to whatever dish you are preparing. Watch for any grit that may have settled at the bottom of the bowl during soaking, and leave it behind.

Asian Broth with Tofu and Brown Rice

that may have settled at the bottom. Add the beef stock and barley, cover the pot, and cook over medium-low heat until the barley is tender, 50 to 60 minutes.

5. Season the soup with salt and pepper to taste, and serve hot.

Note: If you are not planning to serve the soup immediately, let it cool to room temperature; then cover and refrigerate it for up to 5 days. While this soup sits, the hulled barley will continue to absorb the stock. You may find that you need to add more beef stock when you reheat the soup.

Asian Broth with Tofu and Brown Rice

I ESPECIALLY LIKE THIS LIGHT AND HEALTHY SOUP, which is filled with two of my favorite ingredients, brown rice and tofu. The slow simmering infuses every spoonful with the fragrance and flavors of the East, and as a bonus, the soup is a beautiful study of color and texture. ⎯⎯ *Serves 6*

¾ cup brown rice

Salt

1 tablespoon canola oil

½ tablespoon plain sesame oil
   (see sidebar, this page)

1 cup thinly sliced yellow onion

1 tablespoon grated peeled fresh ginger

1 teaspoon minced garlic

1 cup (packed) thinly sliced shiitake
   or white mushrooms

½ cup thinly sliced scallions
   (white part and 3 inches of green)

8 cups Vegetable Stock (page 410) or
   store-bought low-sodium vegetable broth

¼ cup soy sauce

2 tablespoons unseasoned rice vinegar

1 cup firm tofu cubes (½-inch dice)

Cayenne pepper

1. Place the rice in a small saucepan and add water to cover by 1 inch. Add 1 teaspoon salt, cover the pan, and bring to a boil over medium-high heat. Then reduce the heat to maintain a gentle simmer, and cook until the water has been absorbed and the rice is just tender, 30 to 40 minutes. (If the water has been absorbed but the rice is not tender, add ½ cup more water and continue to cook, covered.) Remove from the heat and set aside at room temperature.

2. Heat the canola and sesame oils in a large, heavy pot over medium heat. Add the onion and ginger and cook, stirring frequently, until the vegetables are soft and fragrant, 5 to 8 minutes.

Sesame Oils

Sesame oil is available in two forms: plain and toasted. Plain (or cold-pressed) oil is made from raw sesame seeds and has very little color, aroma, or flavor. Its neutral taste and high smoke point make it a good choice for sautéing. It will keep for up to 6 months at room temperature. Toasted (or roasted) sesame oil, on the other hand, is made from toasted seeds, a technique that draws out a rich fragrance and flavor. It is a deep brown color and should be stored in the refrigerator to avoid spoilage. Unlike plain sesame oil, it should not be used as a cooking oil, although a few teaspoons are often added to a dish at the very end of stir-frying once the pan is off the heat. Use toasted sesame oil for vinaigrettes and cold sauces, too.

3. Add the garlic and shiitakes and cook, stirring frequently, until the mushrooms begin to soften, about 5 minutes. Do not let the garlic brown.

4. Add the scallions and stock, cover the pot, and bring to a boil over medium-high heat. Reduce the heat to medium-low and let the soup simmer until the mushrooms are tender, about 30 minutes.

5. Stir in the cooked rice, soy sauce, rice vinegar, and tofu. Simmer until heated through, 2 to 3 minutes. Season the soup with salt and cayenne pepper to taste. Serve hot. For reheating instructions, see the sidebar on page 4.

Note: The rice can be cooked up to 2 days in advance and refrigerated, covered, until you are ready to make the soup.

Winter Vegetable Soup

THIS IS ONE OF THE FEW SOUPS WHERE I USE BEEF BROTH. I like its rich flavor here, and the way it marries so well with the tomatoes. But feel free to use vegetable broth if you prefer a vegetarian version. In the first step, aromatic vegetables and mushrooms are slowly caramelized to develop a foundation of flavor. Don't rush this, because the intense flavors that develop from the slow cooking impart a rich complexity to the broth. Potatoes and lentils thicken the texture of the soup and give it a rustic, hearty character. To turn this dish into a full meal, spoon cooked whole wheat pasta (shells or penne work well) into individual bowls, and then ladle the soup over it. Soups like this are all about flexibility—using whatever looks good at the farmers' market, produce that might be on sale, or those leftovers lurking in your refrigerator. Substitutions may require an adjustment of cooking times, but you really can't go wrong with this kind of recipe if you start with quality ingredients. I make a huge batch because I like having this soup available for more than one meal, but the recipe is easily halved— the vegetable amounts need not be overly precise. ⟶ *Serves 10 to 12*

3 tablespoons olive oil

About 2 cups diced yellow onion
   (¼-inch dice)

2 small celery ribs, thinly sliced
   (about ½ cup)

2 medium carrots, peeled and cut into
   ¼-inch-thick slices (about 1 cup)

5 ounces shiitake mushroom caps,
   cut in half and sliced ¼-inch thick

12 cups Basic Beef Stock (page 402) or
   store-bought low-sodium beef broth

½ cup French green (du Puy) lentils, rinsed

1 can (28 ounces) diced tomatoes,
   with their juices

3 Yukon Gold potatoes (12 ounces total),
   peeled and cut into ⅓-inch cubes
   (about 2 cups)

2 dried bay leaves

1½ teaspoons dried oregano

1 teaspoon dried basil

¾ teaspoon salt

½ teaspoon garlic powder

¼ teaspoon dried red pepper flakes

1 bunch kale, ribs removed, leaves chopped
   into 1-inch pieces (4 cups packed)

2 cups cauliflower florets

¼ small head green cabbage (8 ounces),
   cored and thinly sliced (about 2 cups)

1½ cups frozen sweet corn

¾ cup chopped fresh flat-leaf parsley

Salt and freshly ground black pepper

Freshly grated Parmesan cheese, for
   garnish (optional)

1. Heat the oil in a large pot over medium heat. Add the onion, celery, carrots, and mushrooms and cook, stirring frequently, until the vegetables are soft and have begun to take on a golden color, about 15 minutes.

2. Add the beef stock and lentils, raise the heat to medium-high, cover the pot, and bring to the start of a boil. Then reduce the heat to medium-low and simmer the soup for 20 minutes.

3. Stir in the tomatoes, potatoes, bay leaves, oregano, basil, salt, garlic powder, and red pepper flakes. Cover and cook for 10 minutes.

4. Add the kale and cook, covered, for 10 minutes. Add the cauliflower and cabbage and cook, covered, until all of the vegetables are tender, about 10 minutes.

LIVING GREEN
Match your pans to the size of the burners on your stove. If the circumference of the burner is larger than the bottom of your pan, you're leaking a lot of unused heat into the air.

how saving time can also save energy

My workdays feel like a whirlwind of activity, so I'm always looking for ways to save time—especially in the kitchen. Before I started writing this book, I'd always thought of my shortcuts as a kind of efficient laziness, but now I realize I'm saving not only my own energy, I'm reducing my household's energy use as well.

I almost always serve directly from the pan I cooked in instead of a serving bowl or platter, considering it one fewer dish I have to wash at the end of a meal. The food usually stays warmer (especially when it's been cooked in and served from a cast-iron pan). It makes for a casual, family-style atmosphere that I like. I also pop a pot of cooled soup right in the fridge instead of putting it in a separate storage container. It saves washing-up time and conserves water. After all, I'm only going to return the soup to that same pot the next day.

Now that I've learned so much more about how important it is to conserve water, especially hot water, which uses a lot of energy, I feel really good about my shortcuts. Every time I decide to wear an apron one more time before I wash it or avoid using another bowl when I am baking, I know I am saving more than just my time; I'm saving energy, too.

5. Add the corn and parsley and cook, uncovered, until heated through, 3 to 5 minutes. Remove from the heat, and season with salt and pepper to taste.

6. To serve, divide the soup among wide shallow bowls, and sprinkle each serving with Parmesan cheese if desired. For reheating instructions, see the sidebar on page 4.

Butternut, White Bean, and Chard Soup

EMBRACE THE BEST OF COLD-WEATHER PRODUCE WITH THIS hearty, satisfying soup. At the Farm Stand, we're adrift in a sea of hard squashes and pumpkins from September to December, and we put our autumn bounty to good use all through the cold months with creations like this delicious soup. It's full of flavor, and the combination of squash, white beans, and chard is simply scrumptious. Although the recipe specifies butternut, Hubbard, Carnival, and other hard squashes will work as well. ⎯⎯ *Serves 6 to 8*

1½ tablespoons canola oil

1½ tablespoons olive oil

1½ cups diced yellow onion (⅓-inch dice)

2 celery ribs, cut into ⅓-inch dice

3 pounds butternut squash, peeled, seeded, and cut into ½-inch cubes (about 4 cups)

8 cups Vegetable Stock (page 410), Chicken Wing Stock (page 403), or store-bought low-sodium vegetable or chicken broth

1 bunch Swiss chard, ribs discarded, leaves chopped into ½-inch pieces (about 4 lightly packed cups)

2 cups cooked white beans, such as navy or cannellini (rinse if using canned beans)

1 tablespoon chopped fresh thyme leaves

Salt and freshly ground black pepper

1. Heat the canola and olive oils in a soup pot or a large saucepan over medium heat. Add the onion and celery, and cook, stirring frequently, until the vegetables are soft but not browned, 5 to 8 minutes.

2. Add the squash and the stock, and bring to a simmer. Reduce the heat to medium-low, cover the pot, and simmer until the squash is just tender, 30 to 40 minutes.

3. Add the chard, beans, and thyme and simmer until the chard wilts and the beans are heated through, 5 to 10 minutes. Season the soup with salt and pepper to taste, and serve hot. For reheating instructions, see the sidebar on page 4.

LIVING GREEN
"Shop" your pantry before you shop the shops. Using food you have sitting in the fridge or pantry saves time and eliminates waste.

Butternut, White Bean, and Chard Soup

the delicious joys of eating local foods **in season**

There are so many reasons to seek out local producers and to choose foods that are in season: Experiencing the incredible flavor of fruits that have fully ripened on tree or vine. Discovering a multitude of colors, shapes, and flavors of varieties unheard of in most supermarkets. Getting to know the people who grow and prepare our food. And supporting your local community—the artisan baker, local farmer, corner butcher, and neighboring beekeeper.

Local food is a small but thriving part of our food economy: In 2009, the USDA estimated there were 4,800 farmers' markets nationwide. We also have the option of buying fresh from the fields at local farm stands or through community supported agriculture programs (CSAs). Buying produce weekly through CSAs, usually from one organic farmer, brings a box of varied produce items that contains whatever was ready to harvest that week. This is a good way to discover new ingredients and challenge yourself to cook with what's available. Plus, when produce is sold directly to the consumer, it cuts down on packaging.

Taste and Variety

When you buy local, you can get flavor and variety that you won't see in produce bred for maximum shelf life and long-distance shipping. Once many fruits are fully ripe, they must be eaten within days, so selling locally is usually the only commercially viable way to offer this produce.

I learned to cook with our organic heirloom raspberries when Drew and I started to farm in 1984 because they had to be used within 48 hours after they were picked. The raspberries we didn't sell at the roadside stand during the day needed to quickly become muffins or jam, or they would spoil. Many years later, when we opened the organic café at our Carmel Valley Farm Stand, one of the motivating factors for building an on-site, certified organic kitchen was to convert excess farm stand produce into tasty meals and baked goods for much the same reason.

Don't assume that just because something is sold at a farmers' market or farm stand, it's organically grown. I was surprised to discover that more than half of the produce at our local farmers' market is not organic. So ask questions just as you would of any supplier, and then go for all the flavor and variety you can find.

Pear and Fennel Soup

JUICY PEARS AND CRISP, ANISE-SCENTED FENNEL may seem like an odd pairing, but this delicate soup is remarkable for its subtle flavor and silken texture. This is the only soup in this cookbook that is meant to be served as a small, elegant starter. Fennel and pears are both at their seasonal best in the cooler months of autumn, and the aromatic, cleansing flavor of fennel perfectly balances the overt sweetness of the pears. In its raw state fennel has a sweet anise taste, but when cooked, its distinctive licorice-like flavor tames and mellows. To subtly reassert some of this elusive flavor, ground fennel and a splash of Sambuca are added to the soup at serving time. For an elegant presentation, garnish each serving with a sprig of feathery fennel fronds. ⁓⁓ **_Serves 4_**

4 cups very thinly sliced fennel
(about 2 large bulbs; see box, page 32)

1 cup pear nectar

3 Bosc pears, peeled, cored, and cut into
½-inch dice

¼ cup heavy (whipping) cream,
or more to taste

¼ teaspoon sea salt, or to taste

1 teaspoon fennel (anise) seed, toasted
(see box) and ground

1 teaspoon fresh lemon juice

1 to 2 teaspoons Sambuca or Pernod
(optional)

1. Combine the fennel and 2 cups water in a medium-size saucepan, cover, and bring to a boil over high heat. Reduce the heat to medium and simmer for 20 minutes.

2. Add the pear nectar and the diced pears, cover the pan, and cook until the pears and fennel are very soft and tender, 20 to 25 minutes. Remove the pan from the heat and let the mixture cool for 10 minutes.

3. Transfer the mixture to a blender or food processor, and puree until smooth. Pass the soup through a fine-mesh sieve set over a clean saucepan; discard any solids. Reheat the soup over medium-low heat. Add the cream and bring to a simmer. Season the soup with sea salt. If the soup seems too thin, cook for 5 to 10 minutes to reduce and concentrate the flavors.

4. Just before serving, add the ground fennel, lemon juice, and Sambuca (if using). (Do not add these in advance of serving because much of the flavor will dissipate.) Divide the soup among four warmed bowls, and serve hot. For reheating instructions, see the sidebar on page 4.

Toasting Nuts and Seeds

Toasting brings out the wonderful flavor and aroma of nuts and seeds and makes them crisp and crunchy. This step takes only a few minutes, but you must watch the nuts and seeds carefully, as they can burn very easily. To reduce the risk of this happening, toast nuts whole or in large pieces.

◆ **IN THE OVEN:** Position a rack in the center of the oven and preheat the oven to 350°F. Spread the nuts or seeds in a single layer on a rimmed baking sheet. Bake them for 5 minutes; then stir. Continue baking until the nuts or seeds are warm to the touch, lightly colored, and fragrant, 2 to 5 minutes longer.

◆ **IN THE MICROWAVE:** Spread the nuts or seeds in a single layer on a microwave-safe plate. Microwave on high power for 1 to 3 minutes, checking and stirring every 30 to 60 seconds, until the nuts or seeds are warm to the touch, lightly colored, and fragrant. The cooking time will depend on the variety of nut, the amount you are toasting, and the wattage of your microwave oven.

◆ **ON THE STOVETOP:** Place the nuts or seeds in a single layer in a heavy skillet, preferably cast-iron, over medium heat. Slowly toast, stirring occasionally, until the nuts or seeds are warm to the touch, lightly colored, and fragrant, 3 to 10 minutes.

Fennel

Revered in Italy, fennel is just starting to become well known in the United States. This sweet, aromatic vegetable with its pale green, celery-like stalks, broad bulbous base, and bright green, feathery fronds is incredibly versatile, juicy, and delicious. The main variety cultivated throughout the Mediterranean and in this country is called Florence fennel (*finocchio*). It is sometimes mislabeled "sweet anise," which deters many who don't like the flavor of licorice from giving this vegetable a try. Fennel, however, is much sweeter and more delicate than anise, with a whispery anise fragrance but none of its sharp licorice taste. Once fennel is cooked, this flavor is even lighter and more elusive than in its raw state.

Fennel is easy to prepare and can be eaten raw or cooked. The bulb is made up of overlapping onionlike layers that encase a sweet-tasting, dense heart. Raw fennel is crisp and crunchy, with a refreshing, clean flavor, and makes a terrific addition to salads. When slow-cooked, its distinctive flavor mellows and the fennel becomes lusciously, meltingly soft. In Tuscany, fennel is the quintessential accompaniment for pork in all of its many guises.

Available year-round, fennel is at its prime from late fall through winter into early spring. Choose large, squat, glossy bulbs with a pale green tint; they should show no signs of cracking, bruising, or browning. The larger the bulb, the less waste is involved, and although it may seem counterintuitive, larger bulbs are often more tender than elongated, slender ones. If possible, buy fennel that still has its stalks and fronds attached, because these parts deteriorate first and are good indicators of freshness. The graceful greenery, which should be bright green, can be used as a garnish or snipped like dill and used as a last-minute flavor enhancer.

At home, refrigerate unwashed fennel in a plastic bag for up to 5 days. To prepare it, wash it thoroughly with cold water. Cut off the feathery fronds and the tubular stalks. Discard the stalks, and reserve the fronds for garnish. Trim the base and remove any discolored layers. (Usually the outer layer of the bulb needs to be discarded, as it can be stringy and tough.) Cut the bulb in half lengthwise. If there is a large core at the base, remove it with a small paring knife. Cut the bulb into wedges, or cut it crosswise into thin slices. Once cut, fennel will discolor from oxidation. To prevent this, squeeze some lemon juice into a bowl of cold water and submerge the cut fennel in it until you are ready to use it.

CHAPTER 2

LEAFY GREEN SALADS

Celebrating Salads

WHEN I WAS GROWING UP IN NEW YORK CITY, I DIDN'T EAT A lot of salads. Which, thinking back, is not too surprising. Most of the salads I remember were made of less-than-fresh iceberg lettuce, a few cold, flavorless tomato wedges, some dry cucumber slices, and maybe a black olive or two . . . usually served with gelatinous Italian or French dressing from a bottle.

I first fell in love with salads when my husband, Drew, and I started growing organic heirloom greens on our farm in Carmel Valley. I never knew lettuces could be so beautiful and delicious! We grew Lola Rosa, which is a light green color near the base that graduates to dark burgundy as the leaves widen toward their frilly-edged tops; bright green and deep red oak-leaf lettuce, with its graceful scalloped edges that really do look like soft, tender oak leaves; and many other varieties that we discovered in seed catalogs.

We experimented with lots of delectable greens, happily sampling the varied tastes and textures— nothing was bland or boring, and I savored them all. There were so many different dressings and ingredients to add that I ended up eating salads all the time, and I still do more than 26 years later. I almost always have a huge salad for lunch,

and then another salad either before, during, or even a couple of hours after dinner. The myriad ways to prepare leafy greens ensure that this healthy fare is always interesting and satisfying. Because I love salads so much, I'm surprised when someone tells me they choose them only when they're trying "to be good and eat healthy" or to lose weight—that flavor isn't their reason for going for the greens. But flavor is *exactly* what we're celebrating in this chapter. I truly believe these delicious recipes are hard not to love.

I urge you to explore a wide variety of salad greens and lettuces, each with its own distinctive flavor and texture. And never compromise on freshness or quality—all the toppings and dressings in the world won't disguise old or wilted lettuce.

Try something different with our Watercress Salad with Crispy Prosciutto, Roasted Tomatoes, and Avocado. The salad itself is

deliciously unique, and the roasted tomatoes will quickly become a recipe gem you'll go back to again and again. Or for a perfect winter salad, try the Escarole with Walnuts, Dates, and Bacon. The intense, rich flavors can serve as a perfect first course to almost any hearty dinner entrée.

In our Salad with Raspberries, Avocado, and Goat Cheese, juicy sweet raspberries perfectly complement the delicate flavor of creamy goat cheese and avocado. Close your eyes and feel the summer sunshine! And if you've never tried strawberries with greens, you're in for a special treat: the Heirloom Lettuce Salad with Strawberries, Walnuts, and Goat Cheese is a favorite of mine. The light balsamic vinaigrette perfectly supports the tangy sweetness of the strawberries and the flavorful heirloom lettuce. Add toasted walnuts and soft goat cheese, and you'll be in salad heaven.

A great way to bring out the best in your salads is to mix your own fresh dressing. Many bottled dressings are made with poor-quality ingredients and often contain additives you don't need or want. Homemade is usually fresher, more flavorful, and often less expensive. I've included fifteen dressing recipes here. Discover the subtle flavors of different olive and nut oils, the surprising variety of vinegars, and the back-to-basic simplicity of lemon juice and fresh herbs. Some of the creamy dressings contain tangy yogurt, tofu, or goat cheese—healthy ingredients that taste great without adding a lot of calories.

Sometimes I think about the difference between the disappointing salad choices I had growing up and the beautiful, nutritious organic salad greens that are available in almost every supermarket across the country today. It's a great feeling to know that Drew and I played a role in that significant and beneficial culinary revolution. I'm so happy to share my passion for salads with you in this cookbook and hope you are as inspired by the infinite choices of leafy greens as I am.

Butter Lettuce Salad with Pears, Pecans, and Gorgonzola (page 68)

Heirloom Lettuce Salad with Strawberries, Walnuts, and Goat Cheese

Heirloom Lettuce Salad with Strawberries, Walnuts, and Goat Cheese

SWEET-TART AND SUCCULENT, STRAWBERRIES are a true joy of spring and summer. This light and delicious salad uses whole heirloom lettuce leaves as a beautiful and flavorful base for the delightful blending of sweet strawberries, creamy goat cheese, and toasted walnuts. The flavors are melded perfectly by a quick-to-make balsamic vinaigrette that features toasted walnut oil. ⸻ *Serves 4 as a side salad*

1 pint fresh strawberries, rinsed, dried, and hulled

Walnut Balsamic Vinaigrette (recipe follows)

7 ounces heirloom lettuce leaves, left whole, or 5 ounces mixed baby greens, rinsed and dried if not prewashed

½ cup walnut pieces, toasted (see box, page 31)

½ cup (about 2 ounces) crumbled goat cheese

1. Cut the strawberries in quarters, place them in a small bowl, and toss them with about 2 tablespoons of the vinaigrette. Set aside.

2. Place all of the lettuce leaves in a large bowl and add 3 tablespoons of the vinaigrette. Toss to lightly coat the leaves; then taste and add more vinaigrette if needed.

3. Transfer the lettuce to individual salad plates. Top the lettuce with the strawberries, toasted walnuts, and crumbled goat cheese, and serve immediately.

THE BASICS

Keeping Lettuce Fresh

To extend the life of leafy greens, wash the leaves and spin them dry to remove all of the moisture. If you plan on using the lettuce within a day, you can leave them in your salad spinner. Otherwise, place the greens in a plastic bag and add a sheet of paper towel, which will absorb any residual moisture. Store in the crisper drawer or if you don't have one, the coolest part of your refrigerator. The greens should stay fresh for up to a week.

Lettuces, left to right: red romaine, red bibb, and green oakleaf.

Nut Oils

Nut oils can turn an ordinary dressing into something extraordinary. Today, most major supermarkets and specialty gourmet shops stock oils made from walnuts, hazelnuts, almonds, pecans, and pistachios. They are not inexpensive, but they do add a depth of flavor and fragrance to salads that can't be beat. Look for toasted or roasted nut oils, and those that have been cold-pressed or expeller-pressed. This indicates that the oil has been extracted through pressure, rather than with heat or solvents.

Nut oils have a short shelf life and can become rancid if not stored properly. After opening one, always refrigerate the oil. Stored in the refrigerator, nut oils will keep for up to 6 months.

Walnut Balsamic Vinaigrette

Good-quality balsamic vinegar and walnut oil make all the difference in this dressing. If you can find a roasted walnut oil, its intensely nutty flavor will not be overpowered by the rich balsamic vinegar. This vinaigrette is delicious paired with Heirloom Lettuce Salad with Strawberries, Walnuts, and Goat Cheese, but it's also light enough to dress delicate baby spinach, mâche, or baby greens. ⁓ **Makes about ½ cup**

2 tablespoons balsamic vinegar
½ teaspoon Dijon mustard
3 tablespoons toasted walnut oil
   (see sidebar)
2 tablespoons extra-virgin olive oil
Salt and freshly ground black pepper

Combine the vinegar, mustard, and both oils in a glass jar and seal the lid tightly. Shake the jar vigorously to combine. Season the vinaigrette with salt and pepper to taste. (The vinaigrette can be refrigerated, covered, for up to 1 month. Let it return to room temperature and shake vigorously before using.)

Spring Mix Salad with Warm Almond-Crusted Goat Cheese

HERE'S AN EASY WAY TO IMPRESS FRIENDS: Serve warm disks of meltingly soft goat cheese, coated with crunchy toasted almonds, on top of a medley of tender baby greens. Some slices of apple and a handful of raisins contribute a hint of sweetness that balances the earthy flavor of the goat cheese. If you prefer a salad without fruit, just leave it out—it will still be delicious. The thyme-accented balsamic vinaigrette pairs well with this combination of ingredients; the Apple Cider Vinaigrette (page 62) is good with this salad, too. ⁓ **Serves 4 as a side salad**

4 ounces plain fresh goat cheese log,
   such as Montrachet

2 tablespoons finely chopped toasted
   unsalted almonds (see box, page 31)

5 ounces (about 6 cups) mixed baby greens,
   rinsed and dried if not prewashed

1 large crisp apple, such as Fuji or Gala,
   quartered, cored, and thinly sliced

About ¼ cup Lemon-Thyme Balsamic
   Vinaigrette (recipe follows)

Salt and freshly ground black pepper

¼ cup raisins

1. Position a rack about 5 inches from the broiler unit and preheat the broiler on high. Line a rimmed baking sheet with parchment paper or aluminum foil.

2. Cut the goat cheese into 4 rounds, each approximately ½-inch thick.

Press the almonds into the top and bottom of each cheese round. Transfer the cheese to the prepared baking sheet.

3. Place the greens and apple slices in a large bowl, and add half of the vinaigrette. Toss to coat, season to taste with salt and pepper, and add more vinaigrette as desired.

4. Broil the cheese until the top begins to brown, watching closely so that the nuts don't burn, 1 to 3 minutes.

5. Divide the greens among four salad plates. Using a spatula, place a cheese round in the middle of each salad. Sprinkle with the raisins, and serve immediately.

THE BASICS

Rinse First

For food safety, if it has not been prewashed, always rinse fresh produce, including herbs and those items that you peel, whether it's organic or conventional.

Lemon-Thyme Balsamic Vinaigrette

Combining two types of oil and two types of acid results in a French-style vinaigrette that is both lighter and more flavorful than single-ingredient dressings. We like the combination of thyme with goat cheese, but basil or oregano, either fresh or dried, can be added to vary the effect. Because the dressing is so light, it's very nice on all tender salad greens. ⌇⌇⌇*Makes about ½ cup*

¼ cup extra-virgin olive oil

2 tablespoons canola oil

2 tablespoons balsamic vinegar

1½ teaspoons fresh lemon juice

½ teaspoon minced shallot

½ teaspoon dried thyme

¼ teaspoon sugar

Place all the ingredients in a glass jar and seal the lid tightly. Shake the jar vigorously to combine. (The vinaigrette can be refrigerated, covered, for up to 1 month. Let it return to room temperature and shake vigorously before using.)

why I am so passionate about organic food and farming

Until I became a farmer myself, I never thought much about how my food was grown. When I bought produce in my local supermarket, the chemicals that were used to grow the items I purchased were odorless and invisible, so I had no idea they were there. But when Drew and I moved onto our farm in 1984 and were taught how to apply all the synthetic fertilizers and potent pesticides stacked in the shed, we both knew without a doubt—in our minds and hearts—that we didn't want to handle these chemicals, apply them to our soil, or eat food grown with them. There was absolutely no question about it. We felt certain that there had to be a way to grow healthier food in cooperation with nature—we just needed to commit to figuring out how! And so began our lifelong journey as organic farmers.

For most of agricultural history, people grew crops using practices we would call organic. Not until the second half of the 20th century did the use of synthetic fertilizers and pesticides become common. Today, this type of farming is called "conventional," meaning that any other practices are outside the norm. At first, these chemical inputs seemed to be extremely effective. They increased yields and decreased crop damage from insects and disease, and farmers saw the potential to be more successful and earn a better living. But like so many things that seem to be silver bullets at the outset, there were unpredicted consequences: health hazards that emerged with the persistence of chemical pesticides in our soil, water, air, and bodies; "dead zones" in major waterways; widespread erosion of topsoil due to a lack of productive organic matter; and ultimately a system of farming that has become dependent on more and stronger chemicals to sustain yields and viability.

In contrast, the principles of organic farming revolve around working with the biological and ecological systems that exist within nature. So rather than add synthetic fertilizers to increase fertility, we build the health of our soil in natural ways. We take advantage of the nutrients in things like compost and cover crops to improve soil quality over time. Instead of using toxic chemical insecticides, we work to build populations of beneficial insects that eat the "pest" insects that damage our crops. Each organic field has flowering habitats nearby, so that beneficial insects will have a place to make their homes. We also practice crop rotation, which means that we don't plant the same crop in the same place season after season. Crop rotation breaks the cycle of pest infestations naturally, without having to resort to poisons. This practice also helps prevent plant diseases from building up in the field and takes advantage of the fact that different crops need different nutrients from the soil. And when it comes to weeds, we deal with them with tractors or by hand—not with toxic herbicides.

Organic farmers use natural methods to enrich the soil and create a healthy ecosystem in which the farm can thrive and produce delicious food. Organic farming complements the local ecology and does not expose our land, air, and water to toxic synthetic chemicals. It's safer for the environment, for the people who farm the land, for the homes and schools nearby, and for those of us who eat the harvest.

Organic for the Health of the Planet

Because atmospheric carbon dioxide (CO_2) contributes significantly to global warming, it's more important than ever to find ways to reduce our "carbon footprint" in everything we do. According to the Rodale Institute, the leading researcher on this topic, organic soil can convert carbon from a greenhouse gas into a food-producing asset. Their studies have shown carbon increases of almost 30 percent in organic soil over 27 years, while conventional farming systems showed no significant increase in soil carbon in the same time period. It is thought that in the conventional system the application of soluble nitrogen fertilizers stimulates organic matter to decay more rapidly and completely, sending carbon into the atmosphere instead of retaining it in the soil as the organic systems do. Organic soils that are rich in carbon also conserve water and support healthier plants that are more resistant to drought stress, pests, and diseases.

Today, land that is farmed organically represents a small percentage of the United States' agricultural output. Even so, the 2.4 million acres managed organically in 2005—just 0.5 percent of all U.S. farmland—captured an estimated 2.4 billion pounds of atmospheric carbon. Imagine the effect if 25 percent, or even 50 percent, of U.S. agricultural farmlands converted to organic production. The land could potentially sequester 120 to 240 billion pounds of CO_2 per year, the equivalent of removing up to 42 million cars from the road.

Organic growers, like the 150 dedicated farmers who grow organic produce for Earthbound Farm, understand the benefits of using natural methods to grow healthy crops and protect our ecosystems. It's hard to believe that the idea of growing food effectively without agricultural chemicals seemed so radical when Drew and I started farming in 1984, even though people had farmed that way for centuries. To me it seems much more irrational to think that we can introduce all these toxic and persistent synthetic chemicals into the environment without significant adverse effects. Organic farming is a passion I've followed and will continue to follow because the stakes are so high—for the future health of our planet with its fragile resources, and for the health of our children. Organic farming produces safer, more nutritious, and more flavorful foods while protecting our precious natural resources for generations to come.

Additional Organic Resources:

National Organic Program (NOP): www.ams.usda.gov/nop/indexIE.htm
Detailed information about USDA organic standards

Organic Center: www.organic-center.org
Scientific research related to organic farming and food

Healthy Child Healthy World: www.healthychild.org
Information to keep children healthy in a toxic world

Environmental Working Group's food information: www.foodnews.org
Current Dirty Dozen and Clean 15 produce lists

The Rodale Institute: www.rodaleinstitute.org
Comprehensive research about organic farming

Natural Resources Defense Council: www.nrdc.org
An effective and powerful environmental action program.

Earthbound Farm: www.ebfarm.com
Organic farming information in the "Why Organic" section

Mixed Baby Greens with Roasted Red Peppers, Walnuts, and Feta

Mixed Baby Greens with Roasted Red Peppers, Walnuts, and Feta

I T'S THE COMBINATION OF SMOKY-SWEET ROASTED RED PEPPERS and the creamy tang of feta cheese that makes this salad so memorable. Toasted walnuts add texture and heighten the nutty nuance of our white wine vinaigrette, which is based on walnut oil. For a pretty combination of colors, use yellow cherry tomatoes. ——— *Serves 4 as a side salad*

5 ounces (6 cups) mixed baby greens, rinsed and dried if not prewashed

¾ cup (3¾ ounces) crumbled feta cheese

¾ cup diced roasted red peppers (page 411) or drained bottled red peppers

1 cup halved cherry tomatoes, preferably yellow

½ cup walnut pieces, toasted (see box, page 31)

White Wine–Walnut Vinaigrette (recipe follows)

1. Place the greens, feta, red peppers, cherry tomatoes, and walnuts in a large bowl and toss to combine.

2. Add half of the vinaigrette and toss to coat the salad. Taste, and add more dressing if needed. Serve immediately.

White Wine–Walnut Vinaigrette

This simple dressing makes a delicious complement to soft, tender greens such as mâche or mixed baby lettuces because it's so light and flavorful. We like it paired with our Mixed Baby Greens with Roasted Red Peppers, Walnuts, and Feta because the walnut oil harmonizes beautifully with the sweet peppers and builds on the flavor of the toasted nuts. The vinaigrette is also terrific drizzled over grilled or steamed vegetables. ——— *Makes about ½ cup*

1 tablespoon white wine vinegar

1 tablespoon fresh lemon juice

½ tablespoon minced shallot

3 tablespoons walnut oil (see sidebar, page 38)

3 tablespoons extra-virgin olive oil

Salt to taste

Combine the vinegar, lemon juice, shallot, and both oils in a glass jar and seal the lid tightly. Shake the jar vigorously to combine. Season the vinaigrette with salt to taste. (It can be refrigerated, covered, for up to 1 month. Let it return to room temperature and shake vigorously before using.)

A Field Guide to Salad Greens

Arugula is a popular aromatic leaf, prized for its nutty flavor and mildly peppery bite. Delicious in salads, it also adds flavor to a variety of soups, pastas, and vegetarian dishes.

Wild Arugula, also known as rocket, is a peppery green that adds a spicy punch to salads. It is distinguished from other arugula varieties by its indented or serrated leaves and its lively taste.

Red and green butter lettuces have soft and supple rounded leaves, which are sweet and delicately flavored. Butterhead lettuces include Boston and Bibb, as well as many heirloom varieties.

Chard comes in many colors, even rainbow. Baby chards make a colorful, nutrition-rich addition to salads, while mature leaves taste similar to spinach when cooked.

Belgian Endive is a petite member of the chicory family, known for its succulent and velvety leaves that have a mildly bitter flavor.

Red Endive is a cross between Belgian endive and radicchio. Its red-edged leaves have a pleasantly bitter flavor.

Escarole, a member of the chicory family, has crisp ruffled leaves that range in color from pale yellow to dark green. It is pleasantly bitter and its piquant flavor works well in salads with assertive ingredients.

Frisée is a chicory that is also known as curly endive. Its long frilly leaves with their green tips and pale inner stems add a fresh, slightly bitter flavor, attractive texture, and loft to salads.

Green and red leaf lettuces are popular spring mix ingredients when picked small. These lettuces are very tender with a mellow, grassy flavor.

Little Gem is a small heirloom lettuce in the romaine family that grows 5 to 8 inches long. It is crisp and crunchy like romaine but its succulent leaves are juicier and have a sweeter, nuttier flavor.

Lola Rosa is a mild-flavored lettuce with intensely ruffled leaves that are light green at the base and dark red at the edges.

Mâche, which is also called lamb's lettuce, has very soft and tender leaves that grow in tiny clusters. It has a mild, nutty flavor and makes a pretty, delicious addition to salads.

Mizuna is a Japanese green with a mild, sweet flavor and a slight mustard tang. Its serrated and deeply fringed baby leaves add elegance to spring mix, while adult leaves can be used in cooking.

Mustard leaves have a pungent flavor that strengthens as they mature. When picked young, baby leaves are mild and have less heat. They make an excellent addition to salads and sandwiches.

Green Oak Leaf lettuce has attractive, deeply lobed leaves that resemble oak leaves. They have a mild, sweet flavor and tender texture.

Red Oak Leaf lettuce is tender and delicate with a beautiful claret color that adds drama to any salad.

Green and White Peacock Kale, which comes in both green-tipped white and red forms, is mildly flavored when picked young. The fringed leaves add an ornamental quality and dimension to spring mix.

Radicchio, also known as Italian chicory, has a pleasantly bitter flavor and earthy taste. Its attractive burgundy-red leaves with distinctive white veins and ribs make a striking addition to salads.

Green Romaine lettuce is prized for its texture and mild, celery-like flavor. It has crisp, sturdy leaves with a crunchy central rib, and is grown in both green and red varieties.

Red Romaine lettuce has the same taste and texture as the green variety. Baby romaine is a popular ingredient in spring mix.

Spinach in its baby form is mild, sweet, and delicate with hints of grassy flavor. Packed with nutrients, it is commonly used in salads, although it is also terrific when cooked.

Tango, a leaf lettuce, has distinctive curly, ruffled leaves which are tender and slightly tangier than other leaf lettuces.

Watercress is a tender, succulent green that has a refreshing, peppery bite when the leaves are young. Use it in salads paired with sweet and salty ingredients to balance its mild tang.

Salad Green Yields

Having trouble figuring out how much lettuce to buy? This table should help. The weight indicated for head lettuce, such as romaine, is the weight before you trim it. The cup measurement is after you have torn the lettuce into bite-size pieces. Plan on serving 1½ cups of greens per person for a side salad and 4 cups per person for a main-course salad.

Type	Amount	Cups
Iceberg	2-pound head	16
Romaine	20-ounce head	8
	8-ounce heart	4
Red or green leaf	16-ounce head	8
Butter (Boston or Bibb)	12-ounce head	10
Radicchio	10 ounces	4
Mixed baby greens	5 ounces	6
Baby spinach	5 ounces	6
Baby arugula	5 ounces	6

Watercress Salad with Crispy Prosciutto, Roasted Tomatoes, and Avocado

T HIS SALAD IS A WONDERFUL COMPOSITION of tastes and textures: peppery watercress, creamy and mellow avocado, crunchy nuts, and crisp, salty prosciutto. The oven-roasted cherry tomatoes take about 2 hours to make but are worth the trouble because they are so intensely flavorful. To maximize the use of this much oven time, you might want to double or triple the quantity—the roasted tomatoes will keep in the refrigerator for a month and are a terrific addition to many salads. On the other hand, if you're short on time, skip this step and just use fresh cherry tomatoes—the salad will still be delicious. If you can't find watercress, arugula makes a perfect substitute.

—— *Serves 4 as a side salad*

8 ounces (about 1½ cups) cherry tomatoes, sliced in half lengthwise

4 ounces (about 8 slices) prosciutto

1 tablespoon white wine vinegar or champagne vinegar

3 tablespoons extra-virgin olive oil

1 teaspoon Dijon mustard

Salt and freshly ground black pepper

5 ounces (about 6 cups) watercress or arugula, rinsed and dried if not prewashed

1 ripe avocado, pitted, peeled, and cut into thin slices

¼ cup pine nuts or chopped toasted Marcona almonds

1. Position a rack in the middle of the oven, and preheat the oven to 225°F.

2. Line a rimmed baking sheet with parchment and arrange the cherry tomatoes on it in a single layer, cut side up. Roast the tomatoes in the oven until they have begun to shrivel and dry out, about 2 hours. The tomatoes should retain some moisture but their flavor will have concentrated and sweetened from the long, slow roasting. Remove the baking sheet from the oven and let the tomatoes cool.

Oven-Roasted Tomatoes

When you have a bounty of tomatoes, or if your tomatoes are less than stellar, oven-roasting is a great way to concentrate their sugar and flavor. Double or triple the quantity specified in this recipe to maximize your oven energy expenditure, and use the tomatoes in other salads and hot dishes, such as Earthbound Farm Health Salad (page 48), Bonnie's Best Salad (page 55), or Baked Mediterranean Shrimp (page 153).

3. Raise the oven temperature to 400°F. Line a rimmed baking sheet with a clean piece of parchment and arrange the prosciutto slices on it in a single layer. Bake until the prosciutto turns crisp, 8 to 10 minutes. Remove the baking sheet from the oven.

4. Combine the vinegar, olive oil, and mustard in a medium bowl and whisk to blend. Season with salt and pepper to taste, and whisk again.

5. Add the watercress to the bowl and toss to coat it with the vinaigrette. Divide the greens among four plates. Divide the avocado slices among the salads. Sprinkle each serving with some of the nuts and oven-roasted tomatoes; then top with the crispy prosciutto, either in whole strips or crumbled. Serve immediately.

usda organic certification: what it means

Prior to October 21, 2002, there was no consistent definition of the term "organic," only a network of private and public organic certification agencies with varying standards. In 2002, the United States Department of Agriculture (USDA) launched its National Organic Program (NOP), created to define and govern uniform standards for organic farming and processing operations. These standards detail the methods, practices, and substances that can be used in producing and handling organic crops. The USDA also created a uniform definition of organic food with standardized product labeling guidelines (page 367). This standardization is important because it ensures the integrity of the organic label for those who purchase organic food. When you buy food labeled "organic," you can be sure that it was produced using strict organic production and handling methods certified by an accredited USDA certifying agency. In addition to ensuring that domestic organic products have met these stringent standards, the USDA requires that any imported product labeled "organic" must be certified by a USDA-approved certifier in accordance with the same standards used in the U.S.

The National Organic Program Standards is a detailed, five-hundred-plus-page document, but in the simplest terms, agricultural crops that meet the organic standards must be grown in fields that have undergone a three-year transition period to organic (if they were previously farmed conventionally). Organic produce is grown with:

- no harmful conventional pesticides;
- no fertilizers made with synthetic ingredients or sewage sludge;
- no genetically modified organisms (GMOs);
- no ionizing radiation;
- clear and appropriate buffers between organic fields and nearby conventional farms;
- specific labeling and record keeping to ensure organic integrity; and
- annual inspection by a USDA-accredited independent certifier.

Earthbound Farm Health Salad

E VERYTHING GOOD FROM THE GARDEN plays a role in this salad, which is not only incredibly nutritious but also colorful and appealing. Carrots and radishes add crunch, cubes of succulent jicama stand in for croutons, creamy avocado contributes a touch of richness, and tamari-roasted sunflower seeds lend a crisp, salty note. What I like best about this raw vegetable salad is its versatility: every vegetable is optional. Substitute kohlrabi for the radishes; add shaved fennel, fava beans, strips of bell pepper, or sliced sugar snap peas. You can even toss in a shredded raw beet, if you don't mind that it'll tint your salad red. The Tofu-Dill Dressing is the perfect partner for the ultimate healthy salad—creamy and flavorful, high in protein, and low in fat. ⸺ *Serves 4 as an entrée or 8 as a side salad*

8 cups chopped or torn romaine lettuce, other sturdy lettuce, or spinach, any heavy stems removed, leaves rinsed and dried if not prewashed

1 small jicama (8 to 10 ounces), peeled and cut into ¾-inch cubes (1½ cups)

½ cup cooked chickpeas (garbanzo beans), rinsed and drained if canned

2 large carrots, peeled and cut into julienne (about 1½ cups)

1 cucumber, peeled, halved lengthwise, seeded, and cut into ⅛-inch-thick slices

1 medium red tomato, cut into bite-size wedges

½ cup thinly sliced radishes

1 ripe avocado, pitted, peeled, and cut into ½-inch cubes

1 cup sunflower or other sprouts (see box, page 50)

¼ cup Tamari-Roasted Sunflower Seeds (see recipe, page 51) or salted raw or toasted sunflower seeds

Tofu-Dill Dressing (recipe follows)

1. Divide the lettuce among the serving plates or place it on a large platter. Arrange the jicama, chickpeas, carrots, cucumber, tomato, radishes, and avocado in separate mounds or rows on top of the lettuce, balancing the colors to make an attractive presentation.

2. Sprinkle the salads with the sprouts and the sunflower seeds, and serve with the Tofu-Dill Dressing on the side.

LIVING GREEN
Recent research has shown that some organic foods are more nutritious than their conventional counterparts. In 2008, the Organic Center conducted a review of peer-reviewed scientific studies, and the results were exciting: Average levels of 11 nutrients (including antioxidants, minerals, and protein) are 25 percent higher in organic produce than in conventional produce, based on 236 scientifically valid comparisons.

Earthbound Farm Health Salad

Tofu-Dill Dressing

This is a really healthy dressing—not much oil, and a good amount of vegetable protein contributed by the tofu. Flavored with garlic and fresh dill, it's very tasty. Although we specify silken or soft tofu, firm will also work, but it adds a bit of a grainy texture. If the dressing is too thick for your liking, thin it with a tablespoon of water. This dressing also makes a delicious dip for raw vegetables. *Makes 2 cups*

2 large garlic cloves, peeled

½ cup fresh dill sprigs, thick stems removed

3 tablespoons fresh lemon juice

2 tablespoons extra-virgin olive oil

1 tablespoon Dijon mustard

8 ounces (about 1 cup) silken or soft tofu, cut in pieces

½ teaspoon salt, or to taste

1. Place the garlic, dill, lemon juice, olive oil, and mustard in a blender and process until the garlic and dill are finely chopped. Add ¼ cup water and the tofu, and run the machine until the dressing is very smooth, stopping once or twice to scrape down the sides of the blender with a rubber spatula.

2. Season the dressing with salt, and transfer it to a bowl or pitcher for serving. (The dressing can be refrigerated in a tightly covered glass jar for up to 1 week. Shake vigorously before using.)

How to Grow Sprouts

Back in my college days, when I shopped at the local co-op and was learning how to cook, I grew my own sprouts, as did many of my friends. Although that fashion may have lapsed for several decades, it seems to be making a comeback. Alfalfa sprouts are generally available in supermarkets everywhere, but growing your own is easy—and best of all, you can grow all your favorite varieties. Almost any grain, bean, or seed can be sprouted. If you like sprouts with a peppery edge, try radish, broccoli, and arugula seeds; for more of a crunch, use chickpeas or sunflower seeds. Small seeds such as alfalfa and arugula grow long silky stems, whereas sunflower seeds, or legumes such as chickpeas and mung beans, yield crunchier, thicker-stemmed sprouts. Look for sprouting seeds or beans at health food and natural foods stores; do not sprout seeds meant for garden cultivation, as these could be treated or coated. It takes only 3 to 5 days to produce homegrown sprouts, and they add interest, flavor, and texture to salads and sandwiches. If you're looking to add more raw foods to your diet, sprouts are a great way. Plus, it's just so satisfying to grow something. All you need is a tiny bit of counter space and a 1-quart canning jar to start sprouting!

Makes about 3 cups

2 to 4 tablespoons sprout seeds or beans, rinsed in cool water

1. Place the seeds or beans in a 1-quart canning jar and add cool water to cover. Let the jar stand, covered with a clean dish towel, at room temperature for at least 5 hours, or overnight.

2. Drain the water from the jar and rinse the seeds or beans thoroughly; drain them again, and return them to the jar. The seeds or beans should be damp but not sitting in water. Place a piece of cheesecloth or a sprouting jar screen over the top of the jar. If you are using cheesecloth, secure the fabric with a rubber band. Lay the jar on its side (to spread out the seeds) and set it in a warm, dark spot.

3. Each day, rinse the seeds or beans thoroughly with cool water, drain them well, and return them to the jar. Cover the jar again with the cheesecloth, and return it to the warm, dark spot. The seeds or beans will begin to sprout in 3 to 5 days.

4. Once the sprouts are about 3 inches tall, place the jar in indirect sunlight for 2 to 4 hours or until the sprouts turn green. The sprouts are now ready to eat. Store them in the jar, tightly covered, or in an airtight container, in the refrigerator for up to 1 week. Rinse the sprouts every day or two to keep them clean and fresh.

Tamari-Roasted Sunflower Seeds

Sunflower seeds are delicious (some might say addictive) when slow-roasted in tamari sauce. They add a wonderful crunch and great flavor to salads.

Makes 4 cups

4 cups raw unsalted sunflower seeds
¾ cup tamari or soy sauce (see sidebar, page 180)

1. Position a rack in the center of the oven and preheat the oven to 300°F. Line a rimmed baking sheet with parchment.

2. Place the sunflower seeds in a small bowl and add the tamari. Stir to coat the seeds completely, and then drain off any excess tamari.

3. Transfer the seeds to the prepared baking sheet and bake, stirring them every 15 minutes to ensure even roasting, until they are crisp, dry, and just starting to color, 30 to 40 minutes. Let the seeds cool completely.

4. Store the sunflower seeds in an airtight container at room temperature for up to 3 weeks.

Spinach Salad with Sesame Vinaigrette

TENDER BABY SPINACH tossed with crunchy carrots, sweet cherry tomatoes, and savory tamari-roasted pumpkin seeds is a great salad combination, and the light and flavorful Asian-inspired dressing is its perfect partner. Fresh spinach is exceptionally nutritious and is a terrific source of vitamins, minerals, and antioxidants. Feel free to improvise—tangerine segments, toasted almonds, and julienned jicama work well as optional additions or substitutions. To turn this salad into an entrée, add shredded cooked chicken breast or cold poached salmon.

Serves 4 as a side salad

5 ounces (about 6 packed cups) baby spinach, rinsed and dried if not prewashed
1 large carrot, peeled and coarsely shredded (about 1 cup)
1 cup cherry tomatoes, halved
About ½ cup Sesame Vinaigrette (recipe follows)
¼ cup Tamari-Roasted Pumpkin Seeds (page 53)

1. Place the spinach in a large salad bowl. Add the carrots, tomatoes, and half of the vinaigrette. Toss to lightly coat the salad, and then taste to see if more dressing is needed.

2. Transfer the salad to a platter or individual salad plates. Scatter the pumpkin seeds over the top, and serve immediately.

Sesame Vinaigrette

This sweet-tart dressing is a Goodman family staple. More than just a vinaigrette for salad greens, it also makes a great marinade for chicken, meat, and seafood, and is delicious drizzled over steamed vegetables. ⁓ *Makes ¾ cup*

2 tablespoons unseasoned rice vinegar

2 tablespoons tamari or soy sauce
   (see sidebar, page 180)

¼ cup toasted sesame oil
   (see sidebar, page 25)

2 tablespoons honey

¼ teaspoon Asian chili sauce

1 tablespoon grated peeled
   fresh ginger

2 teaspoons sesame seeds

Place all the ingredients in a glass jar and seal the lid tightly. Shake the jar vigorously to combine. (The vinaigrette dressing can be refrigerated, covered, for up to 4 weeks. Let it return to room temperature and shake the jar vigorously before using.)

Spinach Salad with Sesame Vinaigrette

Tamari-Roasted Pumpkin Seeds

Salty and crunchy, these roasted pumpkin seeds, also called *pepitas,*
are a delicious snack as well as a topping for salads. Try them with our
Earthbound Farm Health Salad (page 48), or sprinkle them as a garnish on
stir-fries, soups, and steamed vegetables for a quick flavor boost.

Makes 4 cups

4 cups raw shelled, unsalted pumpkin seeds

¾ cup tamari or soy sauce (see sidebar, page 180)

1. Position a rack in the center of the oven and preheat the oven to 300°F. Line a rimmed baking sheet with parchment.

2. Place the pumpkin seeds in a small bowl, add the tamari, and stir to coat the seeds completely. Drain off any excess tamari.

3. Transfer the seeds to the prepared baking sheet and roast, stirring them every 15 minutes to ensure even roasting, until they are crisp, dry, and just starting to color, 35 to 45 minutes.

4. Let the seeds cool completely, and then store them in an airtight container at room temperature for up to 3 weeks.

the environmental benefits of organic farming

Organic farming helps keep toxic chemicals out of the environment and our food supply, conserves petroleum, and helps mitigate global warming. For example, at Earthbound Farm, each year we estimate the ecological benefits of farming our acreage organically. In 2010, working with 150 farmers on more than 35,000 organic acres, we:

- avoided the use of more than 338,000 pounds of toxic synthetic pesticides;
- avoided the use of nearly 11.2 million pounds of synthetic fertilizers;
- conserved an estimated 1.8 million gallons of petroleum by not using petroleum-based pesticides and fertilizers; and
- absorbed carbon dioxide emissions equivalent to taking more than 7,800 cars off the road.

Bonnie's Best Salad

Bonnie's Best Salad

BONNIE SWEAT, THE WIFE OF EARTHBOUND FARM'S CEO, Charles Sweat, is well known for her great salads. Bonnie has a long list of recipes she's created, so I asked her to share her very best salad with us. She says that when she is invited to someone's house for dinner, this is the salad she is almost always asked to bring. I love the crunchiness of the romaine mixed with the soft, peppery taste of arugula and the clean, bright flavor of parsley. Tossed with a lemony shallot vinaigrette and topped with creamy avocado and zesty Parmesan cheese, this is the perfect combination of flavors and textures for a light, fresh salad. If cherry tomatoes are not at their peak, substitute sun-dried, which are packed with flavor, or try our wonderful roasted tomatoes in the recipe on page 46. ⸺ *Serves 8 as a side salad*

6 cups thinly sliced romaine (2 hearts),
   rinsed and dried if not prewashed

4 cups baby arugula

¼ cup chopped fresh flat-leaf parsley

¾ cup freshly grated Parmesan cheese

Lemon-Shallot Dressing
   (recipe follows)

1½ cups halved cherry or pear tomatoes

2 small or 1 large avocado, pitted, peeled,
   and cut into ½-inch cubes

2 cups Bonnie's Garlicky Croutons
   (recipe follows)

1. Place the romaine, arugula, and parsley in a large bowl and toss to combine. Add ½ cup of the Parmesan and toss again.

2. Add some of the Lemon-Shallot Dressing and toss to coat the greens. Taste, and add more as needed. Transfer the salad to a large platter and top with the tomatoes, avocados, and croutons. Sprinkle with the remaining ¼ cup Parmesan cheese, and serve immediately.

THE BASICS

How to Taste Test Salad Dressing

To make sure a dressing is blended to your liking, taste it before pouring it on your salad. Use a lettuce leaf as a dipper. If all is okay, dress the salad as suggested in the recipe. If the dressing needs adjusting, add what's needed a little at a time. To make the dressing less tart, add more oil or a bit of sugar; to make it more tart, add vinegar or citrus juice. Add more herbs or spices to punch up the flavor. Just be sure to taste after each addition.

Lemon-Shallot Dressing

Light and lemony, this dressing harmonizes perfectly with the robust greens, creamy avocado, and nutty Parmesan in Bonnie's Best Salad. Shallots and a touch of Worcestershire balance the lemon tang of this bright, fresh-tasting vinaigrette. Bonnie's secret ingredient is a tablespoon of mayonnaise, which helps emulsify the dressing and adds a bit of creamy smoothness.
⸺ *Makes about 1 cup*

⅔ cup extra-virgin olive oil

¼ cup fresh lemon juice

2 tablespoons finely minced peeled shallots

1 tablespoon mayonnaise

1 small garlic clove, peeled and minced

1 teaspoon Dijon mustard

¾ teaspoon lemon-pepper seasoning

¼ teaspoon freshly ground black pepper

1 teaspoon salt, or to taste

¼ teaspoon Worcestershire sauce

Combine all the ingredients in a glass jar, seal the lid tightly, and shake vigorously to combine. (The dressing can be refrigerated, covered, for up to 5 days. Let it return to room temperature and shake vigorously before using.)

Bonnie's Garlicky Croutons

Croutons are a great addition to salads, adding flavor and crunch, and Bonnie's garlic-infused, buttery croutons are easy to make. This recipe makes more than are needed for one salad, but we suspect having extra on hand will not prove to be a problem. They are terrific as a topping for soups and other salads. ⁓ *Makes about 4 cups*

3 tablespoons butter

3 tablespoons extra-virgin olive oil

3 garlic cloves, peeled and finely minced

¼ teaspoon lemon-pepper seasoning

Pinch of cayenne pepper

1 French batarde or other crusty rustic country bread, such as ciabatta, boule, or pain de campagne, crusts removed, cut into ¾-inch cubes (6 cups)

1. Position a rack in the center of the oven and preheat the oven to 400°F.

2. Combine the butter, olive oil, garlic, lemon-pepper seasoning, and cayenne in a small saucepan, and cook over very low heat until the butter melts and the mixture is warm, 5 to 10 minutes.

3. Place the bread cubes in a large bowl. Pour the butter mixture over them and toss to coat all the surfaces.

4. Transfer the bread cubes to a rimmed baking sheet and spread them out in a single layer. Bake the croutons until they are golden, checking occasionally to make sure that they do not burn, 10 to 12 minutes.

5. If you are not planning on serving the croutons immediately, let them cool completely before storing them in an airtight container in the refrigerator for up to 5 days.

eating organic protecting yourself from unhealthy pesticide residues

While it would be difficult to completely avoid any exposure to synthetic chemicals, choosing organic food can make a big dent in pesticide exposure while also supporting farming practices that protect our environment.

The Environmental Working Group (EWG) compiles a list of commonly consumed fruits and vegetables, ranked by the frequency they're found to contain pesticide residues, based on an analysis of government data. Although this ranking, published in EWG's *Shopper's Guide to Pesticides,* doesn't factor in pesticides' effects on the environment, it is a great resource if you can't find or can't afford all organic produce. You can cut your pesticide exposure from fresh produce up to 90 percent by choosing organic options from the list.

EWG research has found that people who eat the twelve most contaminated fruits and vegetables ingest an average of ten pesticides a day. The Guide helps consumers make informed choices to lower their dietary pesticide load. And choosing organic produce is always a good choice for the environment, lessening the chemical load in our soil, air, water, and wildlife population.

Be sure to check EWG's website for the full list and updates (www.foodnews.org). At our publication date, this is the most current *Shopper's Guide to Pesticides:*

FIFTEEN HIGHEST IN PESTICIDE RESIDUES

1. Celery
2. Peaches
3. Strawberries
4. Apples
5. Blueberries (domestic)
6. Nectarines
7. Bell peppers
8. Spinach
9. Kale
10. Cherries
11. Potatoes
12. Grapes (imported)
13. Lettuce
14. Blueberries (imported)
15. Carrots

TWELVE LOWEST IN PESTICIDES

1. Onions
2. Avocados
3. Sweet corn
4. Pineapple
5. Mangos
6. Sweet peas
7. Asparagus
8. Kiwi
9. Cabbage
10. Eggplant
11. Cantaloupe
12. Watermelon

Jicama and Orange Salad with Orange-Sesame Vinaigrette

T HE RED, GREEN, AND ORANGE COLORS of this salad are eye-catching, and the jicama adds a succulent crunch. The Orange-Sesame Vinaigrette, with its blend of citrus and Asian flavors balanced with just a hint of sweetness, brings all the components into perfect harmony.

Serves 4 to 6 as a side salad

2 medium oranges

1 small jicama (8 ounces; see box, page 246), peeled and cut into 1-inch-long matchsticks (1 cup)

¼ cup thinly sliced red onion

3 cups (about 2½ ounces) baby spinach, rinsed and dried if not prewashed

3 cups rinsed, dried, torn red-leaf lettuce leaves (bite-size pieces)

About ½ cup Orange-Sesame Vinaigrette (recipe follows)

2 tablespoons sesame seeds, toasted (see box, page 31)

1. Using a sharp knife, cut the peel and white pith from the oranges. Working over a mixing bowl, cut on either side of each membrane, releasing the orange segments into the bowl. Remove any seeds, and cut the orange segments in half.

2. Place the orange segments, jicama, red onion, spinach, and lettuce in a large salad bowl and toss to combine. Add ¼ cup of the Orange-Sesame Vinaigrette and toss lightly to coat the salad. Taste to see if more dressing is needed. Sprinkle with the sesame seeds and serve immediately.

Crisp and sweet, jicamas are a refreshing and welcome addition in salads.

Orange-Sesame Vinaigrette

The classic trinity of Asian ingredients—soy sauce, sesame oil, and rice vinegar—gets a boost from fresh orange juice, which adds a hint of sweetness and a bright note to this tasty vinaigrette. It can also do double duty as a quick marinade for shrimp or fish. ⌇⌇⌇ *Makes about ¾ cup*

3 tablespoons canola oil

3 tablespoons toasted sesame oil
 (see sidebar, page 25)

3 tablespoons soy sauce

2 tablespoons fresh orange juice

2 tablespoons unseasoned rice vinegar

1 teaspoon finely grated peeled fresh ginger

1 teaspoon honey

Salt and freshly ground black pepper,
 to taste

Combine the canola oil, sesame oil, soy sauce, orange juice, vinegar, ginger, and honey in a glass jar and seal the lid tightly. Shake vigorously to combine. Taste the dressing, and season with salt and pepper if desired. (The vinaigrette can be refrigerated, covered, for up to 2 weeks. Let it return to room temperature and shake well before using.)

Escarole with Walnuts, Dates, and Bacon

ESCAROLE IS A PERFECT CHOICE FOR WINTER SALADS because it's sturdy and assertive enough to stand up to an array of ingredients and flavors. It has a crisp, juicy texture with a peppery bite, which makes a nice counterpoint to the sweet, chewy dates, mellow toasted walnuts, and smoky pieces of bacon in this salad. If escarole is not available, frisée is a delicious substitute, or use a combination of radicchio and Belgian endive. Complemented with a walnut vinaigrette, this salad makes a refreshing first course for a rich meat meal, such as the Tenderloin of Beef (page 76) or the Greek-Style Lamb Chops (page 103). ⌇⌇⌇ *Serves 4 as a side salad*

1 large head (7 ounces) escarole,
 outer leaves discarded, rinsed, dried,
 and torn into bite-size pieces
 (6 lightly packed cups)

4 ounces (about 5 slices) bacon, cooked
 until crisp, broken into bite-size pieces

⅓ cup chopped pitted dates
 (about 6 dates)

¼ cup walnut pieces, toasted
 (see box, page 31)

Scant ¼ cup thinly sliced red onion

Walnut Vinaigrette (recipe follows)

1. Place the escarole, bacon, dates, walnuts, and red onion in a large bowl and toss to combine.

2. Add half of the vinaigrette to the salad and toss to coat. Add more dressing to taste and serve immediately.

Walnut Vinaigrette

Walnut oil is simply sumptuous and we love it in vinaigrettes, where its rich, nutty flavor really sings. Here it mellows the peppery bite of escarole and amplifies the flavor of the walnuts in our Escarole with Walnuts, Dates, and Bacon, adding an exquisite balance to a hearty salad.

— Makes ½ cup

⅓ cup walnut oil (see sidebar, page 38)

2 tablespoons red wine vinegar

Salt and freshly ground black pepper

Place the walnut oil and vinegar in a glass jar and seal the lid tightly. Shake the jar vigorously to combine. Season the vinaigrette with salt and pepper to taste. (The dressing can be refrigerated, covered, for up to 2 months. Let it return to room temperature and shake vigorously before using.)

FARM FRESH

Escarole

Escarole is a bitter leafy green in the chicory family, closely related to frisée, radicchio, curly endive, and Belgian endive. It forms a head that is open and somewhat flat, with crinkly light to dark green leaves with wide, fleshy stems. It resembles a head of sturdy butter lettuce with curled, ragged edges. Compared to some of its cousins, escarole is mild, and you can eat it both raw and cooked. Raw, it has a chewy, crisp texture and its bitterness is tempered by a slight sweetness. In salads it pairs beautifully with fruits such as pears, apples, or figs, as well with as nuts,

strong-flavored cheeses, and dried fruits. When cooked, its bitterness is more pronounced, although when blanched and then sautéed, it develops a tender, melting texture.

Look for heads of escarole that have crisp, fresh-looking leaves with no sign of browning or wilting. To store, wrap unwashed heads in a moist paper towel or kitchen cloth, and place in a plastic bag. Refrigerate for up to 1 week.

Just before using it, rinse the escarole briefly in cold water. Discard any tough outer leaves, as well as the thick lower ribs near the base of the

head if serving the escarole raw. The inner leaves are more tender and less bitter. Tear the leaves into bite-size pieces for salads.

Escarole with Walnuts, Dates, and Bacon (page 59)

Chopped Autumn Salad

ROMAINE LETTUCE AND RED CABBAGE MAKE A DELICIOUS, crunchy combination. The colors of this salad are beautiful, and every bite is good for you. Apples, pears, persimmons, and pomegranates are the signature fruits of autumn; for a change of pace you can add dried cranberries or sliced grapes. ⎯⎯ *Serves 6 to 8 as a side salad*

12 ounces red cabbage, cored and coarsely
   chopped (about 4 cups)

2 romaine hearts, coarsely chopped (about
   6 cups), rinsed and dried if not prewashed

2 crisp apples, such as Fuji, Gala, or
   Braeburn, peeled, cored, and cut into
   ¼-inch dice (about 2 cups)

2 ripe but firm pears, such as Bosc or Anjou,
   peeled, cored, and cut into ¼-inch dice
   (about 1½ cups)

2 Fuyu persimmons, peeled and cut into
   ¼-inch dice, seeds discarded, if any

Apple Cider Vinaigrette (recipe follows)

Seeds from 1 medium pomegranate
   (optional)

20 fresh mint leaves, cut into thin ribbons

1. Place the cabbage and romaine in a large bowl and toss to combine.

2. Just before serving, add the apples, pears, and persimmons to the cabbage-romaine mixture and toss to combine. Add half of the Apple Cider Vinaigrette and toss again, adding more dressing as desired.

3. Transfer the salad to a large platter and garnish with the pomegranate seeds, if using, and the mint. Serve immediately.

Apple Cider Vinaigrette

This sweet-tart dressing is terrific with sturdy or assertive greens like the romaine and red cabbage in the Chopped Autumn Salad. If you prefer a sweeter flavor, add an extra tablespoon of brown sugar or a tablespoon of honey or agave syrup. ⎯⎯ *Makes about ¾ cup*

½ cup apple cider vinegar

2 tablespoons (packed) light brown sugar

¼ cup extra-virgin olive oil

Pinch of salt, or more to taste

Combine all the ingredients in a glass jar and seal the lid tightly. Shake vigorously to combine. (The vinaigrette can be refrigerated, covered, for up to 2 weeks. Let it return to room temperature and shake vigorously before using.)

Romaine Salad with Snow Peas, Oranges, and Almonds

C RISP ROMAINE LETTUCE IS MORE SUBSTANTIAL than tender leafy greens and lends itself nicely to the addition of fruits, vegetables, nuts, and cheeses in tossed salads. Juicy oranges, crunchy snow peas, and heart healthy almonds combine here for a delicious and nutritious salad. Our light Orange Splash is the perfect dressing for this medley of flavors—not too much oil and just a touch of honey for sweetness. ⎯⎯ ***Serves 4 as a side salad***

2 small oranges

6 cups torn or sliced romaine hearts (about 2 hearts), rinsed and dried if not prewashed

½ cup (2½ ounces) whole almonds (skin on)

3 ounces (about ¾ cup) snow peas, stems and any strings removed, cut on a slight diagonal into ½-inch pieces

Orange Splash Dressing (recipe follows)

1 medium carrot, peeled and shaved into ribbons with a vegetable peeler

1. Cut off a thin slice from the top and bottom of each orange so that the fruit will sit level on a cutting board. Using a sharp paring knife, cut downward, following the contour of the fruit, removing wide strips of the peel and white pith but leaving the flesh intact. Discard the peels. Cut the oranges lengthwise into quarters; then slice the quarters crosswise to make bite-size pieces, removing and discarding any seeds.

2. Place the oranges, romaine, almonds, and snow peas in a large salad bowl and add half of the Orange Splash Dressing. Toss to combine, and taste to see if more dressing is needed. Garnish the salad with the carrot ribbons, and serve immediately.

THE BASICS

Zest

Zest is the colorful exterior of the citrus fruit peel. It contains essential oils, which add an intense flavor and aroma to food. When zesting, use a light touch with a zester, Microplane, or vegetable peeler so you remove only the zest and leave behind the bitter white pith.

It's always wise to wash citrus fruit before removing the zest. In fact, it's a good idea to wash it before doing anything with it— squeezing it for juice, or cutting it into wedges for eating.

Orange Splash Dressing

If you like a light dressing without too much oil, try this one. Freshly squeezed orange juice and a pinch of orange zest turn a basic vinaigrette into one that sparkles with bright flavor. ⎯⎯ ***Makes ⅓ cup***

2 tablespoons fresh orange juice

2 tablespoons extra-virgin olive oil

1 tablespoon champagne vinegar or white wine vinegar

1 tablespoon honey, or more to taste

¼ teaspoon grated orange zest

¼ teaspoon salt, or to taste

Freshly ground black pepper, to taste

Combine the orange juice, olive oil, vinegar, honey, and orange zest in a glass jar and seal the lid tightly. Shake the jar vigorously to combine. Taste, and season with the salt and pepper.

(The vinaigrette can be refrigerated, covered, for up to 1 week. Let it return to room temperature and shake the jar vigorously before using.)

Salad with Raspberries, Avocado, and Goat Cheese

THE COMBINATION OF RASPBERRIES, AVOCADO, AND GOAT CHEESE may seem unusual, but skeptics will be won over when they taste this salad. The peppery arugula matches well with the mild taste and soft texture of butter lettuce. Juicy, sweet-tart raspberries pair nicely with rich and creamy avocado chunks, while crumbles of goat cheese add a tangy note. The delicious vinaigrette is also based on mild, soft goat cheese, contributing another layer of flavor to this salad. ⟶ *Serves 4 as a side salad*

1 small head butter lettuce,
   such as Boston or Bibb
2 cups (2 ounces) baby or wild arugula,
   rinsed and dried if not prewashed
About ½ cup Creamy Goat Cheese
   Vinaigrette (recipe follows)
1 ripe avocado, preferably Hass
½ cup (2 ounces) crumbled mild goat
   cheese
1 cup fresh red or golden raspberries

1. Carefully pull the butter lettuce leaves from the core, tearing off and discarding any damaged parts (you should have about 3 cups). Rinse the leaves under gently running cold water, drain them well, and spin them dry. Wrap the lettuce in a clean kitchen towel and refrigerate until serving time.

2. Just before serving, gently tear the large lettuce leaves into smaller pieces. (Small leaves can be left whole; they'll add volume and texture to the salad.) Place the butter lettuce and arugula in a large bowl, and add about ¼ cup of the vinaigrette. Toss to lightly coat the leaves; then taste to see if more vinaigrette is needed. Divide the greens among four salad plates.

3. Peel the avocado and discard the pit. Cut the avocado into bite-size pieces.

4. Sprinkle the avocado, goat cheese, and raspberries over each serving. Drizzle each salad with a teaspoon of the vinaigrette, and serve immediately.

Creamy Goat Cheese Vinaigrette

Goat cheese, or *chèvre* as it is also known, adds a creamy tang to this simple vinaigrette. It marries beautifully with salads that feature goat cheese and adds interest to an unadorned assortment of greens. The dressing will separate as it sits, so be sure to shake the jar vigorously before using it.

—*Makes about 1 cup*

2 teaspoons chopped shallot

1 tablespoon apple cider vinegar

1 tablespoon red wine vinegar

¼ cup (about 1 ounce) crumbled mild goat cheese

½ cup extra-virgin olive oil

Salt and freshly ground black pepper

1. Place the shallot and both vinegars in a small food processor or a blender, and process briefly. Add the goat cheese and puree.

2. With the machine running on high, add the olive oil in a slow, steady stream. Season with salt and pepper to taste.

3. Transfer the vinaigrette to a glass jar and seal the lid tightly. Shake the jar vigorously to combine. (The vinaigrette can be refrigerated, covered, for up to 2 weeks. Let it return to room temperature and shake vigorously before using.)

using cloth napkins

Over time, I've grown to prefer cloth napkins over paper ones. They're more durable, bigger, prettier, and have a better feel. Once you start using cloth, paper seems like a compromise, like eating with a plastic fork instead of a sturdier metal one. Cloth napkins are also better for the environment. Manufacturing paper napkins uses valuable resources—trees, water, and energy. They also come in wasteful packaging, are shipped via trucks or trains, and generally cannot be recycled.

My "aha" moment with cloth napkins happened at the Tassajara Zen Mountain Center in California's Ventana Wilderness, one of the most special places I've ever been to. The people who run the monastery are incredibly eco-minded, and they've come up with many ways to function well with very limited access to power in their isolated setting. One way they save power and water is to give each guest a cloth napkin in a napkin holder with their name written on it at their first meal.

After every meal, everyone rolls up their cloth napkin and puts it back in the holder to reuse each time they eat. Of course you can ask for a replacement if yours gets noticeably dirty, but I've never had to. Just knowing I will use my napkin again, I take a bit of extra care with it. The ritual became a part of my mindful practice at Tassajara and I carried it home with me—fewer paper napkins to buy and throw away, another way to live more lightly on the Earth.

Sierra Mar Salad with Little Gem Lettuce, Fennel, Feta, and Slivered Almonds

SIERRA MAR IS A WORLD-RENOWNED RESTAURANT AT THE POST Ranch Inn, perched on a mountaintop directly overlooking the Big Sur coast. Craig von Foerster is the acclaimed chef at Sierra Mar, and his seasonally inspired food is highly inventive, expertly prepared, and spectacularly presented. While dinner at Sierra Mar is a special-occasion treat, I go for lunch as often as possible. The lunch menu is fabulous and the views are breathtaking. This salad is always on the menu, and I never fail to order it. Craig generously agreed to share his recipe, which is the essence of simplicity. His choice of ingredients creates a perfect combination of tastes and textures, and it's as healthy and light as it is delicious.

Serves 4 as a side salad

6 small heads Little Gem lettuce, or 2 heads
    butter (such as Boston or Bibb) lettuce
Yogurt Dressing (recipe follows)
½ cup slivered almonds, toasted
1 cup (5 ounces) crumbled feta cheese,
    preferably Valbreso
1 small fennel bulb, shaved into thin slivers
    (see sidebar, this page)
Sea salt

1. Separate the lettuce leaves, and carefully rinse them and spin dry. Transfer the lettuce to a large bowl. Add ¼ cup of the Yogurt Dressing to the bowl and toss to coat the lettuce, adding more dressing as needed.

2. Divide the lettuce among four chilled salad plates. Sprinkle each serving with some of the almonds, crumbled feta, and fennel shavings. Top each salad with a drizzle of dressing and a sprinkling of sea salt. Serve immediately.

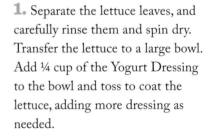

THE BASICS

Shaving Fennel

Wash the fennel bulb and cut off the stalks and fronds, if any, reserving these for use in stock or as a garnish. If the outer layer of the fennel is discolored or thick, discard this layer. Cut the fennel bulb in half lengthwise, and remove and discard the core. Shave the fennel crosswise into paper-thin slices on a mandoline or V-slicer. If you don't have this piece of equipment, use a sharp knife to cut the bulb crosswise into very thin slices.

Yogurt Dressing

The combination of feta cheese and yogurt creates a creamy dressing with a hint of salt and a slight tang. Fresh basil adds a clean, sprightly note as well as a pretty pale green tint to this light and flavorful salad dressing.

~~~ Makes about 1 cup

½ cup plain low-fat yogurt

2 tablespoons white wine vinegar

1 small garlic clove, peeled and minced

¼ cup (1¼ ounces) crumbled feta cheese, preferably Valbreso

¼ cup canola oil

2 packed tablespoons fresh basil leaves

¼ teaspoon freshly ground black pepper

Salt, to taste

Place the yogurt, vinegar, garlic, and feta in a blender and process on high speed until the mixture is smooth, 30 to 60 seconds. With the blender still running on high, add the oil in a slow, steady stream. Then add the basil leaves and process for 15 seconds. Season the dressing with the pepper and salt to taste. (The dressing can be refrigerated, covered, for up to 7 days. Let it return to room temperature and shake to re-emulsify, if necessary.)

YOUR GREEN KITCHEN

Organic Cotton

When you need to buy new dish towels, cloth napkins, and tablecloths, you should consider buying organic rather than conventional cotton. Conventional cotton is the most heavily sprayed crop in the world. Approximately 25 percent of the insecticides and more than 10 percent of the world's agricultural chemicals are used on cotton fields. In contrast, organic cotton is grown without the use of synthetic fertilizers and toxic chemical pesticides—making it healthier for the environment and for the people working in the fields.

Green Bibb lettuce

Butter Lettuce Salad with Pears, Pecans, and Gorgonzola

THERE IS SOMETHING ESPECIALLY WONDERFUL ABOUT THE SOFT, tender leaves of butter lettuce paired with sweet, juicy pears, creamy Gorgonzola, and a sprinkling of sweet and crunchy toasted pecans. Dressed with a light balsamic vinaigrette, this salad makes an elegant start to a meal—especially during the autumn months, when pears are at their prime. Stilton or Roquefort, as well as goat cheese, will also work well with this combination of flavors. ⚬ *Serves 4 as a side salad*

6 cups butter lettuce leaves, torn into bite-size pieces, carefully rinsed and dried

About ⅔ cup Light Balsamic Vinaigrette (recipe follows)

1 ripe pear, quartered, cored, and thinly sliced crosswise

½ cup pecan pieces, toasted (see box, page 31)

½ cup crumbled Gorgonzola cheese

1. Place the lettuce in a large bowl and toss with half of the dressing. Divide the lettuce among four salad plates.

2. Place the pears in the same bowl, drizzle them with a small amount of dressing, and toss to coat. Divide the pears among the salad plates.

3. Sprinkle the pecans and cheese over the salads. Drizzle with additional dressing, if desired, and serve immediately.

Light Balsamic Vinaigrette

Balsamic vinegar makes salad dressings sparkle, and is especially complementary in this salad, with its robust ingredients. It has a rich mellowness that complements the pears, pecans, and Gorgonzola without the assertive bite of some vinegars. But don't stop here—this light and flavorful vinaigrette will enhance just about any salad. ⚬ *Makes about ⅔ cup*

½ cup extra-virgin olive oil

2½ tablespoons balsamic vinegar

2 teaspoons minced shallot

2 teaspoons Dijon mustard

¼ teaspoon salt

Freshly ground black pepper, to taste

Place all the ingredients in a glass jar and seal the lid tightly. Shake vigorously to combine. (The dressing can be refrigerated, covered, for up to 1 month. Let it return to room temperature and shake vigorously before using.)

Butter Lettuce Salad with Pears, Pecans, and Gorgonzola

Chopped Salad with Buttermilk-Avocado Dressing

ONE OF THE GREAT THINGS ABOUT CHOPPED SALADS is their incredible versatility. I am constantly varying the ingredients, depending on what's in season and what's in my refrigerator. Sometimes I substitute ham, turkey, or chicken for the salami, and sometimes I include other favorite vegetables such as hearts of palm, cucumbers, or artichokes. There is no limit to the flavor combinations you can create—just keep in mind that you want a balance of different colors, textures, and tastes to keep the salad lively.

Serves 6 as a side salad or 3 as an entrée

Green romaine

8 cups chopped romaine hearts
(3 romaine hearts), rinsed and dried if not
prewashed

8 ounces sliced salami (¼-inch-thick slices),
cut into ¼-inch dice (2 cups)

1 large tomato, cored, seeded, and diced
(about 1 cup)

5 scallion tops (green part), chopped
(about ⅔ cup)

1 avocado, pitted, peeled, and cut into
¼-inch dice

5½ ounces provolone cheese, cut into
¼-inch dice (1 cup)

1 cup cooked chickpeas (garbanzo beans),
rinsed if canned, chopped

1 cup green or black olives, pitted and
chopped

About ¾ cup Buttermilk-Avocado Dressing
(recipe follows)

1. Just before you plan to serve the salad, place the lettuce in a large salad bowl and add the salami, tomato, scallions, avocado, provolone, chickpeas, and olives. Toss to combine.

2. Add about ½ cup of the Buttermilk-Avocado Dressing. Toss to lightly coat the salad; then taste to see if more dressing is needed. Serve immediately.

Buttermilk-Avocado Dressing

Buttermilk and fresh lemon juice add a subtle tang to this versatile dressing, which gets its creaminess from avocado and mayonnaise. Garlic, cilantro, and jalapeño enliven the dressing, and their robust flavors complement the ingredients in our chopped salad. It also makes a great dip for vegetable crudités. *Makes 1 cup*

¼ ripe avocado, peeled

2 tablespoons chopped fresh cilantro

2 tablespoons chopped scallions
   (white part only)

½ tablespoon chopped jalapeño
   pepper, without seeds

1 small garlic clove, peeled

¼ cup low-fat buttermilk

1½ tablespoons fresh lemon juice

¼ cup mayonnaise

½ teaspoon salt, or more to taste

⅛ teaspoon freshly ground black
   pepper

1. Place the avocado, cilantro, scallions, jalapeño, and garlic in a food processor or blender. Pulse until the mixture is finely chopped, stopping once or twice to scrape the sides of the bowl with a rubber spatula.

2. Add the buttermilk and lemon juice and process until the dressing is smooth. Then add the mayonnaise, salt, and pepper, and blend again. If the dressing is too thick, thin it with a tablespoon of water, or more as needed. (The dressing can be refrigerated, covered, for up to 1 week. Let it return to room temperature and shake vigorously before using.)

THE BASICS

Peeling Hard-Cooked Eggs

If you plan on peeling your eggs immediately after cooking them, drain the hot water from the pot, leaving the eggs in it, and shake the pot back and forth to crack the shells. Then place the eggs in a bowl and add ice water to cover; let the eggs cool. The water will seep in through the cracked shells, allowing them to be slipped off without a struggle. Pat the eggs dry before continuing with the recipe.

Bistro 211 Cobb Salad

BISTRO 211 IS CLOSE TO MY OFFICE, and chef Jon Magnusson's exceptionally good Cobb salad is one of my favorite lunches. Jon was one of our first customers when we started our farm in 1984. Born and raised in Iceland, his motto is "Everything from scratch and always from the heart." This is a composed salad with turkey, cheese, bacon, avocado, tomato, and diced egg arranged in attractive parallel strips. It makes a beautiful presentation. I love the basil vinaigrette, which is also terrific with other salads or as a veggie dip. —*Serves 4 as a main course*

8 cups sliced romaine hearts (2 to 3 hearts),
   rinsed and dried if not prewashed

8 ounces roasted turkey breast, cut into
   ¼-inch cubes

½ cup (2½ ounces) crumbled blue cheese

8 slices bacon, cooked until crisp, crumbled

1 ripe avocado, pitted, peeled, and cut into
   ⅓-inch cubes

1 large tomato, cored and cut into ¼-inch
   dice (about 1 cup)

3 hard-cooked eggs, diced

Bistro 211 Basil Vinaigrette (recipe follows)

1. Spread the lettuce in an even layer on a medium-size platter. Arrange the turkey cubes in a 2-inch-wide strip over the lettuce. Next arrange the blue cheese in a strip, parallel to the turkey. Repeat with the bacon, avocado, tomato, and eggs.

2. Drizzle about ½ cup of the basil vinaigrette over the salad and serve immediately, with extra dressing on the side.

Bistro 211 Basil Vinaigrette

This tasty dressing is a cross between a classic vinaigrette and a creamy dressing. In his restaurant, chef Jon Magnusson uses an egg to emulsify the vinaigrette, but I've substituted plain yogurt to attain a thick, creamy consistency. Lots of fresh basil adds flavor and color. This versatile dressing will complement many salads, but is best used in combination with sturdy greens. ⌇⌇⌇ *Makes about 1 cup*

3 tablespoons red wine vinegar

1 tablespoon fresh orange juice

⅓ packed cup fresh basil leaves

¼ cup chopped yellow onion

2 small garlic cloves, peeled

1 teaspoon Dijon mustard

½ teaspoon salt

⅛ teaspoon freshly ground black pepper

¼ cup plain nonfat yogurt

⅔ cup canola oil

1. Combine the vinegar, orange juice, basil, onion, garlic, mustard, salt, and pepper in a blender, and process until smooth. Add the yogurt and process again for 10 seconds. With the machine running, add the canola oil in a slow, steady stream.

2. Use immediately, or transfer the dressing to a container, cover, and refrigerate for up to 1 week. Let it return to room temperature and shake vigorously before using.

Red leaf lettuce

MEAT AND POULTRY

Memorable Meat Dishes

MANY PEOPLE THINK THAT BECAUSE I AM AN ORGANIC FARMER, I'M ALSO a vegetarian. The truth is that my family and I really enjoy meat and poultry dishes. But I pay close attention to the kinds of meat I buy— seeking out the most eco-friendly, healthy, and humane choices. Also, I look for ways to enjoy the flavors of meat and poultry by focusing on quality rather than quantity—eating smaller portions, savoring the flavors.

Most mainstream meat and poultry are extremely resource- and energy-intensive foods. They also contribute significantly to global-warming gases and pollution. Not all meat and poultry are created equal, however; some ways of raising cattle, pigs, lambs, bison/buffalo, and fowl are much kinder to the environment . . . and to the animals themselves. In this chapter, I include lots of information about different types of meat and their relative eco-impacts so you can choose what feels best for you and your family. I also clarify some eco-labels associated with meat so you can know more about what you're buying.

Like using the extra hot water to take a long bath instead of a quick shower, I know eating meat is a splurge. When I eat meat, I want to enjoy every morsel, so the recipes in this chapter are packed with lots of great flavors and variety. If you feel you've gotten into a bit of a recipe rut, you'll find plenty of inspiration here.

The Buffalo Shepherd's Pie is a true comfort food with a health update, because buffalo (also called bison) or grass-fed beef causes less of an environmental burden and is much leaner and more healthful than typical conventional beef. The tasty filling of the meat complemented by porcini mushrooms, red wine, and fresh thyme is hearty but not heavy.

"Amazing" isn't a word I use lightly, but the flavor of our Amazing Turkey Chili is truly . . . well, amazing. My husband, Drew, was skeptical at first because he's not a big chili fan, but he wound up asking for three helpings! The combination of three types of chile powder—ancho, pasilla, and chipotle—with other spices like cumin, coriander, thyme, and oregano adds a sophisticated flavor to the vegetables and beans. And using lean ground turkey with a touch of lime juice in the sauce makes this dish lighter than your standard "cowboy" chili.

I'm always encouraging people to try new things in the kitchen, but I realized that I had never cooked duck before working on this book. Duck is one of Chef Pam's specialties, and here she reveals her cooking techniques for keeping the meat moist and tender. Braised Duck with Quince and Apples is delicious—the pairing of quince and duck is perfect.

And on a day when you feel like having an adventurous chicken dish, Saigon Caramel Chicken is an outstanding recipe we've created to give you all the flavor of Vietnamese clay-pot cooking without any special equipment. Another favorite is our Chicken Breasts Stuffed with Chard, Gruyère, and Prosciutto.

In addition to protecting the environment, it's important that we honor our food traditions and savor our food memories. They bond us to loved ones and to our past, and carry us into a more grounded future. Two treasured recipes my mother brought with her from Hungary are now saved for my children and grandchildren in this book: Hungarian Goulash and Edith's Stuffed Cabbage. They may sound standard, but my mom tells me that different families have different ways of making these dishes. This is *her* way of making them. I think of all the miles she traveled with these recipes, and the experiences she had. They were never written down because she considered this information so ordinary. According to my mom, who is 81 as I am writing this, "Everybody knows how to roll cabbage and make goulash!" Well, now I've taken the time to document exactly how she does it so this skill and this flavor, my heritage and my food history, from a land I've never been to but tasted all my life, will never be lost.

Herbed Rib Roast of Pork (page 92)

Tenderloin of Beef with Brandied Mushrooms

WHEN YOU WANT TO SPLURGE OR CELEBRATE, one of the most sumptuous and impressive meals you can make is a whole tenderloin of beef. Although this is one of the most expensive cuts in the butcher's shop, a small piece of beef is very satisfying because it's rich tasting and has a succulent texture. Tenderloin is delicious when served unadorned, but the Brandied Mushrooms are easy to make and deeply flavorful—a perfect accompaniment to the tender beef. —*m*— *Serves 4 to 6*

1 small tenderloin of beef (2 to 3 pounds), trimmed, silver skin removed
1 tablespoon extra-virgin olive oil
Salt and freshly ground black pepper
¼ cup fresh tarragon leaves
Brandied Mushrooms (recipe follows)

1. One or 2 days ahead, rub the meat all over with the olive oil. Season it with salt and pepper, and press the tarragon leaves against the meat. Wrap the tenderloin very tightly in plastic wrap and refrigerate it.

2. Two hours before you plan to cook the tenderloin, remove the meat from the refrigerator and let it come to room temperature, still in its wrapping.

3. Position a rack in the middle of the oven and preheat the oven to 450°F.

4. Unwrap the tenderloin and discard the tarragon leaves. Place the tenderloin on a rimmed baking sheet, and roast until the meat is cooked to the desired degree of doneness: An instant-read thermometer should register 130°F for rare, 135°F for medium-rare, and 140°F for medium.

5. Transfer the tenderloin to a cutting board and tent it loosely with a piece of aluminum foil (preferably recycled). Let the beef rest for 10 minutes before cutting it into thick slices. Serve with the Brandied Mushrooms.

Brandied Mushrooms

The combination of dried porcini and fresh cremini mushrooms adds an earthy richness to this dish, which is further enhanced by brandy and red wine. To add depth to these flavors, intensely flavorful chicken stock is reduced with the porcini soaking liquid. If you happen to have homemade veal or beef stock on hand (lucky you!), then either of these can be substituted for the chicken stock. A splash of aged balsamic vinegar and a sprinkling of fresh tarragon perfectly balance the rich, woodsy notes to round out the dish. If you feel indulgent, add the crème fraîche, which will both mellow the flavors and add a bit of creaminess. We love this served with Tenderloin of Beef, but it also complements venison and duck dishes beautifully. —————— *Makes about 1½ cups*

1 ounce (about 1 cup) dried porcini or
   wild mushrooms (see sidebar, page 23)
1 cup very hot water
1½ cups Chicken Wing Stock (page 403)
2 tablespoons unsalted butter
¼ cup finely minced peeled shallots
4 ounces brown (cremini) mushrooms,
   sliced ¼-inch thick (about 2 cups)
Salt and freshly ground black pepper
2 cloves garlic, peeled and crushed
3 tablespoons Cognac or brandy
½ cup dry red wine, such as syrah or
   Zinfandel
1 teaspoon aged balsamic vinegar
2 tablespoons Crème Fraîche
   (optional, page 415)
1 tablespoon chopped fresh tarragon
   or flat-leaf parsley

1. Place the dried porcinis in a small bowl and cover with the hot water. Set aside until softened, about 20 minutes. Place a fine-mesh sieve over a clean bowl, and strain the mushrooms, reserving the soaking liquid. Coarsely chop the porcinis and set aside.

2. Combine the Chicken Wing Stock with the porcini soaking liquid in a small pan and simmer over medium heat until the mixture is reduced by two thirds, about 15 minutes. Set aside.

3. Melt the butter in a medium-size skillet over medium heat. Add the shallots and cook, stirring occasionally, until they begin to soften, about 3 minutes. Add the fresh mushrooms and season with salt and pepper to taste. Cook over medium-high heat, stirring frequently, until the mushrooms exude their juices and soften, 5 to 10 minutes. Add the chopped porcinis and the garlic, and cook for 1 minute, stirring constantly.

4. Add the Cognac to the skillet and cook until the Cognac evaporates, about 2 minutes. Then add the red wine and cook until the wine has almost completely evaporated, 3 to 5 minutes.

5. Add the chicken-porcini stock and the balsamic vinegar. Taste, and season with salt and pepper as needed. Stir in the crème fraîche, if using, and the tarragon. Serve hot. (The mushrooms can be refrigerated, covered, for up to 3 days. Reheat gently over low heat to serve.)

Cremini mushrooms

making eco-friendly meat choices

Like most environmental issues, meat production is a complex one. Eating foods that are high on the food chain is resource-intensive and contributes disproportionately to global warming; for example, industrial feedlot meat production requires about 16 times more fossil fuel energy and generates about 24 times more greenhouse gases than producing the same number of calories of vegetables and rice. The Natural Resources Defense Council estimates that if every American eliminated just 4 ounces of beef a week, the reduction in global-warming gas emissions would be equivalent to taking 4 to 6 million cars off the road!

When you're making meat choices, it's important to consider the type, such as beef or chicken, as well as how that meat was produced. Your food-buying dollars are a powerful force for change in the food industry, and consumer demand drives the popularity of more eco-conscious organic or grass-fed meat.

◆ **Conventional Feedlot Beef: the worst choice for the environment** Thousands of cattle confined in tight quarters, eating large amounts of conventionally produced grain, soy, and silage, result in far-reaching burdens on the environment, which include the use of large amounts of chemical fertilizers and toxic pesticides to grow the animals' feed. Conventional cattle are usually given hormones and regular sub-therapeutic doses of antibiotics to keep them "healthy" in this environment. These feedlots also generate large amounts of animal waste that can pollute water sources and contribute to greenhouse gases.

◆ **Organic Beef: a better option** Organic beef cows must be fed a completely organic diet, so the considerable amount of land dedicated to growing their feed is farmed without toxic pesticides and synthetic fertilizers, which can pollute the environment. Organic farming methods also minimize soil erosion and preserve soil nutrients.

Organic beef cattle are not given hormones or antibiotics, and they are not raised in crowded feedlots. Producers must also maintain organic pasture for the cattle to graze on throughout their lives, and they must adhere to humane standards as required by USDA Organic Standards. Organic beef cattle may be supplemented with organic grain. A cow is still a cow, but just the elimination of a conventional diet, the use of smaller, less crowded herds, and the absence of hormone and antibiotic contamination of soil and water make this choice lighter on the environment. (See page 112 for a definition of the "organic" label for meat.)

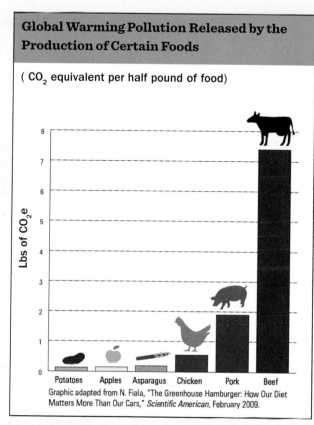

Global Warming Pollution Released by the Production of Certain Foods

(CO_2 equivalent per half pound of food)

Lbs of CO_2 e

Potatoes   Apples   Asparagus   Chicken   Pork   Beef

Graphic adapted from N. Fiala, "The Greenhouse Hamburger: How Our Diet Matters More Than Our Cars," *Scientific American*, February 2009.

This graphic from the NRDC website represents the effects of the production of conventionally produced foods.

◆ **The Grass Is Greener** True grass-fed animal products come from ruminant animals that have eaten only mother's milk, then fresh grass or hay all of their lives. This type of animal husbandry keeps land in permanent pasture, which is more ecologically sound than growing crops and shipping them over long distances to feed cattle. The need for pesticides and herbicides is greatly reduced or eliminated, soil erosion virtually ceases, and soil fertility is enhanced. The need for fertilizers is also minimized on pasture, which protects water supplies from contamination by excessive nitrogen or phosphorous levels. Permanent pasture fixes carbon into the soil, which helps combat the greenhouse effect and global warming. Pastures also provide habitat and additional forage for wildlife. (See page 112 for a definition of the "grass-fed" label.)

◆ **Pork** Pigs are much more resource-efficient and have a smaller carbon footprint than beef. Producing a pound of beef generates nearly 4 times as much climate-warming emissions as a pound of pork. Conventionally raised pigs are fed grains that have been grown with chemical fertilizers and toxic pesticides; they are also routinely given antibiotics. Many swine farms raise pigs in severely crowded conditions and produce large quantities of animal waste. For these reasons, it's best to choose organic pork, which ensures that animals are raised in less crowded, more humane conditions, fed organic feed, and not given antibiotics. (See page 112 for a definition of the "organic" label for meat.)

◆ **Chicken, Turkey, and Duck** As far as greenhouse gas emissions go, fowl have even less of an environmental impact than pork—roughly one third less. And while it takes about 2 pounds of feed to produce 1 pound of chicken, it takes between 10 and 20 pounds of feed to produce a pound of beef. Unless they are certified otherwise, fowl are given conventional grain as feed, and they are usually given doses of sub-therapeutic antibiotics. Organic poultry is usually the best choice. (See page 112 for a definition of the "organic" label for meat.)

Choosing Stew Meat

When it comes to making stew, tough is good. Instead of wasting money on expensive cuts of meat, choose cuts that come from the parts of an animal that get the most exercise, like the shoulder and legs. These cuts are more flavorful and contain a lot of collagen, which when simmered in liquid imparts a luscious texture to foods. The key to tender, melt-in-your-mouth meat in my Hungarian Goulash and the Maklube on page 104 is slow, moist cooking, so that the connective tissues have time to soften.

Hungarian Goulash

MY MOTHER IS HUNGARIAN, and she grew up with goulash made with beef and potatoes. There are many versions of this stew, as different families made it with different ingredients. Some recipes insist on bell peppers, and those can certainly be added if you like. Goulash, like all stews, gets even better a day or two after it's made as its flavors meld together and intensify. It's especially good served over hot egg noodles. ⸺ *Serves 4 to 6*

8 tablespoons olive oil

2 pounds boneless beef stew meat,
    cut into 1-inch cubes

4 cups diced yellow onions (¼-inch dice)

½ cup chopped garlic

2 tablespoons sweet Hungarian paprika

2 tablespoons dried oregano

2 tablespoons dried thyme

1 teaspoon hot Hungarian paprika

Salt and freshly ground black pepper

1 cup tomato sauce

4 to 5 cups cold water

3 pounds Yukon Gold or russet potatoes,
    cut into 1¼-inch cubes (about 6½ cups)

1. Heat 2½ tablespoons of the olive oil in a large, heavy pot or Dutch oven over medium-high heat. Add half of the meat and cook, stirring frequently, until browned all over, 5 to 7 minutes. Transfer the meat and any pan juices to a bowl, and set aside. Repeat with another 2½ tablespoons oil and the remaining beef, and set aside.

2. Add the remaining 3 tablespoons oil to the pot and reduce the heat to medium. Add the onions, garlic, sweet paprika, oregano, thyme, hot paprika, 1 teaspoon salt, and ½ teaspoon black pepper. Cook, stirring frequently, until the onions are soft, 5 to 8 minutes.

3. Add the beef, with any accumulated juices, and the tomato sauce to the pot and raise the heat to medium-high. Add enough cold water to cover the meat, cover the pot, and bring the mixture to the start of a boil. Reduce the heat to maintain a slow simmer and cook until the beef is tender, about 1¼ hours.

4. Add the potatoes and 1 tablespoon salt to the pot. There should be enough sauce to almost cover the potatoes; add ½ cup more water if needed. Cover the pot and simmer the stew until the potatoes are just tender, 20 to 30 minutes. Do not overcook or the potatoes will fall apart.

5. Season the goulash with salt and pepper to taste, and serve hot. (The goulash can be refrigerated, covered, for up to 3 days.)

Edith's Stuffed Cabbage

THERE IS NO DISH I ASSOCIATE MORE WITH MY MOM than her stuffed cabbage. She always makes it in her largest stockpot and cooks a massive quantity so there is plenty for everyone in our family to take some home to eat for days. It was a big challenge to adjust this recipe to serve just six! Whenever she makes it, it feels like a special occasion. In fact, I didn't learn how to make it myself until I wanted to immortalize it in this cookbook, because, frankly, I love it when *she* cooks it for me. That's always been part of the magic of this dish. But now I realize it's equally delicious and full of memories when I make it.

My mom, Edith, showing my daughter, Marea, how to roll stuffed cabbage, a task she learned from her mother when she was a girl in Hungary.

To make these cabbage rolls, ground beef is combined with uncooked rice and liberal amounts of onions, garlic, and spices, then rolled in cabbage leaves and simmered in a rich tomato sauce. Beef and white rice is the classic combination, but as my mom has gotten more health-conscious over the years, she has started to make this dish with ground turkey and brown rice instead of white. She actually prefers it this way now, and I really like it too. If you decide to make the brown rice version, add an extra ½ cup of water since brown rice will absorb a bit more liquid, and cook it for an extra 30 minutes (a minimum of 2 hours). One of the keys to keeping the stuffed cabbage intact is to roll the meat securely and arrange the rolls in a tight circle in the pot. You need a very large pot (at least 12 quarts) for this recipe in order to accommodate the sauce, much of which is absorbed by the rice during cooking. This dish reheats well in the microwave, and can be refrigerated, covered, for up to 3 days. 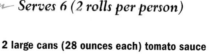 *Serves 6 (2 rolls per person)*

3 large heads of green cabbage

1½ pounds lean ground beef

1½ cups white rice

2 large yellow onions, grated (about 2 cups)

⅔ cup olive oil

⅓ cup chopped garlic

2 tablespoons dried oregano

2 tablespoons dried basil

4 teaspoons salt

4 teaspoons sweet Hungarian paprika

½ teaspoon cayenne pepper

4 cups tomato juice

2 large cans (28 ounces each) tomato sauce

¼ cup ketchup

1. Remove the cores from 2 of the cabbages, leaving the heads intact. Place one of the cored cabbages in a large microwave-safe bowl, and cover it with a kitchen towel. (If you do not have a microwave oven, see the Note on page 84.) Microwave the cabbage on high power until the leaves are pliable and can be detached easily,

6 to 10 minutes. Repeat with the second cabbage. Let the cabbages cool until they can be handled comfortably, at least 15 minutes.

2. Carefully remove the outer leaves of the cabbages, keeping them whole. As you move closer to the center of the heads, the leaves will become smaller. Set aside 12 of the largest leaves. Slice the remaining steamed leaves into 1-inch-wide pieces, and reserve. Core, then cut the remaining uncooked cabbage into 1-inch pieces and set aside. (The cabbage leaves can be prepared to this point up to a day ahead and refrigerated, covered.)

3. Place the ground beef, rice, onions, ⅓ cup of the olive oil, and half of the garlic in a large bowl. Add 1 tablespoon of the oregano, 1 tablespoon of the basil, 1½ teaspoons

of the salt, 2 teaspoons of the sweet paprika, and ¼ teaspoon of the cayenne pepper. Using your hands, knead the mixture together until combined.

4. Place a 1-inch-deep layer of the cut cabbage in the bottom of a 12-quart stockpot, to form a bed for the rolls. Reserve the remaining cut cabbage.

5. With your hands, form about ⅓ cup of the meat mixture (this will vary, depending on the size of the cabbage leaves) into a log. Place the meat in the center of a reserved cabbage leaf. Fold the bottom of the leaf over the filling, and roll the leaf up tightly to create a tidy roll. Using your finger, poke the edges of the leaves into the center of the roll to create a fairly tight and secure

Making Stuffed Cabbage

1. Place the meat mixture in the center of a whole cabbage leaf.

2. Bring the stem end of the leaf over the meat.

3. Begin rolling the meat toward the top of the leaf.

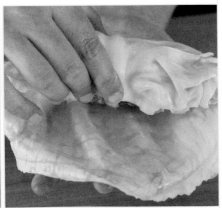

roll. Place the roll, seam side down, along the outer edge of the stockpot. Stuff and roll the remaining cabbage leaves as described, placing the rolls along the outside edge of the pot and then filling in the middle area. The cabbage rolls should be tightly packed in a single layer. Reserve the leftover meat mixture.

6. Cover the rolls with a 2-inch layer of the remaining cut cabbage (you may have some left over). Add the remaining ⅓ cup olive oil, remaining garlic, and remaining 1 tablespoon oregano, 1 tablespoon basil, 2½ teaspoons salt, 2 teaspoons sweet paprika, ¼ teaspoon cayenne pepper, and the leftover meat mixture to the pot. Pour the tomato juice, tomato sauce, and ketchup into the pot. The liquid must cover the cabbage rolls by at least 3 inches;

add water or more tomato juice if needed. Do not stir—just lightly swirl the ingredients together without disturbing the cabbage.

7. Cover and bring the mixture to the start of a boil over high heat. Reduce the heat to medium-low to maintain a simmer and cook for at least 1½ hours. Check once or twice to make sure that the sauce is simmering, not boiling vigorously, and that there is enough liquid to cover the cabbage rolls.

8. Check one of the rolls to see if the rice is fully cooked. This recipe is very forgiving and it is better to cook the cabbage rolls for a few extra minutes rather than undercook them. If the cabbage isn't soft and tender, cover the pot and continue cooking for another 15 minutes, or until the rice tastes fully cooked and the cabbage is soft.

4. Roll the leaf as securely as possible without squeezing the filling.

5. Use your finger to poke one side of the leaf in toward the center

6. Poke in the second side to complete the roll.

A perfect stuffed cabbage, ready to be eaten.

Note: If you don't have a microwave oven, bring a large covered pot of water to a boil. Place a rimmed baking sheet near the stove. Stick a long cooking fork into the core hole of one of the cabbages, and plunge the cabbage (carefully, so you don't splash yourself) into the pot of rapidly boiling water. The outer leaves will begin to fall off. Leave them in the boiling water for a few minutes, until they're limp and flexible enough for stuffing; then take them out one at a time, and place them on the baking sheet. Try not to tear the leaves. After you have removed the outermost 6 or 7 leaves, remove what is left of the cabbage head from the water and set it aside to cool. Repeat with the second head of cabbage. You will need 12 leaves that are soft and pliable enough to be rolled.

9. Turn off the heat and let the cabbage rolls rest for 20 to 30 minutes.

10. Using tongs, carefully remove the cabbage rolls from the pot and transfer them to individual plates or a large platter. Spoon the sauce over the rolls, and serve hot.

7. Place a 1-inch layer of cabbage pieces in the bottom of a large pot and arrange the cabbage rolls, seam side down, in concentric circles in a single layer on the pieces.

8. Cover the rolls with more cut cabbage and sprinkle the remaining spices and meat mixture over the cabbage.

9. Pour on the tomato liquids and you're ready to cook.

Goodman Family Meatloaf

MANY PEOPLE HAVE A MEATLOAF RECIPE THEY'RE LOYAL TO, but I still wanted to share this simple family recipe that my husband, Drew, grew up eating. It is very delicious and easy. One thing that makes it so good is the tomato sauce poured over the meatloaf just before it goes into the oven. The sauce glazes the top and is absorbed into the meat, creating a moist and tasty wonder. Parmesan cheese also adds flavor to the meatloaf, which is terrific eaten cold. If you double the batch, one bonus could be meatloaf sandwiches the next day. ⟶ *Serves 6*

2 pounds lean ground beef, preferably grass-fed

2 teaspoons garlic powder

2 teaspoons onion powder

1½ teaspoons salt

½ teaspoon freshly ground black pepper, or more to taste

1 cup freshly grated Parmesan cheese

1 large egg

1 can (15 ounces) tomato sauce

1. Position a rack in the middle of the oven and preheat the oven to 375°F.

2. Place the beef, garlic powder, onion powder, salt, pepper, ⅔ cup of the cheese, and the egg in a large bowl and stir to combine. (It may be easiest to do this with your hands.)

3. Form the mixture into a loaf shape and transfer it to an 8½ x 4-inch loaf pan, preferably glass. Pour the tomato sauce over the meatloaf, place it in the oven, and bake for 45 minutes.

4. Sprinkle the remaining ⅓ cup Parmesan cheese over the meatloaf and continue baking until an instant-read thermometer inserted into the center registers 165°F, about 15 minutes.

5. Let the meatloaf cool in its pan on a wire rack for 15 minutes to allow it to absorb some of its juices and to firm slightly for easier slicing. Serve hot or warm, with any extra pan juices passed in a pitcher.

TIP

Beef from a steer that has been grass-fed is lower in calories than beef from a grain-fed steer (a 6-ounce steak has almost 100 fewer calories). Grass-fed beef is also rich in health-enhancing omega-3 fats.

my favorite cookware cast-iron

How do I love thee, cast-iron cookware? Let me count the ways. Cast-iron is the most inexpensive, versatile, and eco-friendly cookware available. Ingredients prepared in cast-iron pans cook evenly, and it's easy to achieve a beautiful crisp, browned crust when you want it. Cast-iron pans are generally made from recycled scrap iron and can last (and even get better) over several generations. Also, cast-iron is virtually nonstick when seasoned properly, and there are no chemical coatings to flake or chip off into your food.

Forget about babying your nonstick skillet with plastic or coated spatulas because you're afraid of scratching its finish. I find it intensely satisfying to scrape away at all the crispy goodness in my cast-iron pan with a durable metal spatula. And I love being able to cut things like sausages right in the pan without being afraid of damaging the surface. I use cast-iron to prepare a large variety of foods—baking, braising, grilling, and sautéing at very high, even temperatures without worrying about damaging the pan, which travels seamlessly from stovetop to oven. If you use a protective trivet or small cutting board, the pan can even travel directly to the table, where it will keep the food warm during a meal.

I love that the care I put into my cast-iron cookware actually improves its natural nonstick surface over time, and caring for cast-iron is really easy (see Caring for Your Cast-Iron Cookware on facing page). The more you cook, the smoother the surface becomes. Since cast-iron, if treated well, gets better with age, your grandmother's skillet actually has a better nonstick surface than one purchased in the 1990s. Like organic farming, which improves the soil and makes it more productive over many generations, my *relationship* with my cast-iron cookware is long-term. I think of this cookware as a precious heirloom that wears like . . . well, iron!

Cast-iron cookware was originally designed for use over an open fire, so it's just about indestructible. Its heavy weight ensures a uniformly heated cooking surface from virtually any heat source. And unlike the chemicals that are present in most coated nonstick cookware, the trace amounts of dietary iron in food cooked in cast-iron cookware are actually good for most people.

I've heard some people complain about the weight of cast-iron, but I actually like it—using both hands to work with a skillet feels more mindful and grounded to me. I also love how versatile my cast-iron cookware is. I even turn my skillet over and use it as a baking stone to make pita bread!

If all this affection for cast-iron sounds strange to you, consider a couple of other fans: George Washington's mother thought so much of her cookware that she made special note to bequeath her cast-iron in her will. And in their expedition to the Louisiana Territory in 1804, Lewis and Clark reported that their cast-iron Dutch oven was one of their most important pieces of equipment.

This is a pan that you'll never have to throw away—but you will probably want to give it away, passing it down to a child or grandchild. I started a new tradition in our family when my daughter Marea moved into her first apartment. I sent her off with my first cast-iron skillet. I had cooked everything in that skillet for years, and it was beautifully seasoned. As Marea left to start her own first kitchen, I savored the sweet moment—saying goodbye to an old friend (my pan) and sending all the wonderful food memories, as well as my love, with Marea as she took her first step toward an independent future.

So, if you've been sitting on the fence as to whether or not you should make the jump to cast-iron, think of it first as an investment in the quality of your cooking tools. But it's also an investment in the future—of the environment and, quite probably, of a loved one's cooking experience when it's passed down to them.

Buffalo Shepherd's Pie

SHEPHERD'S PIE IS SOMETHING OF A BRITISH INSTITUTION and definitely falls into the category of comfort food. Ground or diced meat (traditionally lamb or mutton) is combined with gravy and (sometimes) vegetables and topped with mashed potatoes. The "pie" is baked until the potato "crust" browns. It was originally created as an economical way to use leftovers from a Sunday roast, but today shepherd's pie is made any day of the week, with or without leftovers. Our version uses porcini mushrooms, red wine, and beef stock to create a very flavorful base for the meat and vegetables. I like to make this dish with buffalo (bison) because it is a much healthier choice than grain-fed beef, with a lower impact on the environment (see page 91). It tastes great—slightly sweet, rich, and flavorful—but you can substitute ground beef, lamb, or turkey.

One of the things I especially like about this recipe is the way you can vary the flavor by using different toppings. Here we adhere to tradition with a mashed-potato crust. If you want something a little unusual, you can substitute yams for the Yukon Gold potatoes or top the pie with the assertive Celeriac and Potato Mash on page 211. ⌇⌇⌇ *Serves 8*

1 cup (about 1 ounce) dried porcini mushrooms (see sidebar, page 23)

¾ cup hot water

3 tablespoons olive oil

2 pounds ground buffalo (bison) or ground beef, preferably grass-fed

2 cups diced yellow onion (¼-inch dice)

1 medium carrot, peeled and cut into ¼-inch dice (about ½ cup)

1 tablespoon tomato paste

1 tablespoon Worcestershire sauce

2 tablespoons chopped fresh thyme leaves, or 1 tablespoon dried

2 tablespoons unbleached all-purpose flour

1 cup store-bought beef or chicken stock or broth, preferably low-sodium

½ cup dry red wine, such as merlot or zinfandel

1 cup frozen sweet corn (no need to thaw)

Salt and freshly ground black pepper

3 pounds Yukon Gold potatoes, peeled and cut into ¾-inch pieces (about 6½ cups)

3 tablespoons butter, at room temperature

3 tablespoons heavy (whipping) cream

Sweet paprika, for garnish (optional)

1. Place the dried mushrooms in a small bowl and add the hot water. Let the mushrooms soak at room temperature until they soften, about 20 minutes. Drain the mushrooms, reserving ½ cup of the soaking liquid

Caring for Cast-Iron Cookware

GETTING STARTED: Most cast-iron comes pre-seasoned these days, but a new pan still needs to be used a few times to break it in. The first few times you use it, it's especially important to get it nice and hot, and use a generous amount of oil. The cooking oil fills in the pores in the metal, creating a nonstick surface. Until your pan is properly broken in (I find it takes using it about six times), avoid cooking acidic foods like tomatoes.

DAILY CARE: Most of the time I just give my pan a quick rinse with hot water and the scrubby side of a sponge. Then I dry it thoroughly, and rub in a thin coat of vegetable oil before putting it away. Never let your pan air-dry. If I cook something especially sticky or with a strong odor (like fish) in my pan, I'll use a little mild dish soap in addition to hot water. I find that if I wash the pan while it's still warm, it's much easier to clean. When I cook foods that don't stick to the pan (like eggs, grilled cheese, crêpes), I simply wipe the surface clean while it's still warm, treating it more like a grill than a pan (but if it looks dry, I rub in a little vegetable oil). And like a grill, you always preheat your cast-iron pan before cooking, so this kills any germs.

Important reminders: Never put a hot cast-iron pan into cold water. And never soak cast-iron in water or put it in the dishwasher.

and avoiding any grit that may have settled. Chop the mushrooms and set aside.

2. Place a large skillet or Dutch oven over medium-high heat, and when the pan is hot, add 1 tablespoon of the oil. Add the buffalo meat and cook, stirring to break it up, until it is browned, about 5 minutes. Transfer the meat to a bowl and set aside.

3. Add the remaining 2 tablespoons oil to the same skillet and set it over medium-high heat. Add the onion and carrot and cook, stirring frequently, until the vegetables begin to soften, about 8 minutes. Add the tomato paste, Worcestershire sauce, thyme, and flour and stir the mixture for 2 minutes to cook off the raw flour taste. Then add the reserved porcini liquid, the stock, and the wine to the skillet and bring the mixture to the start of a boil. Stir in the buffalo, with any accumulated juices, and the reserved chopped porcinis, and reduce the heat to maintain a simmer. Cook, stirring occasionally, until the mixture thickens and the liquid has reduced by two thirds, 8 to 10 minutes.

4. Remove the skillet from the heat and add the frozen corn. Season the mixture with salt and pepper to taste,

and transfer it to a 9 x 13-inch baking dish or a 2-quart rectangular casserole. Set it aside.

5. Position a rack in the middle of the oven and preheat the oven to 375°F.

6. While the oven is heating, bring a large covered pot of salted water to a boil over high heat, add the potatoes, and cook until tender, 15 to 20 minutes. Drain, reserving about 1 cup of the cooking liquid.

7. Combine the potatoes and the butter in a bowl, and mash them together with a potato masher, adding the cream and some of the reserved potato liquid, as needed, to obtain the correct consistency. Season with salt and pepper to taste.

8. Spread the mashed potatoes over the meat mixture, covering it completely. Swirl the top with a knife to create decorative peaks, or use a fork to crosshatch the top. Sprinkle with paprika, if using.

9. Place the casserole on a rimmed baking sheet and bake the pie until the top is lightly browned and the meat is heated through, 40 to 50 minutes. Serve hot.

Crazy, Messy, Delicious Buffalo Burgers

M Y DAUGHTER, MAREA, TOOK A TRIP TO EUROPE after graduating high school and came home with some interesting food discoveries—such as this burger, which she found in a little restaurant in Berlin. Wanting to be adventurous on her adventure, she tried this unusual menu offering and couldn't believe how good it was—albeit messy, with sauerkraut and barbecue sauce spilling out. She raved about it so much that it was one of the first things we cooked for dinner when she got home, and now we have the burgers often. The combination of cheese, bacon, grilled onions, sauerkraut, and barbecue sauce is unexpected and delicious. Although we prefer buffalo, you can substitute regular ground beef. The easiest way to serve this meal is to cook the patties and then let everyone assemble their own burgers, choosing from an array of condiments. Buffalo meat is very lean, so take care not to overcook it. ⁓ *Serves 4*

LIVING GREEN
It turns out that one of the best ways to save a domesticated species, ironically enough, is to eat it. At the end of the 19th century only about 1,000 bison remained in this country. Now, thanks in large part to a rise in the consumption of buffalo meat, their population has rebounded to nearly a half million.

8 strips thick-sliced bacon

1¼ pounds ground buffalo (bison)

Salt and freshly ground black pepper

3 tablespoons olive oil

1 large yellow onion, cut in half through the stem end, then thinly sliced crosswise

4 slices Swiss cheese

4 good-quality rolls or burger buns, split

½ cup barbecue sauce, warmed

2 cups sauerkraut (packaged in plastic bag or jar), drained and heated until warm

2 ripe tomatoes, cut into thick rounds

Sliced dill pickles

Ketchup

Dijon mustard

1. Cook the bacon in a skillet over medium-low heat, turning it occasionally, until crisp, about 15 minutes. Set the slices aside to drain on a plate lined with paper towels.

2. Gently form the buffalo into 4 round patties. Season the meat on both sides with salt and pepper to taste.

3. Heat 2 tablespoons of the oil in a cast-iron skillet over medium-low heat. Add the onion slices and cook slowly, stirring occasionally, until they begin to caramelize, about 20 minutes. Lower the heat if the onions begin to cook too quickly. Transfer the onions to a plate and set aside. (The caramelized onions can be made 3 days ahead. Cool, cover, and refrigerate.)

4. Return the skillet to medium-high heat, and film the bottom with the remaining 1 tablespoon olive oil. Arrange the buffalo patties in the pan so that they do not touch. Reduce the heat to medium and cook for

Crazy, Messy, Delicious Buffalo Burgers

5 minutes to sear the meat. Turn the patties with a spatula. Place a slice of cheese on each burger, cover the skillet, and cook until the cheese melts and the meat is cooked to your preference, 3 to 7 minutes. (Alternatively, you can grill the buffalo burgers on a barbecue grill.)

5. Set out the rolls, burger fixings, and condiments, and let your guests build their own burgers by adding bacon, caramelized onions, barbecue sauce, sauerkraut, tomato, pickles, ketchup, and mustard as desired.

Setting out the burger fixins.

Bison (Buffalo)

If you haven't tried bison (or buffalo in layman's terms), you're in for a treat. Contrary to what you might expect, there is nothing gamy tasting about buffalo raised for meat production. Bison tastes like high-quality beef, but is richer and sweeter. The meat is naturally flavorful, and can be prepared in the same ways as beef. And when it comes to eating meat, bison is usually a healthier choice than beef. With significantly less fat per gram than other animal proteins, the average cut of grass-fed bison also contains more iron, protein, and minerals than conventional beef. According to the

USDA, while there are 7.4 grams of fat per 100-gram serving of skinless chicken, there are only 2.4 grams in the same size serving of bison. It has 69 percent more iron than beef, and 25 percent more protein as well.

Eating bison is usually eco-friendly. Like grass-fed cattle, most bison graze in open pastures rather than confined to small plots of land. Eating grass is good for them and good for the environment because natural foraging stimulates new grass growth, which in turn helps reduce carbon emissions. Because bison graze on green grass, their meat contains higher levels of

healthy omega-3 fatty acids, iron, and antioxidants such as vitamin E. These fatty acids are deficient in most American diets.

And don't forget that in addition to all the benefits of bison meat, we shouldn't overlook what is not in the meat. Most ranchers abide by the National Bison Association resolution that prohibits the use of growth hormones, steroids, and sub-therapeutic antibiotics (antibiotics given as a preventative measure). So if you want to eat meat that is better for you and the environment, give bison a try.

Herbed Rib Roast of Pork

THE BASICS

Fennel Pollen

The fennel flower produces an edible pollen that can be used to flavor meats and fish to heavenly effect. Hailed as fairy dust for food lovers, this intoxicatingly aromatic and pungent spice is delicious on just about anything. It is much sweeter tasting and more intensely flavored than fennel seed. Although not inexpensive, a pinch or two goes a long way and contributes a real spark of flavor. Dried wild fennel pollen, usually imported from Tuscany, is available at specialty markets and from mail-order sources.

A STANDING RIB ROAST (RACK) OF PORK makes a truly delicious and most impressive centerpiece for a holiday or special-occasion dinner. If you've never seen this cut of meat at your market, don't be surprised—it is generally a custom order, except during the Christmas season. Any market that has an in-house butcher will be able to prepare a rack of pork with a day's notice. Request that the rack be frenched, which means that the meat is removed from the ends of the rib bones to make for a more attractive presentation. This same cut of meat, when 2 racks are tied together in a circle, is called a crown roast of pork. Pork loin on the bone is so juicy and succulent that it needs little enhancement other than a rub of oil, fennel, herbs, and garlic. For maximum flavor, prepare the pork 1 to 3 days ahead of time so that the flavors have time to infuse into the meat; then, before you cook the roast, let the pork sit at room temperature for 2 hours so the meat cooks more evenly. ⁓ *Serves 8*

1 rib roast (rack) of pork (5 pounds), frenched

¼ cup extra-virgin olive oil

Coarse sea salt and freshly ground black pepper, to taste

2 tablespoons ground fennel seed (see sidebar, page 94)

6 large garlic cloves, crushed, peeled, and halved

2 tablespoons chopped fresh thyme leaves

8 fresh sage leaves, thinly sliced

2 tablespoons chopped fresh rosemary leaves

1 tablespoon fennel pollen (see sidebar, this page)

1. At least 1 and up to 3 days ahead, prepare the pork: Massage the pork with the olive oil, rubbing it in with your fingers. (You need the oil so that the herbs will stick to the meat, so don't skimp on the massage.) Sprinkle the meat with sea salt and pepper, and then with the ground fennel. Tuck about half of the garlic between the ribs and into all crevices.

2. Mix the thyme, sage, and rosemary in a small bowl to blend. Press the herbs and the remaining garlic over all the meat and fat sides of the roast. Wrap the pork tightly in plastic wrap so that the herbs and garlic stay pressed against the meat. Place the pork in a baking dish or on a rimmed baking sheet, and refrigerate for at least 1 and up to 3 days.

3. On the day of serving, remove the pork from the refrigerator, and let it sit, still wrapped, at room temperature for 2 hours. Ideally the temperature of the pork should be 50°F at the center of the thickest section when checked with an instant-read thermometer.

Herbed Rib Roast of Pork

4. Position a rack in the lower third of the oven and preheat the oven to 425°F.

5. Unwrap the pork and transfer it to a roasting pan, arranging it bone side down. Sprinkle the fennel pollen, if using, over the meat. Roast the meat until it registers 145°F on an instant-read thermometer or a remote digital thermometer. (The internal temperature of the meat will rise about 10 degrees while it rests.)

6. Remove the pork from the oven and cover the roast loosely with aluminum foil (preferably recycled), or partially cover it with an upside-down metal bowl. Allow the meat to rest for 15 to 20 minutes before carving it between the rib bones.

7. If you like, drizzle some of the pan juices over the slices before serving.

Easy Garlic-Thyme Pork Tenderloin

S O EASY, SO DELICIOUS—THIS IS THE DISH I OFTEN PLAN TO make when I know I'll arrive home from work late, without a lot of time to spend in the kitchen. I've given this simple recipe to many friends who were looking for something quick, easy, and tasty, and they all tell me it's now part of their regular repertoire. The flavors of garlic, lemon, mustard, and thyme complement this cut of meat perfectly. The pork is best if it can be marinated for 8 to 24 hours before cooking, but even 30 minutes will do. This dish is great served with any type of potato. ⸺ *Serves 4*

3 large garlic cloves, crushed and peeled

¼ cup fresh lemon juice, preferably from Meyer lemons

2 tablespoons Dijon mustard

1 tablespoon extra-virgin olive oil

1 teaspoon dried thyme

½ teaspoon salt

Freshly ground black pepper

1 or 2 pork tenderloins (about 1½ pounds total)

1. Combine the garlic, lemon juice, mustard, olive oil, thyme, salt, and black pepper to taste in a small bowl and whisk to blend.

2. Trim any fat off the tenderloin and remove the tough silver-skin membranes, if any. Place the tenderloin in a 1-gallon zip-lock and add the marinade. Seal the

bag, pressing out any excess air, and refrigerate the pork for up to 24 hours, turning the bag occasionally to distribute the marinade evenly.

3. Position a rack in the middle of the oven and preheat the oven to 375°F.

4. Remove the tenderloin from the bag, reserving the marinade.

5. Place a large, heavy ovenproof skillet, preferably cast-iron, over medium-high heat. When the skillet is hot, add the pork and sear it on all sides, turning it with tongs, about 8 minutes.

6. When the meat is nicely browned, add the reserved marinade to the skillet and cook until the sauce begins to simmer. Transfer the skillet to the oven and cook until the tenderloin is slightly pink inside but still moist, and an instant-read thermometer inserted in the center registers 145°F, 10 to 20 minutes.

7. Transfer the tenderloin to a cutting board and let it rest for 10 minutes. Reserve the sauce.

8. Slice the tenderloin into 1-inch-thick pieces and serve with the pan sauce.

Note: Depending on how much time I have, I sometimes vary the way I cook this pork. Although we especially like the brown, seared crust that develops in the cast-iron pan, sometimes I skip the pan-searing step and pop the tenderloin with its marinade right into the oven. Other times, I skip the oven roasting altogether and just cook the pork in the skillet until it's done, then turn off the heat and add the marinade, which bubbles and reduces from the residual heat in the skillet. Then I cut the meat into thick slices, add them to the sauce, and serve the pork right from the skillet rather than dirty more dishes.

Roasting Tips

◆ Choose the correct oven temperature for the food you're roasting. Large roasts, especially those with bones, like prime rib or rack of pork, need low to moderate heat (300° to 350°F) so the meat cooks slowly and evenly. High-heat roasting is recommended for small, tender cuts of meat such as tenderloins, because the high heat creates a seared, browned crust and the meat cooks quickly in a short time.

◆ An instant-read thermometer or a remote digital model is critical for ensuring perfectly roasted meats.

◆ Use a heavy roasting pan with low sides so that the heat is distributed evenly and the pan drippings are less likely to burn. For poultry, an oven rack is recommended to suspend the meat above liquids that are either added or produced during cooking.

◆ Always allow roasted meats to rest for 10 to 20 minutes after removing them from the oven. This allows the meat juices to redistribute; otherwise the juices will spill out and be lost when you begin carving. Tent the roast loosely with aluminum foil (preferably recycled) or with an upside-down bowl propped up on one side (to prevent steaming) while it rests.

Pinwheels of Pork with Spinach and Sun-Dried Tomatoes

THE BASICS

Kitchen String

Kitchen string (also called butcher's string) is a valuable kitchen tool, used mainly to truss poultry and tie meat. When meat is tied, as in our Pinwheels of Pork recipe, it helps maintain the shape of the meat while it's cooking and results in a better-looking finished product. Kitchen string can be found in specialty cookware shops and in mail-order catalogs.

SARAH AND I CAME UP WITH THIS RECIPE FOR A CATERING MENU one holiday season when we wanted a presentation that was both beautiful and unusual. While the red sun-dried tomatoes and the bright green spinach are ideal colors for the winter holidays, this is a dish to enjoy year-round. The tenderloins are pounded thin, layered with the savory spinach mixture, then rolled into a cylinder and baked. When sliced, the pretty pinwheels do double duty—meat and vegetable all in one. The pork is also delicious served cold.

⁓ *Serves 6 to 8*

2 tablespoons olive oil

1 cup diced yellow onion (¼-inch dice)

2 tablespoons minced garlic

12 cups (packed) baby spinach leaves, rinsed and dried if not prewashed

2 ounces sun-dried tomatoes, cut in thin julienne strips (about ⅔ cup), reconstituted in 2 tablespoons warm water if not soft and pliable

2 pork tenderloins (about 1¾ pounds total), trimmed

Salt and freshly ground black pepper, to taste

½ teaspoon sweet paprika

2 tablespoons canola oil

1. Heat the olive oil in a large skillet over medium heat. Add the onion and cook, stirring frequently, until it is soft and translucent, about 8 minutes. Add the garlic and cook until it is fragrant, about 2 minutes.

2. Add the spinach and 1 tablespoon water to the skillet. (It may be necessary to add the spinach in batches.) Cook, stirring frequently, until all the spinach is wilted, about 8 minutes. Stir in the sun-dried tomatoes. Remove the skillet from the heat and let the mixture cool while you prepare the meat.

3. Place the pork tenderloins on a large sheet of parchment paper, arranging them next to each other so that the large end of one is next to the small end of the other. Cover the meat with a large piece of plastic wrap, and using the smooth side of a meat tenderizer or a rolling pin, pound the pork into a ¼-inch-thick rectangle. (The pork pieces need to overlap each other by 1 inch at the seam, so that one large piece of pork is created.) Season the top surface of the pork with salt, pepper, and ¼ teaspoon of the paprika.

4. Position a rack in the middle of the oven and preheat the oven to 350°F.

5. While the oven is heating, spread the spinach mixture over the pork, leaving a ½-inch border all around. Starting from the long side, roll the meat into a tight log. Using kitchen string, tie the roll at 2-inch intervals. If the meat is too long for your skillet, cut it in half to create 2 pieces. Season the exterior of the roll with salt, pepper, and the remaining ¼ teaspoon paprika.

6. Heat the canola oil in a large cast-iron or other heavy ovenproof skillet over medium-high heat. Carefully transfer the pork to the skillet, placing it seam side down. Sear the meat on all sides, 5 to 8 minutes total.

7. Transfer the skillet to the oven and roast until the pork is cooked through, or until an instant-read thermometer inserted into the center of the roll reads 140°F, 30 to 35 minutes.

8. Let the pork rest at room temperature for 15 minutes before removing the string and cutting the roll into ½-inch-thick pinwheels.

Pork Chile Verde

INSPIRED BY THE DISTINCTIVE CUISINE OF NEW MEXICO, this stew combines tender chunks of pork with roasted tomatillos, garlic, and green chiles. We like its rich, complex flavors that evolve through the slow cooking. It's delicious served over rice, and it also makes a terrific filling for burritos or enchiladas. ⁓ *Serves 8*

12 tomatillos, husked and cored
   (see sidebar, page 98)

1 tablespoon olive oil

1 teaspoon dried oregano

Salt and freshly ground black pepper

1 whole garlic head

8 ounces bacon, cut into ¼-inch pieces

¼ cup plus 1 tablespoon unbleached
   all-purpose flour

2 tablespoons ground cumin

3 pounds boneless pork shoulder
   (Boston butt), trimmed and cut into
   1-inch pieces, fat discarded

2 cups diced yellow onion (¼-inch dice)

4 large garlic cloves, peeled and finely
   minced

Pinch of dried red pepper flakes,
   or more to taste

4 cups Chicken Wing Stock (page 403) or
   store-bought low-sodium broth

1 tablespoon tomato paste

1 large can (28 ounces) roasted chopped
   green chiles, drained

¼ cup chopped fresh cilantro, for garnish
   (optional)

8 lime wedges, for garnish (optional)

Tomatillos

The Spanish word tomatillo *means "small tomato," which is what these small green globes resemble. They are members of the nightshade family, cousins of tomatoes and Cape gooseberries. Like gooseberries, the tomatillo is encased in a thin brownish-green papery husk. These papery husks must be peeled off, and the sticky coating that remains should be removed by a thorough rinsing. Averaging 1 to 2 inches in diameter, firm, pale green tomatillos have a tart flavor with hints of apple, lemon, and herbs. They can be eaten raw, but they are generally cooked, at which stage they become lusciously soft, like grilled eggplant. Tomatillos are the main component in* salsa verde, *a staple condiment in Mexican cuisine.*

1. Position a rack in the middle of the oven and preheat the oven to 400°F.

2. Place the tomatillos in a bowl and toss with the olive oil, oregano, and some salt and pepper. Transfer the mixture to a rimmed baking sheet. Cut off and discard the top third of the head of garlic. Wrap the garlic bulb tightly in aluminum foil, and place it on the baking sheet. Bake until the tomatillos have slumped and are juicy, 35 to 40 minutes.

3. Remove the baking sheet from the oven and let the mixture cool for 15 minutes. Then transfer the tomatillos and their juices to a blender. Squeeze the roasted garlic from the skins and add to the blender. Puree until almost smooth. Set aside or refrigerate, covered, for up to 1 day.

4. Place the bacon pieces in a large skillet and cook over medium-low heat until they are crisp, about 15 minutes. Transfer the bacon to a plate lined with several layers of paper towels and set it aside to drain. Reserve all of the bacon fat.

5. Mix the ¼ cup flour, the cumin, and some salt and pepper in a medium-size bowl. Dredge the meat in the flour mixture, a few pieces at a time, until all sides are lightly coated.

6. Add 2 tablespoons of the reserved bacon fat to a large (4-quart) Dutch oven or heavy pot. Set the Dutch oven over medium-high heat, and when the fat is hot, add the pork pieces and cook until the meat is browned, 5 to 8 minutes. Do not crowd the pan; brown the pork in batches if necessary. Transfer the browned meat to a platter and set it aside.

7. Heat another 2 tablespoons of the reserved bacon fat in the same Dutch oven over medium heat. When it is hot, add the onion and cook, stirring frequently, until it is soft, 5 to 8 minutes.

8. Add the garlic cloves and red pepper flakes, and cook until fragrant, 2 to 3 minutes. Return the pork, any accumulated juices, and the tomatillo puree to the Dutch oven, and set it aside.

9. Heat 1 tablespoon of the reserved bacon fat in a large skillet over medium heat. Stir in the remaining 1 tablespoon flour and cook for 2 minutes, stirring constantly, to make a roux (a mixture of flour and fat, used to thicken a sauce or soup). Add the chicken stock, raise the heat to medium-high, and cook, stirring frequently, until the roux is blended in and the stock has thickened slightly. Stir in the tomato paste, the chopped green chiles, and the bacon pieces. Pour the mixture into the Dutch oven and stir to combine.

10. Place the Dutch oven over medium-high heat, cover, and bring to the start of a simmer. Then reduce the heat to low, cover the pan, and simmer gently, stirring occasionally, until the meat is fork-tender, 1¼ to 1½ hours. (Alternatively, you can put the pot in a 300°F oven and cook the pork until tender.)

11. Serve hot, sprinkled with the chopped cilantro and garnished with the lime wedges, if desired. (The stew can be cooled to room temperature, placed in an airtight container or zip-lock bag, and refrigerated for up to 3 days or frozen for up to 3 months. If it is frozen, thaw the stew in the refrigerator for 24 hours before reheating.)

budgeting for eco-friendly meat

There can be real "sticker shock" when you first start buying organic or grass-fed meat, so it's important to understand exactly what you're paying for. It simply costs more for producers to raise animals in a less crowded, more humane environment. It costs more to feed animals organic feed that is grown without chemical pesticides and synthetic fertilizers, protecting the environment in the process. And it costs more to raise animals without using antibiotics and hormones. When you factor in the costs to our environmental and personal health, however, in many ways these more expensive eco-choices are a much better value than non eco-choices.

Most of us can reprioritize our choices and create what I call an eco-budget. When I buy beef, bison, pork, lamb, or poultry that was produced in more humane and sustainable ways, I serve smaller portions accompanied by more vegetable choices. Also, I make an extra effort to serve more meatless meals. In America, we are used to "supersizing," thinking that more is always better. But when we look at what this pattern has done to our collective health, and our environment, it's easy to see that valuing quality over quantity is a wiser, more sustainable strategy.

Italian Sausage with Fennel and Grapes

Italian Sausage with Fennel and Grapes

THE PAIRING OF SAUSAGES AND GRAPES, which may seem unusual, has a long history in Italian cuisine and is really delicious. This hearty country-style dish is very easy to prepare. We like the way the sweetness of roasted grapes, fennel, and onion forms a perfect backdrop for the spicy sausage. Choose whatever type of sausage you like: hot or sweet Italian, chicken and apple, or andouille, for example. This rustic dish makes a great autumn or winter dinner when partnered with some hot crusty bread and a glass of full-bodied red wine. —*Serves 4*

1 tablespoon olive oil

1 pound uncooked sausage, such as sweet or hot Italian, cut on the diagonal into 1-inch-thick slices

1 tablespoon balsamic vinegar

1 to 2 large yellow onions, cut in half through the stem end, then cut crosswise into ¼-inch-thick slices (about 3½ cups)

1 large fennel bulb, cut in half lengthwise, core removed and outer layer discarded if discolored or very thick, then cut crosswise into ⅛-inch-thick slices (about 2 cups)

5 large garlic cloves, crushed, peeled, and halved lengthwise

2 cups seedless red or black grapes, such as Flame grapes

Salt, to taste

2 teaspoons ground fennel seed (see sidebar, page 94)

1. Position a rack in the lower third of the oven and preheat the oven to 400°F.

2. Heat the oil in a large cast-iron skillet or Dutch oven over medium-high heat until it is shimmering hot.

Add the sausage and cook, turning occasionally, until it is well browned and the fat is beginning to render, about 8 minutes. Transfer the sausage to a plate lined with several layers of paper towels and set aside to drain at room temperature. Reserve the fat in the skillet.

3. Place the vinegar in a medium-size bowl and add the onion, fennel, and garlic. Toss to combine. Then add the grapes (leaving them whole), salt, and ground fennel and toss again to coat all surfaces. Transfer the mixture to the skillet and stir to combine. Cook over medium heat, stirring frequently, until the onion and fennel begin to soften, about 8 minutes.

4. Add the sausages, pressing them down into the vegetables so they are partially covered. Transfer the skillet to the oven and roast until the fennel and grapes are tender and the sausage is cooked through, 40 to 50 minutes. Serve hot.

Orzo with Prosciutto, Broccolette, Zucchini, and Peas

THIS IS A DELICATE DISH full of light flavors and contrasting textures. The prosciutto, Parmesan stock, and fresh mint contribute an elegant taste, while the crisp-tender trio of broccolette, peas, and zucchini add a pleasant textural contrast. One great thing about this pasta is that it's just as delicious cold as hot. This is a perfect dish to make for dinner with the idea of saving some for leftovers. Then when you need a quick lunch a few days later, you have a meal all ready to go. The pasta is also a terrific addition to a party or picnic because it tastes so good at any temperature. ⁓ *Serves 4 to 6*

Salt

2 cups (12 ounces) orzo

2 bunches broccolette, trimmed and cut
   into 1-inch pieces (see box, page 169)

2 tablespoons olive oil

1 cup thinly sliced yellow onion

2 small zucchini, cut in half lengthwise,
   then cut into ¼-inch-thick slices
   (about 2 cups)

1 cup shelled fresh English peas

2 cups (8 ounces) diced prosciutto

⅔ cup Parmesan Stock (page 408),
   Chicken Wing Stock (page 403), or
   store-bought low-sodium chicken broth

⅓ cup thinly sliced fresh mint leaves

Freshly ground black pepper

½ cup freshly grated Parmesan cheese

1. Bring 4 quarts water to a boil in a large covered pot over high heat. Add 2 tablespoons salt and the orzo. Stir the pasta for 30 seconds. Then cook for 3 minutes. Add the broccolette and continue cooking, covered, until the broccolette is crisp-tender and the orzo is al dente, 7 to 8 minutes more.

2. Meanwhile, heat the olive oil in a large skillet over medium heat. Add the onion and cook, stirring frequently, until it just begins to soften, about 4 minutes. Add the zucchini and raise the heat to medium-high. Cook, stirring frequently, until the zucchini is just crisp-tender, about 3 minutes. Add the peas, prosciutto, and stock, and cook until the peas are crisp-tender, 2 to 3 minutes.

3. Drain the pasta and broccolette thoroughly in a colander.

4. Add the orzo and broccolette to the skillet and cook, stirring constantly, until the mixture is very hot, about 2 minutes. Add the mint and stir to combine. Season to taste with salt and pepper.

5. Transfer the pasta to a heated bowl or individual serving plates, and sprinkle each serving with some of the Parmesan cheese. Serve hot.

Greek-Style Lamb Chops

A TASTY MARINADE OF OREGANO, LEMON, GARLIC, AND OLIVE OIL adds great flavor to loin lamb chops. Be sure to plan ahead to allow enough time to let the meat marinate for at least 4 hours. In true Greek style, the heady fragrances of oregano and garlic dominate. The herb soaks up much of the marinade, so be sure to generously coat all sides of the lamb with the mixture for maximum flavor. I like to sear the chops in a hot cast-iron skillet, then finish the meat in the oven, but they are also terrific grilled. ⌐⌐⌐ *Serves 4*

⅓ cup olive oil

⅓ cup fresh lemon juice

¼ cup dried oregano

2 tablespoons finely minced garlic

Grated zest of 1 lemon

Salt and freshly ground black pepper

8 lamb loin chops, 1½ to 2 inches thick
(about 2 pounds total)

1. Place the oil, lemon juice, oregano, garlic, lemon zest, 1 teaspoon salt, and ½ teaspoon black pepper in a baking dish and whisk to blend. Add the lamb chops, turning them to coat all sides in the marinade. Cover the dish and refrigerate the meat for at least 4 hours or up to 24 hours.

2. One hour before you plan to cook the chops, remove them from the refrigerator and let them come to room temperature (in the marinade).

3. Position a rack in the middle of the oven and preheat the oven to 375°F.

4. Remove the chops from the marinade, reserving the marinade.

Lightly season the chops with salt and pepper.

5. Place a large cast-iron skillet over medium heat, and when it is hot, add the lamb chops in a single layer, taking care not to crowd the pan. Cook on each side for 3 to 5 minutes to sear the meat until it is nicely browned. Then pour the reserved marinade over the chops, and transfer the skillet to the oven. Cook until the chops are done to your liking, about 5 to 10 minutes for medium-rare. (To test for doneness, insert an instant-read thermometer through the side into the center of a chop, without touching the bone. It will register 145°F when the chop is medium-rare.) Serve hot.

Note: To grill the lamb chops, preheat a barbecue grill to medium. Remove the chops from the marinade and place them on the hot grill grate. Cook them for about 3 minutes on each side, basting with some of the marinade. Then cover the grill and cook the chops, turning them once, until cooked to taste, 4 to 5 minutes more for medium-rare.

Maklube

T HIS RECIPE WAS GIVEN TO ME BY SAMANTHA CABALUNA, a longtime Earthbound Farm employee. Her family has a Middle Eastern heritage,
and this was one of her grandmother's special dishes and Samantha's favorite
growing up. *Maklube* means "upside down," which accurately characterizes this
presentation. Lamb, vegetables, and rice are layered in a Dutch oven. After
cooking and resting, the dish is flipped upside down and the pan is removed.
Maklube is traditionally served with pine nuts and *leban* (Middle Eastern
yogurt), but it tastes great with regular plain yogurt. ⁓ *Serves 6*

7 tablespoons olive oil

**2 pounds boneless lamb stew or leg meat,
    trimmed of fat and cut into 1-inch cubes**

Salt and freshly ground black pepper

1½ teaspoons dried marjoram

3 cups warm water

**2 large eggplants, peeled and cut into
    ¼-inch-thick rounds**

3½ cups thinly sliced yellow onion

3 large cloves garlic, minced

3 large romaine lettuce leaves

**4 large tomatoes, cut into ¼-inch-thick
    rounds**

1½ cups basmati rice

⅓ cup pine nuts, toasted, for garnish

¾ cup plain yogurt, for garnish

1. Place a large skillet, preferably cast-
iron, over medium-high heat, and add
2 tablespoons of the olive oil. Add the
lamb in a single layer, taking care not
to crowd the pan. (It may be necessary
to do this in batches.) Brown the meat,
turning it with tongs to brown all the
surfaces, about 8 minutes total. Season
the meat with salt and pepper to taste,
and sprinkle with the marjoram. Add

the warm water to the skillet, cover,
and reduce the heat to medium-low.
Simmer until the lamb is tender, 1 to
1½ hours.

2. Meanwhile, lightly sprinkle both
sides of the eggplant slices with salt,
and set them aside on a rack or plate
to drain for 1 hour.

3. Using a clean kitchen cloth or
paper towels, blot the water and salt
from the surface of the eggplant
slices. Heat 2 tablespoons of the olive
oil in a large skillet, preferably cast-
iron, over medium-high heat. When
the oil is hot, add half of the eggplant
slices in a single layer, making sure
not to crowd the pan. Cook until
lightly browned, about 2 minutes.
Flip and cook on the other side for
1 to 2 minutes. It is important to
cook the eggplant only until it is
barely crisp-tender; do not overcook
it. Transfer the slices to a baking
sheet lined with several layers of
paper towels.

4. Add 2 more tablespoons of oil to the skillet and repeat with the remaining eggplant.

5. Add the remaining 1 tablespoon oil to the skillet, reduce the heat to medium-low, and cook the onion, stirring frequently, until it is soft and tender, 8 to 12 minutes. Add the garlic and cook, stirring frequently, until fragrant, about 2 minutes. Set aside at room temperature.

6. Line the bottom of a 3-quart Dutch oven with the romaine leaves, arranging the lettuce so that it comes halfway up the sides of the pan. Transfer the lamb to the pan, reserving the pan juices in the skillet. Spread the meat out in an even layer, top it with the eggplant slices, and then cover them with the tomatoes. Scatter the onion mixture over the top, and press lightly with a spatula to compress and even the surface of the layers. Sprinkle the rice over the top.

7. Pour the reserved pan juices into a liquid measuring cup and add enough very hot water to make 3 cups of liquid. Carefully pour the liquid down the sides of the Dutch oven, disturbing the layers as little as possible. Cover the Dutch oven and place it over medium-low heat. Cook for exactly 40 minutes.

8. Remove the Dutch oven from the heat and let it sit, still covered, for 40 minutes to allow the layers to set.

9. To serve, remove the cover of the Dutch oven. Invert a large platter over the Dutch oven, and holding the platter and Dutch oven together firmly, carefully invert the Dutch oven. Lift off the Dutch oven and carefully remove the lettuce. Garnish the Maklube with the toasted pine nuts and yogurt, and serve immediately.

Making Maklube

1. After lining the pot with romaine leaves, spread out the meat in an even layer, then top it with a layer of eggplant slices.

2. Top the eggplant with a layer of tomato slices.

3. Cover the tomatoes with the cooked onions.

4. Complete the layering with a layer of rice, then pour in the liquid, slowly so as not to disturb the layers.

5. After cooking, invert the Maklube onto a platter. Don't worry if it doesn't all stay mounded. The results will be delicious. Remove the lettuce leaves before serving.

Chicken Breasts Stuffed with Chard, Gruyère, and Prosciutto

Chicken Breasts Stuffed with Chard, Gruyère, and Prosciutto

CHICKEN IS ONE OF THE MOST VERSATILE OF MEATS—as highlighted in this recipe, where you pound it thin and add a lively stuffing that combines salty prosciutto, sweet and nutty Gruyère cheese, and earthy chard. The rolls are quickly browned on the stovetop and then finished in the oven. The result is a tender, juicy chicken that is incredibly flavorful. ⎯⎯ *Serves 4 to 6*

3 tablespoons olive oil

1 large bunch Swiss chard, rinsed, stemmed, leaves stacked, rolled, and sliced into 2-inch-wide strips (8 cups)

2 teaspoons minced garlic

1 teaspoon dried oregano

4 skinless, boneless chicken breast halves (8 ounces each)

Salt and freshly ground black pepper

½ cup (2 ounces) grated Gruyère cheese

8 slices (about 4 ounces) prosciutto

1. Heat 1 tablespoon of the olive oil in a large skillet over medium-high heat. Add the chard, garlic, oregano, and 1 tablespoon water, and cook, stirring frequently, until the chard wilts, about 2 minutes. Then cover the skillet and cook until the chard is tender, 3 to 5 minutes more. Remove the skillet from the heat, uncover it, and let the chard cool.

2. Place the chicken, one breast piece at a time, between pieces of plastic wrap or in a large zip-lock bag, and pound the meat with the smooth side of a meat pounder or with a rolling pin until the meat is ¼-inch thick. Repeat with all the chicken.

3. Season one side of each of the chicken breasts with salt and pepper to taste. Sprinkle the cheese over the meat, covering only about two thirds and leaving the end of the chicken that is farthest from you uncovered. Place 2 slices of prosciutto, then add one-quarter of the chard on each breast, again covering only two thirds of the meat. Starting from the end nearest to you, roll the meat up. As you roll, the stuffing mixture will be pushed forward, toward the end of the chicken that was left uncovered. Tightly wrap each roll in plastic wrap, twisting the ends to create a tight, sausagelike roll. Refrigerate for at least 30 minutes or up to 8 hours.

4. Position a rack in the middle of the oven and preheat the oven to 350°F.

TIP

If you buy your chicken where there is a customer-service butcher, you can ask him to pound the breasts for you.

5. Heat the remaining 2 tablespoons olive oil in a large ovenproof skillet, preferably cast-iron, over medium-high heat. Carefully unwrap the chicken rolls and place them, seam side down, in the skillet, resting them against the sides of the pan so that they are less likely to unroll. Sear the meat for 3 minutes. Then turn the rolls with tongs and brown them on all sides, about 8 minutes total. (If the chicken starts to unroll, use toothpicks to pin it closed.)

6. Once all sides have been browned, return the rolls to the seam-down position and transfer the skillet to the oven. Bake until the chicken is cooked through, or until an instant-read thermometer registers 165°F when inserted into the thickest part of the roll, about 10 minutes.

7. Let the rolls rest for 5 minutes before cutting them into ½-inch-thick slices. Serve hot.

Herb-Marinated Chicken Breasts with Pesto

THIS QUICK AND EASY RECIPE PRODUCES MOIST, TENDER CHICKEN breasts with lots of fresh herb flavor. Marinating the breasts requires only 20 minutes, giving you just enough time to toss together a salad and steam a fresh vegetable to round out the meal. If you're looking for a delicious meat dish that's simple to prepare, this one fits the bill nicely. And if there happens to be any left over, the chicken tastes great the next day for lunch. ⟶ *Serves 6*

3 tablespoons chopped fresh basil, or
  2 tablespoons dried
3 tablespoons minced fresh flat-leaf parsley
2 tablespoons chopped fresh sage leaves, or
  1 tablespoon dried rubbed sage
1 tablespoon minced garlic
3 tablespoons olive oil
2 tablespoons fresh lemon juice
6 skinless, boneless chicken breast halves
  (6 ounces each)
1 tablespoon canola oil

½ large lemon
2 tablespoons Pesto (page 164)

1. Place the basil, parsley, sage, garlic, olive oil, and lemon juice in a large mixing bowl and whisk to blend. Add the chicken breasts, and turn them to coat all the surfaces. Cover the bowl with a plate and let the chicken marinate in the refrigerator for 20 to 60 minutes.

2. Position a rack in the middle of the oven and preheat the oven to 375°F.

3. Place a large ovenproof skillet, preferably cast-iron, over medium-high heat, and when it's hot but not smoking, add the canola oil. Arrange the chicken breasts in a single layer in the skillet. (If all the breasts will not fit comfortably without touching, cook the chicken in two batches, adding more canola oil if needed.) Raise the heat to high and cook for 4 minutes to sear the chicken. (Watch to ensure that the garlic does not burn, reducing the heat slightly if necessary.) Turn the breasts over and cook on the other side for 2 minutes. If you've seared the breasts in batches, return all the breasts to the skillet. If they don't fit in a single layer, transfer them to a baking pan.

4. Squeeze the juice from the lemon half over the chicken breasts, and then spread the pesto over them. Transfer the skillet to the oven and bake until the chicken is cooked through, 4 to 6 minutes, or until an instant-read thermometer registers 165°F when inserted into the thickest part of the meat.

5. Let the chicken rest for 5 minutes before cutting it into ½-inch-thick slices. Serve hot.

Chicken and Green Olive Enchiladas

THESE UNUSUAL ENCHILADAS HAVE A ZESTY FLAVOR thanks to the combination of spices and green olives. In our version, we don't cook the tortillas in oil, which makes for a lighter and more healthful dish. If you don't have time to roast a chicken, buy a rotisserie chicken at the grocery store. Remove the meat and save the bones for a quick chicken stock (see page 7). Enchiladas make a great casual supper and are also terrific for a party. Try them with Chili Rice, sour cream, and the very tasty Roasted Tomatillo Salsa, or use a store-bought tomatillo salsa. To save time, you can substitute 2 cans (15 ounces each) of store-bought enchilada sauce for the homemade version. ⁓ *Serves 4 (2 enchiladas per person)*

LIVING GREEN
Reuse aluminum foil whenever possible. If it's dirty, wash it thoroughly in cold water, spread it flat to dry, and fold it neatly to store.

ENCHILADA SAUCE

3 tablespoons canola oil

2 cups diced yellow onion (¼-inch dice)

3 tablespoons minced garlic

1 teaspoon dried oregano

1 teaspoon ground cumin

5 tablespoons chili powder

1½ tablespoons unbleached all-purpose flour

4 cups Chicken Wing Stock (page 403) or store-bought low-sodium chicken broth

Salt and freshly ground black pepper

ENCHILADAS

8 fresh corn tortillas (6-inch diameter)

2⅔ cups shredded cooked chicken

3 cups grated cheddar cheese

1½ cups pitted green olives, chopped

Chili Rice (page 227, optional)

Sour cream

Roasted Tomatillo Salsa (page 418, optional)

1. Prepare the sauce: Heat the oil in a large skillet or Dutch oven over medium heat. Add the onion, garlic, oregano, and cumin, and cook, stirring frequently, until the onion is soft but not browned, about 8 minutes. Stir in the chili powder and flour, and cook, stirring constantly, for 1 minute to eliminate the raw flavor of the flour.

2. Slowly add the stock, whisking to blend. Raise the heat to medium-high and cook, uncovered, until the sauce begins to thicken, 15 to 20 minutes. (You need about 3½ cups of sauce.) Season with salt and pepper to taste. Transfer the sauce to a medium-size bowl and let cool.

3. Position a rack in the middle of the oven and preheat the oven to 350°F.

4. Spread ½ cup of the enchilada sauce over the bottom of a 9 x 13-inch baking dish.

5. Prepare the enchiladas: Dip both sides of 1 tortilla into the sauce in the bowl, and shake off any excess. Transfer the tortilla to the baking dish. Place ⅓ cup of the shredded chicken at one end of the tortilla. Top the mixture with ¼ cup of the cheese and 2 tablespoons of the olives. Roll the tortilla up tightly and place it, seam side down, at one end of the baking dish. It's okay if the tortillas crack during the rolling process. Repeat with the remaining tortillas.

6. Cover the tortillas with the remaining sauce, and sprinkle with the remaining cheese. Cover the baking dish with aluminum foil (preferably recycled), and bake until the sauce is bubbling and the filling is hot, about 20 minutes. Serve with Chili Rice, sour cream, and Roasted Tomatillo Salsa, if desired.

Note: You can make the enchiladas a day ahead. Place them in the baking dish, pour the sauce over the rolled tortillas, and refrigerate, covered with aluminum foil. The next day, let them sit for an hour at room temperature before baking.

Chicken and Green Olive Enchiladas

understanding eco-labels for meat

Some of the labels you see on meat packaging can be confusing when you're trying to make better choices for the environment and your health. What's the difference between "Natural" and "Organic"? Does organic beef come from 100-percent grass-fed cattle? These issues become more complicated because some standards for labels do overlap. Humane treatment for animals is built into USDA Organic Standards, which is the most inclusive eco-label. Organic standards do not, however, cover all label claims in this section. Grass-fed animals are never given grain or soy. Organic production methods require access to pasture, but allow feeding of organic grain and hay. So if you want to be assured that your meat is organic and grass-fed, both labels must be present.

It is important to remember that all these labels have separate certifiers and their own sets of standards. While I can't list all the requirements for these labels here, this overview of the broad points will help you to navigate these claims.

♦ **Natural** The USDA definition of "natural" is "Meat that is minimally processed and free of additives such as preservatives, artificial flavors, or colors." This is a processing claim for the finished product only (the meat after slaughter) and has nothing to do with how the animal was raised or handled.

♦ **USDA Certified Organic** This is the strictest and most regulated label. Animals certified under the USDA National Organic Program (NOP) must be fed a 100-percent organic diet; they are never given hormones or antibiotics; they are never exposed to synthetic

pesticides. Cattle may be pasture-fed their entire lives, or be fed a combination of grass and organic grain. Organic feed may not contain animal by-products. Standards require that all animals be raised in a humane manner with access to the outdoors, shade, shelter, exercise areas, fresh air, and sunlight. Only meats that have been produced and processed in strict compliance with USDA Organic Standards may bear the organic seal. The Organic Seal does not claim that animals were 100-percent grass fed.

♦ **American Grassfed Association** This organization defines grass-fed products from ruminants—including cattle, bison, goats, and sheep—as those foods from animals that have eaten nothing but their mother's milk and fresh grass or grass-type hay. Many products are marketed as "grass-fed" when grass has been only part of the animal's diet. Animals may also have been confined, given grain, antibiotics, or synthetic hormones. For this reason the Association is the only seal that provides assurance that the products you purchase are from 100 percent grass-fed animals. The grass-fed label does not claim that the meat is also organic.

♦ **Certified Humane Raised and Handled** Overseen by the Humane Farm Animal Care since 2003, this certification program ensures that a producer meets humane standards for animals from birth through slaughter. Animals must have ample space, shelter, gentle handling to limit stress, ample fresh water, and a healthy diet of quality feed, without added

antibiotics or hormones. Therapeutic administration of antibiotics under the care of a veterinarian is allowed. Cages, crates, and tie stalls are among the forbidden practices, and animals must be free to do what comes naturally. Chickens, for example, must be able to flap their wings and dust-bathe, and pigs must have the space to move around and root. The program also requires higher standards for humane slaughtering methods. This label does not claim that the meat is organic or grass-fed.

◆ **American Humane Certified** (formerly Free-Farmed) Overseen by the American Humane Association, a 133-year-old humane agency that has been offering this certification since 2000, certification includes third-party verification that science-based standards are being met as well as a monthly auditing process. Standards include the following: Animals must be free to move around and express normal behavior. Producers must provide proper medical care, diet, and water. No antibiotics or hormones may be given in feed; therapeutic administration of antibiotics under the care of a veterinarian is allowed. Animals must be free from fear and distress, and be provided with appropriate shelter for comfort and rest. This label does not claim that the meat is organic or grass-fed.

◆ **Raised Without Antibiotics** "Raised without antibiotics" is a general claim, which implies that subtherapeutic antibiotics were not used in the production of a food product. The USDA has defined "raised without antibiotics" to mean that animals used for meat were raised entirely without the use of low-level (subtherapeutic) doses of antibiotics. Claims on these products do imply that the manufacturer has gone beyond USDA regulations for conventional meat production.

◆ **Hormone Free** "No hormones administered" and "hormone free" are general claims that imply that no hormones were given to meat or dairy animals. There is currently no standard definition for the term except for meat products. Unless otherwise specified, there is no organization independently certifying this claim.

It's important to note that the USDA prohibits the use of hormones for pigs and poultry in the United States. Therefore producers who label pork and poultry products as "no hormones administered" are not doing anything beyond what all conventional producers are required to do.

Saigon Caramel Chicken

I F YOU'RE FAMILIAR WITH VIETNAMESE CUISINE, you may know that clay pot cooking is a standard technique. With this recipe, we've re-created one of our favorite restaurant dishes for the home kitchen—and it works perfectly well without any special equipment. Tender pieces of chicken are cooked in a deceptively simple combination of chicken stock, sugar, soy sauce, and fish sauce, with a result that is rich and full of complex flavors—sweet, salty, and hot, all at once. Fish sauce is a mainstay of Vietnamese cuisine and is a key element of this dish. Look for it in Asian markets, as high-quality brands are rarely carried in mainstream grocery stores. The chicken needs to marinate for a few hours before being cooked, so plan ahead. Serve the chicken over steamed jasmine rice or cellophane noodles in shallow bowls. —*mm*— *Serves 4*

Fresh cilantro

MARINADE AND CHICKEN

¼ cup canola oil

2 tablespoons soy sauce, preferably low-sodium

2 tablespoons fish sauce (see box, page 156)

2 tablespoons grated peeled fresh ginger

2 tablespoons finely minced fresh lemongrass (from 2 stalks; see sidebar, page 19)

1½ pounds boneless, skinless chicken breast or thigh meat, cut into ¾-inch cubes

SAUCE

¼ cup (packed) dark brown sugar

1¾ cups Chicken Wing Stock (page 403) or store-bought low-sodium chicken broth

½ jalapeño pepper, seeds and ribs removed if desired, or 2 or 3 dried hot chiles

3 large garlic cloves, peeled and halved

4 slices (¼-inch thick) peeled fresh ginger

3 tablespoons fish sauce (see box, page 156)

1 tablespoon soy sauce, preferably low-sodium

1 bunch (6 to 8) scallions, top 2 inches discarded, remainder cut on a diagonal into 1-inch lengths

GARNISH

2 tablespoons chopped fresh cilantro (optional)

1. Prepare the marinade: Place the oil, soy sauce, fish sauce, ginger, and lemongrass in a medium-size bowl and stir to combine.

2. Add the chicken to the marinade and stir to coat the pieces. Cover the bowl and refrigerate for 2 to 3 hours to allow the flavors to develop.

3. Remove the chicken from the marinade and rinse the pieces in cold water. Discard the marinade. Set the chicken aside to drain while you prepare the sauce.

4. Prepare the sauce: Place the dark brown sugar in a small, heavy-bottomed saucepan, and cook over medium-high heat until the sugar is hot to the touch and starting to melt around the edges. Add the chicken stock and stir until the sugar dissolves. Add the jalapeño, garlic cloves, and ginger slices, and cook, uncovered, until the liquid has reduced by half, 5 to 8 minutes. Remove the pan from the heat and let the mixture sit for 15 minutes to infuse the flavors.

the solids. Return the pan to the stove and add the fish sauce, soy sauce, and scallions. Reheat over medium heat until the sauce is hot. Then add the chicken, reduce the heat to medium-low, and gently poach the chicken, stirring occasionally, until it is cooked, 5 to 8 minutes.

5. Set a sieve over a clean saucepan and pour the mixture into it, discarding

6. Serve the chicken and sauce garnished with the cilantro, if desired.

Chicken Puttanesca Pasta

T HIS IS MY VARIATION ON THE TRADITIONAL ITALIAN *PUTTANESCA*, a spicy sauce, generally served with pasta, that combines tomatoes with a vibrant cast of ingredients—onion, garlic, anchovies, black olives, and capers. We love the depth and complexity of flavors in this dish—it's so vivacious that my family never tires of it. The last-minute addition of fresh basil and parsley adds a crucial flash of freshness—you'd miss the herbs if they weren't there. —*mm*— *Serves 4 to 6*

¼ cup olive oil

1 cup diced yellow onion (¼-inch dice)

4 large garlic cloves, peeled and minced

Pinch of dried red pepper flakes, or to taste
   (optional)

Salt

1 pound dry short-cut pasta such as penne
   or rigatoni

1¼ pounds boneless, skinless chicken
   breasts, cut into ¾-inch cubes

1 large can (28 ounces) and 1 medium
   can (15 ounces) crushed tomatoes,
   with their juices

3 tablespoons tomato paste

5 canned anchovy fillets, finely chopped,
   or 2 tablespoons anchovy paste
   (see sidebar, this page)

Freshly ground black pepper

¾ cup (packed) Kalamata olives, pitted,
   rinsed, and cut in half lengthwise

3 tablespoons capers, rinsed

½ cup chopped fresh basil

⅓ cup chopped fresh flat-leaf parsley

1 cup shredded mozzarella cheese

½ cup freshly grated Parmesan cheese,
   for garnish

Anchovies

Anchovies are a member of the herring family, native to the Mediterranean and southern European coastlines. They are sold in two forms: filleted and packed in oil, or whole and packed in salt. Filleted anchovies are the easiest to use and are readily available in most supermarkets. Whole anchovies require more work to remove the heads, tails, and backbones, and they must also be rinsed of excess salt. Once the tin has been opened, refrigerate anchovies, covered in either oil or salt, in an airtight container. For the best flavor, use them within 6 months of opening.

1. Place a large, deep skillet over medium heat, and when it is hot, add the olive oil. Add the onion and cook, stirring occasionally, until it has softened, 5 to 8 minutes. Add the garlic and red pepper flakes, if using, and cook, stirring frequently, until the garlic is fragrant, about 2 minutes. Set the onion mixture in the skillet aside.

2. Bring at least 4 quarts of water to a boil in a large covered saucepan over high heat. Add 2 tablespoons salt and the penne, and stir constantly for 30 seconds. Cook, stirring occasionally, according to the package directions until the pasta is al dente, 10 to 12 minutes.

3. While the pasta is cooking, place the skillet with the onion mixture over medium-high heat and add the chicken. Cook, stirring frequently, until the chicken is no longer pink on the outside, about 5 minutes. Stir in the tomatoes and their juices, and bring the mixture to a simmer. Reduce the heat to medium-low, cover the skillet, and cook until the tomatoes begin to soften, about 10 minutes.

4. Meanwhile, drain the pasta, return it to the pot, and cover to keep it warm.

5. Add the tomato paste, anchovies, ¾ teaspoon salt, black pepper to taste, the olives, and the capers to the chicken mixture. Simmer over medium heat, uncovered, stirring occasionally, until the tomatoes are tender, the chicken is cooked through, and the sauce has thickened, about 10 minutes. Stir in the basil and parsley, and remove the skillet from the heat. (If you need to, you can prepare the sauce several hours before you're ready to cook and serve the pasta. Reheat the sauce while you cook the pasta.)

6. Spread the hot chicken puttanesca sauce in an even layer in the skillet, and immediately sprinkle the mozzarella over it. Cover, and let the mixture sit for a few minutes to allow the cheese to melt.

7. Divide the hot pasta among individual serving bowls, and top with the puttanesca sauce. (Alternatively, place the pasta in a large bowl, add the sauce, and toss to completely coat.) Sprinkle each serving with Parmesan, and serve immediately.

Amazing Turkey Chili

THREE DIFFERENT KINDS OF CHILES—ancho, pasilla, and chipotle—add depth of flavor and subtle heat to this perennial crowd-pleaser. Everyone has a favorite chili recipe, but this version, with its blend of spices, vegetables, and stock, is so rich and complex that it is outstanding. The chili can be also be made with beef, but ground turkey is a lower-calorie, lower-fat option, and the chili is so flavorful that no one will know the difference. We like a combination of light and dark turkey, but the recipe will work with either cut. The quantities specified here result in a mildly spicy chili. If you like yours south-of-the-border hot, add more chipotles and cayenne pepper. Serve bowls of steaming hot chili with grated cheddar or Monterey Jack cheese, and garnish each serving with dollops of sour cream. The chili freezes well; defrost it overnight in the refrigerator before reheating. ━━ *Serves 8*

¼ cup canola oil

2 medium yellow onions, cut into ¼-inch dice

1 green bell pepper, stemmed, seeded, and cut into ¼-inch dice

3 tablespoons ancho chile powder (see sidebar, this page)

1 tablespoon pasilla chile powder (see sidebar, this page)

2 tablespoons ground cumin

2 tablespoons ground coriander

1 tablespoon sugar

2 teaspoons dried thyme

2 teaspoons dried oregano

½ teaspoon cayenne pepper, or more to taste

5 garlic cloves, peeled and finely minced

2½ pounds ground turkey

2 cups store-bought low-sodium chicken broth

1 large can (28 ounces) diced tomatoes, with their juices

1 cup tomato sauce

¼ cup tomato paste

2 chipotle peppers in adobo sauce, with or without seeds, minced (see sidebar, page 418)

2 cans (15 ounces each) pinto beans, rinsed under cold water and drained

1 tablespoon apple cider vinegar

2 tablespoons fresh lime juice

Salt, to taste

1. Heat the oil in a large stockpot or Dutch oven over medium heat. Add the onions and bell pepper and cook, stirring frequently, until the vegetables soften, 10 to 15 minutes.

2. Meanwhile, combine the chile powders, cumin, coriander, sugar, thyme, oregano, and cayenne pepper in a small bowl.

3. When the vegetables are soft, add the herb/spice mixture and the garlic, and stir constantly until the mixture is

THE BASICS
Chili Powder
The kind of generic chili powder that you find in the supermarket is a blend of several spices. While there is no established formula for making chili powder, it typically consists of about 80 percent chile pepper blended with garlic powder, oregano, ground cumin, sometimes salt, and occasionally monosodium glutamate. Some blends even include traces of clove, allspice, anise, and coriander. Ethnic and specialty markets carry chile powders made from specific varieties of chile, usually without other additives, and that's what's called for in Amazing Turkey Chili.

Duck Breasts with Dried Cherry Sauce

hot and fragrant, about 3 minutes. Add the ground turkey and cook, breaking up the meat, until the meat is browned, about 10 minutes.

4. Add the broth, diced tomatoes, tomato sauce, tomato paste, chipotle peppers, pinto beans, and vinegar. Stir

to blend, and simmer the chili over medium-low heat, stirring occasionally, until it is cooked through and has begun to thicken, 30 to 45 minutes.

5. Remove the pot from the heat, and stir in the lime juice and salt to taste. Serve hot.

Duck Breasts with Dried Cherry Sauce

DOMESTIC DUCKS CAN BE DISAPPOINTINGLY DRY AND TOUGH, but I've found that a short period of brining tenderizes and adds moisture to the meat. This step requires at least 3 hours, so plan accordingly. Duck is traditionally paired with fruit, and our dried cherry sauce offers a delicious, slightly sweet counterpoint to this robust meat. The basis of the sauce is called a *gastrique* in French, a syrupy reduction of caramelized sugar and vinegar, to which fruit is generally added. Tart dried cherries stand up beautifully to the *gastrique* and perfectly balance the richness of the duck. ⎯⎯⎯ *Serves 4*

BRINE

2 teaspoons fennel seeds

1 teaspoon whole black peppercorns

1 tablespoon agave nectar (see box, page 321) or honey

2 teaspoons coarse (kosher) salt

4 cups cold water

DUCK AND SAUCE

4 boneless, skinless duck breast halves (6 to 8 ounces each)

3 tablespoons sugar

3 tablespoons red wine vinegar

½ cup dried tart cherries, such as Morello

3 tablespoons olive oil

¼ cup thinly sliced peeled shallots

1 cup dry red wine, such as Pinot Noir or Merlot

1 cup Duck Stock (page 404) or Chicken Wing Stock (page 403)

¼ cup heavy (whipping) cream

Salt and freshly ground black pepper

1. Prepare the brine: Place the fennel seeds and peppercorns in a small dry skillet over low heat and toast until hot and fragrant, 2 to 4 minutes. Transfer the mixture to a medium-size

Dutch Ovens

A good Dutch oven is a kitchen essential. Dutch ovens are heavier and thicker than a stockpot, allowing them to conduct heat more effectively. And they're deeper than a skillet, so they can accommodate large quantities of meat and liquid. These qualities make Dutch ovens the best choice for braises, pot roasts, and stews, especially as they can be used both on the stovetop and in the oven.

not crowd the pan or the meat will steam; it may be necessary to do this in batches. Transfer the duck to a plate and set aside. When the meat is cool enough to handle, discard the skin from the breast pieces.

3. Discard all but 1 tablespoon of fat in the Dutch oven. Add the onion, garlic confit, bay leaf, thyme leaves, and brandy, and bring to a simmer over medium-high heat. Cook for 2 minutes. Then add the duck stock, cover, and bring to a simmer. Add the duck pieces and any accumulated juices, cover the Dutch oven, and cook at a very slow simmer over medium-low heat until the duck is very tender, 1 to 1½ hours.

4. Meanwhile, peel and core the whole quince, and chop it into small pieces. Place the pieces in a small saucepan and add ¾ cup water. Cook over medium heat until the quince is very soft, 10 to 15 minutes. Drain and mash the quince. Add the quince puree to the Dutch oven.

5. Combine 2 tablespoons of the butter and 2 teaspoons of the sugar in a medium-size skillet, and cook over medium heat until the butter has melted and the sugar has dissolved. Add the apples, cut side down, and cook until the apple flesh is golden brown, about 10 minutes. Flip the apples and cook on the other side until they are just tender, 8 to 10 minutes.

Remove from the skillet and set aside at room temperature. When cool enough to handle, remove the seeds and cores.

6. Heat the remaining 2 tablespoons butter and 2 teaspoons sugar in the same skillet. Add the quince wedges and cook, turning to cook all sides, until the fruit is golden brown and just tender, about 10 minutes. Set aside at room temperature. The skillet will be used again, so there is no need to wash it.

7. When the duck is very tender, use tongs to transfer the meat to a platter, and tent it loosely with aluminum foil. Strain the braising liquid through a fine-mesh sieve into a clean saucepan, and discard the solids. Place the pan over high heat and cook, uncovered, to concentrate the flavors and slightly thicken the sauce, 7 to 10 minutes.

8. While the sauce is reducing, reheat the apple halves and quince wedges in the skillet until warmed through.

9. Remove the sauce from the heat, and whisk in the crème fraîche and parsley. Season with salt and pepper to taste.

10. To serve, arrange 2 pieces of duck on each plate or shallow bowl. Nap them with the sauce, and arrange an apple half and several wedges of quince next to the meat. Serve hot.

CHAPTER 4

FISH AND SHELLFISH

RECIPES

ECO-MINDED LIVING

SELECTED PRIMERS

Plus 12 more useful tips.

Sensational, Sustainable Seafood

I REMEMBER WITNESSING THE FIRST TIME MY DAUGHTER, MAREA, DISCOVERED the wonders of the ocean. She was thirteen months old and her eyes were filled with the joy of a young child. As I watched her playing on the beach, I felt the strong pull to preserve this natural beauty. We pointed to the ocean and told her that was the fishes' real home, creatures she had seen only in books or aquariums. For days, she kept saying, "Shhhhh, shhhh" and we soon realized that she wasn't telling us to be quiet; she was saying "fish" and just couldn't quite manage the "f" sound. After "mama" and "dada," "fish" was her first word!

Many years later, that memory still reminds me of just how fragile our oceans are and how important it is to protect them for future generations. Watching a child dance on that boundary of land and water is a perfect image of the direct link between the health of our oceans and the health of all life on our planet.

The oceans supply more than 50 percent of the Earth's oxygen—that's more than 2½ times the amount produced by the rain forests. And like the rain forests, what we know about our oceans is dwarfed by what we've yet to discover. If our oceans continue to deteriorate, food sources, medicinal compounds, and vital knowledge about our planet are just a few of the things we could lose before we ever discover them.

Happily, one of the best ways to protect our oceans is by choosing environmentally responsible seafood. Like the organic movement, the sustainable seafood movement is profoundly influenced by consumer demand. Once we start asking for sustainable seafood and stop purchasing those foods that deplete species or damage our oceans, we are well on our way to reforming an entire industry and ensuring that our children and their children will inherit healthy oceans and bountiful sea life.

The recipes in this chapter represent a delicious variety of seafood flavors. For the most part, fish and shellfish are light, nutrition-rich, and very fast to prepare. This chapter has some wonderful recipes to try—with spices and condiments that will take your taste buds on a delicious world tour from Southeast Asia, to the Mediterranean, to Mexico. I've included simple, family-style favorites like Fish Tacos with freshly prepared Farm Stand Pico de Gallo. Or you can choose the unique flavors of a Seared Tuna with French Lentil Salad, which combines the extra flavor and nutrition of cumin-flavored lentils with the fresh taste of mint, offset by the white creaminess of crumbled feta cheese. One of my favorite recipes is the Coconut-Crusted Salmon, which combines heart-healthy omega-3-rich fish and a crispy light crust. Drizzle a bit of Coconut Chile Sauce over it for a dish you'll want to make over and over again.

As with all cooking and eating, I urge you to be adventurous! Try the Mussels Provençal—a fast, easy, and nutritious meal that is also an excellent sustainable seafood choice. Mussels are one of the most environmentally friendly foods on the planet. They are generally produced using very low-impact aquaculture methods. They filter algae and other particles from the water, so their cultivation can actually improve water quality and the health of other species in that environment.

Making sustainable seafood choices can be confusing, so I've included a lot of information and resources in this chapter. With the help of the Monterey Bay Aquarium's Seafood Watch Program, I explain when (and why) farmed seafood is a bad choice and when it may be a good one. You'll find out when to ask your grocery store or fish market where something comes from and also how it was caught, and when to avoid certain types of fish or shellfish entirely. You'll also read about why frozen fish is often your best alternative with regard to both quality and environmental impact.

In many ways we are still at the frontier of a sustainable seafood revolution. Unlike organic foods, there is no central government certification agency for fish and shellfish, and many times where your seafood comes from and how it was caught is not readily apparent. There are, however, private sustainable seafood certification agencies—such as the Marine Stewardship Council—that are doing a very good job at setting standards for wild fisheries, encouraging consumer education, and promoting seafood eco-labeling (see page 144). As we become more knowledgeable about ocean issues and begin to demand sustainable choices, we have the ability to halt and reverse damaging practices and restore our oceans for generations to come.

Mussels Provençal (page 148)

Black Cod with Summer Succotash

BLACK COD IS THE COMMON NAME for the sleek, slender, coal-black sablefish, a species found in the North Pacific. The flesh ranges from ivory to pale tan and its texture is tender, moist, and flaky when cooked. This full-flavored, high-fat fish is very high in omega-3 fatty acids, which have been shown to have numerous health benefits. Black cod is similar in richness and sweet flavor to Chilean sea bass, but is a much more sustainable choice. It's at its peak season in summer, so we've paired it here with a variation on the classic succotash. Served cold, our succotash makes a unique and interesting contrast with the hot fish, and the combination of fresh sweet corn, cucumbers, tomatoes, and basil is delicious and very healthy. Lima beans are traditional, but we prefer edamame (soybeans) because we like their bright green color and fresh, nutty flavor. When summer-ripe corn and tomatoes are not available, pair the fish with any vegetable of your choice, and serve it with Brown Rice with Barley (page 226). ⎯⎯ *Serves 4*

4 skinless black cod fillets (6 ounces each)

1 tablespoon plus 2 teaspoons extra-virgin olive oil

Salt and freshly ground black pepper

1 teaspoon garlic powder

1 teaspoon dried tarragon

½ teaspoon sweet paprika

Summer Succotash (recipe follows)

1. Dry the fish fillets with paper towels. Using your fingers, rub both sides of the fish with 2 teaspoons of the olive oil. Season the fish with salt and pepper on both sides.

2. Stir the garlic powder, tarragon, and paprika together in a small bowl. Sprinkle all of this seasoning mixture on one side of each fillet.

3. Heat a cast-iron or heavy-bottomed skillet over medium-high heat. Add the remaining 1 tablespoon olive oil to the skillet. Arrange the fillets, spice mixture down, in the skillet, taking care not to crowd the pan. (If necessary, use two skillets.) Cook the fish for 3 minutes. Then flip the fillets over and continue cooking until they just firm up and the very last flakes on the tail end start to separate, 2 to 3 minutes. (Alternatively, the fish can be seared on one side, and finished in a 375°F oven.) When perfectly cooked, the fish will offer some resistance and will spring back when pressed with a fingertip. Avoid overcooking or the soft flesh will fall apart.

4. Top each fish fillet with a generous scoop of Summer Succotash, and serve immediately.

Summer Succotash

Sweet corn, nutty edamame, juicy tomatoes, and crunchy cucumber star in this colorful vegetable medley. It makes a terrific salsalike sauce for our black cod, and it is also a delicious side dish, great for a summer barbecue or picnic.
—*Serves 4*

Salt

1 cup shelled edamame, English peas, or
    fava beans, fresh or thawed if frozen

2 cups fresh corn kernels (from 3 large ears)

1½ cups diced peeled cucumber
    (¼-inch dice)

2 large Roma tomatoes, seeded and
    cut into ¼-inch dice (about 1 cup)

½ cup extra-virgin olive oil

¼ cup chopped fresh basil

1 tablespoon chopped fresh tarragon

Freshly ground black pepper

1. Bring 8 cups water to a boil in a covered saucepan over high heat. Stir in 1 tablespoon salt and the edamame. Cook, covered, for 2 minutes. Add the corn and remove the pan from the heat. Let the vegetables sit for 1 minute, and then drain them in a colander or sieve. Run cold water over the vegetables until they have cooled to room temperature; drain well.

2. Place the cucumber, tomatoes, olive oil, basil, and tarragon in a large mixing bowl. Add the edamame-corn mixture, stirring to combine. Season with salt and pepper to taste. The succotash can be refrigerated, covered, for 1 day.

YOUR GREEN KITCHEN

Tips on Buying Fresh Sustainable Seafood

Understanding how to select fresh, healthy, and sustainable seafood may seem like a daunting task, and it's easy enough to feel overwhelmed at the fish counter. Maybe that helps to explain why more than half of Americans seldom, if ever, eat fish. This is a shame because fish is easy to cook at home, and can confer substantial health benefits. Here are a few simple guidelines to help you choose the best:

◆ Shop in markets that specialize in seafood and where fish is labeled with its country of origin, whether it is wild or farmed, and whether it is fresh or previously frozen.

◆ The store should be clean, with no unpleasant, fishy odors.

◆ Fish and shellfish should always be displayed on plenty of ice.

◆ Seafood should be moist and glistening, not dull and dry. Eyes should be clear and bright, and gills red or bright pink, not pale or brownish.

◆ Clams, oysters, and mussels should be tightly closed. Live bivalves will close their shells if they are touched. Discard any shellfish whose shells remain open when handled.

◆ Pre-packaged fish shouldn't have pools of liquid in the package.

◆ Ask if the seafood you are buying is considered sustainable and if it has been caught or farmed in environmentally friendly ways. Your local fishmonger may be able to guide you. If not, refer to the Monterey Bay Aquarium's Seafood Watch guide for your area (visit www.SeafoodWatch .org to download their handy regional Seafood Watch pocket guides) or look for seafood that bears the seal of respected sustainable certifiers, such as the Marine Stewardship Council (see page 144).

Herb-Crusted Halibut with Tomato-Caper Sauce

Herb-Crusted Halibut with Tomato-Caper Sauce

HALIBUT IS A WONDERFUL FISH that is still plentiful in the northern Pacific waters. It is low-fat, with very white flesh that is firm and mild-flavored, and is available fresh year-round in most areas, as well as frozen. Sold in either fillets or steaks, it is very versatile and can be prepared in any manner. I like this simple treatment, where a light dusting of herbs and bread crumbs creates a thin crust. The sauce—made with wine, tomatoes, and capers—has a rich, luscious texture. ⟶ *Serves 4*

½ cup fine dry bread crumbs

3 tablespoons minced fresh tarragon

1 tablespoon minced fresh flat-leaf parsley

2 cups dry white wine

2 tablespoons chopped shallots

6 fresh tarragon sprigs

¾ cup heavy (whipping) cream

¼ cup peeled, seeded, and finely diced
   tomatoes (see sidebar, this page)

3 tablespoons capers, drained

Salt and freshly ground black pepper

4 skinless Pacific halibut fillets
   (about 6 ounces each)

Juice of 1 lemon

2 tablespoons canola oil

1. Place the bread crumbs, 1 tablespoon of the minced tarragon, and the parsley in a small bowl and stir to combine. Set aside.

2. Combine the wine, shallots, and tarragon sprigs in a small pan and bring to a simmer over medium heat. Cook, uncovered, at a slow simmer until the liquid has reduced to 2 tablespoons, about 20 minutes. Add the heavy cream and cook over medium heat until the sauce has reduced by half, 5 to 8 minutes.

3. Strain the sauce through a fine-mesh sieve into a bowl. Discard the solids and return the sauce to a clean pan. Add the remaining 2 tablespoons minced tarragon, the tomatoes, and the capers. Season to taste with salt and pepper. Keep the sauce warm while you cook the halibut.

4. Position a rack in the middle of the oven, and preheat the oven to 375°F.

5. Sprinkle both sides of the halibut fillets with the lemon juice and season them with salt and pepper. Spread the bread crumb mixture on a plate and dip one side (only) of each fillet into the crumbs, pressing lightly so they adhere.

THE BASICS

How to Peel and Seed a Tomato

To peel a tomato, use a small knife to cut around and remove the core from the stem end. Then cut a small X through the skin on the bottom of the tomato. Submerge the tomato in boiling water just until the skin begins to loosen, about 30 seconds. Quickly remove the tomato from the boiling water and plunge it into a bowl of ice water to stop the cooking process. Drain, and remove the skin (it should slip off easily).

To seed a tomato, cut it in half through the stem end (lengthwise), and squeeze the juices and seeds into a sieve set over a bowl. Reserve the juices, if desired, and discard the seeds.

6. Heat the canola oil in a large ovenproof skillet (preferably cast-iron) over medium-high heat. Arrange the fish fillets, crumbed side down, in the skillet, making sure not to crowd the pan. Cook the fillets until the crumbs are golden, 2 to 3 minutes.

7. Carefully turn the fillets over and transfer the skillet to the oven. Bake until the fillets are just opaque and can be flaked with a fork, 4 to 6 minutes, depending on the thickness of the fish.

8. Serve the fillets warm, drizzled with the sauce.

six reasons to protect our oceans

Unless you live by the coast, it can be easy to forget about the oceans and why their health is so important to us. So here's a reminder.

1. The ocean produces roughly half of the Earth's oxygen.

Ocean plants (especially floating single-celled phytoplankton) provide more oxygen than the rain forests.

2. The ocean absorbs carbon emissions from our atmosphere—an estimated 22 million tons a day!

During photosynthesis, phytoplankton remove carbon dioxide (CO_2) from seawater and release oxygen as a by-product. This allows the oceans to absorb additional carbon dioxide from the atmosphere. If fewer phytoplankton existed, atmospheric carbon dioxide would build up at a faster rate.

3. The ocean provides most of our fresh water.

Although we don't usually think of our oceans as drinking water, they contain roughly 97 percent of the water on the planet. When ocean water evaporates, it returns to the planet surface as rain or other types of precipitation, leaving the salt behind.

4. The ocean is the Earth's climate control.

Our oceans are actually one interconnected body of water. This water circulates around the globe, moving from shallow to deep waters and back again, spreading the heat from the sun throughout the entire planet. Without such perpetual motion, the blistering heat delivered daily to the tropics would render them uninhabitable, and the rapid spread of ice caps from the North and South Poles would bring harsher weather to both northern and southern latitudes.

5. The ocean is a major source of food and jobs.

Fish from the ocean are the primary source of protein for one in six people on Earth. In addition, nearly a million people in the U.S. have jobs that directly depend on the ocean.

6. The ocean provides medicines and the promise of knowledge for the future.

Researchers have developed anti-leukemia drugs from sea sponges, bone-graft materials from coral, and anti-infection agents from shark skin, to name a few medical gifts from the sea. And there is still so much in the oceans that is unexplored and undiscovered. Like the rain forests, our oceans hold the promise of many compounds that exist nowhere else on Earth; the loss of undiscovered ocean creatures and their habitats would be incalculable.

Yogurt-Marinated Mahi Mahi with Curry and Herbs

A SIMPLE MARINADE MADE WITH YOGURT, FRESH LEMON, HERBS, and spices imparts a complex and intriguing taste to the firm, flavorful flesh of this warm-water fish. Just a short period of marinating produces moist, tender fish with flavors reminiscent of Indian tandoori oven cooking. Try this marinade with other firm fish such as Pacific halibut, striped bass, and wild salmon, or even with chicken. Serve the mahi mahi with your favorite rice pilaf and a simple salad for a satisfying meal that's both healthy and delicious.
—*Serves 4*

2 teaspoons canola oil

1 cup plain nonfat yogurt

2 tablespoons fresh lemon juice

1 tablespoon minced fresh cilantro

1 tablespoon minced fresh dill

1 teaspoon salt

½ teaspoon curry powder, preferably Madras

½ teaspoon sweet paprika

1½ pounds skinless, boneless U.S.-caught mahi mahi, cut into 4 pieces

1. Line a rimmed baking sheet with a piece of parchment paper, and brush the paper with the canola oil. Set aside.

2. Combine the yogurt, lemon juice, cilantro, dill, salt, curry powder, and paprika in a medium-size bowl and whisk to blend.

3. Dip each piece of mahi mahi into the yogurt mixture, coating the fish on all sides. Transfer the fish pieces to the prepared baking sheet, and pour any excess marinade over the fish. Marinate in the refrigerator for 20 to 30 minutes.

4. Position a rack in the middle of the oven and preheat the oven to 375°F.

5. Bake the mahi mahi until it is cooked through, 15 to 20 minutes depending on the thickness of the fish. Serve hot, with the pan juices on the side.

THE BASICS

Panko Crumbs

Panko are Japanese bread crumbs that resemble fresh bread crumbs at first glance. They are dry, however, irregularly shaped, and coarser than regular bread crumbs. When used for frying, they produce a light, crunchy coating that is tender and delicate. They seem to absorb less oil and to stay crisp longer than regular crumbs. Panko crumbs are widely available in supermarkets now, in both regular and whole wheat versions.

To make panko at home, remove the crusts from slices of fresh, firm-textured white or whole wheat sandwich bread. Using the coarse shredding disk of a food processor or the coarse side of a box grater, grate the bread. Transfer the crumbs to a rimmed baking sheet and bake in a 300°F oven until dry but not toasted, about 5 minutes.

Coconut-Crusted Salmon

THIS IS THE KIND OF CRUSTED FISH DISH that's seen on menus at high-end restaurants, yet this recipe is surprisingly easy. It's quick enough to whip up any time you crave a special treat—or want to impress dinner guests. The Asian-inspired crisp topping of coconut and Japanese tempura-style bread crumbs contrasts beautifully with the flaky, nutrition-rich salmon. This is the perfect time to use your favorite cast-iron skillet, which will go seamlessly from stovetop to oven. A light drizzle of our Coconut Chile Sauce makes a beautiful presentation and tastes sublime. ⁓ *Serves 6*

½ cup shredded unsweetened coconut
   (see sidebar, page 139)
¼ cup panko (see sidebar, this page)
Salt and freshly ground black pepper
6 skinless salmon fillets (6 ounces each),
   preferably wild, pinbones removed
2 tablespoons fresh lime juice
2 tablespoons peanut oil
Coconut Chile Sauce (page 416, optional)

1. Position a rack in the middle of the oven and preheat the oven to 375°F.

2. Combine the shredded coconut, panko, ½ teaspoon salt, and ¼ teaspoon pepper in a small bowl. Toss well, and then spread the mixture on a plate.

3. Brush the top side of the salmon fillets with the lime juice. Lightly season the fish with salt and pepper. One piece at a time, dip the top side of each fillet in the coconut-panko mixture, making sure the surface is coated. Pat the mixture onto the fish, if necessary.

4. Set a large, heavy-bottomed skillet, preferably cast-iron, over medium heat. When the skillet is hot, add the peanut oil. Arrange half of the salmon fillets, coconut side down, in the skillet and cook for 3 minutes to sear the fish and brown the topping. Carefully flip the fish over and cook on the other side for 3 minutes. Using a spatula, transfer the fish to a baking sheet. Repeat with the remaining 3 fillets.

5. Transfer the baking sheet to the oven and bake until the salmon is just firm to the touch and the interior is nearly opaque but still moist, 2 to 4 minutes depending on the thickness of the fish. (Alternatively, use an instant-read thermometer; the fish is done when the thermometer registers 130°F when inserted into the thickest part of a fillet.)

6. Place each fillet of salmon on a warmed plate. Drizzle with Coconut Chile Sauce, if using, and serve.

Coconut-Crusted Salmon

Seared Salmon with Chipotle-Lime Butter

I LOVE DISHES THAT ARE QUICK TO COOK, full of flavor, and good for you. This simply seared salmon fits all three criteria. A 1-hour marinade in fresh citrus juice balances any hint of fishy flavor the salmon may have, and the fillets sear up beautifully in a hot cast-iron skillet. The Chipotle-Lime Butter adds a bit of heat and a touch of richness to the fish, but it's completely optional. I recommend serving the salmon with rice and some Grilled Corn Salsa for a great mix of flavors, colors, and textures. ⟶ *Serves 4*

½ jalapeño pepper, seeded and finely chopped
2 tablespoons fresh lemon juice
2 tablespoons fresh lime juice
4 teaspoons canola oil
4 skinless salmon fillets (6 ounces each), preferably wild, pinbones removed
Salt and freshly ground black pepper
Chipotle-Lime Butter (recipe follows, optional)
Grilled Corn Salsa (page 419, optional)

1. Place the jalapeño, lemon and lime juices, and 2 teaspoons of the canola oil in a glass baking dish or shallow bowl. Add the salmon and turn the fish to coat all surfaces with the marinade. Let it rest at room temperature for 1 hour.

2. Heat a large cast-iron skillet over medium-high heat until it is very hot. Add the remaining 2 teaspoons canola oil to the skillet. Remove the salmon from the marinade, reserving the marinade. Season both sides of the fillets with salt and pepper.

3. Arrange the fish in the skillet so that the pieces do not touch. Cook the salmon until the flesh is golden on the bottom, about 3 minutes. Then turn the fillets over, reduce the heat to medium, and cook until the salmon is almost cooked through, 2 to 3 minutes, depending on the fillets' thickness. Add the reserved marinade and cook until it reduces to a glaze, about 1 minute.

4. Top each fillet with a teaspoon or more of Chipotle-Lime Butter, if using, and serve immediately with Grilled Corn Salsa, if desired.

Chipotle-Lime Butter

Simple to make, compound butters are a terrific way to add flavor and spice to many different dishes. Start with soft butter and mix in fresh or dried chopped herbs, minced garlic, grated citrus zest, or spices for whatever flavors strike your fancy. Here we've used smoky chipotle chiles combined with lime to create a zesty butter that melts and forms a simple sauce for the salmon. Compound butters can be frozen for several months, so keep it handy to dress up fish, poultry, meat, or vegetables. ⟶ *Makes about ⅓ cup*

4 tablespoons (½ stick) unsalted butter, at room temperature

1 tablespoon finely minced chipotles in adobo sauce (see sidebar, page 418), plus 1½ teaspoons of the adobo sauce

Grated zest of 1 lime

1 teaspoon salt

1. Using a fork, blend the butter, chipotles, adobo sauce, lime zest, and salt in a small bowl. Use within an hour, or see Step 2.

2. If you are not planning to use the butter within an hour, transfer it to a piece of parchment paper that is about 8 inches long, form it into a cylinder, and roll it up securely; refrigerate the butter until firm. (It can be stored in the refrigerator for up to 3 days. For longer storage, wrap the butter in a second layer of plastic wrap or in aluminum foil and freeze it for up to 3 months.) To serve the chilled butter, unwrap it, and using a sharp knife that has been dipped in hot water, cut as many slices as you need. Return any leftover butter to the refrigerator or freezer.

THE BASICS

Frozen vs. Fresh Fish

It may seem counterintuitive, but the truth is that fish that has been frozen at sea is sometimes fresher and of better quality than fresh. Flash-freezing at sea is a good guarantee of quality and flavor because the industrial freezing methods used today are extremely quick and are done at very low temperatures. That prevents ice crystals from forming inside the fish, which can ruin its texture. This technique also ensures that flash-frozen fish is far superior to fresh fish that you freeze at home.

Although you won't find the same variety of fish that you'd expect to see fresh in your fishmonger's display case, many of the most popular varieties are now available in supermarket freezers. When buying frozen fish such as salmon, tilapia, cod, or halibut, look for labels that indicate the fish has been responsibly sourced.

Some frozen fish fillets are best cooked in their frozen state, so be sure to follow the package instructions. If defrosting is necessary, put the fish on a plate, cover it, and let it thaw in the refrigerator for several hours. Avoid defrosting at room temperature or in cold water—all this does is draw out the flavor of the fish, along with some of its moisture.

THE BASICS

Thai Curry Pastes

There are a number of different types of Thai curry paste, but the most common ones are red and green. Based on a blend of fresh chiles and other spices and herbs, they tend to be very hot and aromatic. Green curry paste generally contains green chiles, coriander seeds, cumin seeds, lemongrass, ginger, galangal, garlic, onion, and shrimp paste, along with some other ingredients. Red curry paste is based on a puree of red chiles, which gives it its distinctive color, with the addition of kaffir lime leaves, turmeric, cinnamon, and peppercorns. The degree of heat of the curry paste depends on the variety of chile that is used. Thai chiles, both red and green, in general pack a fiery punch, so a little curry paste goes a long way.

Thai-Style Salmon Cakes

SALMON CAKES WITH NO BREAD CRUMBS IN SIGHT! This recipe uses fresh salmon that is finely chopped and combined with an array of ingredients that are the hallmark of Thai cuisine: ginger, lemongrass, chiles, fish sauce, and curry paste. The moist, vibrantly flavorful cakes are bound with egg white, which makes them delicately textured and melt-in-your-mouth tender. Be sure to allow time for the salmon mixture to refrigerate for at least an hour; this lets the flavors develop and makes the delicate mixture easier to handle. Tasty enough to stand on their own, the salmon cakes are also delicious served with a drizzle of Coconut Chile Sauce or with a dash of sweet chili sauce. ⎯⎯

Makes 8 cakes; serves 8 as an appetizer or 2 as an entrée

12 ounces skinless salmon fillet, preferably wild, pinbones removed

1 tablespoon finely grated peeled fresh ginger

1 stalk lemongrass (pale, tender part only), very finely chopped (see sidebar, page 19)

1 garlic clove, peeled and minced

1 tablespoon sweet chili sauce, such as sriracha (a hot and slightly sweet condiment prized in Thai and Vietnamese cuisine)

1 tablespoon fish sauce (see box, page 156)

1 teaspoon red curry paste

1 large egg white

¼ cup minced scallions (white part and 2 inches of green)

1 tablespoon fresh lime juice

1 tablespoon finely minced jalapeño pepper, seeds removed, or to taste

½ cup canola oil, or more as needed

Lime wedges, for garnish

Coconut Chile Sauce (page 416, optional)

1. Cut the salmon into 1-inch pieces and place them in a food processor. Pulse until the fish is coarsely ground. (Alternatively, you can chop the fish by hand.) Transfer the salmon to a large bowl and add the ginger, lemongrass, garlic, sweet chili sauce, fish sauce, curry paste, egg white, scallions, lime juice, and jalapeño. Stir thoroughly to combine. The mixture will be very wet. Refrigerate, covered, for at least 1 hour, or up to 8 hours.

2. Heat the oil in a large skillet (preferably cast-iron) over medium-high heat. When the oil is hot but not smoking, drop ½-cupfuls of the salmon mixture into the pan. Lightly flatten each cake with the back of a spoon so that they are ⅓-inch thick. (If necessary, work in batches so the salmon cakes do not touch.) Cook until the bottom is golden brown, about 4 minutes. Turn the cakes over and cook until golden brown and cooked through, 3 to 4 minutes. Transfer to a plate lined with several thicknesses of paper towels.

3. Serve hot or warm, with lime wedges on the side and drizzled with Coconut Chile Sauce, if desired.

Unsweetened Coconut

Packaged coconut, in both sweetened and unsweetened versions, is sold in plastic bags. Baking coconut, which comes shredded or flaked, is very moist and has been highly sweetened. For savory dishes, dry-textured unsweetened coconut is a better choice. If your supermarket does not carry unsweetened coconut, look for it in natural foods stores or in Asian markets.

Fish Tacos with All the Fixins

FISH TACOS ARE A FUN, casual, do-it-yourself kind of meal and are the perfect menu for an informal get-together. Just double or triple the recipe to accommodate a crowd. I marinate and cook the fish, then set out the cheese, cabbage, Pico de Gallo, and warm tortillas. Other accompaniments such as guacamole, sour cream, rice, beans, coleslaw, or Grilled Corn Salsa (page 419) can also be offered. Everyone makes their own creation, adding what they like. Tilapia is an excellent choice for tacos and if it's U.S. farmed, it's also one of the most sustainable species you can buy. The white to pink flesh is sweet, mild-tasting, and very fine-textured. A classic citrus marinade keeps the fish moist and succulent, and is then used to sauté the onions, caramelizing them in a most delicious way. ◦—◦ *Serves 4 (2 tacos per person)*

2 tablespoons olive oil

2 tablespoons fresh lime juice

2 tablespoons fresh orange juice

2 garlic cloves, peeled and finely minced

1 teaspoon dried oregano

½ large yellow onion, thinly sliced

1 pound (about 4) skinless tilapia fillets

1 tablespoon canola oil, plus more for warming the tortillas

8 corn tortillas

1 cup (3 ounces) shredded cheddar cheese

2 cups thinly shredded green cabbage or romaine lettuce

1 cup Farm Stand Pico de Gallo (page 421)

1. Place the olive oil, lime and orange juices, garlic, oregano, and onion slices in a medium-size bowl and stir to combine. Place the fish fillets in a shallow glass baking dish and add the marinade mixture, turning the fish so that all surfaces are coated. Cover the dish and refrigerate for 1 hour.

2. Heat the canola oil in a large skillet (preferably cast-iron) over medium-high heat. Remove the fish from the marinade, reserving the marinade (including the onions). Arrange the fish in the skillet in a single layer; do not crowd the fish or it will steam. Cook for 3 minutes. Then carefully flip the fish over and cook on the second side until it is done, 2 to 3 minutes. Transfer the fish to a platter and keep it warm.

Farm Stand Pico de Gallo and Grilled Corn Salsa

3. Add the marinade, with the onions, to the skillet and cook, stirring frequently, until the onions are caramelized and tender, about 7 minutes. Set aside.

4. To warm the tortillas, lightly film a skillet with canola oil, and place it over medium heat. Sprinkle the tortillas lightly with water, and stack one tortilla on top of another in the skillet, using 2 tortillas per stack. Heat them for 1 minute, then flip them over and warm the other side. Remove the tortillas from the skillet, cover them with a towel to keep them warm, and repeat with the remaining tortillas.

5. Break the fish into pieces. Set out the warm tortillas, caramelized onions, cheese, cabbage, Pico de Gallo, and fish for your guests to create their own tacos.

Fish Tacos topped with Grilled Corn Salsa

Linguine with Spinach, Tuna, and Bacon

THIS IS PAM'S ALL-TIME FAVORITE PASTA RECIPE. It was taught to her by her friend Pete Johnson. She calls it "Pete's Pasta." Don't be deterred by the unusual combination of spinach, tuna, and bacon, because the resulting dish is utterly delicious; the cooking technique allows the ingredients to meld together in an amazing way. We suggest using pole-caught albacore tuna packed in oil rather than other varieties, because albacore tuna is considered one of the best choices for ocean sustainability by the Monterey Bay Aquarium Seafood Watch. ⎯⎯ *Serves 2 to 3*

Salt

10 ounces dry linguine or spaghetti

4 strips thick-sliced bacon, cut into ½-inch squares

2 tablespoons olive oil

Dried red pepper flakes, to taste

4 garlic cloves, peeled and minced

⅓ cup dry white wine

1 can (6 ounces) pole-caught albacore tuna in oil, drained (see sidebar, this page)

1 pound fresh baby spinach, well rinsed and dried if not prewashed

Shaved or grated Parmesan cheese (optional)

1. Bring a large covered pot of water to a boil over high heat. Add 1 tablespoon salt to the water, add the linguine, and cook, uncovered, until it is al dente, about 9 minutes.

2. While the pasta is cooking, place the bacon, olive oil, and red pepper flakes in a large skillet (preferably nonstick), and cook over medium heat, stirring occasionally, until the bacon is crisp. Add the garlic to the skillet and cook, stirring frequently, for 2 minutes.

3. Add the wine and raise the heat to medium-high. Stir in the tuna and the spinach, and cook until the spinach wilts, 6 to 8 minutes (it may be necessary to add the spinach in batches, adding more as it cooks down).

4. By this time the linguine should be ready. Using tongs, transfer the pasta to the skillet; reserve ¾ cup of the pasta cooking water. Cook the pasta-tuna mixture for 3 to 4 minutes, stirring constantly, so that the pasta absorbs the oil in the skillet. Add some of the reserved pasta water if the mixture seems dry.

5. Divide the pasta among warmed bowls, and garnish with Parmesan cheese if desired. Serve hot.

YOUR GREEN KITCHEN

Choosing Sustainable Tuna

When purchasing tuna, it's helpful to know which species are environmentally sustainable and which are highly endangered. Troll- or pole-caught albacore is your best choice. Ahi tuna, or yellowfin as it is also called, is considered a good alternative if it is troll- or pole-caught. Avoid bluefin tuna because it's in such high demand that its population has severely declined. Any tuna species caught on long-lines is not considered sustainable and should be avoided. Unfortunately, other than the premium pole-caught tuna products, this information is generally not readily available to consumers, so ask your fishmonger to be sure you know what you're buying.

Seared Tuna with French Lentil Salad

Seared Tuna with French Lentil Salad

THIS RECIPE IS ONE OF MY FAVORITES—I love the way the tuna pairs with the healthy, flavorful lentil salad. The lentils are moistened with a delicious cumin-spiced vinaigrette and studded with sweet roasted peppers, salty feta cheese, and the bright zing of fresh mint. The aromatic flavor of cumin is echoed in the tuna—the vinaigrette does double duty as a marinade for the fish. Cumin is the predominant flavor, so if you're not a big fan, reduce the amount to 1 teaspoon. The salad can be served warm or at room temperature—it's up to you. You can make the salad up to a day ahead: refrigerate it, covered, and then bring it to room temperature before serving. ⟶ *Serves 4*

CUMIN VINAIGRETTE

- **2 tablespoons fresh lemon juice**
- **2 tablespoons fresh orange juice**
- **½ cup extra-virgin olive oil**
- **½ tablespoon ground cumin**
- **Salt and freshly ground black pepper**

TUNA AND LENTILS

- **1½ pounds fresh tuna, preferably pole-caught albacore (see sidebar, page 141), cut 1½ inches thick**
- **1½ cups French lentils (see sidebar, page 144), rinsed**
- **Salt**
- **4 cups cold water**
- **1 cup diced roasted red peppers (¼-inch dice; see page 411)**
- **1 cup thinly sliced scallions (white and light green parts)**
- **3 tablespoons chopped fresh mint**
- **½ cup (about 2 ounces) crumbled feta cheese**
- **Freshly ground black pepper**
- **About 2 teaspoons olive oil**

1. Prepare the vinaigrette: Place the lemon and orange juices, the oil, and the cumin in a glass jar and seal the lid tightly. Shake the jar vigorously to combine. Season the dressing with salt and pepper to taste. (The vinaigrette can be refrigerated, tightly covered, for up to 2 weeks. Let it return to room temperature and shake before using.)

2. Prepare the tuna and lentils: Place the tuna in a shallow pan and brush all sides with about 2 tablespoons of the vinaigrette. Cover the pan and let the tuna marinate at room temperature for 1 hour.

3. Meanwhile, place the lentils, 2 teaspoons salt, and the cold water in a medium-size saucepan. Cover the pan and bring to the start of a boil over high heat. Reduce the heat to low to maintain a simmer, and cook the lentils, stirring occasionally, until they are tender, 25 to 35 minutes.

A Tuna Reminder

On a health note, albacore tuna has high levels of heart-healthy omega-3 fatty acids, but is also rated as having moderate levels of mercury. Large species of fish are the most likely to bio-accumulate higher levels of mercury. This means that because environmental mercury from land-based sources accumulates in smaller fish, and these smaller fish are eaten by larger fish, mercury is accumulating at a more concentrated level in the flesh of larger carnivorous fish. A U.S. National Academy of Sciences report in 2000 concluded that for the majority of people, the risk of harm from eating fish was low; however, the dangers of mercury exposure to pregnant women, infants, and children should not be minimized. Although tuna is delicious, it's best to enjoy eating it only a few times a month. Children under six years of age and pregnant women should avoid tuna altogether—both canned and fresh.

4. Drain the lentils and transfer them to a medium-size bowl. Let them cool slightly. Then add the red peppers, scallions, and mint, and toss to combine. After the salad has cooled to warm, add the feta (if the lentils are still hot, the cheese will melt).

5. Add ⅓ cup of the cumin vinaigrette to the lentil mixture, tossing to combine. Add more vinaigrette if desired, and season with salt and pepper to taste. Keep the salad warm.

6. Discard the marinade, and season the tuna on both sides with salt and pepper.

7. Place a cast-iron skillet over high heat and when it is hot, add the olive oil (enough to film the bottom of the pan). Reduce the heat to medium and add the tuna. Cook the fish for 3 minutes. Then turn the tuna over and cook until it reaches the desired degree of doneness, 3 to 4 minutes for medium-rare.

8. Immediately transfer the tuna to a cutting board. Let it rest for 2 to 3 minutes while you divide the lentil salad among four plates. Cut the tuna into ½-inch-thick slices, and arrange them on top of the lentil salad. Drizzle each serving with some of the remaining vinaigrette, and serve.

THE BASICS

Lentils

Lentils are legumes and are always sold dried. They are a high-protein food and have been a staple part of diets throughout Europe, the Middle East, and India for centuries. Lentils are an excellent meat substitute and provide a fair amount of fiber, iron, and vitamins A and B. With a bag in your pantry, you'll always have the makings of a nutritious and satisfying meal or side dish.

The small green French lentil (also called lentille du Puy) *is sold with its seed coat still on and cooks a bit more slowly than other types, retaining a firm al dente texture when cooked. It has a slightly peppery flavor and is good in dishes where a firm texture is desirable, such as salads and unpureed soups.*

Brown lentils, also called "regular" or "continental," are the most common and readily available variety in supermarkets. They have a slightly nutty, earthy taste and will turn mushy if overcooked.

Red lentils are small and round in shape, and do not have a seed coat. They lack any discernible flavor but become creamy when cooked, which makes them ideal for purees, soups, and other dishes where the lentils don't have to retain their shape.

Black lentils are sometimes called "beluga" because they sparkle like beluga caviar when cooked. Small and round, they hold their shape well when cooked. Like brown lentils, they have an earthy flavor, and like French lentils, they are best in salads and unpureed soups where their color, shape, and texture really shine.

Lentils should be stored in an airtight container at room temperature for up to a year. They cook quickly (usually in 40 minutes or less), and unlike beans and peas, they do not need to be soaked before cooking, which is a convenience.

to farm or not to farm fish

The Answer Is Sometimes Yes and Sometimes No...

The United Nation's Food and Agriculture Organization (FAO) estimates that more than 70 percent of the world's wild fish stocks are now fully fished, overfished, or depleted. Many believe that aquaculture—the practice of raising (farming) fish in enclosed ocean pens or freshwater ponds or tanks—is needed to fill the gap and to meet the shortfall of seafood in future decades. But a fish farming operation's positive or negative impact on the environment depends on the fish or shellfish being raised, how they are raised, what they are fed, and where the farm is located. There are pros and cons to farmed fish; when you know the issues, you can make informed purchases.

An Example of Aquaculture at Its Worst

Farmed salmon that is raised in open-water pens can pose serious environmental threats: pollution and disease from overcrowded farms; escape of farmed fish that then compete with wild fish populations; use of antibiotics, colorants, and other chemicals; and inefficient use of wild fish for food.

Some Examples of Aquaculture at Its Best

Responsible fish farming practices exist, and they tend to take advantage of the animals' natural traits. For example, bivalve shellfish like clams, mussels, scallops, and oysters feed by filtering algae and other microorganisms from the water and help keep water clean—a benefit to the surrounding environment.

Inland fish farms with closed systems of recirculating water are also a good form of aquaculture, particularly if the fish receive a grain-based diet that includes little or no wild fish. Tilapia, catfish, and carp are all currently being sustainably farmed in land-based tanks. Not far behind are inland farms that raise trout, char, sturgeon, and U.S.-farmed freshwater Coho salmon. These fish require a diet of grain and wild fish, but producers are constantly working to decrease the amount of wild fish in their food.

Pros of Fish Farming:

◆ It can be a viable source of fish protein for much of an ever-expanding global population.

◆ It relieves pressure and demand on stocks of over exploited wild fish, allowing species to recover.

◆ Aquaculture is an important part of the economy in many developing nations.

◆ Farmed fish is widely available and reasonably priced.

Cons of Fish Farming:

◆ Carnivorous species are raised on fish meal made from decreasing stocks of smaller wild fish.

◆ Some aquaculture operations are managed poorly, resulting in a range of environmental problems.

◆ When fish are raised in open-water pens, harmful organisms can migrate from farmed species to wild fish, and non-native species escape to compete with and contaminate wild populations.

◆ Some large industrial fish-farming operations set prices so low that sustainable fisheries and fish-farming operations have difficulty competing in the marketplace.

Resources:

Monterey Bay Aquarium:
www.seafoodwatch.org
Oceana:
www.oceana.org

Cal's Dungeness Crab Salad with Persimmon "Carpaccio"

THE BASICS

Mâche

Mâche, which is also called lamb's lettuce, is a very tender salad green with a mild, nutty flavor. It has been popular in Europe for decades and is now widely available in the United States as well. Mâche grows in tiny clusters, like a rosette. In the market, it may be sold with its leaves still clustered together or separated. With its delicate teardrop-shaped leaves and deep green color, mâche makes a very pretty addition to salads and is delicious on its own.

CAL STAMENOV, CHEF AT BERNARDUS LODGE IN CARMEL VALLEY, California, created this elegant dish in which crab and persimmon co-star in a visually stunning salad that's full of surprises. The crab is dressed with a simple citrus vinaigrette. A puddle of ginger aioli hides beneath a circle of thinly sliced persimmons—a "carpaccio" of fruit. The ginger in the creamy aioli contributes a subtle heat, and the persimmons balance the acidity of the vinaigrette. The sum of all the elements results in a complexity of flavors and textures in a dish that's light and extremely fresh.

For an artful presentation, the crabmeat should be in large pieces, so use the claws and larger legs and save the remaining smaller crab legs and the meat from the bodies for another use, such as the Dungeness Crab Bisque on page 16. Or you can blend the leftover crab with some of the unused Ginger Aioli to make a quick crab cocktail. Be sure to save all of the shells to make Crab Stock (page 17), so that none of the crab is wasted. ⟶ *Serves 4*

YUZU VINAIGRETTE

Finely grated zest of 2 yuzu
  (see sidebar, facing page) or limes

2 teaspoons fresh lemon juice, or more
  if needed (see Step 1)

1 tablespoon yuzu or lime juice

Sea salt and freshly ground black pepper

3 tablespoons fruity extra-virgin olive oil

GINGER AIOLI

2 teaspoons finely grated peeled fresh
  ginger

3 tablespoons fresh lime juice

2 teaspoons soy sauce

½ cup mayonnaise

Kosher salt and freshly ground white pepper

4 cooked Dungeness crabs, about
  1¾ pounds each (see Note)

Salt and freshly ground black pepper

3 ripe Hachiya persimmons, or 2 ripe mangos

3 ounces (about 4 cups) mâche
  (see sidebar, this page)

1. Prepare the vinaigrette: Combine the yuzu zest, lemon and yuzu juices, and a pinch of salt and pepper in a small bowl. Slowly whisk in the olive oil. Taste, and add more oil or salt and pepper as required. (If you're not using yuzu juice, increase the amount of lemon juice by 1 teaspoon to approximate the same acidity level.) Set the vinaigrette aside at room temperature.

2. Prepare the Ginger Aioli: Combine the ginger, lime juice, soy sauce, and mayonnaise in a small bowl. Season with salt and pepper to taste.

Refrigerate it, covered, while you proceed with the recipe. (The aioli can be made 1 day in advance.)

3. Remove the two claws from each crab. Cut off the small knuckles at the joint where they attach to the main claw; save these small pieces for making crab stock. Using a wooden mallet or a small hammer, very lightly tap the shells of the crab claws until they crack in several places, taking care not to smash the meat in the process. Bend each small pincer claw away from its larger counterpart until it snaps; then very gently twist it in order to release the tiny piece of crab inside the shell. Carefully extract the claw meat from the broken shells. Set the crabmeat aside while you work on the legs.

4. Remove the four largest (front) legs from the crabs. For this recipe, use only the largest segments, those closest to the body. Cut off the lower, smaller pieces at the first joint and save them for another use. Tap the shells of the larger leg pieces as you did for the claws, and carefully extract the fingers of meat. Add the leg meat to the claw meat, cover, and refrigerate. Each salad should have 6 whole pieces of crab: 2 claws and 4 leg pieces.

5. Place the crab in a medium-size bowl and season lightly with salt and pepper. Whisk the vinaigrette and pour it over the crab. Very gently blend the ingredients with a rubber spatula,

taking care not to break the crab pieces.

6. Cut off and discard the top (the stem end) of the persimmons. Remove the skin from the fruit with a vegetable peeler. Cut the persimmons crosswise into thin slices, ⅛ to ¼ inch thick.

7. To assemble the salads, place a generous dollop of Ginger Aioli in the center of each plate. Spread the sauce out into a 3-inch round. Arrange a layer of mâche leaves on top of the sauce, leaving a small round of aioli uncovered in the center. Arrange 5 slices of persimmon on top of the mâche, overlapping the pieces slightly to create a circle of fruit. The aioli will be covered, except for a small area in the center.

8. Arrange 3 pieces of crab on top of the persimmons in the center of the circle. (Use any less-than-perfect pieces on this bottom layer.) Top with 3 more pieces of crab. Serve immediately.

Note: With the exception of soft-shell blue crabs, fresh crab generally comes to the market in cooked form. If you do find it live (your best bet is in Chinese markets in major cities), ask the fishmonger to cook, clean, and crack the crab for you.

THE BASICS

Yuzu

Yuzu is a Japanese citrus fruit valued for both its juice and its rind. Ranging in color from dark green to bright yellow, depending on its ripeness, the fruit is the size of a tangerine. The rind is rough and bumpy, but extremely fragrant. The flavor of the juice is tart—stronger than lemon—with undertones of lime, tangerine, and pine. Yuzus are prized in Japanese cuisine and are a key ingredient in the dipping sauce known as ponzu. Yuzus are in season from November through May and are found mainly in Asian and specialty markets. Yuzu juice and candied rind are available through mail order.

Mussels Provençal

MUSSELS ARE NOT DIFFICULT OR TIME-CONSUMING TO COOK.
They are also one of the most sustainable seafood choices you can make.
A bowl of steaming mussels makes a great first course, or you can pair
them with a big green salad and a loaf of crusty garlic bread for a light supper.
The secret to this dish is the very tasty broth—a combination of butter, wine,
and Pernod. Pernod is a French liqueur with a light anise (licorice) flavor.
Unfortunately, it's expensive and has few other uses in cooking. The mussels will
still be good without the liqueur, but if you plan on making this dish fairly often,
consider adding Pernod to your liquor cabinet. ⎯⎯ *Serves 4*

3 pounds mussels

1 cup dry white wine

3 garlic cloves, peeled and finely minced

⅓ cup thinly sliced leek (white and light
green parts only)

2 small ripe tomatoes, cut into ¼-inch dice
(about 1 cup)

2 tablespoons Pernod (optional)

4 tablespoons (½ stick) butter, cut into
4 pieces

3 tablespoons finely minced fresh flat-leaf
parsley

1 tablespoon chopped fresh tarragon leaves

Salt and freshly ground black pepper

1. Scrub the mussels in cold water and
scrape off any hairy fibers with a small
knife.

2. Place the wine, garlic, and leek in a
saucepan that is large enough to hold the
mussels. Bring to a boil over high heat
and cook, uncovered, for 5 minutes.

3. Add the mussels and cover the pan
tightly. Cook for 4 minutes. Then add
the tomatoes, Pernod if using, butter,
parsley, and tarragon. Continue to cook,
uncovered, until the broth has reduced
by about half and the mussels are open,
about 5 minutes.

4. Remove the mussels with tongs
and divide them among four warmed
bowls. Discard any mussels that have
not opened. Return the saucepan to
high heat and reduce the broth to
concentrate the flavors, about 2 minutes.
Season the broth with salt and pepper
to taste, pour it over the mussels, and
serve immediately.

Debearding Mussels

*Some mussels have stringlike
fibers protruding from their shells.
These fibers are linked to the
interior flesh of the mussel and
are what help attach the shellfish
to surfaces underwater. Remove
the beards right before cooking.
Holding the shell in one hand and
grasping the beard with the fingers
of your other hand, pull the beard
quickly and firmly toward the
hinge of the mussel. If the beard is
particularly recalcitrant, cut it by
gently scraping along the edge of
the shell with a small sharp knife.*

Mussels Provençal

Seared Sea Scallops with Carrot-Citrus Sauce

I F YOU'RE LOOKING FOR AN ELEGANT DINNER that comes together in minutes, look no further: pan-seared scallops perched atop a bed of wilted baby spinach, drizzled with a sauce composed of just three ingredients—carrot juice, orange juice, and butter. The recipe for this delectable carrot-citrus sauce comes from our friend Cal Stamenov, executive chef at Bernardus Lodge. Cal's acclaimed cuisine is based on intense flavors and the freshest of ingredients, and this dish is a wonderful case in point. Light and brightly flavored, the sauce forms a perfect counterpoint to the richness of the scallops and the austerity of the spinach. Moreover, the presentation is visually stunning with its contrast of colors and textures. The sauce is also delicious paired with any mild-flavored white fish, such as halibut, sole, or tilapia. ⟶ *Serves 4*

Freshly harvested and rinsed red carrots

1¼ cups fresh carrot juice (see Note)
1¼ cups fresh orange juice (see Note)
1½ pounds fresh baby spinach, rinsed and
　　dried if not prewashed
Kosher salt and freshly ground black pepper
Pinch of freshly grated nutmeg
4 tablespoons (½ stick) cold unsalted butter
1½ pounds wild sea scallops, preferably
　　diver caught, tough side muscles
　　removed
¼ cup unbleached all-purpose flour
About 3 tablespoons olive oil

1. Place the carrot and orange juices in a shallow saucepan and simmer the mixture over medium-low heat until the liquid has reduced to ¾ cup, 15 to 20 minutes. Scrape the sides of the pan with a rubber spatula occasionally, stirring the concentrated residue that forms on the pan back into the juices. Set the reduction aside.

2. Place 1 tablespoon water in a very large skillet over medium-high heat. Add the spinach and cook, stirring frequently, until it wilts, about 8 minutes. (It may be necessary to do this in batches). Season the spinach lightly with salt and pepper and the nutmeg. Set it aside.

3. Just before you cook the scallops, bring the carrot juice mixture to the start of a simmer over medium heat. Remove the pan from the heat and whisk in 1 tablespoon of the butter. When this has melted, whisk in a second piece of butter. Continue, adding the remaining 2 tablespoons butter, whisking constantly until each piece is incorporated. If the sauce gets too cold, return it to the stove briefly. Do not leave the pan on the heat too long, however, because if the sauce gets too hot, the butter will separate out.

Season with salt and pepper to taste. Set the sauce aside, off the heat, while you cook the scallops.

4. When you are ready to cook the scallops, return the spinach to medium heat to reheat it.

5. Pat the scallops dry with paper towels. On a flat plate, whisk the flour with a pinch each of salt and pepper. Dip the top and bottom (flat sides) of the scallops in the flour mixture.

6. Place a large skillet (preferably cast-iron) over medium-high heat. When the skillet is hot but not smoking, add the olive oil. Arrange the scallops in a single layer, one flour side down, and cook without turning or moving them until the bottom surface is browned, 1½ to 2 minutes. Carefully turn the scallops over (tongs work well) and cook to the desired degree of doneness, 1 to 3 minutes more.

7. Divide the spinach among four plates, arranging it in the center of the plates. Arrange some of the scallops on top of the spinach. Ladle some of the carrot-citrus sauce around the spinach (if the sauce is too cold, return it briefly to the stove), and serve immediately.

Note: If you're making your own carrot juice, peel the carrots; the skin can have a slight bitterness. If you're squeezing fresh oranges, discard the seeds, but don't strain the juice, as the pulp adds body to the sauce.

THE BASICS

Buying Sea Scallops

If you have a choice when purchasing sea scallops, look for wild diver-caught scallops. "Diver-caught" is a term that refers to scallops harvested by divers and brought to land on the same day. Hand harvesting, as opposed to dredging, is one of the most environmentally friendly fishing methods. Unfortunately, most commercial scallop fisheries use dredging, which involves dragging heavy nets across the ocean floor. This technique can result in the capture of sea turtles and other sea life, and also damages the seafloor habitat.

Commercial boats are at sea far beyond the 3-mile limit, and spend anywhere from 3 to 14 days out of harbor. In contrast, diver-caught scallops are removed by hand from the inshore rocky coastline on short trips of 24 hours or less.

Scallops deteriorate quickly. When they cannot be brought to shore within a day, they are shucked soon after harvest and are usually frozen on board the ship. Frozen scallops typically are treated with phosphates (sodium tripolyphosphate in particular) to whiten them and reduce their moisture loss. Soaked in phosphates, scallops absorb additional water—increasing their weight and the price per pound. Beware of buying frozen scallops that are not diver-caught, or any scallops sold as fresh that are starkly white in color. This indicates they've been treated with chemicals and soaked in water to increase their weight. Diver-caught or dry-pack (untreated) scallops will have a naturally sweet-briny smell and a creamy color, and are worth the extra expense.

Baked Mediterranean Shrimp

Baked Mediterranean Shrimp

ALL THE FLAVORS AND AROMAS OF THE MEDITERRANEAN— tomatoes, basil, olives, and garlic—are combined to delicious effect in this very easy dish. Serve it warm or at room temperature as a first course (with lots of fresh bread for mopping up the sauce), or toss it with angel hair pasta and serve with a salad for a more substantial meal. ⟶ *Serves 6 to 8 as an appetizer or 4 as an entrée*

1 pound large shrimp (16 to 20 count per
   pound), peeled and deveined

2 tablespoons extra-virgin olive oil

2 tablespoons white wine

4 large garlic cloves, peeled and minced
   (about 1 tablespoon)

2 tablespoons capers (see sidebar,
   this page)

½ cup pitted and sliced Kalamata olives

2 medium tomatoes, peeled, seeded
   (see sidebar, page 131), and cut into
   ½-inch dice

¼ cup chopped fresh basil

2 tablespoons chopped fresh flat-leaf parsley

1 cup (4 ounces) crumbled fota cheese

¼ teaspoon dried red pepper flakes, or
   to taste

Grated zest of 1 lemon

1. Position a rack in the middle of the oven and preheat the oven to 375°F.

2. Place all the ingredients in a large bowl and stir gently to combine.

3. Transfer the mixture to a 9 x 12-inch baking dish. Bake until the shrimp is just cooked through, 15 to 25 minutes depending on the size of the shrimp.

4. Remove the baking dish from the oven, and divide the shrimp and sauce among shallow bowls. Serve warm or at room temperature.

A flowering caper and whole caperberries

Easy Shrimp Scampi

HRIMP SCAMPI IS AN ITALIAN CLASSIC that combines pan-seared shrimp, garlic, wine, and butter. A simple sauce forms in the skillet and clings to the shrimp like a glaze. This is a terrific dish when you want a quick and delicious meal—it comes together in a matter of minutes with just a handful of ingredients. If your fishmonger has already peeled and deveined the shrimp for you, prepping the garlic is the most time-consuming step. My family likes their shrimp crispy; it's important to use a hot skillet and high heat to attain this texture. Shrimp Scampi is wonderful tossed with pasta, spooned over rice, or served with a light, crusty bread to soak up the delicious sauce.

Serves 4

TIP

If you're not a fan of peeling and deveining shrimp, or you have limited time, ask your fishmonger to do the job for you.

3 tablespoons olive oil

¼ cup minced garlic
    (about 8 large cloves)

1½ pounds large shrimp
    (16 to 20 count per pound),
    peeled and deveined

⅔ cup dry white wine or dry white
    vermouth

Pinch of dried red pepper flakes

3 tablespoons unsalted butter,
    cut into 3 pieces

2 tablespoons fresh lemon juice,
    or more to taste

⅓ cup minced fresh flat-leaf parsley

Salt

1. Place a large skillet (preferably cast-iron) over medium heat and add the olive oil. When the oil is warm, add the garlic and reduce the heat to low. Cook, stirring frequently, until the garlic softens, 1 minute; do not let it burn.

2. Meanwhile, pat the shrimp dry with a clean kitchen towel or paper towels.

3. Place the skillet over medium heat, and when the oil is hot but not smoking, stir in the shrimp in a single layer. (It may be necessary to do this in two batches so that the pan is not crowded.) Cook the shrimp until golden, 2 to 3 minutes. Then turn the shrimp and cook on the other side until cooked through, 1 to 2 minutes, depending on the size of your shrimp. (If your shrimp are very large, turning them up on edge—tails up—will help them cook more evenly.) Transfer the shrimp to a platter.

4. Remove the skillet from the burner and set it aside for 1 minute to let it cool slightly. Then return it to medium heat and add the wine and red pepper flakes. Cook until the wine has reduced by half, 1 to 2 minutes.

Add the butter, one piece at a time, whisking until each piece has melted before adding the next piece. Then add the shrimp, lemon juice, and parsley and cook for 1 minute, stirring to coat the shrimp with the sauce. Season with salt to taste, and serve immediately.

Vietnamese Shrimp and Bok Choy Curry

CURRIES ARE A MAINSTAY OF SOUTHEAST ASIAN COOKING, with regional variations unique to each country. This Vietnamese-inspired version is redolent with the heady fragrances of lemongrass and coriander, enlivened by the bite of ginger and chiles, and tempered with coconut milk and baby bok choy. Several simple steps build layers of flavor and contribute to the complexity of the dish: shrimp shells are used to infuse the coconut-stock base; and spices are dry-toasted, then cooked with oil to awaken their flavors and aromas. Adding baby bok choy and fresh herbs at the final stage of cooking preserves their vibrant color and lively taste. Vietnamese fish sauce, called *nuoc mam*, while not easily discernible as an ingredient, is an indispensable element and adds a rich intensity to this dish. This is a curry where the whole is much more than the sum of its individual parts—and like many curries, it is best served over rice.

Serves 4

1 pound large shrimp (16 to 20 count per pound), unpeeled

1 can (14 ounces) unsweetened light coconut milk

3 stalks fresh lemongrass, minced (see sidebar, page 19)

2 scallions (white and green parts), thinly sliced

3 tablespoons finely grated peeled fresh ginger

1 tablespoon thinly sliced jalapeño chile (seeds optional), or more to taste

2 teaspoons ground coriander

1 teaspoon ground cumin

1 teaspoon ground turmeric

3 tablespoons peanut or canola oil

3 tablespoons Vietnamese fish sauce (nuoc mam; see box, page 156)

1 small red bell pepper, stemmed, seeded and cut into ¼ x 1-inch strips (1 cup)

5 heads baby bok choy, leaves separated

¼ cup chopped fresh mint

2 tablespoons chopped fresh cilantro

1 tablespoon fresh lime juice

THE BASICS

Toasting Herbs and Spices

Gentle toasting of dried herbs and spices (in ground or seed form) enhances their aroma and flavor. Place spices in a small skillet and cook over medium-low heat until they're warm to the touch and noticeably fragrant, 1 to 2 minutes. Don't leave the stove unattended because herbs and spices can quickly scorch.

1. Peel and devein the shrimp, reserving the shells. Cover and refrigerate the shrimp. Place the shrimp shells in a medium-size saucepan and add the coconut milk, ¾ cup water, and the lemongrass, scallions, ginger, and jalapeño. Cook over medium heat until the mixture is reduced by about one third, 15 to 20 minutes. Remove the pan from the heat and let the mixture cool to room temperature.

2. Place a sieve over a clean bowl and pour the coconut-shrimp stock into it,

pressing firmly on the solids with a rubber spatula to extract all of the liquid. Discard the solids and set the stock aside.

3. Combine the coriander, cumin, and turmeric in a small skillet and set it over medium-low heat. Toast the spices until they are hot to the touch and fragrant, 1 to 2 minutes, taking care not to let them burn. Add 1 tablespoon of the peanut oil, 2 tablespoons of the fish sauce, and 1 tablespoon water to the skillet. Cook, stirring frequently, until the

THE BASICS

Vietnamese Fish Sauce

Fish sauce is a defining element of Vietnamese cuisine. Its use as an ingredient or a condiment compares to salt in Western cooking or soy sauce in Chinese and Japanese cuisines. The best Vietnamese fish sauce, called nuoc mam, *is a thin, amber-colored liquid derived from merely two ingredients: fish and salt. However, the simplicity of its composition belies its unique complexity of taste. To Western sensibilities, "fermented fish juice" sounds anything but appealing. Don't allow this to deter you, because fish sauce heightens the richness and intensity of a dish, unifying its diverse and complex flavors.*

Traditional production techniques, although basic, are time-consuming.

Small fresh fish, usually anchovies, are dried on trays in the sun until they begin to ferment. They are then packed between layers of salt in wooden vats or clay jugs. Left in a hot place for many months or more than a year, the fish slowly exudes its juice. This liquid is drained from the vat and constitutes the first extraction, which is the most prized (and very rarely available in the U.S.). To increase production yields, salted water is generally added back to the fish in the vat, and after a shorter fermentation period, the liquid is once again extracted. The fish sauce usually available in the U.S. is the diluted version, which is the accepted standard for everyday use in cooking.

Fish sauce is also used in other Asian countries, primarily in Thai cuisine. Thai fish sauce (nam pla) *is the source of most brands sold in the United States. In general, Thai fish sauce has a stronger and saltier taste than its Vietnamese counterpart. If you substitute Thai fish sauce for Vietnamese* nuoc mam, *use less to avoid overwhelming the other flavors of your dish. Look for Vietnamese fish sauce in Asian markets, and once the jar is opened, store it in the refrigerator. If you are unable to find* nuoc mam, *look for the Thai-produced Vietnamese-style brand called Viet Huong's Three Crabs; it is a delicate, fragrant, and pleasant-tasting substitute.*

sauce reduces to a thick paste and becomes aromatic, about 5 minutes. Add the paste to the coconut-shrimp stock, and stir to blend.

4. Heat 1 tablespoon of the peanut oil in a large skillet (preferably cast-iron) over medium-high heat until it is hot but not smoking. Add the shrimp and cook, stirring frequently to coat them in the oil, until they are partially cooked, 1½ to 2 minutes. Transfer the shrimp to a plate and set aside.

5. Heat the remaining 1 tablespoon peanut oil in the same skillet over medium-high heat. Add the red pepper strips and the remaining 1 tablespoon fish sauce, and stir-fry until the pepper strips soften slightly, 2 to 3 minutes. Add the stock mixture and the bok choy, and bring to the start of a boil. Then reduce the heat to medium, cover the skillet, and cook until the bok choy is just tender, 3 to 5 minutes.

6. Add the shrimp to the skillet and simmer over medium-low heat until they are cooked through, 2 to 4 minutes. Remove the skillet from the heat and stir in the mint, cilantro, and lime juice. Serve hot.

voting for the environment with your dollar

Sometimes we all feel small and ineffective in the face of our planet's problems, but we should never underestimate our power as consumers. As someone who's been in the retail produce business for more than a quarter century, I see firsthand how the demands of even a few consumers can change the market. I've seen huge retailers start carrying a new product because of requests from one or two persistent shoppers.

The rise of organic foods in the marketplace is a prime example. When retailers saw that they risked losing shoppers to competitors who offered organic choices, they started carrying organic products in their stores.

When what you want isn't available, it makes a very powerful statement to leave a shop without making a purchase. I've walked out of a seafood shop because they had only Atlantic farmed salmon and no wild Alaskan salmon or U.S. freshwater-farmed Coho salmon. I let the fishmonger know the reasons I prefer the wild salmon, telling him I would be happy to buy my fish there instead of having to go elsewhere. If a few other consumers did the same, I would be surprised if the store didn't change their offerings. Our dollars can truly change the way food is produced in this country . . . one purchase at a time.

Baby Bok Choy

Bok choy is an Asian member of the cabbage family, cultivated in China since ancient times (it is sometimes called Chinese cabbage). It is now grown in North America, where cooks prize it for its versatility. In mainstream supermarkets you are most likely to encounter only bok choy and baby bok choy, although there are other varieties such as *choy sum* and *gai choy*. Baby bok choy is the immature version of bok choy. It is about 7 inches long, with stalks that are whitish green and dark green oblong leaves with smooth edges. Joined at the base in a bulblike cluster, the stalks are larger and heartier on the outside, encasing a more petite heart with smaller ribs and leaves. Baby bok choy has crunchy, juicy stalks with a slightly peppery edge that is balanced by a subtle sweetness. The flavor of the leaves is mild and sweet. Baby bok choy is less fibrous and more tender than its more mature counterpart.

At the market, where it is available year-round, look for crisp, plump stalks and bright green leaves that are not wilted. To prevent wilting during storage, poke holes in a plastic bag with the tip of a knife and refrigerate the bok choy, unwashed, in the bag for up to 4 days.

To prepare it, trim off and discard about ¼ inch of the base. Baby bok choy is most often used with its leaves still attached, the bulb either left whole or cut lengthwise in half or quarters. Wash it thoroughly in cool water, gently separating the leaves to dislodge any dirt. Baby bok choy can be eaten raw, stir-fried, steamed, microwaved, braised, or boiled. It has a high water content, so it becomes limp very quickly if you overcook it. To prevent that from happening, cook it at a high temperature so the leaves become tender and the stalks stay crisp. Baby bok choy adds crunch and color to a wide variety of dishes, and it is a good source of calcium, potassium, and vitamins A and C. It may be one of the lowest-calorie vegetables on earth—1 cup of shredded bok choy has just 9 calories.

VEGETARIAN ENTREES

Bon Appétit . . . Without the Meat

WHILE I'M NOT A VEGETARIAN, MY FAMILY AND I ENJOY EATING meatless meals on a regular basis. I try to be aware of where my food comes from and its effect on the environment, so during the week I'm mindful of trying to balance our meals with vegetarian options. But to tell you the truth, most of the time I choose a meat-free soup, crêpe, pasta, or salad because I'm craving the delicious taste of that particular dish. I'm not thinking we need to "deprive" ourselves of meat for that meal.

Eating vegetarian is a great way to tread more lightly on the earth. Generally speaking, it takes more than 11 times as much fossil fuel to make 1 calorie of animal protein as it does to make 1 calorie of plant protein. And if every American who eats meat daily committed to eating meat-free one day a week, it would be the CO_2-reducing equivalent of taking 8 million cars off the roads!

If you're new to vegetarian entrées, I hope you'll be pleasantly surprised by the wonderful flavors of healthy whole grains, vegetables, beans, nuts, and soy in this chapter. I think you will agree that these recipes are so delicious and satisfying, no one will ask, "Where's the meat?" Even if you've been cooking vegetarian for years, there's plenty of inspiration here, with a wide variety of flavorful ingredients and taste combinations that I hope will soon become dishes your family asks for again and again.

One of my all-time favorite foods is savory crêpes, and I've included a recipe for one particularly tasty variation: Spinach, Mushroom, and Gruyère Crêpes. Making crêpes takes a bit of practice, but they're well worth the effort. For me these delicate, super-thin "pancakes" are special not only because they're so tasty, but also because they're full of delicious memories. My first date with my husband, Drew, was at a crêpe restaurant in Berkeley after a concert. I was surprised, and impressed, that he ordered two entrées: crêpes florentine and a huge spinach salad with warm bacon dressing. There was just something so appealing about someone with such an appetite for really good food. I also met Trudy, my first friend in Carmel, at a restaurant that sold crêpes. She was a waitress there,

Summer squash so fresh their blossoms are still attached.

and we started a conversation after Drew ordered his usual two entrées. She said that her boyfriend was the only other person she knew who did that. Trudy is now one of my longtime nearest and dearest friends, so you could say that in my life, eating crêpes and getting to know special people seem to go together!

Another of my favorite recipes is the Rigatoni with Eggplant and Buffalo Mozzarella. I fell in love with this dish on a family trip to Italy and learned to duplicate it at home. The tender chunks of eggplant, fresh basil leaves, light tomato sauce, and buffalo mozzarella—which magically retains both its resilient texture and its creaminess—vividly bring back the flavors of Italy. Served over al dente rigatoni pasta, this dish is a joy to the senses. Maybe it will even send your taste buds traveling to a place where the pace is less hurried, and meals are lingered over and savored.

And I think you'll find our Homemade Veggie Burgers deliciously satisfying, with a flavor and texture you just can't find in frozen ready-made veggie burgers.

For me, this kind of food represents wonderful flavors to be shared with family and

friends. Eating lower on the food chain does have a powerful impact on the environment, but it's appetite-appeal that draws me to these dishes. As I look over the recipes in this chapter, I just want to get cooking. Wait till you taste our Springtime Whole Wheat Spaghetti with Fresh Favas, Peas, and Asparagus. Experience the comfort-food satisfaction of autumn-inspired Pumpkins Stuffed with Quinoa, Butternut, and Cranberries, and splurge by treating yourself to the creamy, slightly nutty flavor of the Roasted Cauliflower Tart. I hope you will enjoy exploring these recipes and other meatless options throughout this book. There are dozens more vegetarian recipes in the Soup, Leafy Green Salads, Vegetable and Grain Salads, and Side Dishes chapters. So *bon appétit* . . . without the meat!

Spinach, Mushroom, and Gruyère Crêpes (page 175)

Springtime Whole Wheat Spaghetti with Fresh Favas, Peas, and Asparagus

How to Peel Fava Beans

Fava beans require a little extra work, but their fresh, delicate taste is reward enough for the effort. Shell the beans, discarding the thick pods. Blanch the beans in boiling salted water for 30 seconds if they are tiny, or 60 seconds if they are large. Immediately drain the beans and plunge them into a bowl of ice water to stop the cooking. Drain the beans again in a colander. When the beans are cool enough to handle, peel off the tough outer skins to release the tender inner beans.

GREEN IS THE COLOR OF SPRING. To celebrate the beautiful green vegetables that epitomize the season, we've combined fava beans, fresh English peas, and tender asparagus in a very light and healthful pasta dish. The Parmesan Stock adds great flavor, but if you don't have time to make it, a good-quality vegetable broth will suffice. Whole wheat spaghetti is my pasta of choice; it's a much more nutritious option than pasta made from white flour and we like its nutty flavor. Look for thin whole wheat spaghetti so the dish stays light and the focus remains on the glorious green vegetables. ⚋ *Serves 4 to 6*

Salt

1½ cups shelled fresh English peas

16 asparagus spears, woody ends trimmed, spears peeled if desired, cut on the diagonal into 2-inch lengths

1 pound thin whole wheat spaghetti

2 tablespoons olive oil

2 medium leeks (white and light green parts only), cut in half lengthwise, then thinly sliced crosswise and rinsed well

Pinch of dried red pepper flakes, or to taste

4 large garlic cloves, peeled and minced

⅓ cup white wine

About 1 cup Parmesan Stock (page 408), Vegetable Stock (page 410), or store-bought low-sodium vegetable broth, heated

Grated zest of 1 lemon

1½ tablespoons minced fresh tarragon

2 tablespoons butter (optional)

1 cup shelled and peeled fava beans (see sidebar, this page)

Freshly ground black pepper

½ cup freshly grated Parmesan cheese

1. Fill a medium-size bowl with ice water and set it aside.

2. Fill a medium-size saucepan with salted water, cover, and bring it to a boil over high heat. Blanch the peas in the boiling water for 30 seconds. Using a slotted spoon, transfer the peas to the ice water and submerge them to stop the cooking.

3. Blanch the asparagus in the same saucepan of boiling salted water, cooking the spears for 60 seconds. Drain, and plunge the asparagus into the ice water. Drain the vegetables, and set them aside.

4. Bring at least 4 quarts water to a boil in a large covered saucepan over high heat. Add 2 tablespoons salt to the boiling water, and stir in the pasta. Cook the pasta according to the package directions until it is al dente, 5 to 8 minutes.

5. Meanwhile, heat the olive oil in a large skillet over medium-low heat. When the oil is warm, add the leeks and red pepper flakes. Cook, stirring frequently, until the leeks are soft, about 5 minutes, taking care not to let them color. Then add the garlic and cook, stirring frequently, for 2 minutes.

6. Add the wine to the skillet and raise the heat to medium-high. Cook until the wine has evaporated, 3 to 5 minutes. Add ½ cup of the hot Parmesan Stock, the lemon zest, and the tarragon.

7. Using tongs, transfer the cooked spaghetti to the mixture in the skillet (or drain it in a colander and then add it to the skillet). Cook the pasta, stirring constantly, until it is coated with the sauce, about 2 minutes. If the pasta seems dry, add another ¼ cup stock to the skillet.

8. Stir in the butter (if using), the reserved peas and asparagus, and the fava beans. Cook until heated through, 1 to 2 minutes, adding the remainder of the stock if needed. Season with salt and black pepper to taste.

9. Divide the pasta among shallow bowls, and garnish each serving with a sprinkling of Parmesan cheese. Serve hot.

THE BASICS

Blanching

Blanching is the process of immersing food (usually vegetables, fruits, and herbs) briefly in boiling water, then plunging it into ice water to stop the cooking. Blanching firms the flesh, loosens the skins, and sets the color and flavor of food. You can blanch delicate spring vegetables like peas and fava beans and pat them dry before putting them in the freezer, where they will keep for up to 3 months.

Pasta Cooking Tips

◆ Cook pasta in plenty of water in a large pot. As a rule of thumb, use at least 4 quarts of water for every pound of pasta.

◆ Add coarse sea salt or kosher salt to the water when it reaches a boil, and wait for the boiling to resume before adding the pasta. Use 2 tablespoons salt for every 4 quarts water. If you don't add enough salt, the pasta will be bland or tasteless.

◆ Never add oil to the pasta water. This prevents the sauce from adhering properly to the pasta.

◆ Once the pasta is added to the boiling salted water, it is important to stir it immediately so that it doesn't stick to the pot. Stir continuously for about 30 seconds. If cooking small shells or short tubular pastas, stir periodically until done.

◆ The pasta water must boil briskly during cooking. Adjust the heat setting on your stove to maintain a boil. Cook the pasta from start to finish without interruption.

◆ To determine doneness, taste the pasta several times while it is cooking. It is done when it is no longer hard or chalky in the middle, but retains a little bite. The Italians called this *al dente*—literally meaning "to the teeth."

◆ Before draining the pasta, remove a cup of the cooking water, which you may want to add to your sauce to thin it out. Never rinse pasta, or you'll wash off the starch that helps the sauce adhere. Drain the pasta quickly but not overly thoroughly; in most cases the pasta should remain moist.

◆ Pasta cools off quickly, so it's best served in warmed bowls. To warm serving dishes, let them sit in hot water or place them in a warm oven while you are cooking.

Whole-Grain Pasta

The USDA now urges Americans to eat at least three servings of whole grains a day. Filling some of that quota with whole-grain pasta is a tasty way to meet your body's needs. Unlike traditional pastas made with refined durum or semolina wheat, whole-grain noodles haven't lost their bran and germ during processing. Bran, the outer skin of a whole grain, and the germ, or embryo of the grain, carry considerable amounts of healthy fats, protein, antioxidants, fiber, and B vitamins. Fiber is especially good for those who are looking to cut back on their caloric intake: Fiber fills you up much more quickly, so you are less likely to eat as much. You also feel satisfied much sooner than when you eat refined foods. Whole-grain pastas, from whole wheat to kamut to farro, are increasingly available in supermarkets, so it's easy to enjoy their firm bite, nutty flavor, and terrific nutritional benefits.

Farro Penne with Pesto

MY FAMILY IS A HUGE FAN OF FARRO PASTA. We eat much less white pasta since we discovered it a few years ago. Farro pasta retains the nutty flavor of the grain, but it has a smooth texture with no hint of graininess. I make big batches of pesto when basil is flourishing, and with the pesto ready to go, pasta with pesto is one of my fastest, yet most appreciated, meals. Sometimes I throw in a handful of toasted pine nuts or chopped sun-dried tomatoes to vary the dish a bit. Chopped grilled vegetables are a delicious addition as well. ⸻ *Serves 4*

Coarse sea salt or kosher salt

4 cups (about 9 ounces) farro penne

About 1 cup Pesto (recipe follows)

Freshly ground black pepper

1 cup freshly grated Parmesan cheese

1. Bring 4 quarts of water to a boil in a large covered pot over high heat. Add 2 tablespoons coarse sea salt, and stir in the penne. Cook, stirring once or twice, according to the package directions until al dente, 10 to 12 minutes.

2. Drain the pasta in a colander, setting aside 1 cup of the cooking water. Return the pasta to the pot. Add ¾ cup of the Pesto and stir to combine. If the pasta is too dry, add ⅓ cup or more of the reserved cooking water.

3. Taste the pasta, and season with coarse sea salt and pepper to taste. Add more Pesto if desired.

4. Divide the pasta among four warmed bowls, and sprinkle each serving with the Parmesan cheese.

Pesto

Pesto is an all-purpose sauce based on fresh basil, olive oil, Parmesan cheese, and lots of garlic that enhances everything it encounters, from pasta, pizza, and vegetables to grilled meats and fish. Even though commercial preparations are readily available in markets today, they rarely compare to homemade pesto. ⸻ *Makes about 3 cups*

3 large garlic cloves, peeled

6 cups (packed) fresh basil leaves

¼ cup (packed) fresh flat-leaf parsley leaves

½ cup pine nuts

1 cup olive oil, plus more if storing the pesto

1 cup (3 ounces) fresh finely grated Parmesan cheese

1 teaspoon salt, or more to taste

Freshly ground black pepper, to taste

1. Place the garlic, basil, parsley, and pine nuts in a food processor and pulse until coarsely chopped.

2. With the machine running, add the 1 cup olive oil in a slow, steady stream, processing until the pesto is smooth and stopping when needed to scrape the sides of the bowl with a rubber spatula.

3. Transfer the pesto to a medium-size bowl. Add the Parmesan, and season with the salt and pepper.

Use immediately, or store for up to 1 month in the refrigerator. To preserve its vivid green color while it is stored, pour a thin film of olive oil over the pesto to seal out the air, and then cover the container. Pesto can also be frozen for up to 3 months; cover the top layer with olive oil as described. For handy small portions, freeze the pesto in ice cube trays and then transfer the cubes to a zip-lock freezer bag or a plastic container; defrost the frozen cubes for several hours in the refrigerator.

THE BASICS

Peeling Garlic

The simplest way to peel a clove of garlic is to put it on a cutting board and give it a good whack with the flat side of a large knife or cleaver. This loosens the skin and you can then easily slip out the clove.

want to reduce your carbon footprint? eat less meat

It's true—we would use considerably fewer resources if we ate less meat. A landmark 2006 report from the United Nations Food and Agriculture Organization ranked livestock as one of the top contributors to critical environmental problems, such as deforestation, loss of biodiversity, water pollution, and greenhouse-gas emissions that contribute to global warming.

Consider the following:

◆ According to the Food and Agricultural Organization of the United Nations, the global production of animals for food is the single biggest source (about 18 percent) of human-generated greenhouse-gas emissions—more than all the cars, planes, ships, trucks, and trains in the world combined.

◆ Industrial feedlot meat production requires about 16 times more fossil fuel energy than does production of the caloric equivalent of vegetables and rice.

◆ Raising animals for food consumes more than half of all the water used in the U.S. It can take 2,500 gallons of water to produce a pound of meat, but only 155 gallons for a pound of wheat.

What you can do and what your actions can accomplish:

◆ Go vegetarian at least once a week. The Center for the New American Dream calculated that for every 1,000 people who choose to eat a meatless meal once a week, we'll save 70,000 pounds of grain for human food use, prevent the erosion of 70,000 pounds of topsoil, and save 40 million gallons of water a year.

◆ Cut down your portions. On average, Americans eat about 8 ounces of meat per day (roughly twice the global average). Whenever you choose to eat meat, try to consume less. It's healthier for the planet, and for most of us, too. The USDA reminds us that a standard serving of meat is 4 ounces. Meat is also wonderful as a seasoning or highlight in dishes; it doesn't have to be the center of the meal.

◆ Look at the trade-offs of choosing more eco-friendly meat. (See page 78 for more information about more eco-friendly meat options.)

Keep in mind that there are other factors to consider when choosing meat, such as the humane treatment of animals and the way they are raised. All meat is not created equal. There's a big difference between feedlot beef and organic grass-fed beef, for example.

Buckwheat Pasta with Tofu and Sesame Vegetables

THE KEY TO THIS RECIPE lies in having everything prepped and ready to go before you start cooking. First the tofu is sautéed to give it a golden crust; then while the pasta is cooking, the vegetables are quickly stir-fried. The result is an easy vegetarian dish loaded with tasty vegetables, beautiful colors, and varying textures. One thing that I especially appreciate about this dish is that it's great hot, at room temperature, or cold right out of the fridge. This is a perfect budget-friendly recipe that's great to remember when you need to make a dish for a potluck or a party. ⚊⚊ *Serves 4 to 6*

½ cup soy sauce

1 tablespoon fresh lemon juice

2 tablespoons unseasoned rice vinegar

2 tablespoons toasted sesame oil (see sidebar, page 25)

1 teaspoon ground ginger

1 teaspoon garlic powder

14 to 16 ounces firm tofu, drained and cut into ½-inch-thick slices

2 tablespoons kosher salt

8 ounces buckwheat (soba) noodles

3 tablespoons plain sesame oil

3 tablespoons minced shallots

1 tablespoon finely grated peeled fresh ginger

1 tablespoon minced garlic

2 cups (6 ounces) broccoli florets

1 red bell pepper, stemmed, seeded, and cut into ⅛-inch-thick strips (about 1½ cups)

1 large carrot, peeled and cut into ⅛-inch-thick rounds (about 1 cup)

1 small zucchini, cut in half lengthwise and then cut crosswise into ⅛-inch-thick slices (about ¾ cup)

Salt, to taste

2 teaspoons sesame seeds, toasted (see box, page 31)

1. Place the soy sauce, lemon juice, vinegar, toasted sesame oil, ginger, and garlic powder in a large bowl and whisk to blend. Add the slabs of tofu and let marinate for 5 minutes.

2. Heat a large skillet, preferably cast-iron, over medium-high heat and add the tofu (reserving the bowl of marinade). Cook on one side until browned, about 2 minutes. Then turn the tofu over with a spatula and cook until nicely browned on the other side, 2 minutes. Transfer the tofu to a cutting board and cut it into ¾-inch cubes. Return the tofu to the bowl containing the marinade.

3. Bring 4 quarts of water to a boil in a large covered pot over high heat. Add 2 tablespoons salt, and stir in the noodles. Cook according to the package directions until al dente, about 7 minutes.

Buckwheat Pasta with Tofu and Sesame Vegetables

4. While the pasta is cooking, heat the plain sesame oil in a cast-iron skillet over medium-high heat. Add the shallots, ginger, and garlic, and cook, stirring constantly, until aromatic, about 1 minute. Then add the broccoli, bell pepper, carrot, and zucchini and stir-fry until the vegetables begin to soften, about 4 minutes. Cover the skillet and cook until the vegetables are crisp-tender, another 2 to 4 minutes.

5. Meanwhile, drain the noodles and add them to the tofu.

6. Season the vegetable mixture with salt, and add it to the tofu and pasta. Toss to combine, sprinkle with the sesame seeds, and serve.

Orecchiette with Broccolette

Broccolette tops resemble broccoli florets.

ORECCHIETTE MEANS "LITTLE EARS" IN ITALIAN; the shell-shaped pasta is a terrific vehicle for flavorful sauces. The classic Italian trio of oil, garlic, and anchovies forms the flavor base of this pasta dish, which goes together in a flash. Once the water boils, the pasta will be ready to serve in less than 20 minutes. And you only need to use one pot, because the broccolette is cooked with the pasta. This is one presentation where the starring vegetable is not meant to be al dente, or crisp-tender—the broccolette needs to be fully cooked so that it melts into a creamy sauce. Be sure to save some of the pasta cooking water if you drain the orecchiette and broccolette, as it both thickens and flavors the dish. ⸻ *Serves 4*

Coarse sea salt or kosher salt

4 cups (12 ounces) orecchiette

10 ounces broccolette (see box, facing page), ends trimmed, stalks cut into 1½-inch pieces (4 cups)

¼ cup olive oil or oil from Garlic Confit (page 414)

5 canned anchovies, mashed to a paste with a fork

4 garlic cloves from Garlic Confit, smashed; or 4 fresh garlic cloves, peeled and minced

Pinch of dried red pepper flakes, or more to taste

Grated zest of 2 lemons, preferably Meyer lemons

1½ cups freshly grated Parmesan or Pecorino Romano cheese

1. Bring 4 quarts water to a boil in a large covered pot over high heat. Add 2 tablespoons coarse sea salt, and stir in the orecchiette. Cook, stirring once or twice, for 7 minutes. Then add the broccolette and cook until the pasta is al dente and the broccolette is tender, 9 to 12 more minutes.

2. A few minutes before the pasta and broccolette are cooked, pour the olive oil into a large skillet (at least 12 inches in diameter) and heat it over medium heat. When the oil is hot, add the anchovies, garlic cloves, and red pepper flakes. Cook, stirring frequently, until the anchovies dissolve and the mixture is hot, about 2 minutes.

3. Using a large slotted spoon, transfer the orecchiette and broccolette to the skillet. (Alternatively, reserve 1 cup of the cooking liquid, then drain the contents of the pot in a colander. Transfer the mixture to the skillet.) Cook the mixture for 2 or 3 minutes, stirring frequently, adding some of the hot pasta cooking water to the skillet if the mixture seems dry. Add the lemon zest and 1 cup of the cheese, stirring to coat.

4. Transfer the pasta to a warmed platter, and sprinkle with the remaining ½ cup cheese. Serve hot.

FARM FRESH

Broccolette

Broccolette, also called "broccolini" and "baby broccoli," is a hybrid cross between broccoli and *gai lan* (confusingly known as both Chinese broccoli and Chinese kale). This elegant, versatile vegetable has long, slender, juicy green stalks topped with clusters of tiny florets. Although broccolette does resemble miniature broccoli, its stalks are sweeter and less fibrous, and do not require peeling. It tastes like broccoli but with an intriguing hint of pepper and mustard and none of broccoli's cabbage-y flavor.

Broccolette is sold in small bunches in most supermarkets and specialty stores and is available year-round. Look for slim, vibrant green stalks that are firm and crisp; the heads should have tightly closed buds. If the stalks are thicker than a pencil, it is best to cut them in half lengthwise so that the stems and florets will cook in the same amount of time. Store unwashed broccolette in a perforated plastic bag in the refrigerator; it will keep for up to 14 days.

Broccolette is as versatile as broccoli and can be steamed, stir-fried, roasted, or eaten raw. Be careful not to overcook it—it should remain juicy and crunchy for most recipes. It generally needs no preparation other than trimming about ½ inch off the bottom of the stems. Rinse it under cold water and pat it dry with a clean kitchen towel. One cup (about 8 stalks) contains only 35 calories and provides 130 percent of the daily recommended requirement for vitamin C, as well as significant amounts of fiber and vitamin A.

Rigatoni with Eggplant and Buffalo Mozzarella

Rigatoni with Eggplant and Buffalo Mozzarella

I DISCOVERED THIS AMAZINGLY SIMPLE but intensely flavorful pasta dish when our family traveled to Italy a few summers ago. It was so memorable that it made the top of my list of recipes to try to replicate. Chunks of succulent eggplant get a quick sauté to set their flavor, then are simmered in a light marinara sauce until tender. At the last minute, cubes of *mozzarella di bufalo* are added, quickly becoming soft and creamy as they melt into the sauce. This dish goes together in no time, especially if you have marinara sauce on hand. If you don't have time to make my Heirloom Tomato Sauce or the Quick Tomato Sauce, you can fast-track the recipe by using a store-bought version.

A word about the eggplant, which is at the heart of this dish: Salting is not required, but it's important to sauté the eggplant over high heat in the amount of oil specified. You need very high heat to force the eggplant to brown and develop flavor. In the absence of high heat, the vegetable will simply soak up the oil, become soggy, and taste flat.

I serve this dish with a warmed baguette to sop up the extra sauce, and with a light salad of lettuce and endive dressed only with olive oil, balsamic vinegar, and salt and pepper. —*Serves 4*

4 tablespoons olive oil

Pinch of dried red pepper flakes, or to taste

1 large eggplant (1¼ pounds), peeled or unpeeled, cut into ½-inch dice

3 cups Myra's Heirloom Tomato Sauce (page 416), Quick Tomato Sauce (page 417), or good-quality store-bought marinara sauce

Salt and freshly ground black pepper

12 ounces rigatoni pasta, or other short tubular pasta such as penne or ziti

1 ball (4 to 5 ounces) imported mozzarella di bufalo or fresh milk mozzarella, cut into ½-inch cubes (about ¾ cup)

6 fresh basil leaves, roughly torn

½ cup freshly grated Parmesan or Pecorino Romano cheese

1. Bring 4 quarts water to a boil in a large covered pot over high heat.

2. While the water is heating, heat the olive oil in a large skillet over high heat. When the oil is very hot, add the red pepper flakes and the eggplant. Cook, turning the eggplant frequently, until it begins to brown and soften slightly, about 2 minutes.

3. Add the tomato sauce to the skillet and reduce the heat to low. Simmer gently until the mixture is hot and the eggplant is almost tender, 2 to 3 minutes. Remove the skillet from the heat.

Season with salt and pepper to taste.

4. Add 2 tablespoons salt to the boiling water, and stir in the rigatoni. Cook, stirring once or twice, according to the package directions until the pasta is al dente, 10 to 12 minutes. Just before the rigatoni is done, reheat the eggplant mixture over medium heat.

5. Drain the pasta and immediately transfer it to a warmed bowl. Pour the sauce over the rigatoni, and toss thoroughly to distribute the sauce evenly and coat all the pasta. Add the mozzarella and basil, and toss to combine. Serve hot, with the grated cheese on the side.

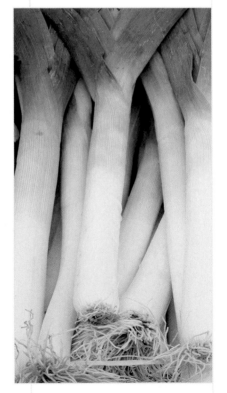

Soil tends to lodge in between the layers of a leek, so rinse them thoroughly before using.

Leek and Feta Risotto Cakes

ARBORIO RICE MAKES A GREAT BASE for this tasty combination of leeks, feta, and Parmesan. If you happen to have leftover risotto, this is a great way to turn it into another meal or a first course: Just add minced cooked vegetables, herbs, and cheese for a quick batch of risotto cakes. It's important to note that the cakes need to be completely cold before you cook them, or they will fall apart in the skillet. Chilling the cakes allows the starches to harden and makes them fry-able. For a satisfying meal, serve the risotto cakes with a vegetable side or two. ⌇⌇⌇ *Makes 12 cakes; serves 4 to 6*

4 tablespoons olive oil

½ cup finely chopped yellow onion

2 large leeks (white part only), well-rinsed and finely chopped (about 2 cups)

2 teaspoons minced garlic

1 tablespoon butter

1 cup Arborio or Carnaroli rice

¼ cup white wine

3 cups Vegetable Stock (page 410) or store-bought low-sodium vegetable broth, heated

½ cup crumbled feta cheese

¼ cup freshly grated Parmesan cheese

2 large eggs, lightly beaten

¼ cup snipped fresh chives

2 tablespoons chopped fresh flat-leaf parsley

Salt and freshly ground black pepper

1. Heat 2 tablespoons of the olive oil in a medium-size saucepan over medium heat. Add the onion, leeks, and garlic, and cook, stirring frequently, until the vegetables are soft, 6 to 8 minutes.

2. Add the butter and the rice. Cook, stirring constantly, until the rice is hot, 1 to 2 minutes. Then stir in the wine and cook until all of the liquid has evaporated, about 2 minutes.

3. Add 1 cup of the vegetable stock, stirring constantly to bring out the starch in the rice. When almost all of the stock has been absorbed, add another cup. Repeat until all of the stock has been absorbed, about 20 minutes total. (The risotto is meant to be fully cooked and not al dente for this recipe.) Remove the pan from the heat and let the mixture cool for 20 minutes.

4. Stir the feta, Parmesan, eggs, chives, and parsley into the risotto. Season the mixture with salt and pepper to taste. When it is cool enough to handle, form the mixture into twelve ½-inch-thick cakes, about ⅓ cup each, and refrigerate them, uncovered, until they are completely cold, at least 4 hours. (The cakes can be refrigerated, well wrapped, for up to 2 days before cooking.)

5. Just before serving, heat the remaining 2 tablespoons olive oil in a large nonstick skillet, preferably cast-iron, over medium-high heat. Arrange the cakes in the skillet so that they do not touch (it may be necessary to do this in two batches), and cook until the bottom is crisp and browned, about 3 minutes. Turn the cakes over and cook on the other side until golden and warmed through, about 3 minutes. Serve immediately.

LIVING GREEN
Concerns persist over the safety of nonstick cookware, although many experts are confident that cooking with nonstick is safe if it is used properly. Because nonstick coatings break down and can release potentially toxic fumes when heated above 500°F, don't use heat settings higher than medium-high. Because some of the chemicals used to create the nonstick surface are potentially toxic, it is recommended that pans that are chipped or scratched be discarded.

Barley "Risotto" with Spinach and Mushrooms

LOVE THE RUSTIC FLAVOR and chewy texture of barley, yet I realized that I hardly ever eat it except in mushroom barley soup. So I thought it was time to figure out a vegetarian barley entrée that my family would enjoy, and this one gets rave reviews from everyone. A variation on the traditional Italian rice dish, barley risotto is rich and satisfying enough to work as a main course when served with a big salad and whole wheat rolls. It is also great as a side dish for any meat, especially pork or lamb. I splurge on organic Parmigiano-Reggiano to go with it because the aged cheese adds tons of flavor. —*mm*— *Serves 4*

¼ cup olive oil

About 1½ cups diced yellow onion
   (¼-inch dice)

2 garlic cloves, peeled and finely chopped

4 cups (8 ounces) sliced brown (cremini) or
   white mushrooms (⅓-inch-thick slices)

2 teaspoons fresh thyme leaves

2 cups hulled barley (see box, this page),
   rinsed

6 cups Vegetable Stock (page 410) or
   store-bought low-sodium vegetable broth

1 teaspoon salt

Pinch of freshly ground black pepper

8 ounces (6 cups packed) baby spinach,
   well rinsed and patted dry if needed

1 teaspoon soy sauce

½ cup freshly grated Parmigiano-Reggiano
   cheese, plus more for garnish

1. Pour the olive oil into a large saucepan or Dutch oven, and place it over medium heat. When the oil is hot, add the onion and cook, stirring frequently, until it is soft and translucent, 7 to 10 minutes. Add the garlic and cook, stirring frequently, for 1 to 2 minutes, taking care not to burn the garlic.

2. Add the mushrooms and thyme, and cook until the mushrooms soften, about 5 minutes. Add the barley and cook, stirring constantly, until the grains are hot to the touch, 2 to 3 minutes. Add the vegetable broth, and salt, and pepper. Cover the pan and bring the mixture to the start of a boil. Then reduce the heat to low, cover the pan, and simmer, stirring occasionally, until the barley is tender and most of the liquid has been absorbed, about 1 hour.

3. Remove the lid and raise the heat to medium. Stir in the baby spinach and the soy sauce. Cook, uncovered, stirring frequently, until the spinach wilts, about 3 minutes. Then stir in the cheese, remove the pan from the heat, and let the barley risotto sit, covered, for 2 minutes.

4. Divide the risotto among warmed shallow bowls, and sprinkle with additional cheese.

THE BASICS

Hulled vs. Pearled Barley

There are two forms of barley that you are likely to encounter when shopping: hulled and pearled, or pearl. Hulled barley has been minimally processed to remove its inedible hull. The grains have a distinctive tan color and are chubby. Hulled barley still has most of its protein-rich bran layer and is sometimes called "barley groats." After barley grains are hulled, they can be further refined by an abrasive polishing process called "pearling." Pearling strips off the germ and most or all of the bran. The more the grains have been pearled, the paler, smaller, and less nutritious the barley will be. Pearled barley is widely available in supermarkets, whereas you are more likely to find hulled barley or semi-pearled barley (which still retains some of its outer bran coating) in specialty stores. Hulled barley does take longer to cook, but it has much more protein, fiber, and B vitamins than the pearled variety.

Spinach, Mushroom, and Gruyère Crêpes

CREPES ARE ONE OF MY ALL-TIME FAVORITE FOODS. I fell in love with them as a teenager when my family took a trip to Paris. French crêpes—*wow!* So delicious! I taught myself to make crêpes years later, and now it's one of my family's most anticipated dinners. At home I make them for one person at a time, filling them and finishing them right in the pan—and then we make dessert crêpes with any leftover batter. But it's also easy to make the crêpes ahead of time and then fill them —especially if you're cooking them for company or for a larger group. Spinach, mushrooms, and Gruyère cheese make a fabulous filling, but crêpes are incredibly flexible. Add anything you might use in an omelet or pizza— including small amounts of leftovers that might otherwise go to waste. If you like a creamy filling, add the crème fraîche. Make sure you plan for enough time to refrigerate the batter. ——— *Serves 4 (2 crêpes per person)*

TIP

Crêpes made with buckwheat flour are also delicious with the filling described here. Be sure to try them, too. You'll find a recipe for Buckwheat Crêpes on page 429.

WHOLE WHEAT CREPES

(Makes about 8 crêpes)

1 cup whole wheat pastry flour

⅛ teaspoon salt

1¼ cups whole milk, divided

2 large eggs, lightly beaten

2 tablespoons unsalted butter, melted

FILLING

2 tablespoons olive oil

½ cup minced shallots

3½ cups (10 ounces) chopped white, cremini, or other fresh mushrooms

½ cup dry white wine

Salt and freshly ground black pepper

1 pound baby spinach, well rinsed and patted dry if needed

⅓ cup Crème Fraîche (page 415; optional)

ASSEMBLING

¼ cup milk, if needed

2 tablespoons unsalted butter, melted, for cooking the crêpes

2 cups (7 ounces) grated Gruyère cheese

1. Prepare the crêpe batter: Place the flour and salt in a medium-size bowl and whisk to combine. Add the milk and the eggs, and whisk to combine. Add the melted butter and whisk until the batter is smooth. You can also make the batter in a blender or with an immersion blender if you prefer. Cover the bowl with a plate and refrigerate 1 to 3 hours.

2. Prepare the filling: Heat the olive oil in a large skillet over medium heat. Add the shallots and cook, stirring frequently, until they soften, about 3 minutes. Add the mushrooms and wine, and season with salt and pepper to taste. Cover the skillet and cook, stirring occasionally, until the wine has evaporated and the mushrooms are tender, 8 to 10 minutes.

3. Add the spinach to the mushroom mixture and cook, covered, stirring frequently, until the spinach wilts, about 5 minutes. (It may be necessary to add the spinach in two or three batches, depending on the size of your skillet.) Remove the cover and continue cooking until all the liquid has evaporated, about 5 minutes. Add the crème fraîche, if using, and stir to combine. Set the filling aside and keep warm.

Making Crêpes

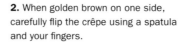

1. Pour the batter into a cast-iron skillet or crêpe pan and tilt to get a round shape.

2. When golden brown on one side, carefully flip the crêpe using a spatula and your fingers.

3. While the second side cooks, sprinkle cheese down the middle of the crêpe, then add a strip of filling.

4. Fold the top and bottom of the crêpe in toward the middle.

5. Fold the two sides in toward the middle.

6. Once folded, flip the crêpe over. Cook until both sides are golden brown.

4. When you're ready to make the crêpes, if the batter is too thick—it should have the consistency of thin pancake batter—add 2 tablespoons of milk and whisk to combine.

5. Place a 12-inch cast-iron skillet, or a crêpe pan over medium heat and when the pan is hot, brush with some of the melted butter. Pour or ladle ¼ cup of batter into the center of the pan, lift the pan off the stove, and tilt and swirl the pan so that the batter spreads thinly across the bottom of the pan in a widening circle; don't worry if the crêpe is not a perfect circle. There may be some small holes, but again this is not of consequence as the crêpes are meant to be thin. If the holes are large, you can immediately dot a bit of batter on them to fill them. Cook until tiny bubbles begin to appear in the crêpe batter; depending on how hot the pan is, the crêpe will be ready to flip in 15 to 30 seconds. With a spatula, lift up one corner of the crêpe to check if the cooked surface is lightly golden around the edges, and if so, flip the crêpe.

6. Sprinkle the cooked side with ¼ cup of cheese, and spoon a scant ⅓ cup of warm filling in a strip down the middle. By this time the second side of the crêpe should be a light golden brown. Fold all four sides of the crêpe into the center to enclose the filling. Turn the crêpe over with a spatula, and cook until both sides are golden brown, about 1 minute.

Serve immediately, folded side down. Alternatively, keep the crêpe warm in a 250°F oven while you repeat with the remaining crêpes and filling.

7. Repeat with the remaining batter and filling, whisking before making each crêpe. Make sure to also grease the pan lightly between each crêpe. The batter may thicken as it rests. If so, thin it with a tablespoon or two of milk as needed.

Spinach, Mushroom, and Gruyère Crêpes (page 175)

White Bean and Radicchio Gratin

White Bean and Radicchio Gratin

THIS UNUSUAL DISH has its roots in Italy, where both white beans and radicchio are popular ingredients. The beans are cooked with onion and garlic to infuse them with flavor. Then half of the bean mixture is pureed with the cooking liquid, which creates a creamy base for the radicchio. A mixture of nutty Gruyère cheese and bread crumbs creates a tasty topping for this unique vegetarian dish that is loaded with protein and nutrients.

Serves 8 to 10

1 pound dried Great Northern or cannellini beans (about 2½ cups)

10 to 12 cups cold water

About 4 cups diced yellow onions (¼-inch dice)

1 tablespoon plus ½ teaspoon minced garlic

2 tablespoons olive oil

1 tablespoon white wine vinegar

2 teaspoons salt, or to taste

½ teaspoon freshly ground black pepper

1 small head (4½ ounces) radicchio, cut in half through the core, then thinly sliced crosswise (2 cups)

1 cup dry unseasoned bread crumbs (see sidebar, this page)

1 cup grated Gruyère cheese

½ teaspoon dried thyme

½ teaspoon dried basil

1. Pick through the beans, discarding any stones, and rinse them in a colander under cold running water. Place the beans in a large saucepan and add enough cold water to cover by 2 inches. Cover the pan and bring the water to a boil over high heat. Then reduce the heat to medium-low, partially cover the pan, and cook the beans for 30 minutes.

2. Add the onions and the 1 tablespoon garlic, and continue to cook until the beans are tender, 30 to 45 minutes, depending on the age of your beans.

3. Position a rack in the middle of the oven and preheat the oven to 425°F.

4. Drain the beans, reserving 1 cup of the cooking liquid, and transfer half of the beans to a large bowl and puree them with an immersion blender or by hand with a potato masher. (Alternatively, puree them in a food processor.) Add the remaining whole beans, the reserved cooking liquid, and the olive oil, vinegar, salt, pepper, and radicchio. Stir to combine. Transfer the mixture to an 8 x 10-inch baking dish.

THE BASICS

Making Bread Crumbs

Bread crumbs are a great way to avoid wasting bread. Bread crumbs can be made from toasted (dry) or fresh bread.

To make toasted crumbs, toast leftover bread, cool it completely, then break into pieces. For fresh bread crumbs, cut bread into 1-inch pieces. Process either fresh or toasted bread in a food processor for fine or coarse crumbs.

Homemade bread crumbs keep best stored in an airtight container in the freezer.

5. Combine the bread crumbs, Gruyère, remaining ½ teaspoon garlic, thyme, and basil in a bowl, and stir to blend. Cover the bean mixture with the bread crumb topping.

6. Bake the gratin until the mixture starts to bubble and the topping turns golden brown, 20 to 30 minutes. Serve hot.

7. The gratin can be refrigerated, covered, for up to 5 days. Reheat in the microwave to serve.

Sesame-Ginger Asparagus with Tofu

ASPARAGUS IS PERFECTLY SUITED to quick and easy stir-fry cooking. High heat, combined with a short cooking time, ensures that the spears retain their fresh flavor and bright emerald color. An Asian combination of ginger, garlic, and sesame oil subtly flavors the asparagus and tofu mixture here. The simple sauce concentrates to become a light glaze. If you can find black sesame seeds (available at Asian markets and some supermarkets), sprinkle a combination of white and black seeds over the asparagus to make an especially attractive presentation. Serve it over brown rice or noodles.

Serves 4

1½ pounds fresh asparagus, woody ends trimmed, spears peeled if desired
2 tablespoons canola oil
1 tablespoon plain sesame oil (see sidebar, page 25)
7 ounces firm tofu, cut into ½-inch cubes (about 2 cups)
1 tablespoon grated peeled fresh ginger
2 garlic cloves, finely minced
Pinch of dried red pepper flakes, or to taste
2½ tablespoons soy sauce or tamari (see sidebar, this page)
1½ tablespoons mirin (Asian sweet rice wine)
1 tablespoon fresh lemon juice
2 tablespoons sesame seeds, toasted
Brown rice or noodles, for serving

1. Slice the asparagus spears on the diagonal into 1½-inch-long pieces, and set them aside (see Note).

2. Heat a wok or a large skillet, preferably nonstick, over medium-high heat. When the wok is hot, add the

Sesame-Ginger Asparagus with Tofu

canola and sesame oils and heat until the oil is shimmering but not smoking. Add the tofu and stir-fry until it starts to turn golden, 2 to 3 minutes.

3. Add the ginger, garlic, and red pepper flakes, and cook, stirring frequently, until the mixture is fragrant, about 1 minute. Add the asparagus and stir-fry until it is just crisp-tender, 3 to 5 minutes, depending on the thickness of the spears.

4. Add the soy sauce, mirin, and lemon juice and cook, stirring

frequently, until the liquid reduces and lightly glazes the mixture, 2 to 3 minutes.

5. Transfer the mixture to a warmed platter, sprinkle with the sesame seeds, and serve hot over brown rice or noodles.

Note: If your asparagus spears are fat, stir-frying might leave them too crunchy. You can either cut the spears in half lengthwise or blanch the spears in boiling water for 45 to 60 seconds to parboil them slightly before adding them to the skillet.

FARM FRESH

Asparagus

Asparagus is a member of the lily family and is related to leeks and onions. Green asparagus is the most commonly found variety in the United States. Europeans are very fond of white asparagus, which is identical to green except for its growing method: To ensure that greening does not occur, the plants are covered with soil as they grow, to interrupt the process of photosynthesis.

The peak season for domestic asparagus runs from February through June, although hothouse varieties are available year-round in some markets. Choose firm, bright green spears with tight, dry, compact tips. Select spears that are roughly equal in size so they

will cook in the same amount of time. Inspect the stem ends and avoid any asparagus that is wrinkled, split, or dried out. Give the bunch a squeeze—if the stalks squeak when rubbed together, they're fresh.

Asparagus is fragile, and its natural sweetness begins to diminish from the moment it is harvested. Try to use it the day you buy it. If you must store it, the best way to maintain its bright color and crisp texture is to store it standing upright in a glass of water: Trim off the bottom ½ inch of the spears, place the spears in a glass that will hold them comfortably, add enough cold water to cover the bottom of the spears by 1 inch, and refrigerate. Asparagus stored

in this fashion should remain fresh for 3 days. Re-trim the bottom of the stalks before using.

Although debate rages over the virtues of thin versus fat spears, the fact is that thick asparagus has plenty of flavor and succulence. Peeling is optional, but it speeds the cooking time with thick spears, preventing the tips from getting overcooked. Use a sharp vegetable peeler to remove the skin, starting about 2 inches below the asparagus tips.

One cup of asparagus contains a mere 40 calories. In addition to vitamins B_6 and C, asparagus is high in fiber, potassium, and folate and is a natural diuretic.

a quick primer on global warming

A big part of being an Earthbound Cook is becoming more mindful of how our actions affect the planet. For this reason, it's important to understand the basics of global warming to better visualize why and how changing some simple everyday things we do can help. Here's a simplified explanation.

The sun's radiation travels to the Earth in the form of light waves. Most of this radiation is absorbed and warms the Earth before being radiated back out into space as infrared heat. Some of this heat is trapped by naturally occurring gases in our atmosphere. This occurrence, called the greenhouse effect, keeps our planet at a relatively stable temperature, warm enough for us to live here. If our atmosphere weren't able to keep some of this heat, our Earth would be a frozen desert.

Problems arise, however, when we thicken our atmosphere with a blanket of excess man-made emissions from sources like fossil-fuel power plants (burning coal, fuel oil, or natural gas), gas-burning vehicles, and intensive conventional farming practices. Deforestation is also a big part of this problem because vegetation that usually absorbs some of the heat-trapping carbon dioxide (CO_2) in the atmosphere is eliminated. Our planet's natural heat-exchange system is thrown out of balance when a greater concentration of greenhouse gases—such as CO_2, methane, nitrous oxide, and ozone—trap excess heat in our atmosphere instead of allowing it to radiate into space.

The result is rising global temperatures that contribute to a number of serious environmental problems, which include increasingly frequent and severe droughts and floods, declining snow accumulation, more frequent and more violent storms, melting polar ice caps, and severe coastal erosion from rising seas. According to the Natural Resources Defense Council, rising global temperatures could also lead to health problems, such as increased spread of infectious diseases and more lung problems; weather changes, such as fiercer and more frequent hurricanes and deadly heat waves; and serious shortages in food supplies caused by drought and the destruction of marine-life habitat.

As each of us goes about our daily lives, we leave a carbon footprint that is made up of the CO_2 and other greenhouse gases generated by the energy and resources we use to do everything from driving our cars and powering our homes to bathing, clothing ourselves, and so much more. The foods we choose to eat and how we prepare them can have a big impact on our carbon footprint. So with every meal, we have the opportunity to tread more lightly on the planet.

Sweet Dumpling Squash Stuffed with Quinoa, Butternut, and Cranberries

Pumpkins Stuffed with Quinoa, Butternut, and Cranberries

SMALL EDIBLE PUMPKINS AND WINTER SQUASHES make gorgeous serving dishes, especially festive during the holiday season. I've chosen sugar pie pumpkins, which are easy to work with and readily available in the autumn months. Sweet Dumpling and acorn squash can also be used, or if you're in a hurry, serve the quinoa stuffing on its own—it's delicious either way. If you're unfamiliar with quinoa, it's an easy-to-prepare grain that makes a nice change from rice or couscous. Quinoa was the staple grain of the Incas and it remains an important ingredient in South American cuisines to this day. You can feel virtuous eating it, too—quinoa has more protein than any other grain. ⟿ *Serves 4*

3 tablespoons olive oil

About 1 cup diced yellow onion (¼-inch dice)

2 teaspoons ground cumin

1 cup quinoa (see sidebar, this page), rinsed in cold water and drained

2 cups Vegetable Stock (page 410), or store-bought low-sodium vegetable broth

½ cup dried unsweetened cranberries

4 small edible pumpkins, Sweet Dumpling squash, or small acorn squash (1½ to 2 pounds each)

1½ cups diced butternut squash (¼-inch dice)

¼ cup pepitas (raw pumpkin seeds), pine nuts, or chopped walnuts, toasted (see box, page 31)

½ teaspoon ground cinnamon

1 teaspoon fresh lemon juice

Salt and freshly ground black pepper

1. Place 2 tablespoons of the olive oil in a heavy-bottomed saucepan or Dutch oven, and heat over medium heat. When it is hot, add the onion and ground cumin and cook, stirring frequently, until the onion is soft and golden brown, about 10 minutes.

2. Add the quinoa to the saucepan and stir to coat the grains. Add the stock and raise the heat to high. When the liquid comes to a boil, reduce the heat to low, add the cranberries, and cover the pan. Cook at a slow simmer until the liquid has been absorbed, 15 to 25 minutes.

3. Meanwhile, cut the top off each pumpkin, reserving the tops, if desired, for decorative effect. Scoop out and discard the seeds and fibers. If the pumpkins do not sit flat, trim a small slice off the bottom to create a flat base. Place the pumpkins on a rimmed baking sheet and set it aside.

THE BASICS

Quinoa

Quinoa (pronounced keen-wah) is a nutritional powerhouse, with high levels of lysine, an amino acid essential for the synthesis of protein. Not only is quinoa high in protein (6 grams per ¼ cup as opposed to 4 grams for brown rice), but the protein it supplies is a complete protein, meaning that it includes all nine essential amino acids. Quinoa also provides vitamin E, iron, magnesium, potassium, and fiber, and is higher in unsaturated fats and lower in carbohydrates than most grains.

4. Place the remaining 1 tablespoon oil in a large skillet, preferably nonstick, and heat it over medium-high heat. When it is hot, add the cubed butternut squash and cook without stirring until the squash is browned on the bottom, 2 minutes. Toss to turn the pieces (or use a spatula to accomplish this) and cook, stirring frequently, until the squash is just tender, about 2 minutes more. Set aside.

5. When the quinoa is cooked, remove the pan from the heat and stir in the toasted pepitas, cinnamon, and lemon juice. Add the butternut squash, and season with salt and pepper to taste.

6. Position a rack in the lower third of the oven and preheat the oven to 375°F.

7. Divide the quinoa filling among the pumpkin shells; do not pack the mixture. Transfer the baking sheet to the oven and roast until the quinoa is hot and the flesh of the pumpkins is tender when pierced with a skewer or fork, 45 to 60 minutes. Avoid overcooking, because the pumpkins may collapse. If you intend to use the pumpkin tops, add these to the oven during the last 15 minutes of cooking.

8. Serve immediately, with the tops (if using) leaning against the stuffed pumpkins.

YOUR GREEN KITCHEN

Be Oven Savvy

Use your oven wisely—it's an energy hog. Heating the oven uses a lot of kilowatts, so it makes good sense (and cents) to minimize the time it runs and maximize the energy expenditure. Here are some tips to help you use your oven efficiently:

◆ Buy an oven thermometer. The one built into your oven may not be accurate, and the actual temperature may be much higher than the oven control indicates. If that's the case, you are using more energy than you need, as well as running the risk of overcooking your food.

◆ If you have a double oven, use the smaller oven if the dish fits. Save the larger oven for multiple pans or large items.

◆ For small items that need baking or reheating, use a countertop oven, such as a toaster oven. These appliances preheat faster and have a lower output of watts.

◆ The longer an oven is turned on but not used, the more energy it wastes. Preheating accounts for much of an oven's energy use. Start preheating the oven just 10 to 15 minutes before you need to use it.

◆ Look for ways to maximize the use of your oven. Instead of cooking just one dish at a time, if you're baking an entrée, choose a vegetable or potato you can cook at the same time.

◆ Resist peeking: Opening the oven door drops the temperature by at least 25°F, and the oven has to switch back on again to replace it.

◆ If you have a convection feature on your oven, it uses about 20 percent less energy than a standard electric oven and has a shorter warm-up time.

◆ Self-cleaning ovens are more energy efficient than standard ovens because of their thicker insulation. This means they lose less heat to the surrounding air. If you have a self-cleaning model, don't clean it too often: this is the most energy draining of the oven's functions.

Homemade Veggie Burgers

I F YOUR MISSION IS TO EAT MORE MEATLESS MEALS, this recipe is a
very good starting point. These veggie burgers are bold and satisfying, with
a surprisingly complex flavor. Full of super-healthy ingredients like walnuts,
bulgur, and pinto beans, and flavored with Middle Eastern spices, the patties have
good texture and a dynamic taste. The egg whites can be eliminated if you wish:
The mixture will taste the same but the texture of the burger will be a bit heavier.
The burger patties do need to be refrigerated until they are completely chilled
before cooking, for at least 4 hours, so be sure to plan accordingly.

 I enjoy these with a side of Yogurt Sauce with Red Onion and Cucumber.
You can sandwich the burger and sauce in a whole wheat pita (see recipe,
page 287), or serve the burgers on whole wheat buns with lettuce, tomatoes,
and red onion slices. —ww— ***Makes 6 burger patties; serves 4 to 6***

½ cup bulgur wheat

1½ teaspoons salt

1½ cups walnut pieces

2 large garlic cloves, peeled

1 cup (packed) fresh cilantro leaves

2 cups cooked pinto beans (see box,
 page 422), rinsed and drained if canned

3 tablespoons soy sauce

1½ teaspoons ground cumin

¼ teaspoon cayenne pepper

2 large egg whites

2 tablespoons canola oil

Yogurt Sauce with Red Onion and
 Cucumber (recipe follows), for serving
 (optional)

*It's always a good idea to assemble your
ingredients before you start to cook.*

2. Place the walnuts,
garlic, and cilantro in
a food processor and
process until the mixture
is roughly chopped.
Add the bulgur, pinto
beans, soy sauce, cumin,
remaining 1 teaspoon
salt, and cayenne pepper,
and process until the
mixture is finely chopped.

3. Add the egg whites
and process again until
combined.

1. Place the bulgur, 1 cup water, and
½ teaspoon of the salt in a saucepan.
Cover and bring to a boil over high
heat. Reduce the heat to medium-low
and simmer until the water has been
absorbed, 10 to 15 minutes. Let the
bulgur cool for 10 minutes.

4. Refrigerate the mixture, covered,
until it is completely cold, at least
4 hours or as long as overnight.

5. Form the mixture into 6 patties,
each about 3½ inches in diameter
(about ½ cup per patty).

6. Heat the canola oil in a large skillet, preferably cast-iron, over medium to medium-high heat. Add the burgers and cook until they are browned and crisp, 4 to 6 minutes. (Do not crowd the pan; cook in two batches if necessary.) Carefully turn the patties over and cook on the other side until browned and heated through, about 5 minutes.

7. Serve the burgers hot, with Yogurt Sauce with Red Onion and Cucumber on the side if desired.

Yogurt Sauce with Red Onion and Cucumber

I enjoy this chunky sauce all by itself, but it goes especially well with our Homemade Veggie Burgers. The smoky flavor of grilled red onion is distinctive, and the tahini-mint dressing, which relies on yogurt rather than oil for its creaminess, mellows the piquancy of the capers. If you are in a hurry, skip the grilling step and just use raw red onion—the sauce will still taste great. Use any leftover sauce on grilled or smoked salmon. ⟶ *Makes about 2 cups*

1 red onion, cut into 1-inch-thick rounds
1½ tablespoons olive oil
Salt and freshly ground black pepper
1 cucumber, peeled, seeded, and
    thinly sliced
2 tablespoons capers, drained
½ cup plain yogurt
1 tablespoon tahini
1 tablespoon fresh lemon juice
1 teaspoon minced garlic
¼ teaspoon ground cumin
¼ cup chopped fresh mint

1. If you will be grilling the onion, preheat a grill to medium-high.

2. Brush the onion slices with some of the olive oil, and season them lightly with salt and pepper. Grill them over medium-high heat (or cook them on a cast-iron grill pan on the stovetop), turning them once, until the slices are tender, about 10 minutes.

3. When the onion slices are cool enough to handle, chop them into ½-inch dice and place them in a bowl. Add the cucumber and capers, and stir to blend.

4. To make the sauce, combine the yogurt, the remaining olive oil, and the tahini, lemon juice, garlic, and cumin in a small bowl and whisk to blend. Stir in the mint, and season with salt and pepper to taste.

5. Add half of the sauce to the onion mixture, stirring to coat. Then add more dressing if desired. Serve immediately, or refrigerate the sauce, covered, for up to 5 days.

Vegetarian Three-Bean Chili

THIS CHILI IS SO HEARTY AND SATISFYING, you'll never miss the meat. Jalapeño peppers vary in heat intensity, so if you don't like your chili spicy, reduce the cayenne pepper to ¼ teaspoon. Although canned beans make this quicker to prepare, cooking your own from scratch is super-easy and eco-friendly, too. See page 422 for instructions; you'll need 1¾ cups cooked beans (6 ounces, or a scant 1 cup, uncooked) of each of the three varieties. *Serves 4*

2 tablespoons olive oil

About 1 cup diced yellow onion (¼-inch dice)

1 cup diced red bell pepper (¼-inch dice)

1 jalapeño pepper, seeded and finely chopped

1 tablespoon ground cumin

1 tablespoon dried oregano

1 teaspoon ground coriander

½ teaspoon cayenne pepper, or to taste

1½ teaspoons chili powder

1 cup Vegetable Stock (page 410), store-bought low-sodium vegetable broth, or water

1¾ cups cooked red kidney beans, rinsed and drained if canned

1¾ cups cooked white beans, rinsed and drained if canned

1¾ cups cooked black beans, rinsed and drained if canned

1 cup canned tomato puree

1 large can (28 ounces) diced tomatoes, with their juices

1½ cups fresh or frozen corn kernels (no need to thaw)

1 tablespoon salt, or to taste

Freshly ground black pepper, to taste

1. Heat the oil in a large stockpot or Dutch oven over medium heat. Add the onion, bell pepper, and jalapeño, and cook, stirring frequently, until the vegetables soften, 6 to 8 minutes.

2. Add the cumin, oregano, coriander, cayenne, and chili powder to the pot and cook, stirring constantly, for 1 minute to blend the spices. Then add the stock, all the beans, and the tomato puree, diced tomatoes, and corn. Cook over medium-low heat, stirring often to prevent the mixture from burning, until the chili thickens, 20 to 30 minutes. If the mixture seems too dry as it is cooking, stir in ½ cup water and cover the pot.

3. Season with the salt and pepper, and serve hot. The chili can be refrigerated, covered, for up to 5 days. Reheat over low heat or in the microwave to serve.

How to Conserve Virtual Water

Some food and manufactured goods may not look liquid, but they still "contain" the virtual water used to produce them. Virtual water takes into account the water used to grow plants, take care of and feed animals, and process goods to get them ready for market.

A good tip for conserving virtual water is to eat lower on the food chain: more plant-based foods, less meat. According to a recent article in *Discover* magazine,

it takes about 155 gallons of water on average to grow a pound of wheat. A pound of beef, however, can contain as much as 2,500 gallons of virtual water; a pound of chicken, 468 gallons. Using the calculator on Waterfootprint.org, a UNESCO-run website, we can determine the amount of virtual water used to produce just about everything: a cup of coffee is 37 gallons; an apple, 19 gallons; a banana, 27; a slice of bread, 10.

There is also virtual water in paper products and packaging. The amount varies according to what is being produced, but a good rule of thumb is to purchase products (such as paper towels and napkins) and packaging (such as cardboard and plastic) that have a high percentage of post-consumer recycled content (PCR). It generally takes much less water and energy to manufacture goods using recycled rather than new materials.

Curried Chickpeas

I LOVE DISHES THAT ARE FAST AND SIMPLE yet have a real depth of flavor. In this recipe, chickpeas are simmered in a tomato sauce that's been spiced up with the heat of ginger and curry. My favorite way to eat these is over brown rice and topped with a generous dollop of plain yogurt. Serve the chickpeas hot or at room temperature with some steamed vegetables, and you have a very satisfying and nutritious meal. ⟞⟝⟞⟝ *Serves 4*

2 tablespoons canola oil

1 small red onion, cut into ¼-inch dice (about 1 cup)

1½ tablespoons finely grated peeled fresh ginger

½ tablespoon minced garlic

1 tablespoon curry powder

3 cups cooked chickpeas (garbanzo beans; see box, page 422), rinsed and drained if canned

2 cups Myra's Heirloom Tomato Sauce (page 416), Quick Tomato Sauce (page 417), or good-quality store-bought marinara sauce

2 tablespoons chopped fresh flat-leaf parsley

1½ teaspoons salt

1. Heat the oil in a large skillet, preferably cast-iron, over medium heat. Add the onion, ginger, and garlic and cook, stirring frequently, until the onion is soft, 6 to 8 minutes. Add the curry powder and cook for another minute, stirring constantly.

2. Add the chickpeas and tomato sauce and cook, stirring occasionally, until the sauce has thickened, about 5 minutes.

3. Remove the skillet from the heat, and stir in the parsley and salt. Serve hot or at room temperature.

Eggplant Parmesan

HAD ALMOST FORGOTTEN about this classic, timeless dish until a summer trip to Italy a few years ago. It was served frequently there, as was a version using zucchini instead of eggplant. It does take a bit of time to cook the eggplant, but this step creates the special melt-in-your-mouth texture and is worth the effort. Whatever sauce you choose to pair with the eggplant, it should be light and fresh-tasting so that it doesn't overwhelm the delicate flavor of the vegetable. —— *Serves 6*

1 large eggplant (about 1¼ pounds),
   peeled or unpeeled

Kosher salt

⅔ cup unbleached all-purpose flour

Freshly ground black pepper

2 large eggs

1 tablespoon cold water

1 cup fine dry unseasoned bread crumbs

About 6 tablespoons olive oil

2½ cups Myra's Heirloom Tomato Sauce
   (page 416), Quick Tomato Sauce
   (page 417), or store-bought marinara
   sauce

20 fresh basil leaves, torn

1 cup freshly grated Parmesan cheese

1 tablespoon chopped fresh flat-leaf parsley

8 slices (about 7 ounces) provolone cheese,
   or ¾ cup grated provolone

1. Slice the eggplant into ¼-inch-thick rounds. Sprinkle both sides of the eggplant slices with about 2 tablespoons kosher salt, and set them aside to drain on a rack or in a colander for 30 minutes.

2. Using a clean kitchen towel, thoroughly blot the liquid and salt from the eggplant slices.

3. Spread the flour on a piece of parchment paper or on a flat plate,

LIVING GREEN

If you spend some time seeing how long it takes your oven to preheat to various temperatures, you'll save energy down the road by no longer preheating too far in advance. Most ovens will get to 350°F within 15 minutes, and newer ovens will heat up faster. No need to preheat it 30 minutes in advance and waste the heat!

season it with kosher salt and black pepper to taste, and stir to combine. Combine the eggs and the cold water in a small shallow bowl, and whisk to blend. Spread the bread crumbs on a piece of parchment paper or on a flat plate.

4. Position a rack in the middle of the oven and preheat the oven to 350°F.

5. Dip the eggplant slices in the seasoned flour, coating both sides lightly. Then dip the eggplant in the egg, coating both sides completely. Finally, dip the eggplant in the bread crumbs, pressing them lightly with dry fingers to ensure that the coating sticks. Set the breaded eggplant aside on a baking sheet.

6. Heat 3 tablespoons of the olive oil in a large skillet, preferably cast-iron, over medium-high heat. If you have two skillets, heat another 3 tablespoons oil in the second one and you can cook all of the eggplant simultaneously. Otherwise, when the oil is hot, add half of the breaded eggplant slices in a single layer, making sure not to crowd the skillet. Cook until the coating is lightly browned, about 2 minutes. Flip the slices over, and cook on the other side for 1 to 2 minutes. It is important to cook the eggplant only until it is barely crisp-tender; do not overcook it. Transfer the slices to a baking sheet lined with several layers of paper towels.

7. Add the remaining 3 tablespoons oil to the skillet and repeat with the remaining eggplant slices.

8. Arrange half of the eggplant in a 9-inch square or a 7 x 10-inch baking dish. If necessary, cut some of the slices to fill in the gaps so you create a single layer of eggplant without any large holes. Cover the eggplant with about 1 cup of the tomato sauce. Sprinkle half of the basil over the sauce, and cover with ½ cup of the grated Parmesan.

9. Arrange the remaining eggplant slices in over the Parmesan, cover

Eggplant, ripe and ready for picking.

with the remaining 1½ cups tomato sauce, and sprinkle with the remaining basil and the parsley. Cover with the remaining ½ cup Parmesan cheese. Top with the slices of provolone cheese, cutting the cheese as required to cover the entire dish (or scatter the grated provolone over the top).

10. Bake until the cheese melts and the sauce bubbles around the edges of the dish, 15 to 20 minutes. Let sit for 10 minutes before cutting and serving. In the unlikely event that you have some left over, it can be refrigerated, covered, for up to 3 days. Reheat it in a 350°F oven until hot, 15 to 20 minutes.

Note: For a change of pace, try this classic dish with zucchini: Cut 1¼ pounds medium-size zucchini lengthwise into ¼-inch-thick slices, and cook as described starting at Step 3 of the recipe. Be sure not to overcook the zucchini when sautéing it, as it will continue to cook as it drains on paper towels and while it bakes.

we are what we eat . . . and so is our planet

Honey retains the flavor of the flowers that bees have dined on. Beef from grass-fed animals has a different taste and nutrient profile than beef fattened on grain. And someone once told me about her goats getting into a patch of eucalyptus leaves and turning the evening's milk menthol-flavored! "We are what we eat" has become a cliché—to the point that it's sometimes the stuff jokes are made of. But if we really think about the intimate ways food affects our bodies, it's not such a laughing matter. Researchers have found pesticide residues in the urine of children who eat conventional produce; it disappeared three days after switching to organic fruits and vegetables. And diets heavy in processed foods that are loaded with sugar and trans fats have resulted in a countrywide crisis of obesity, heart disease, and diabetes.

I try to stay mindful of what's on my plate, for my own health and also the health of the planet. If I don't want chemical pesticides in my body, it makes perfect sense that I don't want them in the food I eat. And I don't want them in the air and water either. Eating organic is a great start, as is staying away from overly processed foods—especially those that have unpronounceable ingredients no one would stock in a family kitchen.

Roasted Cauliflower Tart

Roasted Cauliflower Tart

CREAMY WHITE CAULIFLOWER is available year round, and I'm always looking for new and interesting ways to cook it. This elegant, decadently rich tart certainly puts a new spin on a vegetable that's often unappreciated. Who knew that cauliflower could taste so sumptuous: roasted until golden brown and crispy, then combined with sweet caramelized onions in a rich cheesy custard. The cauliflower and onions can be prepared up to 2 days in advance of assembling the tart, and the pastry crust can be prebaked early in the day before you fill and bake the tart. The finished tart does not keep well, however, because if it sits too long the crust gets soggy (even with the blind baking step), so serve it the same day it's made. ⚬⚬⚬ **_Makes one 9-inch tart_**

1 small head of cauliflower (about 1 pound), separated into 1 inch florets (about 5 cups)

2 tablespoons truffle oil (see box, page 217) or olive oil

Sea salt and freshly ground black pepper

Flaky Multigrain Pie Crust dough for a single-crust pie (page 426), wrapped in parchment and refrigerated

Unbleached all-purpose flour, for rolling the dough

1 tablespoon Dijon mustard

2 tablespoons olive oil

1 large yellow onion, cut in half through the stem end and then cut crosswise into ⅛-inch-thick slices (about 3½ cups)

2 large eggs

1 cup mascarpone cheese

½ cup heavy (whipping) cream

¼ teaspoon freshly ground white pepper

Pinch of freshly grated nutmeg

1 cup (3½ ounces) shredded Gruyère cheese

⅔ cup (about 1½ ounces) freshly grated Parmesan cheese

1. Position a rack in the middle of the oven and preheat the oven to 425°F.

2. Place the cauliflower florets in a large bowl, add the truffle oil, and toss to coat. Transfer the florets to a rimmed baking sheet, arranging them so they don't touch one another, and season generously with sea salt and black pepper. Roast for 15 minutes. Then flip the florets with a spatula and continue cooking until the cauliflower is tender and browned, 15 to 20 minutes. Set the florets aside to cool.

3. Reduce the oven temperature to 375°F.

4. Remove the dough from the refrigerator and open the parchment paper to a flat rectangle. Let the dough sit at room temperature for 10 to 20 minutes to soften. (If the

THE BASICS

Blind Baking

"Blind baking" refers to the preliminary baking of a pastry crust before it is filled. The crust is usually lined with parchment or aluminum foil, and then filled with dried beans or ceramic pie weights to prevent it from blistering and puffing. The beans and paper are removed after 15 or 20 minutes, and the crust is returned to the oven for a few more minutes of baking, until it dries slightly and begins to brown. Blind baking is specified when a pie shell will be filled with a liquid mixture, like a quiche or custard; the prebaking prevents the crust from being soggy and raw tasting.

dough is too cold or firm, it will crack when you try to roll it out.)

5. Lightly dust a rolling pin and the top surface of the dough with flour. Roll the dough into an 11-inch round, and transfer it to a 9-inch tart pan with a removable bottom. Line the tart shell with parchment, and fill it with pie weights or dried beans. Place the tart pan on a rimmed baking sheet and bake for 20 minutes.

6. Remove the baking sheet from the oven and lift out the paper and pie weights. Lightly prick the bottom of the pastry with a fork, and return the baking sheet to the oven. Bake the pastry until it dries slightly and begins to take on a faint color, 8 to 10 minutes.

Nestled within their greens sit firm white heads of cauliflower.

7. Remove the baking sheet from the oven, set the tart pan on a wire rack, and allow the crust to cool slightly, about 10 minutes. Then carefully brush the bottom and sides of the pastry shell with the mustard. Set it aside at room temperature.

8. Heat a large skillet, preferably cast-iron, over medium-low heat. When it is warm, add the olive oil. Add the onion slices and cook, stirring frequently, until they soften and caramelize, 30 to 40 minutes. Be patient and do this slowly: The onions should be golden, not brown.

9. While the onions are cooking, thinly slice the roasted cauliflower florets and set them aside.

10. Transfer the caramelized onions to the prebaked tart shell and spread them out in a thin layer. Top with the sliced roasted cauliflower. Transfer the tart pan to a rimmed baking sheet.

11. Combine the eggs, mascarpone, cream, white pepper, and nutmeg in a medium-size bowl, and whisk to combine. Stir in the Gruyère. Pour the mixture over the cauliflower and onions in the tart shell, and sprinkle the Parmesan over the top. Bake until the tart is puffed, set in the center, and golden brown, 30 to 40 minutes.

12. Transfer the tart to a wire rack and let it cool for at least 15 minutes before serving.

CHAPTER 6

SIDE DISHES

Sides with Star Quality

WHEN I'M THINKING GREEN, IT'S OFTEN THE SMALL THINGS I DO over and over that really add up to the greatest payoff for the environment. In the kitchen, side dishes provide the perfect opportunity and flexibility to put many of my eco-actions into practice. Vegetable side dishes are one of the easiest ways to eat with the seasons. And this chapter has enough variety—from summer's bounty of crops to winter's hearty choices—to inspire you to choose your ingredients when they are at their freshest. Fruits and vegetables in season are generally less expensive and more flavorful.

Just seeing produce at its peak of freshness and abundance can inspire you to try something you've never tasted before, like kale or baby bok choy. You'll soon be looking forward to what each season has to offer rather than lamenting the scarcity of certain out-of-season foods.

Wonderful vegetable dishes are included here, many of which can be "upsized" to entrées for a vegetarian meal. I think our choices for winter vegetables are particular standouts. Many people think winter is the season of scarcity, but I find this to be quite the contrary. Try our Cauliflower "Couscous," which has the texture and versatility of couscous but is all vegetable—and deliciously different. Serving this dish is a wonderful way to both cut calories and put an extra serving of vegetables into any meal. And if you haven't eaten turnips lately, I think you'll be pleasantly surprised by the Creamy Baby Turnips—a very tasty alternative to mashed potatoes.

I'm always looking for ways to cut down my family's meat

Cauliflower—delicious in the couscous-like dish on page 210.

consumption without everyone feeling deprived, and eating a lot of vegetable side dishes is a satisfying way to do just that. I often aim for a plate that's about half veggies, a quarter whole grains, and a quarter protein. Eating this way is delicious and healthy for both people and the planet.

Sometimes I spend most of my cooking time creating a special side dish, and then quickly grill a piece of fish or a chicken breast for a wonderful meal. I especially love our Summer Squash with Tomatoes and Basil served with halibut or chicken that's been cooked quickly and simply in a cast-iron skillet with just olive oil, salt, and pepper.

Side dishes are ideal for using leftovers. Drew's Crispy Pasta turns cold pasta into a yummy side dish. Or try our Fried Brown Rice with any combination of cooked vegetables, meat, or tofu that's stashed in your refrigerator. This is a perfect technique for turning leftovers into a new dish. Using up the many odds and ends in my fridge feels good because it's economical, good for the environment, and delicious.

Summer Squash with Tomatoes and Basil (page 230)

Kathy's Gingered Bok Choy

REW'S STEPMOTHER, KATHY GOODMAN, is a terrific cook, and the recipes she contributed to my first book, *Food to Live By*, garnered rave reviews. In this recipe of Kathy's, I really like the way the ginger and olive oil create a fragrant broth that delicately flavors the baby bok choy. The result is an exceptionally light, tasty, and healthful dish in which the olive oil takes the place of butter to add body and richness. Kathy suggests serving this vegetable with Seared Salmon with Chipotle-Lime Butter (page 136) or any grilled fish. ~~~ *Serves 4*

1 piece fresh ginger (4 inches), peeled
    and julienned
2 tablespoons olive oil
1 teaspoon salt
2½ pounds baby bok choy, rinsed, trimmed,
    and cut into ½-inch pieces
2 tablespoons tamari or soy sauce
    (see sidebar, page 180)

1. Place the ginger, olive oil, salt, and 1 cup water in a large pot. Cover the pot and bring to a simmer over low heat. Simmer for 5 minutes.

2. Add the bok choy and cook, covered, until it is tender, 5 to 7 minutes.

3. Drain the bok choy mixture and transfer it to a warmed serving dish. Sprinkle with the tamari, and serve immediately.

Asian Broccoli, Asparagus, and Shiitake Stir-Fry

HE SECRET TO SUCCESS FOR ANY STIR-FRY RECIPE is to make sure you have all the ingredients measured and ready to go before you heat your pan. I love this health-conscious combination of broccoli florets, tender asparagus, and earthy shiitakes, with its lively glaze of ginger, garlic, and tamari. Serve it as a side dish for roast chicken or grilled fish, or over brown rice for a tasty lunch. ~~~ *Serves 4*

2 teaspoons canola oil

2 teaspoons toasted sesame oil

½ cup finely diced yellow onion

1 tablespoon grated peeled fresh ginger

1 teaspoon minced garlic

2½ cups broccoli florets

6 ounces (15 medium) asparagus spears,
   peeled and cut on the diagonal into
   1½-inch lengths (about 1½ cups)

5 ounces shiitake mushroom caps,
   cut into bite-size pieces (2 cups)

2 tablespoons tamari or soy sauce
   (see sidebar, page 180)

1 tablespoon unseasoned rice vinegar

Salt and freshly ground black pepper

1. Heat the canola and sesame oils in a large skillet over medium heat. Add the onion, ginger, and garlic, and cook, stirring frequently, until the onion softens and the mixture is fragrant, 3 minutes.

2. Add the broccoli florets and ⅓ cup water, cover the skillet, and cook for 3 minutes. Then stir in the asparagus, mushrooms, and 3 tablespoons water. Cover the skillet and cook until the vegetables are crisp-tender, about 4 minutes. If the mixture is too dry, add another tablespoon or two of water.

3. Add the tamari and vinegar and cook, uncovered, stirring constantly, until the sauce thickens and glazes the vegetables, 2 to 3 minutes. Season with salt and pepper to taste, and serve hot.

warming up to the microwave

When microwave ovens started gaining popularity in the '80s, I remained suspicious. This technology seemed too good to be true, and I was worried that it had some hidden health risks. Now, decades later, most health experts assure us that microwaves are safe to use, as long as we don't cook or reheat in plastic. And since learning that microwaves help save energy as well as time, I've embraced them wholeheartedly. Microwaves are an especially good choice when cooking for one or two people. A great example is corn on the cob—one of my favorite summertime foods. I often cook a single ear for myself in the microwave (husk and all) for 2 minutes, and when I remove the husk, the corn is perfect. If I had cooked that same ear of corn in a pot of boiling water, I would have waited longer for my food and used 12 times more energy. I would also have used a significant amount of water to boil the corn and more to wash the pot afterward. Another great example is a baked potato.

The microwave takes 5 minutes, while baking in an oven takes 50 minutes and uses 20 times more energy.

Using the microwave also makes environmental sense when you are reheating small portions of food cooked in big batches—like soup, stew, or hot cereal. You're eating something homemade and healthy, saving a lot of energy, and washing only the bowl you would have used anyway. A great time-*and* energy-saver, the microwave is a true eco-hero!

Garlic Roasted Broccolette

Garlic Roasted Broccolette

ROASTING IS A SIMPLE METHOD that really brings out the sugars and flavors of many vegetables, including broccolette. If you aren't familiar with this vegetable, you're in for a treat. Broccolette, which is also known as broccolini and baby broccoli, is actually a cross between broccoli and *gai lan* (Chinese broccoli). I love it because unlike broccoli, the stems are long, thin, and tender. Tossed with slivers of garlic, a splash of olive oil, and a sprinkling of sea salt, the preparation couldn't be easier. Oven-roasting makes the garlic soft and sweet and browns the broccolette tops lightly, but leaves the stems crisp-tender. ⟶ *Serves 4*

2 bunches broccolette (see box, page 169), rinsed and patted dry
10 garlic cloves, peeled and thickly sliced
2 tablespoons extra-virgin olive oil
Sea salt

1. Position a rack in the middle of the oven and preheat the oven to 375°F.

2. Cut off and discard the bottom inch of the broccolette stems. If any of the stems are thicker than a pencil, slit them lengthwise, starting from the bottom and cutting upward for 2 or 3 inches. (This will allow the thicker stems to cook in the same amount of time as the thinner ones.)

3. Place the broccolette on a rimmed baking sheet, and add the garlic slices and olive oil. Using your hands, toss to coat all the vegetables. Spread the broccolette out in a single layer on the baking sheet, and sprinkle with sea salt to taste. Roast for 10 minutes.

4. Stir the vegetables with a spatula, and continue roasting for another 10 minutes. Stir again, and roast for 5 more minutes.

5. Check to see if the broccolette is tender, browned, and crisp. If it is not, continue cooking for up to another 5 minutes. Serve hot.

THE BASICS
Roasting Vegetables

Roasting vegetables at a high temperature really brings out their sweetness. This cooking method works exceptionally well with all root vegetables, as well as with Brussels sprouts, fennel, cauliflower, and onions. Cut the vegetables into a uniform size, toss with olive oil, and season with salt and pepper. Spread in a single layer on a rimmed baking sheet and roast at 400°F, stirring occasionally, until the vegetables are tender and lightly caramelized.

recycling basics

We are all truly earthbound in the sense that we share a bountiful yet finite planet. There is no "away" when we throw our garbage out. One way or another it stays on our planet. When we consider dealing with waste, we have three broad options: reuse it, recycle it, or store it in a landfill. Recycling makes sense for the environment, but according to the Environmental Protection Agency, our national recycling rate is just 30 percent. Recycling isn't hard to do once you develop a system. And it feels good to make a difference, both locally and globally.

Not all waste management facilities have the same recycling capabilities or requirements, so contact your local recycling center for information. To find the recycling center nearest you, call 1-800-CLEANUP. Or you can go to www.earth911.com and use their search function.

Here are some kitchen items you can recycle:

Paper and Cardboard Packaging

This material is highly recyclable, and most curbside collectors are happy to take it—just remember to keep it dry and clean. Many recycling centers now accept paperboard milk and juice cartons as well; ask locally. Plastic- or waxy-coated cardboard, and wet or greasy cardboard, such as pizza boxes, cannot be recycled because it will clog the sorting machines.

Do not include carbon paper, stickers, plastic-laminated paper, plastic-laminated cardboard, fast-food wrappers made from plastic, dirty or food-stained paper tissues or napkins.

Plastic

Plastic can be recycled to make many diverse products, but recycling centers vary in the types of plastic they accept, depending on the market for them. Check with your local recycling center. Also, when shopping for plastic goods, please look for ones that are recyclable and/or are made with recycled content. Plastic goods are assigned different numbers to help identify them for recycling.

◆ #1 (PET) and #2 (HDPE) are the plastics that are recycled the most. Plastic bottles are made from these types of plastic, as are many yogurt, cottage cheese, and sour cream tubs.

◆ #3 PVC, #4 LDPE, #5 PP, #6 PS, and #7 are the least recycled plastics. They aren't any less recyclable; it's just that there's little demand for them. And it often costs recycling companies more to go through the expense of sorting them out than they can recoup from selling them.

Most plastic grocery bags are made from #4 LDPE, and many grocery stores have bins where customers can drop off used plastic bags for recycling. An even better option is to keep a stash of them in the car and reuse them when you go grocery shopping.

Some yogurt, cottage cheese, margarine, and vitamin containers are made from #5 PP plastic. It is also used in food wraps and bottle tops. Few curbside recycling companies accept #5 PP plastic, so it's difficult to recycle. Ask your local recycling company about your best options.

Styrofoam (polystyrene) cups, food trays, egg cartons, and coffee cup lids are made from #6 PS plastic. Some recycling centers now accept polystyrene for recycling, although this is fairly rare. Hard plastic goods, such as five- and ten-gallon water bottles, sunglasses, DVD cases, signs and displays, and certain food containers have traditionally not been recycled.

Glass

Glass can be recycled almost an indefinite number of times, and there is a high demand for recycled glass.

Some recycling centers ask you to sort glass according to color; most, however, do the sorting at the facility. Paper labels can be left on the glass.

Aluminum Foil and Foil Packaging

These are important to recycle, but they must be clean. Check with your local facility. Aluminum foil can be reprocessed into mechanical components, such as engine parts.

Aluminum Cans

Aluminum is a highly recycled material and can be reused an indefinite number of times. Some recycling centers request that the cans not be crushed flat. Check locally.

Steel Cans

Steel is a highly recycled material. The steel industry relies on recycled steel scrap to save both natural resources and energy. To check a can for steel, use a magnet. If the magnet sticks to your can, the can is made with steel. If you can, rinse food cans and remove labels before recycling.

Closing the Loop

It's important to remember that simply putting items in your recycling bin doesn't guarantee that they will actually be recycled and used for something else. Purchasing recycled products completes the recycling loop. By purchasing products with a high percentage of post-consumer recycled content (PCR), you are creating a demand for more environmentally sound products, which in turn encourages manufacturers to meet that demand by using more and more recycled materials. (See the box on page 291 for more information about PCR paper products.)

Roasted Butternut, Fennel, and Cranberries

ROASTING IS A TERRIFIC TECHNIQUE for intensifying the flavor of vegetables, creating crisp, golden brown exteriors and moist, meltingly tender insides. Here I've combined some favorite ingredients—vitamin-rich butternut squash, sweet fennel, tart apples, and dried cranberries—in a rustic dish that epitomizes autumn. After a quick toss in maple syrup–laced olive oil and a sprinkling of fresh herbs, the mixture is roasted in a hot oven to coax out the sweetness and flavor of the vegetables. For best results, cut the vegetables in uniform-size pieces to ensure even cooking. Winter vegetables such as carrots, parsnips, rutabagas, cipollini onions, shallots, and yams would also work well in this dish. Pancetta (Italian bacon) adds a rich, smoky-salty flavor that complements the vegetables, but this ingredient is optional and can be eliminated if you prefer a vegetarian or vegan dish. Try chopping some of our Savory Nut Mix (page 431) and sprinkling it over the medley as a garnish—it makes a tasty addition, contributing crunchy texture and another layer of complexity to the dish. ⚬⚬⚬⚬ *Serves 8 to 10*

3½ pounds butternut squash, peeled, halved lengthwise, seeded, and cut into ½-inch dice (about 6 cups)

3 large fennel bulbs, halved lengthwise, cored, and cut into ½-inch dice (about 3 cups), fronds reserved

3 crisp apples such as Fuji or Granny Smith, peeled, cored, and cut into ½-inch dice (about 2 cups)

¾ cup dried cranberries, preferably organic

½ cup (4 ounces) finely minced pancetta (optional)

2 tablespoons extra-virgin olive oil

1 tablespoon pure maple syrup

1 tablespoon fresh thyme leaves

1 tablespoon chopped reserved fennel fronds or fennel pollen (see sidebar, page 92)

Coarse sea salt or kosher salt and freshly ground black pepper

1. Position a rack in the center of the oven and preheat the oven to 400°F.

2. Place the squash, fennel, apples, cranberries, and pancetta, if using, on a rimmed baking sheet.

3. Place the olive oil and maple syrup in a small bowl, and whisk to combine.

4. Pour the oil mixture over the vegetables and toss to coat. Add the thyme and fennel fronds, and season

Roasted Butternut, Fennel, and Cranberries

with coarse salt and black pepper to taste. Spread the mixture out. Do not crowd the vegetables as this will cause them to steam rather than brown—use two pans or cook in batches if necessary.

5. Roast the vegetables until they are lightly caramelized and tender, 30 to 45 minutes. As they are roasting, shake the baking sheet

or stir the vegetables occasionally so they develop a crisp crust on each side.

6. Transfer the vegetables to a warmed platter and serve immediately.

7. Refrigerate leftovers, covered, for up to 3 days. Reheat over low heat or in a microwave before serving.

THE BASICS

Sorting Out Salts

Salt is an indispensable condiment that heightens and harmonizes the flavors of food. It comes in a variety of forms, shapes, and colors, each with its own attributes and uses. In my recipes, I often specify coarse sea salt or kosher salt. These salts have a clean, slightly mineral flavor with no lingering aftertaste. Because most common table salts (what we find in salt shakers across America) contain additives like iodine, or chemicals that act as flow agents to prevent caking, I prefer to use sea salt or kosher salt to avoid any harsh, iodine flavors.

__Kosher salt__ has large, irregular-shaped grains. Chefs favor these coarse flakes because their size allows them to control how much they are sprinkling over food. Kosher salt is either sold flaked

or coarsely ground, and comes in boxes. Look for brands without any anti-caking additives.

__Sea salt,__ in its simplest form, is created when ocean waters flood shallow beds along coastlines. The water evaporates and leaves large salt crystals behind. The varying complexity of the different waters and minerals from the surrounding land lend unique flavor and color to these flaky salts. Specialty sea salts, such as Maldon, Fleur de Sel, Sel Gris, or Hawaiian black salt, tend to be more expensive than other kinds of salt, so are best used as finishing salts, sprinkled on dishes just before serving. These salts are not used for baking because they don't dissolve quickly, are less uniform in shape, and may have a more predominant mineral flavor.

Carrot Risotto

FRESH CARROT JUICE gives this unusual risotto a beautiful color and an intriguing hint of sweetness. Carrots are incredibly good for you, and although juicing them removes the fiber, you're still getting all the carotenoids, vitamins, and potassium. This risotto makes a good side dish for roast chicken or fish, taking the place of potatoes or conventional rice. If you don't have an extraction juicer, use fresh unsweetened carrot juice, which is available in the produce department at most markets. ⎯⎯ *Serves 4*

2 tablespoons olive oil

1 medium yellow onion, cut into ¼-inch dice (about 1½ cups)

1 teaspoon minced garlic

1 cup Arborio or Carnaroli rice

⅓ cup dry white vermouth or dry white wine

2½ cups fresh carrot juice

About 1 cup Chicken Wing Stock (page 403), Vegetable Stock (page 410), or store-bought low-sodium chicken or vegetable broth

1 tablespoon fresh lemon juice

1 tablespoon butter

1 tablespoon fresh thyme leaves or chopped fresh dill, or 1 teaspoon dried thyme or dried dill (optional)

Coarse (kosher) salt and freshly ground black pepper

1. Heat a large skillet, preferably nonstick, over medium heat. When it is hot, add the oil and the onion and cook, stirring frequently, until the onion softens and becomes translucent, 7 to 10 minutes.

2. Add the garlic and rice to the skillet and cook, stirring frequently, for another 2 minutes, taking care not to burn the garlic. Then add the vermouth and cook, stirring frequently, until the liquid evaporates, about 5 minutes.

3. Begin adding the carrot juice, ½ cup at a time, stirring frequently and cooking until it is absorbed before adding the next ½ cup. This should take 30 to 35 minutes in all. When you've incorporated all the juice, add ½ cup of the stock and stir it in. At this point the risotto may be done. The rice should be tender but still have a bit of firmness, and the risotto should be creamy, not dry. Add more stock and cook further as needed to attain this consistency.

4. Remove the skillet from the heat and stir in the lemon juice, butter, and thyme if using. Season with coarse salt and black pepper to taste, and serve immediately.

Cauliflower "Couscous"

THIS IS A DELICIOUS, HEALTHY, AND UNUSUAL WAY to prepare cauliflower. The cooking technique borrows from risotto, but the dish resembles couscous in appearance. The cauliflower is chopped into small pieces and slow-stirred with additions of hot stock, a technique that ensures a creamy texture but still maintains a bit of chew. Just about any diced vegetable or fresh herb can be added to the recipe, so use your imagination and clean out your refrigerator! The cauliflower "couscous" can be served either as a vegetable or as a low-carb substitute for rice or potatoes. —— *Serves 4 to 6*

1 head of cauliflower (1¼ pounds), cut into
    ¾-inch florets (about 4 cups)
2 tablespoons extra-virgin olive oil
1 cup finely sliced leeks (white and light
    green parts), rinsed well
3 cloves garlic, peeled and minced
2 cups Chicken Wing Stock (page 403),
    Vegetable Stock (page 410), or store-
    bought low-sodium chicken or vegetable
    broth, heated
1 large carrot, peeled and cut into ¼-inch
    dice
2 small zucchini, cut into ¼-inch dice (about
    2 cups)
¾ cup freshly grated Parmesan or Pecorino
    Romano cheese
2 tablespoons minced fresh flat-leaf parsley
Salt and freshly ground black pepper

1. Place half of the cauliflower florets in a food processor and pulse until they are chopped into small "grains." (Do not overprocess, or the vegetable will turn to mush. You want the cauliflower "grains" to resemble rice. Alternatively, you can finely chop the cauliflower by hand.) Transfer the cauliflower to a bowl and repeat with the remaining florets.

2. Heat the olive oil in a large skillet over medium heat. When the oil is hot, add the leeks and cook, stirring frequently, until they soften, about 4 minutes. Add the garlic and cook, stirring frequently, for 1 minute.

3. Add the cauliflower and cook, stirring frequently, until the mixture is warm to the touch, about 2 minutes. Add 1 cup of the chicken stock and cook, stirring frequently, until the chicken stock is absorbed, about 10 minutes.

4. Meanwhile, bring a small pan of water, covered, to a boil over high heat. Add the diced carrot and cook for 3 minutes. Drain, and set the carrot aside.

5. Add the remaining 1 cup stock, the zucchini, and the blanched carrots to the cauliflower, cover the skillet, and cook until the vegetables are crisp-tender, about 5 minutes. Remove the cover and cook until almost all of the stock has been absorbed, 3 to 5 minutes.

6. Stir in the Parmesan and parsley. Season with salt and pepper to taste, and serve hot.

Celeriac and Potato Mash

CELERIAC, OR CELERY ROOT AS IT IS ALSO KNOWN, is a homely gnarled root that is prized in Europe but little known in this country. It tastes like a cross between parsley and celery. Despite its name, it is not the root of common stalk celery; rather, it is cultivated from a special variety of celery. Celeriac is delicious both raw and cooked, imparting a refreshing clean flavor to salads, soups, and stews. Serve it with roasted meat and poultry, as either a vegetable side or as a substitute for potatoes. Partner it with potatoes, as in this recipe, for a wonderful combination. ⁓ *Serves 6*

2 pounds celeriac, peeled and cut into ½-inch pieces (about 4½ cups)

2 pounds Yukon Gold potatoes, peeled and cut into ¾-inch pieces (about 4½ cups)

Salt

4 tablespoons (½ stick) butter, at room temperature

¼ cup heavy (whipping) cream

Freshly ground black pepper

Sweet paprika, for garnish (optional)

1. Place the celeriac and potatoes in a large pot. Add 1 teaspoon salt and enough water to cover them by 1 inch. Bring to a boil, covered, over high heat. Then reduce the heat to medium-low and simmer until the vegetables are fork-tender, 15 to 20 minutes.

2. Drain the celeriac and potatoes, reserving about 1 cup of the cooking liquid. Return the vegetables to the pot and place it over medium heat for 1 to 2 minutes to dry them a bit.

3. Remove the pot from the heat and add the butter. Mash with a potato masher, adding the cream and as much of the reserved cooking liquid as needed to obtain the desired consistency. Season with salt and pepper to taste.

4. If necessary, reheat the mash over low heat. Serve hot, sprinkled with the paprika if desired.

TIP

Once peeled or cut, the flesh of a potato can discolor. The speed with which this occurs varies with variety, but discoloration doesn't affect the taste of the potato. To prevent this from happening, you can immerse peeled or cut potatoes in a bowl of ice water for up to 2 hours until you are ready to cook them.

food miles: why the carbon footprint of your food isn't always as simple as measuring from point A to point B

The term "food miles" refers to the distance food travels from farm to plate. Now that we are able to bring greens grown in Arizona to New Yorkers who are hungry for fresh salads in January, many people are eating a more healthful diet. But there are also the carbon emissions from these road miles to consider. In the United States, the most frequently cited statistic is that food travels an average of 1,500 miles from farm to consumer, so food miles definitely matter.

What troubles me is the assumption by some that how far food has traveled is the most important determinant of food's ecological impact, when in fact *how* our food is produced, and *what* we choose to eat, often have a much bigger effect on the environment. Another question that's important to ask is "Are all food miles created equal?" Food miles tell you only the distance a food has traveled. This figure doesn't tell you how much fuel per unit is used for transportation—such as gallons of diesel consumed per pound of fruit or vegetables transported. It's easy to understand that people traveling 100 miles by mass transit share with their co-travelers the total amount of carbon emissions it took to get them to where they're going. By contrast, a single person traveling 100 miles in a car is responsible for the total amount of carbon emissions it takes to reach the destination. But this truth is often overlooked when it comes to food-mile assumptions.

For example, imagine someone purchasing an apple in Manhattan who is faced with the choice between a local conventionally grown apple from Westmoreland, New York, and an organically grown apple from Wenatchee, Washington. In food miles the calculation is simple: 250 versus 2,750. But the person choosing the apple might not consider the gallons of fuel per unit used to bring that apple to market. The apple from Washington state may have traveled across the country in a class VIII refrigerated truck packed with 30 pallets, or a total of 94,080 apples. The truck gets 6.5 miles per gallon, so it uses 423 gallons to bring the apples to market. That's 0.0045 gallons per piece of fruit, or 1 gallon for every 222 apples.

Let's assume that the local New York apple traveled on a 10-foot flatbed truck with 2 pallets containing 6,272 apples, and the truck gets 8.5 miles per gallon. The 30 gallons used by the flatbed truck sound like a lot less than the 423 consumed traveling from Washington until you consider the fuel per apple. The New York fruit arrives at market responsible for 0.0048 gallons per apple, or 1 gallon for every 208 apples delivered.

Based on these variables, the carbon emissions of the Washington apple are slightly less than the local apple. Add to this that the Washington apple was organically produced, whereas the one from New York was conventionally produced, and the ecological gap is much larger in favor of the Washington apple. When it comes to fresh produce, I believe local *and* organic is often the best choice (see Joys of Eating in Season, page 30). But, I'm concerned when I hear recommendations for choosing nonorganic local produce over organic produce because it will reduce your carbon footprint. Choosing organic provides so many environmental and health benefits that I believe advocating local above all else is doing consumers and the planet a disservice.

Another oversimplification of just counting food miles is the assumption that all agricultural land can be equally productive, thus energy efficient. In fact the soil, temperature, rainfall, and sunlight of different regions have a direct impact on the amount of energy, land, and agricultural inputs needed to produce crops.

So how can you reduce the carbon footprint of the food you eat? It has been substantiated that eating lower on the food chain yields a much bigger environmental benefit than just buying local. A 2008 Carnegie Mellon University study reported that if you reduced your food miles to zero, you would cut associated greenhouse-gas emissions by roughly the equivalent of driving a car 1,000 fewer miles over the course of a year. By comparison, if you replaced red meat and dairy with chicken, fish, or eggs for only one day per week, you would save the equivalent of driving 760 miles per year. And going vegetarian only one day a week would be like driving 1,160 fewer miles during the year. The study proposes that a dietary shift can be a much more effective way to lower an average household's food-related carbon footprint than buying local, and it's a much more attainable goal.

We should consider the impact of food miles, but not as our sole yardstick for protecting the environment. There are many good reasons to buy local organic produce, but I hate to think that someone would forgo eating fresh vegetables and fruits during the winter because of their commitment to reducing food miles, choosing instead something that was less healthy for the planet and their bodies. Food miles is an oversimplified yet very emotional issue for many people, and it presents a good example of how important it is to look at environmental issues from many different angles. What I've come to understand is like a well-varied diet, local food and food shipped longer distances can each have a place in a menu that's healthful for people and the planet.

A baby greens harvester works alongside a flatbed truck that will transport the greens quickly for processing.

Green Beans with Shiitakes and Bok Choy served over buckwheat noodles

Green Beans with Shiitakes and Bok Choy

FRESH, CRISP STRING BEANS are one of my favorite vegetables, especially during the summer, when I can pick them fresh out of my garden. My family loves green ones, yellow ones, purple ones, and Romanos, and we frequently enjoy fresh beans in some fashion (often raw). This recipe combines tender green beans with two other terrific vegetables—shiitake mushrooms and baby bok choy. Sesame, ginger, and tamari create a light and delicious sauce. The bright green hue of the beans does not last very long because the vinegar leaches the color, so for best results, serve this stir-fry hot off the stove. For a main course, serve the vegetables over soba (buckwheat) noodles or brown rice.

Serves 6 to 8

1 pound tender green beans, trimmed

Salt

1 tablespoon plain sesame oil (see sidebar, page 25)

1 tablespoon canola oil

1½ tablespoons minced shallot

1 tablespoon finely grated peeled fresh ginger

1½ teaspoons minced garlic

4 cups thinly sliced shiitake mushroom caps (about 8 ounces)

3 small heads baby bok choy, trimmed and sliced into ½-inch-wide ribbons (4 cups)

3 tablespoons tamari or soy sauce (see sidebar, page 180)

1 tablespoon unseasoned rice vinegar

2 tablespoons sesame seeds, toasted (see box, page 31)

1. Fill a large bowl with cold water and ice, and set it aside.

2. Bring a large covered pot of water to a boil over high heat. Add the beans and 1 teaspoon salt, and cook until the beans are just crisp-tender, 4 to 5 minutes. Immediately drain the beans in a colander, then plunge them into the bowl of ice water to stop the cooking. Drain the beans again and set aside.

3. Heat the sesame and canola oils in a large skillet over medium-high heat until hot and shimmering. Add the shallot, ginger, garlic, shiitakes, and bok choy. Cook, stirring constantly, until the mushrooms have softened slightly and the ginger is fragrant, 2 to 3 minutes. Then reduce the heat to medium-low and add the drained beans, tamari, and vinegar. Cook, stirring constantly, until the beans are hot, about 3 minutes.

4. Remove the pan from the heat, stir in the sesame seeds, and serve hot.

THE BASICS

Parboiling

To parboil is to partially cook food by boiling it briefly in water, then plunging it in ice water to stop the cooking. Foods that are parboiled can be added to quick-cooking ingredients at the last minute. Parboiling ensures that all the ingredients will finish cooking at the same time.

Prepping Kale

To prepare kale, strip the leaves from the tough central stems by folding the leaves in half lengthwise and then tearing, snipping, or slicing the stems off. (Cut into small pieces, the stems can be added to soups, stocks, or stir-fry dishes.) Stack several leaves together, and slice or roughly chop. As a rule, 1 pound will yield about 12 cups of chopped kale. Like most greens, kale is composed largely of water, so it shrinks considerably when heated.

Dinosaur kale

Truffled Kale Casserole

KALE MAY WELL BE THE HUMBLEST OF GREENS, dismissed by many who perceive it to be bitter, but this preparation is sure to convert those who doubt its charms. We like cooking with dino kale (also known variously as Lacinato, dinosaur, *cavolo nero*, or Tuscan kale) because its dark green leaves are tender and sweet, but any variety of kale will taste terrific in this preparation. The earthy, rich flavor and aroma of truffle oil elevate this rustic green to new heights. Add a layer of nutty Gruyère cheese and a crisp topping of panko crumbs, and you have a vegetable dish that will have everyone begging for seconds.

—— Serves 4

4 tablespoons olive oil

1 medium yellow onion, halved lengthwise, then thinly sliced crosswise

2 large garlic cloves, finely minced

1 pound kale, center ribs removed, leaves chopped (about 12 cups lightly packed)

⅓ cup Chicken Wing Stock (page 403), Vegetable Stock (page 410), store-bought low-sodium chicken or vegetable broth, or water

1 cup panko (Japanese-style bread crumbs; see sidebar, page 134)

1 tablespoon minced fresh tarragon

1 tablespoon white or black truffle oil (see box, facing page)

Salt and freshly ground black pepper

1½ cups (5 ounces) grated Gruyère or Comté cheese

1. Heat 2 tablespoons of the olive oil in a large skillet over medium heat. When the oil is hot, add the onion and cook, stirring frequently, until softened, about 8 minutes. Add the garlic and cook, stirring constantly, for 2 minutes. Add the kale and chicken stock, cover the skillet, and cook until the kale is tender, 10 to 20 minutes depending on the variety of kale.

2. While the kale is cooking, position a rack in the middle of the oven and preheat the oven to 350°F.

3. Meanwhile, heat the remaining 2 tablespoons olive oil in another skillet and stir in the panko. Cook over moderate heat, stirring often and watching closely so that the crumbs do not burn, until the panko is lightly golden, about 5 minutes. Set aside.

4. When the kale is tender, remove the skillet from the heat and stir in the tarragon and truffle oil. Season with salt and pepper to taste. Transfer the mixture to a 1-quart ceramic or glass baking dish. Sprinkle the cheese over the kale, and then top with the panko. Bake until the crumbs are golden and the cheese has melted, 20 to 25 minutes. Serve hot.

Beautiful, curly leaves of kale.

THE BASICS

Truffle Oil

Truffles are rare culinary delicacies that grow beneath the roots of certain hardwood trees. The best white and black truffles are unearthed by pigs and dogs in Italy and France, and they command exorbitant prices during their short seasons. Truffle oil is a modern culinary ingredient, popular with chefs and diners alike, that is intended to impart the flavor and aroma of truffles to a dish.

Most truffle oils are not, in fact, made from actual truffles; they are a synthetic product that combines one or more aromatic odorants found in real truffles with an olive oil base. Despite the fact that commercial truffle oil is not an extraction of pressed truffles, it is a wonderfully fragrant oil that adds an intense, earthy perfume and distinctive trufflelike flavor to dishes. Fresh truffles are very costly, but the oil, which costs a fraction of the price of the real fungi, stands in quite nicely. Truffle oil should be used sparingly, as a little goes a long way. Try it drizzled over pasta dishes and soups, or brush it over vegetables before roasting them.

Both black and white truffle oils are now widely available. The black oil has a slightly more pungent aroma than the white, and is a bit less expensive. Store truffle oil in a cool, dark place for up to 6 months. If stored for long periods, even high-quality truffle oil will lose its aroma and flavor, so it's best to purchase the oil in small quantities.

Black truffles

Herbed Sugar Snap Peas

I F YOU'RE LOOKING FOR A QUICK VEGETABLE DISH with lots of flavor, sugar snap peas are a great starting point. Crisp and juicy, both the edible pods and the peas inside are very sweet. Brief cooking is the best way to handle sugar snaps so they retain their signature crunch and color. Here we suggest a preliminary blanching, followed by a sauté in butter. Tarragon, dill, and mint partner nicely with sugar snaps; add any herbs in Step 4 with the chives. ⎯⎯ *Serves 4*

Sugar snap peas

Sea salt
1 pound sugar snap peas, strings removed,
    if needed
1 tablespoon butter
2 tablespoons finely minced shallots
2 tablespoons snipped fresh chives
Grated zest of 1 lemon

1. Fill a large bowl with cold water and ice, and set it aside.

2. Bring a large covered pot of water to a boil, and add 1 tablespoon salt. Add the sugar snaps and cook for 2 minutes. Drain, and immediately plunge the sugar snaps into the bowl of ice water to stop the cooking process. When the sugar snaps are cool, drain them again and set them aside.

3. Melt the butter in a large skillet over medium heat. Add the shallots and cook, stirring occasionally, until they are soft and translucent, about 3 minutes.

4. Add the sugar snaps to the skillet and raise the heat to medium-high. Cook, stirring frequently, until the peas are hot, about 3 minutes. Stir in the chives and lemon zest and cook, stirring constantly, for 1 minute. Season with salt to taste, and serve hot.

YOUR GREEN KITCHEN
Reusable Shopping Bags

Each year we use more than 100 billion plastic and 10 billion paper shopping bags in the U.S. alone. It takes an estimated equivalent of 12 million barrels of oil just to make that many plastic bags. And the numbers are exponentially higher if you count bag consumption around the world—well over 500 billion plastic bags are used annually, which works out to be almost 1 million bags a minute. Every reusable bag we use saves resources, reduces pollution, and helps reduce costs (one of the reasons many stores offer shoppers a credit for using their own bags). So when the checker asks, "Paper or plastic?" tell him or her you brought your own. If every person in America used a reusable tote for just one shopping trip a week for a year—just one!—we could keep about 16 billion bags out of our landfills.

Baby Spinach with Garlic and Lemon

THIS IS THE WAY SPINACH IS COOKED IN ITALY—with lots of garlic and a hint of red pepper. Baby spinach is mild and tender, so it cooks in a flash. Infusing the olive oil with garlic before adding the greens builds flavor, and by removing the cloves and then returning them at the finish of the dish, you avoid burning the garlic. Raw spinach is voluminous, so use your largest skillet. Add the spinach in handfuls, stirring in more as each batch wilts, until you have fit the entire quantity into the pan. A squeeze of fresh lemon juice just before you serve the dish adds a nice note of brightness and balances the richness of the oil.

If you substitute mature spinach in this recipe, be sure to remove the stems and blanch it first, taking care to squeeze out all of the moisture before you add it to the oil in the skillet. ⟶ *Serves 4*

3 tablespoons olive oil

4 large garlic cloves, lightly smashed

Pinch of dried red pepper flakes, or to taste

1½ pounds baby spinach, well rinsed and patted dry if needed

Sea salt

1 lemon, halved

1. Warm the olive oil in a very large skillet over medium-low heat, and add the garlic and red pepper flakes. Cook, stirring occasionally, until the garlic is lightly golden and softened, 5 to 7 minutes. Remove the garlic from the skillet with a slotted spoon and chop it fine; set it aside.

2. Raise the heat to high and add a large batch of spinach to the skillet. Once the spinach begins to wilt, add more, and continue in this manner until all the spinach is wilted, 7 to 10 minutes. Drain the pan of any liquid that may have accumulated. Stir in the reserved chopped garlic, and season with salt to taste.

3. Squeeze lemon juice to taste over the spinach, and serve immediately.

Baby spinach, about a week from harvest.

Green Beans with Walnuts and Tarragon

THIS DISH IS SUPERB when it's made with young, tender green beans. To keep the beans green, they're first blanched to set their vibrant color and to parboil them. An infusion of shallots and walnut oil forms the basis of a quick and flavorful sauce in which the beans are gently sautéed. Don't be tempted to cook this dish over high heat—the delicate flavor and aroma of the walnut oil will be lost. Tarragon partners beautifully with green beans, and the sprinkling of chopped walnuts amplifies the flavor of the oil as well as adding a bit of crunch to the dish. *Serves 4*

Sea salt

1 pound fresh green beans, trimmed

3 tablespoons walnut oil (see sidebar, page 38)

2 tablespoons finely minced shallots

2 tablespoons minced fresh tarragon

Freshly ground black pepper

⅓ cup chopped toasted walnuts (see box, page 31), for garnish

1. Fill a large bowl with cold water and ice, and set it aside.

2. Bring a large covered pot of water to a boil over high heat, and add 1 tablespoon salt. Add the beans and cook for 2 minutes. Drain, and immediately plunge the beans into the bowl of ice water to stop the cooking process. When the beans are cool, drain them again and set them aside.

3. Heat the walnut oil in a large skillet over medium-low heat. When the oil is warm, add the shallots and cook, stirring occasionally, until they are soft and translucent, about 3 minutes.

4. Add the green beans to the skillet, and raise the heat to medium. Cook, stirring frequently, until the beans are hot, about 4 minutes. Stir in the tarragon, and season the beans with salt and pepper to taste.

5. Transfer the beans to a platter and sprinkle the chopped walnuts over them. Serve hot or at room temperature.

Creamy Baby Turnips

I F YOU'RE UNSURE WHETHER OR NOT YOU LIKE TURNIPS, just give this recipe a try, because I suspect you'll give them a thumbs-up afterward. Golf-ball-size baby turnips are the best choice, but if they're not available, look for ones that are less than 2 inches in diameter. (As a general rule, as turnips age, their flavor becomes stronger and their texture more woody. Mature turnips can be bitter and are not recommended for this recipe.) A long, slow simmer in cream tames the peppery bite of turnips into a mellow sweetness. Truffle salt and a drizzle of truffle oil intensify the earthy flavors of the dish, but even without this flourish, the humble turnip has never tasted better! ―――― **Serves 4**

1½ pounds baby turnips, peeled and cut into ¼-inch dice (about 4 cups)

¾ cup heavy (whipping) cream

Truffle salt (see sidebar, this page) or sea salt

Freshly ground black pepper

Truffle oil (optional; see sidebar, page 217)

1. Place the turnips in a medium-size saucepan and add the cream. Place the pan over low heat, cover, and simmer until the turnips are very soft and the cream has been absorbed, about 40 minutes.

2. Mash the turnips with a potato masher or an immersion blender until smooth.

3. Season with truffle salt and black pepper to taste. Serve hot, with a drizzle of truffle oil if using.

THE BASICS

Truffle Salt

For those of us who love the aroma and taste of truffles but can't afford the price tag, truffle salt is a wonderful compromise and a great item to have in the pantry. Sea salt combined with ground black or white truffles makes a fragrant, flavorful condiment that is widely available in specialty food stores or online. I like it as a seasoning for roasted vegetables such as asparagus and cauliflower, sprinkled on popcorn, or tossed with pasta.

YOUR GREEN KITCHEN

Why Using Leftovers Saves More Than Food

Americans throw away more than 25 percent of prepared food—approximately 96 billion pounds each year. In fact, by weight, food leftovers are the single largest component of waste in the landfills in the United States. As a nation, we spend $1 billion a year to dispose of uneaten food from residences, restaurants, and cafeterias.

When food winds up in our landfills, it is left to decompose anaerobically (without oxygen), so it produces methane, a greenhouse gas that is 21 times more potent than carbon dioxide. Landfills are the largest human-related source of this gas in the United States, producing 34 percent of all methane emissions.

So, what can you do?
1. Shop wisely; don't overbuy.
2. Store food properly, and keep track of perishable items.
3. If you have a lot of extra fresh vegetables, it's a great time to make soup.
4. Compost food scraps (see page 247), or look into food waste collection services in your community.

Skillet-Roasted Parsnips and Carrots

INSTEAD OF TURNING ON THE OVEN to caramelize root vegetables, try this easy stovetop technique. First the parsnips and carrots are browned in hot oil; then a flavorful liquid, in this case tangerine juice and honey, is added to braise and tenderize the vegetables; a sprinkling of sugar toward the end of cooking gives them an appealing glaze. Feel free to experiment with other root vegetables, juices, sweeteners, and herbs to vary the results. For example, baby turnips and rutabagas are delicious cooked in this manner with apple cider, a splash of maple syrup, and a sprinkling of fresh thyme. — *Serves 4*

THE BASICS

Caramelizing

Strictly speaking, to caramelize means to cook sugar until it liquefies and browns. Caramelization is a chemical reaction that occurs when the sugar in food is heated to the point where molecules are transformed, generating an array of complex flavors. Today, "caramelization" is also used to refer to the technique of browning fruits and vegetables in the oven, under the broiler, or on the grill or stovetop so that the high-temperature cooking "caramelizes" the natural sugars in the food.

---

3 tablespoons olive oil

1 pound parsnips, peeled and cut on the diagonal into ¾-inch pieces (about 2½ cups; see Note)

1 pound carrots, peeled and cut on the diagonal into ¾-inch pieces (about 2½ cups; see Note)

¼ cup fresh tangerine juice or orange juice

½ cup hot water

2 teaspoons mild honey, such as tupelo

2 teaspoons sugar

2 tablespoons chopped fresh flat-leaf parsley

Sea salt and freshly ground black pepper

1. Place the olive oil in a large skillet and heat it over medium-high heat. When it is hot, add the parsnips and carrots, and cook, stirring occasionally, until the vegetables turn golden brown, 12 to 15 minutes.

2. Meanwhile, combine the tangerine juice, hot water, and honey in a small bowl, and stir to dissolve the honey.

3. Add the juice mixture to the skillet and bring to the start of a simmer. Then reduce the heat to medium, cover the skillet, and cook, stirring occasionally, until the vegetables are almost tender, about 10 minutes.

4. Remove the cover, raise the heat to medium-high, and cook, stirring frequently, until the liquid evaporates, about 5 minutes.

5. Sprinkle the sugar over the vegetables and cook until they are glazed and caramelized, 3 to 5 minutes. Stir in the parsley, and season with sea salt and black pepper to taste. Transfer to a warm platter, and serve hot.

Note: To ensure even cooking time, select parsnips and carrots that are the same diameter, if possible. Halve or quarter the thicker parts so that all the pieces will be similar in size. If the parsnips are larger than an inch wide at the top, remove and discard the tough core.

Skillet-Roasted Parsnips and Carrots

Savory Roasted New Potatoes

NEW POTATOES ARE SIMPLY YOUNG POTATOES of any variety. They are called "new" because they are picked at an immature stage, before their sugar content has fully converted into starch. Consequently, they have a firm, waxy texture and very thin skins. They are often small (compared to russets, for instance), but size is not necessarily an indicator. New potatoes lend themselves perfectly to pan-roasting, as specified in this recipe, because they retain their shape during cooking and are meltingly tender, not mealy. Tossed in a simple combination of spices, Worcestershire sauce, and olive oil, these potatoes have a hint of heat, which you can turn up or cool down by modifying the quantity of paprika. —— *Serves 4 to 6*

12 small new potatoes (about 1¼ pounds
   total)
½ teaspoon garlic powder
½ teaspoon Hungarian hot paprika
½ teaspoon salt
¼ teaspoon freshly ground black pepper
1 tablespoon Worcestershire sauce
2 tablespoons olive oil

1. Position a rack in the middle of the oven, and preheat the oven to 375°F.

2. Scrub the potatoes and then dry them with a clean kitchen towel. Cut the potatoes in halves or quarters, depending on their size. Transfer the potatoes to a shallow baking pan.

3. Mix the garlic powder, paprika, salt, and pepper in a small bowl until blended. Sprinkle the spice mixture over the potatoes, and toss to coat all surfaces.

4. In the same small bowl, whisk the Worcestershire sauce and olive oil together until combined. Drizzle the mixture over the potatoes, and toss to coat. Bake until the potatoes are browned and tender, 25 to 35 minutes. Serve hot.

Freshly dug potatoes of all sizes and shapes.

How to Cook Potatoes and Sweet Potatoes (Yams)

There are hundreds of varieties of potatoes in a wide assortment of colors, shapes, and sizes, and they can all be baked, roasted, boiled, steamed, or mashed. Potatoes are generally divided into two categories: waxy and starchy. Use waxy varieties like reds and fingerlings when you want the potatoes to retain their shape when cooked—in salads and soups, for instance. Potatoes, such as russets and Yukon Golds, are starchier and are best used for baking or in gratins, where their starch thickens the liquid to make a creamy sauce.

BAKING: Large floury potatoes like russets and Yukon Golds are good for baking in their skins because when cooked they have a light, fluffy texture. Sweet potatoes (yams) are also baked as described here:

◆ Position a rack in the middle of the oven and preheat the oven to 425°F.

◆ Scrub the potatoes under cold running water. Remove any eyes with the tip of a knife or vegetable peeler.

◆ Prick each potato several times with a fork to prevent bursting. Place the potatoes directly on the oven rack or on a baking sheet (an aluminum foil–lined baking sheet is important for sweet potatoes because they leak during baking).

◆ Bake for 1 to 1¼ hours, or until soft all the way through. Test by gently squeezing a potato with your fingers.

◆ Cut each potato open, fluff the flesh with a fork, and top it with any of the following: grated cheese, butter, sour cream, snipped chives or green onions, bacon crumbles, or sautéed vegetables.

OVEN-ROASTING: Every type of potato is suitable for oven-roasting. For a delicious vegetable medley, combine potatoes with yams or root vegetables such as carrots, rutabagas, or parsnips; cut all the vegetables the same size for even cooking.

◆ Position a rack in the middle of the oven and preheat the oven to 425°F.

◆ Cut the potatoes into wedges (or cubes) and place them in a roasting pan or casserole dish. Add just enough olive oil to coat the potatoes, then sprinkle with kosher or sea salt and freshly ground black pepper. Toss to coat.

◆ Cook, turning them with a spatula a few times during cooking, until they are fork-tender and golden brown, 30 to 45 minutes. Serve hot or at room temperature.

BOILING: Any type of potato can be boiled. Yukon Golds and russets are often boiled to make mashed potatoes (they can also be steamed).

◆ For about 4 servings, peel 2 pounds of potatoes and cut them into 1-inch cubes or leave them unpeeled, if you prefer.

◆ Place the potatoes in a large saucepan and add just enough cold water to cover. Bring to a boil, covered, over high heat, and add 1 teaspoon salt. Reduce the heat to medium and re-cover the pan.

◆ Cook at a gentle simmer until the potatoes feel tender when pierced with the tip of a paring knife, about 15 minutes. Drain immediately.

◆ If you are making mashed potatoes, return the potatoes to the pot. Pour ½ to 1 cup hot milk over the potatoes (depending on how thin you like them), and add 3 tablespoons butter or olive oil. Mash vigorously with a potato masher, or use an immersion blender or handheld electric mixer. Mix until the potatoes are as smooth as you like them.

◆ Season to taste with salt and freshly ground black pepper.

STEAMING: Steaming potatoes over simmering water is a good technique for delicate new potatoes because it does not dilute their sweet taste and ensures that they retain their shape when cooked.

◆ If you will be mashing the potatoes, peel and cut them into 1-inch cubes. If you are making potato salad and using new potatoes, peeling is optional. Small potatoes can also be served whole.

◆ Place a steamer basket into a large pot and add water to a depth of 2 inches to the pot. (Make sure the water does not touch the bottom of the basket.) Transfer the potatoes to the basket, cover, and bring the water to a boil over high heat.

◆ Reduce the heat to a simmer and cook until the potatoes are tender when pierced with the tip of a knife, 15 to 20 minutes. Remove the steamer insert from the pot.

◆ If you are making mashed potatoes, pour the water from the pot and return the potatoes to it. Add the hot milk, butter, and salt and freshly ground black pepper to taste (see above). Otherwise, toss the potatoes with fruity olive oil or butter, season with sea salt to taste, and sprinkle with fresh herbs.

Drew's Crispy Pasta

THIS IS ONE OF MY HUSBAND'S BEST INVENTIONS, and we serve it often as either a side dish or a main course. The high-heat cooking results in a chewy crunch and lets the garlic flavor really shine. Both white and whole wheat pasta also work well in this dish. And it's a great way to use up any that's been left over. The dish is extra-good with a sprinkling of Parmesan on top, but this is strictly optional. ~~~ *Serves 4*

Coarse (kosher) salt

4 cups short-cut farro pasta,
    such as shells or penne

¼ cup olive oil

2 tablespoons chopped garlic

Freshly grated Parmesan cheese,
    for serving (optional)

1. Bring 4 quarts of water to a boil in a large covered pot over high heat. Add 2 tablespoons salt and the pasta, and stir to combine. Cook according to the package directions until al dente, 8 to 10 minutes. Drain the pasta in a colander, and set it aside.

2. Heat the olive oil in a large skillet, preferably cast-iron, over medium heat. Add the garlic and cook, stirring constantly, until fragrant, about 1 minute.

3. Add the pasta to the skillet and stir to coat it with the oil. Salt the pasta to taste, and cook over medium to medium-high heat, stirring occasionally, until it is golden and crisp, 8 to 10 minutes. Take care not to burn the garlic.

4. Serve hot, with Parmesan cheese on the side if desired.

Brown Rice with Barley

BARLEY AND BROWN RICE are a serendipitous pairing, not only healthy and nutritious, but also nutty and delicious. I especially like this dish with our Black Cod with Summer Succotash (page 126), but it's also a great accompaniment to a whole variety of grilled meats, poultry, and steamed vegetables. ~~~ *Serves 4*

1 cup short-grain brown rice

½ cup hulled barley

1 tablespoon olive oil

1½ teaspoons salt

1 teaspoon dried thyme

Place 2½ cups water in a medium-size saucepan, add all the ingredients, cover the pan, and bring the mixture to a boil over high heat. Reduce the heat to low and simmer until all the liquid has evaporated and the rice is tender, 30 to 40 minutes. Serve hot.

Chili Rice

TINTED A PRETTY RED COLOR by the addition of crushed tomatoes and chili powder, this rice dish makes a great accompaniment to Chicken and Green Olive Enchiladas (page 109) or Vegetarian Three-Bean Chili (page 189). The flavors are mellow and the spices are subtle; if you like, you can turn up the heat by adding more jalapeño. ⎯⎯ *Serves 4 to 6*

¼ cup olive oil

¾ cup diced yellow onion (¼-inch dice)

1 small red bell pepper, stemmed, seeded
    and cut into ¼-inch dice (about ½ cup)

1½ tablespoons minced garlic

1½ tablespoons minced jalapeño pepper

1½ cups long-grain white rice

1½ teaspoons dried oregano

1½ teaspoons ground cumin

1 teaspoon chili powder

2⅔ cups Chicken Wing Stock (page 403),
    Vegetable Stock (page 410), or store-
    bought low-sodium chicken or vegetable
    broth

⅓ cup canned crushed tomatoes

1½ teaspoons salt

⅓ cup thinly sliced scallion tops (green
    part only)

1. Heat the olive oil in a large skillet over medium heat. Add the onion, bell pepper, garlic, and jalapeño and cook, stirring frequently, until the vegetables soften, about 6 minutes.

2. Add the rice, oregano, cumin, and chili powder and cook, stirring frequently, until the rice is hot, about 2 minutes.

3. Add the chicken stock and the crushed tomatoes, raise the heat to high, cover the skillet, and bring the mixture to a boil. Then reduce the heat to low, and simmer until all of the liquid has been absorbed, 18 to 25 minutes.

4. Stir in the salt and scallions, and fluff the mixture with a fork. Serve hot.

Fried Brown Rice

D ON'T LET LEFTOVER RICE GO TO WASTE! It's terrific the next day, or even when it's a few days old, especially if served stir-fried in a skillet. Any kind of rice will work, but I prefer the nutty flavor and chewy texture of short-grain brown rice, and you can't argue with its whole-grain nutrients and fiber. Fried rice makes a flavorful side dish, and it can be turned into a complete meal by adding leftover cooked chicken, turkey, pork, tofu, or even shrimp, along with other cooked vegetables and greens. Just be sure to start with chilled rice so that the starch has hardened—this makes it fry-able. ⁓ *Serves 4*

A variety of summer squash.

3 tablespoons canola or olive oil

1 tablespoon plain sesame oil

1½ cups thinly sliced shiitake mushroom caps

¼ cup diced red onion (¼-inch dice)

1 heaping tablespoon finely grated peeled fresh ginger

1 heaping tablespoon minced garlic

4 cups cooked brown rice, cold

2 large eggs, lightly beaten (optional)

1½ cups assorted leftover cooked meats or vegetables, cut into chunks or dice (optional)

2 tablespoons soy sauce

1. Heat a large skillet, preferably cast-iron, over medium heat, and add the canola and sesame oils. Add the mushrooms, red onion, and ginger, and cook, stirring frequently, until the mushrooms soften, about 5 minutes. Then add the garlic and cook, stirring constantly, until it's fragrant, about 1 minute.

2. Add the rice and stir to coat the grains with the oil. Using the back of a large spoon, press the rice onto the bottom of the skillet, creating an even layer. Let the rice cook without stirring until it starts to get golden and crispy on the bottom, 6 to 7 minutes.

3. Stir the rice, and then press the grains onto the bottom of the skillet once again. Cook without stirring until the rice begins to get golden and crispy on the bottom, 6 to 7 minutes.

4. If you are using the eggs, make a small well in the center of the rice and pour in the eggs. Stir the eggs, gradually scrambling and incorporating them into the rice. If you are not using the eggs, simply stir the rice.

5. Press the rice onto the bottom of the skillet once again and cook without stirring until it is golden and crispy on the bottom, about 5 minutes.

6. Meanwhile, reheat any leftover meat or vegetables, if using.

7. Remove the skillet from the heat and stir in any meat or vegetables and the soy sauce. Serve hot.

Making Fried Brown Rice

1. Add the cooked brown rice to the pan once you've allowed the mushrooms, onions, ginger, and garlic to soften. Stir the rice, making sure all of it gets coated with oil. If you're adding eggs, wait until all the rice is crispy. Then, make a well in the center of the rice layer and pour them in. (If you aren't adding eggs, just stir the rice at this point.)

2. Use a fork to gradually incorporate the eggs into the rice.

3. Press the rice into an even layer and cook 5 minutes more before serving.

Here I've dressed up the brown rice with some leftover chopped tomatoes, zucchini, and yellow summer squash. All delicious additions.

Summer Squash with Tomatoes and Basil

DURING THE LONG HOT DAYS OF SUMMER, when summer squash are plentiful and sun-ripened tomatoes are juicy and sweet, this combination of vegetables and basil is a perfect celebration of the season's bounty. I make this dish all through the summer months, and my whole family loves it. The vegetables are easy to prepare and cook, and the dish tastes incredibly light and healthy. The tomatoes make the consistency just a little bit saucy, so you can use the medley as a terrific topping for pasta or as a sauce for grilled fish or chicken. The key to success is to cook the zucchini just until it's crisp-tender, adding the tomatoes and basil at the end so the tomatoes don't completely fall apart and the basil retains its bright, vibrant flavor. We like it sprinkled with freshly grated Parmesan, but this is optional. For a zestier dish, add dried red pepper flakes, capers, or olives with the zucchini in Step 2. ⎯⎯ *Serves 6 to 8*

Zucchini with its blossom.

2 tablespoons olive oil

1 cup diced yellow onion (¼-inch dice)

1½ tablespoons minced garlic

1¾ pounds zucchini or yellow summer squash, cut in half lengthwise and then cut crosswise into ⅓-inch-thick slices (about 6 cups)

4 medium vine-ripened tomatoes, cored and cut into ½-inch dice (about 2½ cups)

½ cup (lightly packed) chopped fresh basil leaves

Salt and freshly ground black pepper

½ cup freshly grated Parmesan cheese

1. Heat the oil in a large skillet, preferably cast-iron, over medium heat. Add the onion and cook, stirring occasionally, until it softens, about 6 minutes. Add the garlic and cook, stirring frequently, until it is fragrant, about 2 minutes.

2. Add the zucchini, cover the skillet, and cook, stirring occasionally, until it is crisp-tender, about 5 minutes.

3. Add the tomatoes and cook, covered, for 2 minutes. Stir in the basil, and season with salt and pepper to taste. Cover, and cook for 1 minute. Then add two thirds of the Parmesan to the mixture and stir to combine. Sprinkle the remaining cheese on top, and serve hot.

Summer Squash with Tomatoes and Basil

Roasting Winter Squash Seeds

Almost very type of winter squash seed can be roasted, not just pumpkin seeds. They're a healthy and delicious snack, so it makes sense not to waste such a nutritious part of the plant.

To roast: Scoop the seeds and stringy pulp from your squash. Wash the seeds in warm water to remove as much of the pulp as possible. Spread the wet seeds in a single layer on a rimmed baking pan and sprinkle with salt. Bake in a preheated 350°F oven for approximately 20 minutes, checking and stirring every 5 minutes, until the seeds are a light golden brown. Check doneness by removing a sample, cooling to a safe temperature, and tasting—if the insides of the seeds are dry, they're done. Add more salt if needed. Eat warm, or allow the seeds to cool completely, and store them in an airtight container or plastic bag.

Yam and Winter Squash Casserole

WINTER SQUASH AND YAMS make a serendipitous pairing. Both orange-colored vegetables are filled with healthy vitamins and antioxidants, but their succulent flesh is so moist and sweet, you'd never guess you were eating something very nutritious. If you like to offer a sweet vegetable dish with your holiday feast, this is a recipe worth trying. The walnut crumble topping adds a delicious crunch to the smooth puree. ⎯⎯ *Serves 6 to 8*

3 large Garnet or Jewel yams
    (sweet potatoes; see page 368)
2 pounds butternut, acorn, or Hubbard
    squash, cut in half, seeds and strings
    removed
1 teaspoon olive oil
⅔ cup (10 ⅔ tablespoons) unsalted
    butter, melted
4 large eggs
⅓ cup milk
1 teaspoon pure vanilla extract

TOPPING
¼ cup (½ stick) unsalted butter, melted
⅔ cup (packed) light or dark brown sugar
⅓ cup walnut halves, coarsely chopped
3 tablespoons unbleached all-purpose
    flour
½ teaspoon ground nutmeg
½ teaspoon ground cinnamon

1. Position a rack in the middle of the oven and preheat the oven to 425°F.

2. Poke the yams in several places with a fork, and place them on a rimmed baking sheet lined with aluminum foil, preferably recycled.

3. Brush the cut surfaces of the squash with the olive oil. Place the squash, cut side down, on the same baking sheet and bake until the squash is soft and tender, 35 to 45 minutes.

4. Remove the squash from the baking sheet and set it aside. Return the baking sheet to the oven and continue baking the yams until they are very soft, another 10 to 15 minutes. Let the squash and yams cool to room temperature.

5. Peel the yams, discarding the skin, and place them in a large bowl. Mash them roughly with a potato masher or an immersion blender, and measure out 2 cups of mash. Reserve the remainder for another use.

6. Peel the squash, discarding the skin, and place the flesh in a large bowl. Mash roughly with a potato

masher or an immersion blender, and measure out 2 cups of mash. Reserve the remainder for another use.

7. Combine the mashed yams and squash in a large bowl and puree with a potato masher or immersion blender until smooth. Add the melted butter, eggs, milk, and vanilla, and beat with a whisk or a wooden spoon until blended. Transfer the mixture to an 8-inch square baking dish.

8. Preheat the oven to 350°F.

9. Prepare the topping: Place the melted butter, brown sugar, walnuts, flour, nutmeg, and cinnamon in a small bowl, and stir to blend. Sprinkle the topping over the squash mixture.

10. Cover the baking dish with aluminum foil and bake for 30 minutes. Then remove the foil and continue baking until the topping is golden, about 20 minutes more. Serve hot.

Yam and Winter Squash Casserole

Quick Shiitake Sauté

I LIKE MUSHROOMS OF ALL VARIETIES, but shiitakes are a particular favorite because they have so much flavor and texture. Best of all, they need very little in the way of seasoning to prepare them. The taste of shiitakes is more assertive than most cultivated mushrooms, and they make an excellent accompaniment to roasts, such as our Herbed Rib Roast of Pork (page 92), or to grilled meats, like the Greek-Style Lamb Chops (page 103). Always start with a hot pan and cook the mushrooms at a relatively high heat for the first few minutes so they'll give off moisture and brown a bit before they soften. —*mm*—
Serves 4

(page 92); (page 103)

3 tablespoons olive oil
1 pound fresh shiitake mushrooms, stemmed,
  caps cut into ¼-inch-thick slices
Coarse (kosher) salt
2 tablespoons finely minced shallots
1 large garlic clove, peeled and minced
½ cup dry white wine
1½ tablespoons minced fresh tarragon
Freshly ground black pepper

1. Heat a large skillet over medium-high heat, and when it is hot, add the olive oil. Add the mushrooms and cook without stirring until they begin to release their moisture, 2 to 3 minutes. Then sprinkle the mushrooms with salt to taste, and stir them briefly. Continue cooking the mushrooms without stirring until they are golden and have begun to soften, another 2 to 3 minutes.

2. Reduce the heat to medium and add the shallots. Cook, stirring frequently, until the shallots are tender, about 2 minutes. Add the garlic and cook, stirring constantly, until it is fragrant, about 1 minute.

3. Add the wine, raise the heat to medium-high, and cook until it has evaporated, 3 to 5 minutes. Stir in the tarragon, and season the shiitakes with salt and pepper to taste. Serve immediately.

THE BASICS

Rinsing Mushrooms

You may have heard that raw mushrooms should never touch water, the idea being that they will soak up the liquid like a sponge and become soggy. However, tests have shown that cultivated mushrooms submerged in water for 5 minutes barely absorb any measurable liquid.

Place the mushrooms in the basket of a salad spinner and rinse them with cold water, swishing them to remove the dirt and grit. Then simply spin to remove the excess moisture.

VEGETABLE AND GRAIN SALADS

Innovative Salads with Substance

EARTHBOUND FARM'S ORGANIC CAFE IS PART OF OUR FARM STAND, located in Carmel Valley, California. There, surrounded by farm-fresh organic produce, and equipped with a pantry stocked with many types of organic whole grains and pastas, our Executive Chef, Sarah LaCasse, makes sure that the popular all-organic salad bar always includes about eight delicious vegetable and grain salads. She prepares them to reflect the season, using whatever is at its peak of freshness and flavor. I am there almost every day to get my favorite lunch—a *huge* salad from our salad bar—I always include a mix of these hearty salads to add variety, texture, and enough substance to fill me up.

All but one of the recipes in this chapter are vegetarian, so as a whole, they are light on the environment, as well as deliciously filling. Included are several unusual salads to satisfy your craving for something crunchy, like the Baby Turnip and Carrot Salad, which combines super-thin slices of carrots and sweet-and-peppery baby turnips in a simple but refreshingly light dressing of shallots, lemon juice, and a mixture of olive and canola oils. Another different crunchy combination is the Fennel, Apple, and Radish Salad, which mixes sweet apples, the subtle heat of radishes, and the distinctive anise flavor of fennel. And if you feel like eating something colorful and light, our Thai Cabbage Salad is perfect: a beautiful mix of red cabbage, English cucumbers, mint, and basil in a light Asian-style vinaigrette.

I've also included a variety of scrumptious salads featuring whole grains. The Brown Rice and Chickpea Rainbow Salad, flavored with a zesty pesto vinaigrette, is a visual feast that includes red tomatoes, pale green cucumbers, and dark Kalamata olives. With the protein and fiber of chickpeas and brown rice, this dish is filling and delicious. If you haven't discovered farro yet, I highly recommend it.

Beets—try them in our Roasted Beet Salad alla Caprese (page 242).

This ancient grain quickly became one of my family's all-time favorites. Try the Farro Salad with Edamame and Arugula—a great choice both for taste and nutrition. And I can't seem to get enough of the Bulgur and Grilled Vegetable Salad. When there is a batch in my fridge, I'll heat a bowlful as an entrée, eat it at room temperature to complement a half sandwich, or add a couple of cold heaping tablespoons to a salad to make it more flavorful and filling. The bulgur salad also makes a beautiful appetizer, scooped onto whole lettuce leaves, like Bibb or romaine hearts, and arranged in an attractive pattern on a platter.

Nearby farms supply our organic café with a beautiful array of potatoes, and the potato salad recipes in this chapter explore the flavors, colors, and textures of different potato varieties. The German Potato Salad showcases Yukon Gold, Red Bliss, or Yellow Finn potatoes. And as pleasing to the eye as to the taste buds, the Three-Color Potato Salad adds colorful vegetables, such as tomatoes and fresh green beans, to the mix.

Actually, harvesting fresh potatoes is one of my favorite things to do. It's like a treasure hunt: carefully loosening the ground with a pitchfork, then kneeling down and sinking my hands elbow-deep in the fragrant, warm earth to look for the small new potatoes. As many times as I've done this, it's still exciting to find the potatoes and carefully brush away the excess soil from the tender skins. When digging for potatoes, it's especially comforting to know they were grown organically. The joy of digging and eating these tasty root vegetables isn't marred by worries about pesticides on my hands or in my food.

Like harvesting fresh organic potatoes, the salads in this chapter are all wonderfully satisfying. Whether you're going for extra crunch, a light side dish, a more filling addition to a leafy salad, or a delicious meatless entrée, these salads offer endless possibilities.

Three-Color Potato Salad (page 258)

Fennel, Apple, and Radish Salad

Fennel, Apple, and Radish Salad

THE SUBTLE ANISE FLAVOR OF FRESH FENNEL partners perfectly with sweet-tart apple, and the radish slices add a spark of peppery heat. Both the fennel and apple will discolor after slicing, so be sure to toss these ingredients with the dressing immediately after prepping them. The concept of this fabulously fresh-tasting salad is really simple: Cut an assortment of seasonal raw vegetables into paper-thin slices, toss them with a light dressing, and add a shower of fresh herbs. Experiment to create your own versions, keeping in mind that you'll want a balance of color, texture, and flavor. We prefer the super-thin, even slices you get by using a mandoline (see the sidebar on page 240), but if you cut the vegetables by hand and your slices are thicker, the salad will still be delicious. ⌒⌒⌒ *Serves 4 to 6*

1 large fennel bulb

¼ cup extra-virgin olive oil

2 tablespoons fresh lemon juice

1 tablespoon unseasoned rice vinegar

½ teaspoon snipped chives or minced
   scallion tops (green part)

Salt and freshly ground black pepper

1 large crisp apple, such as Fuji or Gala

12 large radishes, trimmed and thinly sliced
   (about 2 cups)

1. Snip enough of the fennel fronds to measure 1 tablespoon. Set the fennel bulb aside.

2. Combine the olive oil, lemon juice, vinegar, fennel fronds, chives, ¼ teaspoon salt, and black pepper to taste in a glass jar and seal the lid tightly. Shake the jar vigorously to combine. (Any leftover vinaigrette can be refrigerated, covered, for up to 1 week. Let it return to room temperature and then shake vigorously before using.)

3. Trim the fennel bulb, cut it in half lengthwise, and then thinly slice the halves. Quarter and core the apple, then thinly slice it.

4. Place the fennel, radish, and apple slices in a large bowl and add three-quarters of the vinaigrette to the vegetables. Toss to lightly coat the salad, and then taste to see if more dressing is needed. Season the salad with salt and pepper to taste. Transfer the salad to a platter or individual salad plates. (The salad will lose its crunchiness over time, but it can be refrigerated, covered, for up to 2 days.)

THE BASICS

Fresh Parsley

You may notice that I specify flat-leaf parsley in my recipes. Even though there are more than thirty varieties of America's most recognizable herb, you'll most likely find only two types in your grocery store: curly-leaf and flat-leaf (also called Italian). Curly-leaf parsley is the most popular, but chefs prefer flat-leaf. It has a sweet, bright flavor that is preferable to the bitter, grassy tones of curly-leaf. Flat-leaf parsley is also much more fragrant than its curly cousin.

Baby Turnip and Carrot Salad

Mandolines

A mandoline is the secret to achieving uniform, wafer-thin slices of vegetables. This handy tool, also called a V-slicer, is sold in most cookware shops and housewares departments, in a range of styles and prices. For home use, inexpensive plastic models work perfectly well, so don't feel that you need to invest in a $200 stainless-steel import. Look for a slicer that has interchangeable slicing blades, usually ranging from ¹⁄₁₆ inch to ¼ inch, as well as a julienne blade for cutting vegetables into matchstick-size strips. Because the blades are extremely sharp, it's important to choose a mandoline that comes with a safety guard to protect your fingers.

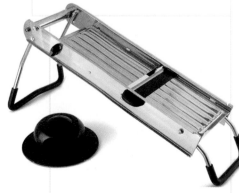

PAPER-THIN ROUNDS OF RAW BABY TURNIPS AND CARROTS are moistened with a fresh lemon-parsley dressing to make an unusual and remarkable salad. Baby white turnips are sweet and juicy, with a mild hint of pepperiness. They are a world removed from their mature cousins, which are often hard and stringy and have a very sharp bite. Mid-March through June is the peak season for tender baby turnips. Look for very small turnips with a diameter about the same as the carrots'. If you can find purple or red carrots, use an assortment of hues to add a colorful note. This salad benefits from a short marination, up to 2 hours, to allow the flavors to develop and meld. Anything much longer than this, however, and the salad will begin to lose its appealing crunch and vivid colors. —ʍʍ— *Serves 4*

6 baby white turnips, golf-ball-size, washed
　and trimmed
2 large carrots, peeled
¼ cup minced fresh flat-leaf parsley
½ tablespoon minced shallot
¼ teaspoon minced garlic
2 tablespoons fresh lemon juice
3 tablespoons extra-virgin olive oil
2 tablespoons canola oil
Sea salt and freshly ground black pepper,
　to taste

1. Using a mandoline (see sidebar, this page), slice the turnips into paper-thin rounds. (Alternatively, use a sharp knife to slice the turnips as thin as possible.) Transfer the turnips to a medium-size bowl. Slice the carrots in the same manner, using only the thickest part of the carrots so that all the rounds are approximately the same size. Add the carrots to the bowl. (Unused parts of the carrots can be saved for stocks, soups, or healthy snacks.) You want roughly equal quantities of turnip and carrot for the salad. Stir in the parsley.

2. Combine the shallot, garlic, and lemon juice in a glass jar and seal the lid tightly. Let this mixture marinate at room temperature for 10 minutes.

3. Add the olive and canola oils to the shallot mixture, seal the lid tightly, and shake vigorously to combine. Season to taste with sea salt and pepper. (The dressing can be refrigerated, covered, for up to 5 days. Let it return to room temperature and then shake vigorously before using.)

4. Add the dressing to the turnip-carrot mixture, tossing to coat. Season the salad with sea salt and pepper to taste. Refrigerate the salad, covered, for up to 2 hours before serving.

5. Transfer the salad to a platter or individual salad plates, and serve.

growing your own food

Luscious vine-ripened tomatoes, raspberries hanging like red jewels among green foliage, or new potatoes emerging from loose earth that you gently rub away to reveal their pretty red or yellow or purple skins. With just footsteps between your ingredients and your kitchen, organic produce that you grow at home is by far the freshest, most satisfying, and most eco-friendly food choice. It just doesn't get much greener.

Gardening is a decision to link yourself more closely with the cycles of nature. It's exciting and extremely rewarding to watch your vegetables grow beautiful and strong, but there's also risk involved. In my California garden, I have experienced the heartbreak of losing a lettuce patch to snails overnight, or a thriving squash plant to a gopher. But I find that being in such an intimate relationship with nature is grounding and invigorating—it's thrilling to join in an adventure starring the weather, insects, soil, and seeds.

I feel a sense of accomplishment when I'm turning the soil, enriching it with compost, breaking up all the large soil clumps with my hands, and gently planting seeds and little seedlings with wishes for them to grow strong and healthy. A bag of produce from the supermarket may be healthful and tasty, but I'll never have the same "maternal" affection for it that I have for the basket of summer squash, vine-ripened tomatoes, Romano beans, and fresh basil I carry into the kitchen from my garden. That basketful is bursting with the life I helped develop, and I feel pride in the results of my hard work. Also, my hunger to prepare and eat this produce has been intensifying all the weeks and months I've watched it grow!

Gardening isn't only healthy exercise for the body and good relaxation for the mind; it's also an activity that binds you more closely with your family and community. Some people are surprised when they hear that my kids enjoy eating lots of fruits and vegetables. I'm sure part of the reason for this is that even though we have a big organic farming business, they grew up with a home garden— working the soil, deciding what they wanted to plant every summer, harvesting it, and then eating it at its peak of freshness and flavor. Vegetables were always a true treat in our home, never a punishing prerequisite for dessert.

These days my son, Jeffrey, and I put in the garden as a team, and we spend some of our best time together during collaborative trips to the nursery. Then we work side by side planting, weeding, watering, and talking. Sharing your extra produce with friends and neighbors is also a great gift. And sharing a new plant variety or a successful way to deal with a garden pest creates immediate common ground and connection with a fellow gardener you never met before.

Growing your own garden is also a wonderful way to explore new varieties of produce. You can grow carrots of all colors, tomatoes of all shapes, and herbs with fresh flavors to seduce the senses. Even if you live in an apartment in the city, you may be able to grow some herbs in little pots on the windowsill to flavor your food as you cook. Growing anything at all can be very gratifying. And don't be intimidated if you've never gardened before. When Drew and I started Earthbound Farm in 1984, there was no Internet to help educate us about how to grow food or troubleshoot problems, so we got all our information from the staff at our local nursery and from *Rodale's Encyclopedia of Organic Gardening.* I still recommend those two sources to get you going, in addition to what you'll find on the Web. So whatever plot you have to work with, I urge you to break ground. A whole world of flavor and satisfaction is waiting just under the surface.

Roasted Beet Salad alla Caprese

Beet Greens

Whenever you can, purchase beets with their greens still attached—they're a good indicator of how fresh the beets are. Many people cook only the beet bulb and toss away the greens. Rather than waste the leafy tops, add them to soups and stir-fries, toss them in pasta, or use them raw in salads. The greens are very nutritious, with significant levels of calcium, iron, and vitamins A and C.

When trimming beets, leave about 1 inch of beet greens attached to the top, and do not cut the tap root. If cut before cooking, beets bleed and stain everything in proximity a bright crimson.

INSALATA CAPRESE, THE SUBLIME ITALIAN CLASSIC that marries tomatoes, basil, and *mozzarella di bufalo*, is spectacular when sun-ripened tomatoes are in season. But from December to June, when tomatoes are lackluster, sweet earthy beets make an excellent substitution. In our unorthodox version of this popular salad, disks of meltingly soft mozzarella alternate with roasted beets and rounds of juicy citrus. Drizzled with an orange-scented vinaigrette, the salad is a beautiful study in colors and textures as well as a pleasure for the palate. Be sure to use soft fresh milk or buffalo milk mozzarella sold in water, not the hard mozzarella that is used for grating and has a plastic texture. If fresh basil is not available, use arugula or parsley as a winter substitute. —*mm*— *Serves 4 to 6*

4 medium beets, preferably 2 red and
    2 golden, scrubbed and trimmed
    (see sidebar, this page)
1 tablespoon olive oil
Salt and freshly ground black pepper,
    to taste
2 tablespoons red wine vinegar
Grated zest of 1 orange
1 tablespoon fresh orange juice
1 teaspoon Dijon mustard
1 teaspoon honey, or more to taste
⅓ cup extra-virgin olive oil
2 balls (4 to 6 ounces each) fresh milk or
    buffalo milk mozzarella cheese, drained
    and patted dry
2 medium oranges
Sea salt, to taste
¼ cup fresh basil leaves, sliced in very thin
    ribbons, or opal basil sprigs

1. Position a rack in the middle of the oven and preheat the oven to 400°F.

2. Dry the beets with paper towels and rub them with the tablespoon of olive oil. Season them with salt and pepper, and then wrap each beet individually in aluminum foil, sealing it tightly. Place the beets directly on the oven rack and roast until they are very tender, 50 to 60 minutes, depending on their size.

3. Remove the beets from the oven and let them cool on a rack (still in their foil packets) until they are cool enough to handle, 30 to 40 minutes. (The cooked beets can be refrigerated, tightly wrapped, for up to 2 days in advance. Return the beets to room temperature before proceeding with the recipe.)

4. Peel the beets or rub off the skins with a clean kitchen towel. Cut the beets into ¼-inch-thick rounds, discarding the top and bottom pieces.

Roasted Beet Salad alla Caprese in a casual, family-style presentation

5. Place the vinegar, orange zest, orange juice, mustard, honey, and extra-virgin olive oil in a glass jar. Cover the jar tightly with a lid and shake it vigorously to combine. Season the dressing with salt and pepper to taste, and add more honey if you prefer a sweeter flavor. Set the dressing aside at room temperature while you finish the salad (or refrigerate it for up to 5 days).

6. Cut the mozzarella into ¼-inch-thick slices. Place the cheese on a platter and drizzle with some of the vinaigrette. Let stand at room temperature for 20 to 30 minutes.

7. Cut off a thin slice from the top and bottom of each orange so that the fruit will sit level on a cutting board. Using a sharp paring knife, remove wide strips of the peel and white pith by cutting downward, following the contour of the fruit. Leave the flesh intact. Cut the oranges crosswise into ¼-inch-thick slices.

8. To assemble the salad, arrange slices of beets, cheese, and oranges in an attractive overlapping pattern. Drizzle the salad with some of the vinaigrette, and season it lightly with sea salt and freshly ground pepper. Scatter the basil ribbons over the salad, and serve at room temperature. The beets will bleed and color the cheese, but that is part of the effect.

A colorful display of carrots.

Carrot-Apple Slaw

THERE'S NO SHORTAGE OF CRUNCH in this tasty and colorful slaw. The simple mayonnaise-based dressing can be made up to 3 days ahead of assembling the salad, and the slaw itself can be made a day ahead, then covered and stored in the refrigerator. Don't add the cashews until serving time, though, because they will get soggy if they are tossed with the slaw ahead of time.
—*Serves 6 to 8*

4 medium carrots, peeled and grated (about 3 cups)

1 cup finely shredded red cabbage

1 crisp apple, such as Gala or Fuji, cored, peeled, and grated

⅓ cup raisins

½ cup mayonnaise

¼ cup apple juice

2 tablespoons apple cider vinegar

1 tablespoon fresh lemon juice

Salt and freshly ground black pepper

½ cup salted cashews, chopped

1. Place the carrots, cabbage, apple, and raisins in a large bowl.

2. Combine the mayonnaise, apple juice, cider vinegar, and lemon juice in a small bowl, and whisk to blend.

3. Add the mayonnaise mixture to the carrot mixture and stir to combine. Season with salt and pepper to taste. Just before serving, stir in the cashews. Serve immediately.

Pineapple and Jicama Salad with Honey Vinaigrette

SWEET CUBES OF FRESH PINEAPPLE meld with crunchy, juicy jicama, creamy avocado, and toasted pecans in an unusual and refreshing salad that is great for picnics or as an accompaniment to spicy Mexican dishes. The vinaigrette marries all the disparate elements of this salad. The honey flavor is quite predominant, so pick a mild honey or one whose flavor you know you like. For the best results, let the pineapple and jicama marinate in the dressing for at least an hour before finishing and serving the salad. ⎯⎯ *Serves 4 to 6*

HONEY DRESSING

⅓ cup mild-flavored honey

1 tablespoon hot water

Grated zest of 1 orange

¼ cup apple cider vinegar

1 teaspoon salt

Freshly ground black pepper, to taste

1½ tablespoons extra-virgin olive oil

SALAD

½ fresh pineapple, peeled, cored,
    and cut into ¼-inch cubes

12 ounces jicama, peeled and cut into
    ¼-inch cubes

½ small red onion, very thinly sliced

⅓ cup thinly sliced fresh mint leaves
    (optional)

2 ripe avocados, preferably Hass, pitted,
    peeled, and cut into ⅓-inch cubes

1 cup pecan halves, toasted (see box,
    page 31)

1. Prepare the dressing: Combine all the dressing ingredients in a glass jar and seal the lid tightly. Shake the jar vigorously until the honey dissolves. Let the dressing sit at room temperature while you assemble the salad.

2. Prepare the salad: Place the pineapple, jicama, and red onion in a medium-size bowl. Toss with ⅓ cup of the dressing, stirring to coat. Cover the bowl with a plate or a clean kitchen towel and refrigerate the salad for 1 hour, or up to 4 hours, stirring to coat the fruit and vegetables several times.

3. Add the mint, if using, to the salad and stir to blend. Transfer the salad to a serving bowl or platter. Arrange the avocados and pecans on top of the salad, drizzle with more of the dressing, and serve immediately. (Serve the remainder of the dressing on the side.) The salad can be refrigerated, covered, for up to 2 days.

FARM FRESH

Jicama

Jicama is a round tuber that can vary in weight from 4 ounces to 6 pounds. It is native to Central America and is a cousin of the sweet potato. Covered in a thin, nondescript brown skin, the flesh inside is white and exceptionally crisp and juicy, with an applelike texture. It is mildly sweet and has hints of nutty flavor reminiscent of fresh water chestnuts. By itself jicama is somewhat bland, but its fresh, clean taste marries beautifully with other ingredients. Most often eaten raw, jicama adds texture to salads and makes a crunchy addition to vegetable trays. Try it with our Hummus (page 413) as a low-calorie alternative to bread or crackers, or dunk it in your favorite dip. For something out of the ordinary, serve it as they do in Mexico: cut into sticks and sprinkled with fresh lime juice, chile powder, and salt for a refreshing snack. Jicama can also be cooked in stir-fries, braises, and soups, where it absorbs flavors without losing its characteristic crunch.

Jicamas are generally imported from Mexico or South America and are available year-round. Select small to medium-size jicamas with smooth, unblemished skins; large specimens can be fibrous, tasteless, and starchy. Avoid any that show signs of shriveling or cracking. The skin should be thin, not thick and desiccated. Jicamas can be stored in a cool, dry place, uncovered, for up to 1 week, or refrigerated, uncovered, for up to 2 weeks. Once peeled or cut, wrap it tightly, refrigerate it, and use it within a week.

Jicama is an excellent source of vitamin C and contains calcium, potassium, magnesium, and vitamin A—all for a mere 49 calories per cup. If that isn't enough to convince you of the health advantages of this vegetable, consider that 1 cup also contains more than 6 grams of fiber!

To prepare jicama, remove the skin as well as the fibrous flesh directly under the skin, using a vegetable peeler or a sharp knife. If the jicama is very fresh, the skin will simply pull off.

composting your kitchen scraps

Growing up in New York City, I can't remember ever hearing the word "compost." In fact, I ate so few fresh fruits and vegetables in those days I wouldn't have had much to compost anyway! But now that I live on a farm and generate a lot of fruit and vegetable trimmings, I am grateful to have space for a compost pile where I can turn kitchen scraps into this valuable soil amendment for my garden.

I realize that composting may not be possible for everyone, and I don't mean to instill guilt in city dwellers for not doing it. Just think how much fuel they save walking to their local market, while those of us in more rural areas get into our cars and drive many miles to do our shopping.

If you're able to give composting a try, here is some basic information I hope will encourage you to get started.

What is compost?

Compost is organic matter (things like kitchen scraps and garden clippings) that has fully decomposed. The result is a valuable soil amendment gardeners often call "black gold." Compost improves soil structure, aids in necessary microbial activity, attracts beneficial soil organisms like earthworms, and holds its nutrients in a slow-release form. To make compost, we balance the mixture of organic ingredients, make sure they're not too wet or too dry, and turn the mixture regularly to make sure it gets enough oxygen. While there are many ways to compost, there is really no best method. You can find many types of bins to hold your scraps and clippings—some that rotate, some that store the compost in layers, others that use worms to break down your scraps—but if you have the room, you can also use a simple backyard compost pile.

There are abundant online resources explaining how to compost, ranging from instructions for setting up a small kitchen worm-compost bin, to advice on managing a basic compost pile in your backyard. You can also check with your local waste management facility. Many offer reduced prices on compost bins made from recycled materials.

Why it's important to compost

Since food waste decomposes in a relatively short amount of time, many people don't consider this waste to be much of an environmental problem. But when food is buried in the landfill, it decomposes anaerobically (without oxygen) and produces methane, a greenhouse gas 21 times more potent than carbon dioxide (CO_2). A recent study by the independent nonprofit agency WRAP (Worldwide Responsible Accredited Production) found that 25 percent of a typical American household's garbage is comprised of discarded food and trimmings, generating roughly 96 billion pounds of food waste each year. And food waste in our landfills, combined with other materials that decompose, such as yard clippings, is the second largest man-made source of methane in the United States, accounting for 34 percent of total methane emissions.

What about garbage disposals? These keep waste out of the landfills, but they pass it along to our water treatment facilities, resulting in the greater use of energy and water. (See page 249.) If your house uses a septic tank system, waste from the garbage disposal is added to the rest of the sewage sludge in your tank. In fact, in terms of water and septic-tank use, some building codes consider a garbage disposal the equivalent of adding another bathroom. So until there's a better system for city dwellers, if you can't compost your scraps, it is better to include them with your other garbage than to put them down the garbage disposal.

But if you do have the space, composting your non-meat kitchen scraps is the most environmentally friendly way to deal with this kind of waste. You'll experience the joy of knowing that what used to be your garbage—coffee grounds, egg shells, and banana peels, for example—is now nourishing your garden or your houseplants!

Thai Cabbage Salad

Choose cabbages with the tightest heads and the deepest red leaves.

I LOVE THE CRUNCH OF THIS BEAUTIFUL SALAD as well as its brilliant colors. The combination of sugar, citrus, and jalapeño pays homage to the elemental Thai trinity of sweet-sour-spicy. The salty crunch of peanuts is the crowning touch, but be sure to add them just at serving time so they don't get soggy. ⎯⎯ *Serves 4*

About 8 ounces red cabbage, thinly sliced
   (2 cups)

2 medium carrots, peeled and coarsely
   chopped (about 1½ cups)

½ cup coarsely grated seedless (English)
   cucumber (peeled or unpeeled)

3 tablespoons finely diced jalapeño pepper,
   with or without seeds (see sidebar, page 12)

3 tablespoons chopped fresh mint or cilantro

3 tablespoons chopped fresh basil

2 tablespoons fresh lime juice

2 tablespoons canola oil

1 teaspoon minced peeled garlic

2 teaspoons fish sauce (see box, page 156)

2 teaspoons sugar

¼ teaspoon dried red pepper flakes,
   or to taste

1 cup salted dry-roasted peanuts (optional)

1. Place the cabbage, carrots, cucumber, jalapeño, mint, and basil in a large bowl and stir to combine.

2. Combine the lime juice, oil, garlic, fish sauce, sugar, and red pepper flakes in a small glass jar and seal the lid tightly. Shake the jar vigorously to combine. (The vinaigrette can be refrigerated, covered, for up to 1 week.)

3. Add three-quarters of the dressing to the cabbage mixture, and toss to combine. Taste, and add more dressing if needed. Just before serving, stir in the peanuts if using.

Sesame Soba Noodle Salad

SOBA ARE LONG, THIN, FLAT JAPANESE NOODLES made from a combination of buckwheat and wheat flours. The buckwheat gives them their distinctive beige-brown color and nutty flavor. Slivers of crunchy radish and carrot add texture and color to this salad, which is very light and fresh tasting, with a subtle hint of sesame flavor. It goes well with grilled chicken or fish. ⎯⎯ *Serves 6 to 8*

8 ounces dry soba (buckwheat) noodles

¼ cup plain sesame oil (see sidebar, page 25)

½ cup unseasoned rice vinegar

3 cups julienne-cut, seeded, peeled cucumber

2 cups grated carrots

2 cups grated radishes (about 16 radishes)

6 scallions (white part and 3 inches of green), thinly sliced

1½ teaspoons salt

Freshly ground black pepper, to taste

2 tablespoons sesame seeds, toasted (see box, page 31)

1. Bring a large pot of salted water to a boil over high heat. Reduce the heat to medium and add the noodles. Cook at a slow simmer until the noodles are just tender, 7 to 10 minutes. Transfer the noodles to a colander and set it under cold running water to stop the cooking. Drain well, and transfer the noodles to a large bowl.

2. Mix the sesame oil and vinegar together in a small bowl.

3. Add the cucumber, carrots, radishes, and scallions to the noodles, and toss to combine. Add the dressing, salt, and pepper, and toss to coat. Transfer the salad to a serving platter, sprinkle with the sesame seeds, and serve. The salad can be refrigerated, covered, for up to 5 days.

garbage disposals: how some friendly advice turned out to be not so environmentally friendly . . .

Decades ago, when I was newly married and still figuring out my way around the kitchen, Drew and I visited his aunt and uncle in Miami. Helping his aunt clean up after dinner, I was instructed to scrape all the plates into the sink so all the waste could go down the garbage disposal. When I threw something into the garbage can, I was firmly reminded that all the waste possible was to go down the disposal. Since her husband owned a trash disposal company, I was pretty confident she would be an expert on handling waste, and I was grateful to learn this new protocol.

Because of those lessons long ago, I kept my garbage disposal very busy until I started doing research for this book. It turns out that garbage disposals are not at all green! They use a great deal of water and electricity; the solid waste either becomes sludge in your septic system or travels to a wastewater treatment plant where the solid matter has to be filtered out (again using lots of water and electricity); and eventually the sludge from either location must be transported to a disposal site. So if you have a garden, or even a few pots on a balcony, it's much better to compost what you can to make rich fertilizer for your plants (See Composting Your Kitchen Scraps, page 247). If you don't make compost, minimizing food waste and putting scraps in the garbage is the next best option.

Chicken Salad with Two Rices

Chicken and Wild Rice Salad

WILD RICE IS DARK AND GLOSSY, with a rich, nutty flavor and a chewy texture. Admittedly, it is expensive, but a little goes a long way. Here we've added tender strips of chicken, toasted pecans, and the sweet burst of citrus to the rice to create a one-dish meal. Roast your own chicken or use a store-bought rotisserie chicken for this salad. Oranges are easier to eat in a salad when you remove the bitter white pith that snuggles beneath the peel, so it's worth the time to segment the fruit instead of slicing it into rounds.
— *Serves 4*

¾ cup wild rice, rinsed well
   (or 3 cups cooked wild rice;
   see sidebar, page 253)
1 teaspoon salt
About 3 cups cold water
2 cups cooked chicken, shredded or
   cut into ½-inch dice
⅔ cup diced celery (½-inch dice)
½ cup pecans, toasted and coarsely
   chopped (see box, page 31)
2 large oranges
½ cup Golden Balsamic Vinaigrette
   (recipe follows)
¼ cup chopped celery leaves

1. Place the wild rice and the salt in a medium-size saucepan, add enough cold water to cover by ½ inch, cover the pan, and bring to a boil over high heat. Then reduce the heat to medium and cook slowly until the rice is tender, 40 to 50 minutes. Drain the rice and let it cool to room temperature.

2. Place the rice, chicken, celery, and pecans in a large bowl and stir to combine.

3. Cut off both ends of each orange to create a flat surface so that the fruit can sit level on a cutting board. Using a sharp paring knife, remove wide strips of the peel and pith by cutting downward, following the contour of the fruit. Leave the flesh intact. Holding the orange over a bowl to catch the juice, slice between the white membranes to release the fruit in segments. Cut the orange segments in half crosswise to form bite-size pieces. Add the oranges and the reserved juice to the salad.

4. Add the vinaigrette and celery leaves and toss gently to combine. Serve immediately, or refrigerate, covered, until serving time. The salad is best eaten the day it is made.

Chicken Salad with Two Rices

For a more economical version of Chicken and Wild Rice Salad, you can use white rice, such as long grain, jasmine, or basmati, in place of two-thirds of the wild rice. In Step 1, place ¼ cup wild rice and the salt in a medium-size saucepan, add 2 cups cold water, and simmer, covered, for 25 minutes. Then add ½ cup white rice and an additional ½ cup water. Continue to cook, covered, until the rice is tender, about 15 minutes more. Uncover the pan and let the rice cool to room temperature. Continue with the recipe at Step 2.

Golden Balsamic Vinaigrette

If you have never tried golden balsamic vinegar, do! It is lighter and fresher tasting than the traditional dark balsamic vinegar—still intense, but with a hint of fruitiness. And it won't darken foods the way regular balsamic does.

Makes about 1 cup

½ cup extra-virgin olive oil

¼ cup plus 2 tablespoons golden
   balsamic vinegar

¼ cup canola oil

1½ teaspoons sugar

1 teaspoon minced garlic

1 teaspoon minced shallot

½ teaspoon dried thyme leaves

¼ teaspoon salt

¼ teaspoon freshly ground black pepper

Place all the ingredients in a glass jar and seal the lid tightly. Shake the jar vigorously until the sugar dissolves. (The vinaigrette can be refrigerated, covered, for up to 1 month. Let it return to room temperature and then shake vigorously before using.)

using cold water helps us get out of environmental hot water

Sometimes cold (or cooler) water works just as well as hot water, and there's a lot of energy savings involved. Here are a few tips.

Turn down your water heater.

The thermostat on the water heater in a typical household is set at 140°F. But did you know that water heated to 120°F is usually hot enough? Lowering your water heater temperature also lowers levels of global-warming CO_2. Any time you burn fossil fuel, greenhouse gases like CO_2 are produced. (See page 183 for more information about global warming and greenhouse gases.) According to Power Scorecard (founded by leading environmental organizations and scientists), each 10-degree reduction for an electric water heater (most electricity is generated by the burning of a fossil fuel) means we lessen the amount of CO_2 produced per year by 600 pounds; for a gas heater, it saves 440 pounds of CO_2. This is the CO_2 equivalent of driving a small car over 1,000 miles for the electric water heater and 745 miles for the gas heater.

And here's another interesting tidbit from Power Scorecard: "If every household turned its water heater thermostat down 20 degrees, we could prevent more than 45 million tons of annual CO_2 emissions—the same amount emitted by the entire nation of Kuwait or Libya."

When possible, do laundry with cold water.

If everyone in the U.S. used cold water to do their laundry, we could prevent somewhere in the realm of 60 million tons of CO_2 emissions each year. There are many good cold-water detergents available, and an added benefit is that our washables will last longer.

Use more cold water in the kitchen.

When you think of it, there are many times when we don't need to use hot water in the kitchen—for example, when rinsing dishes. Being mindful of using hot water can really help lower your energy bills and help cool global warming.

Wild Rice and Shiitake Salad

WILD RICE, WHICH REALLY ISN'T RICE AT ALL, has a terrific chewy texture and nutty flavor. Unlike true rice, which can get mushy when tossed with vegetables and salad dressing, it holds up beautifully in composed salads. In this hearty salad, crunchy toasted almonds boost the nuttiness of the rice, shiitake mushrooms add a rich, earthy note, and dried cranberries lend a touch of sweetness to every bite. This salad makes great picnic or barbecue fare, and it can be served as a room-temperature side dish with grilled fish or roast chicken. ⟶ *Serves 6 to 8*

1 cup wild rice, rinsed well
 (or 4 cups cooked wild rice;
 see sidebar, this page)
Salt
About 4 cups cold water
3 tablespoons canola oil
8 ounces shiitake mushrooms,
 stems removed, caps thinly sliced
 (about 4 cups)
1 cup whole almonds (skins on),
 toasted and coarsely chopped
¾ cup dried unsweetened cranberries
¼ cup thinly sliced scallions
 (white part and 3 inches of green)
About ¾ cup Golden Balsamic Vinaigrette
 (facing page)
Freshly ground black pepper

1. Place the rice and 1 teaspoon salt in a medium-size saucepan and add enough cold water to cover by ½ inch. Bring to a boil, covered, over high heat. Then reduce the heat to medium and cook gently until the rice is tender, 40 to 50 minutes. Drain the rice and transfer it to a large mixing bowl.

2. Heat the oil in a large skillet over medium-high heat. Add the mushrooms and cook, stirring frequently, until they are tender, 6 to 8 minutes. Add the mushrooms to the rice, and stir in the almonds, cranberries, and scallions.

3. Add about ½ cup of the Golden Balsamic Vinaigrette to the rice mixture, stirring to combine. Taste, and add more dressing (sparingly) if needed. Season with salt and pepper to taste. The salad can be served at room temperature or cold. (It can be refrigerated, covered, for up to 5 days.)

THE BASICS

Wild Rice

Wild rice is technically not a true rice; it is the seed of an aquatic grass that grows in marshy areas, native to the Great Lakes region. The grain was once a favorite food of Native Americans, who harvested the grass from dugout canoes. Commercial production today is limited to the Midwest states, California, Australia, and Canada, where the grass is grown in shallow freshwater bays, rivers, and lakes, or in man-made paddies. Mechanical harvesting is now the norm, but in some areas the rice is still hand-harvested, which contributes to its lofty price tag. From a nutritional standpoint, wild rice has more protein than other rices and is a good source of a number of the B vitamins. Wild rice is often mixed with other rices or grains, such as bulgur, to stretch its yield. Be sure to rinse wild rice in cold water to remove any debris before cooking. Cook it slowly so the slender grains don't overcook and turn starchy.

Brown Rice and Chickpea Rainbow Salad

THE TITLE OF THIS RECIPE just hints at how special this salad is. True, brown rice and chickpeas play starring roles, but tomatoes, cucumbers, red onion, and Kalamata olives add beautiful color, texture, and flavor to the dish. Moistened with a zesty Pesto Vinaigrette, this is a deliciously different, nutritious salad that makes a great addition to a picnic or barbecue and suffices as a stand-alone vegetarian meal. *Serves 6 to 8*

Versatile chickpeas are a good source of protein.

1 cup short-grain brown rice
Salt
1 cup cooked chickpeas (garbanzo beans; see box, page 422), rinsed and drained if canned
2 medium tomatoes, cored, seeded, and cut into ¼-inch dice (about 1¼ cups)
1 cucumber, peeled, seeded, and cut into ¼-inch dice (1 cup)
1 small red onion, cut into ¼-inch dice (about 1 cup)
¾ cup Kalamata olives, pitted and sliced
½ cup chopped fresh flat-leaf parsley
1 tablespoon fresh lemon juice
About ¾ cup Pesto Vinaigrette (recipe follows)
Freshly ground black pepper

1. Place the rice, 2¼ cups water, and 1 teaspoon salt in a small saucepan, cover, and bring to a boil over medium-high heat. Reduce the heat to maintain a simmer and cook until the water has been absorbed and the rice is tender or nearly so, 30 to 40 minutes. Check the water level once or twice during cooking to make sure that it has not evaporated, and add a little more water if needed.

2. Remove the pan from the heat, and spread the rice on a rimmed baking sheet so that it will cool quickly. (You should have about 3 cups.)

3. Place the rice, chickpeas, tomatoes, cucumber, red onion, olives, parsley, and lemon juice in a large bowl and stir to combine.

4. Add ½ cup of the Pesto Vinaigrette to the mixture, and toss to coat. Taste, and add more dressing if needed. Season with salt and pepper to taste, and serve chilled or at room temperature. (The salad can be refrigerated, covered, for up to 5 days.)

Pesto Vinaigrette

The deep emerald-green color of this salad dressing matches the vibrancy and intensity of its flavor. Similar to pesto in taste, but with a bit more acidity, the vinaigrette stands up well to hearty salads. It's also delicious in pasta salads and in green salads based on sturdy lettuces such as radicchio, romaine, or iceberg.
—◠◠◠— *Makes about ¾ cup*

½ cup (packed) fresh basil leaves

¼ cup unseasoned rice vinegar

1 small shallot, halved

1 tablespoon pine nuts

1 tablespoon freshly grated Parmesan
   cheese

1 large clove garlic, peeled

1 teaspoon salt

½ teaspoon freshly ground black pepper

¼ cup extra-virgin olive oil

2 tablespoons canola oil

1. Place the basil, vinegar, shallot halves, pine nuts, Parmesan, garlic, salt, and pepper in a blender or food processor. Pulse until the mixture forms a finely chopped coarse paste, stopping once or twice to scrape the sides of the bowl with a rubber spatula.

2. With the machine running, add the olive and canola oils in a slow, steady stream, and process until fully emulsified. (The vinaigrette can be refrigerated, covered, for up to 1 week. Let it return to room temperature before using.)

Mediterranean Spinach and Orzo Salad

L IGHT, SATISFYING, AND VISUALLY APPEALING, this salad combines an assortment of delicious ingredients that are staples of Mediterranean cuisine—spinach, sun-dried tomatoes, olives, and feta cheese. In the time it takes to cook the orzo, you can assemble the other components and make the vinaigrette. As an added bonus, this salad can be made a day ahead, covered, and refrigerated. For the best flavor, let the chilled salad come to room temperature before serving. —◠◠◠— *Serves 4 to 6*

Sun-dried tomatoes

1 cup orzo pasta, preferably whole wheat

4 ounces fresh baby spinach, well rinsed
   and patted dry if needed

⅓ cup oil-packed sun-dried tomatoes,
   chopped

½ cucumber, peeled, seeded, and diced

¼ cup Kalamata olives, pitted and chopped

2 teaspoons chopped fresh oregano, or
   ¾ teaspoon dried

Red Wine Vinaigrette (recipe follows)

Salt and freshly ground black pepper

2½ ounces feta cheese, crumbled (½ cup)

1. Bring a large covered saucepan of salted water to a boil over high heat. Add the orzo and cook according to the package directions until just tender, 9 to 11 minutes. Drain, and rinse under cold running water until the pasta cools to room temperature. Drain well again, and transfer the orzo to a large bowl.

2. Add the spinach, sun-dried tomatoes, cucumber, olives, and oregano to the orzo and toss to combine.

3. Add half of the Red Wine Vinaigrette and toss again. Taste, and add more dressing if desired. Season with salt and pepper to taste.

4. Transfer the salad to a platter, and sprinkle with the feta. Serve at room temperature.

Red Wine Vinaigrette

This classic vinaigrette, with its vibrancy and assertive flavors, is delicious paired with all leafy greens and is robust enough to stand up to heartier grain or pasta salads. —*Makes about 1 cup*

½ cup extra-virgin olive oil

¼ cup canola oil

¼ cup red wine vinegar

1 teaspoon minced shallot

½ teaspoon minced garlic

½ teaspoon sugar

½ teaspoon salt

¼ teaspoon dried thyme

¼ teaspoon dried oregano

¼ teaspoon freshly ground black pepper

Place all the ingredients in a glass jar and seal the lid tightly. Shake the jar vigorously to combine. (The vinaigrette can be refrigerated, covered, for up to 1 month. Let it return to room temperature and then shake vigorously before using.)

Note: This vinaigrette recipe makes double the amount you need for the Mediterranean Spinach and Orzo Salad. But it stores well and is a great dressing to have on hand for just about any type of salad.

Potatoes

It's not surprising that potatoes are America's most popular vegetable when you consider how great tasting and versatile they are. They can be served at every meal, starting with hash browns or home fries at breakfast, then on to potato chips as a snack food, and potato gratin for dinner. And is there any better comfort food than mashed potatoes?

Potatoes come in an array of sizes, shapes, textures, and colors. In the United States the vast majority can be loosely divided into five categories: russet, long white, round red, round white, and yellow-fleshed.

- **RUSSET POTATOES** are the most widely used variety in this country. This is a large, all-purpose potato with a high starch and low moisture content. When baked they have a light, fluffy flesh, sometimes described as mealy. Russets are generally the potato of choice for French fries, gratins, and baking. They tend to fall apart, however, when cut and boiled for salads, soups, or stews.

- **FINGERLINGS** are a newly popular potato, although they are actually a form of long whites. The name refers to the shape rather than a type of tuber, and they can be found in a range of skin and flesh colors. These small, thumb-shaped potatoes generally boast thin skins and a rich,

buttery texture. Russian Banana and French Fingerlings are the most common, and are excellent for baking, grilling, roasting, and steaming.

- **ROUND RED AND ROUND WHITES** are medium-size potatoes, distinguishable mainly by the color of their skins. Both are considered boiling potatoes, although they truly are all-purpose tubers, great for pan roasting, braising, grilling, and mashing. Thin-skinned, with white, waxy flesh characterized by a medium to low starch content, they have a moist, creamy texture when cooked.

- **YELLOW-FLESHED POTATOES,** such as Yukon Gold, German Butterball, and Yellow Finn, have skins and flesh that range from

yellow to gold. These are considered boiling potatoes because of their high moisture content. Their dense, creamy texture and buttery flavor make them a popular choice for mashed potatoes.

Numerous potatoes are marketed as "new" potatoes. These are simply any variety that has been harvested young, before the sugars convert to starch. They are prized for their crisp, waxy texture, sweet taste, and thin, papery skins. They are ideal for soups and potato salads because they hold their shape well and don't need peeling. They also work well when grilled or pan-roasted.

Many are heritage or heirloom varieties that have been around for centuries but not grown for commercial consumption. Look for blue and purple potatoes, most closely related to those cultivated by the Incas in the 16th century. They have an earthy, nutty flavor, and their flesh ranges in color from dark bluish purple or lavender to white. Many varieties will stain your hands while peeling. If this is a concern, you should wear rubber gloves.

When selecting potatoes, look for firm tubers that are free of cracks and soft brown spots. Avoid green-colored skins, excessive eyes, and sprouting. Ideally, potatoes should not be refrigerated; store them in a brown paper, perforated plastic, or mesh bag in a cool, dark, well-ventilated place. Use them as soon as possible, within 10 days to 2 weeks of purchasing. If you need to store them for a longer time, refrigeration will extend their shelf life. For information about cooking potatoes, see page 225.

Three-Color Potato Salad

GROW DIFFERENT TYPES OF NEW POTATOES in my garden, and this recipe may be my favorite way to serve them. The salad is a glorious combination of potatoes with green beans, tomatoes, olives, capers, and parsley. It's a perfect dish to bring to a picnic or potluck. —ᴍᴍ— *Serves 6 to 8*

1½ pounds small new potatoes, preferably in assorted colors such as red, purple, and yellow, scrubbed (peeling optional)

Salt

About 4 cups cold water

About 8 ounces fresh green beans or wax beans, or a combination of both, trimmed, blanched (see sidebar, page 163), and cut into 1-inch lengths (1½ cups)

2 large ripe tomatoes, cored and cut into ½-inch dice

1 small red onion, halved through the stem end, then very thinly sliced crosswise

½ cup Kalamata olives, pitted and halved

⅓ cup chopped fresh flat-leaf parsley

2 tablespoons capers, drained

Pinch of dried red pepper flakes

¼ cup extra-virgin olive oil

1 tablespoon fresh lemon juice

1 teaspoon dried oregano

Freshly ground black pepper

1. Place the potatoes in a large pot, and add 1 tablespoon salt and enough cold water to cover. Cover the pot and bring the water to a boil over high heat. Then reduce the heat to medium-low and simmer until the potatoes are tender, 20 to 30 minutes, depending on their size.

2. While the potatoes are cooking, place the green beans, tomatoes, red onion, olives, parsley, capers, and red pepper flakes in a large mixing bowl, and stir gently to combine.

3. Combine the olive oil, lemon juice, and oregano in a small glass jar and seal the lid tightly. Shake the jar vigorously to combine. Season the vinaigrette with salt and pepper to taste, and set it aside at room temperature.

4. When the potatoes are tender, drain them immediately, and then let them cool until they can be handled. Cut the potatoes into small pieces, and add them to the bean mixture. Pour the vinaigrette over the vegetables, and toss gently to coat thoroughly. Season with salt and pepper, if desired. The salad can be served at room temperature or chilled. (It can be refrigerated, covered, for up to 3 days.)

LIVING GREEN
It's best to avoid using disposable cups, plates, and utensils. Most paper disposables can't be recycled due to the coating that helps them resist heat and moisture, so they end up in landfill. Just like getting in the habit of bringing your own bags to the supermarket, why not bring your own plates and silverware on a picnic? They are sturdier, more enjoyable to eat with, and don't generate waste—so many reasons to feel good.

Three-Color Potato Salad

German Potato Salad

If you scrub the potato skins well, there's no need to peel them off.

POTATO SALAD IS A PERENNIAL FIXTURE at picnics and barbecues, popular with just about everyone. There are as many versions as there are cooks; this one is a classic German preparation, enlivened with bacon and vinegar. The potatoes are steamed rather than boiled, so that they retain their shape and vitamins. If you prefer more crunch in your potato salad, customize the recipe by adding diced celery, red onion, dill pickles, or whatever you like best. ⁓ *Serves 6 to 8*

2 pounds thin-skinned waxy potatoes, such as Yukon Gold, Red Bliss, or Yellow Finn, cut into ¾-inch chunks (peeling optional)

8 ounces thick-sliced bacon, cut into ½-inch pieces

2 tablespoons distilled white vinegar

1 cup mayonnaise

1 bunch scallions, thinly sliced (white part and 3 inches of green, about ½ cup sliced)

¼ cup chopped fresh flat-leaf parsley

Salt and freshly ground black pepper

1. Pour water to a depth of about 1 inch into a saucepan, cover the pan, and bring the water to a boil over medium-high heat. Place the potatoes in a steamer basket, set it over the boiling water, cover the pan, and steam the potatoes until they are tender when pierced with the tip of a knife, 10 to 15 minutes.

2. Meanwhile, cook the bacon in a skillet over medium-low heat, turning it occasionally, until crisp, about 15 minutes. Transfer the bacon to paper towels to drain. Turn off the heat, and discard all but 1 tablespoon of the fat. Add the vinegar to the skillet and stir to blend.

3. Place the mayonnaise in a small bowl, and add the vinegar-fat mixture, stirring to combine.

4. Drain the potatoes in a colander and transfer them to a large bowl. Add half of the mayonnaise mixture to the still-hot potatoes and stir to combine; reserve the remaining mayonnaise mixture. Let the potatoes cool to room temperature.

5. When the potatoes are at room temperature, add the bacon, scallions, parsley, and the remaining mayonnaise mixture, and stir to combine. Season with salt and pepper to taste. Serve immediately, or refrigerate the salad, covered, until serving time. (It can be refrigerated for up to 3 days.)

Lemon Couscous Salad with Spinach

LIGHT AND LEMONY, this simple preparation makes a nice side dish that goes with just about everything. The spinach is blended into the warm couscous, so it wilts just a bit. The lemon dressing and fresh dill perk up the couscous, giving it brightness and flavor, while toasted walnuts add crunch to the medley. The salad can be made a day ahead, but add the walnuts just before serving so they don't get soggy. For maximum flavor, let the salad come to room temperature before serving. *Serves 6*

1¼ teaspoons salt

1½ cups couscous

2 cups (3 ounces) packed baby spinach leaves, well rinsed and patted dry if needed, cut into thin ribbons

4 scallions (white part and 3 inches of green), thinly sliced

3 tablespoons chopped fresh dill

¼ cup extra-virgin olive oil or walnut oil

3 tablespoons fresh lemon juice

¼ teaspoon freshly ground black pepper

½ cup walnut pieces, toasted

1. Bring 2 cups water and ½ teaspoon of the salt to a boil in a small saucepan over high heat.

2. Place the couscous in a large heatproof mixing bowl and add the boiling water. Immediately cover the bowl with a kitchen towel. Let it sit until the water is absorbed, about 7 minutes. Fluff the couscous with a fork.

3. While the couscous is still warm, add the spinach, scallions, and dill, stirring to combine.

4. In a small bowl, whisk together the olive oil, lemon juice, remaining ¾ teaspoon salt, and the pepper. Add the dressing to the couscous, stirring to coat. Add the walnuts, and serve at room temperature. (The salad can be refrigerated, covered, for up to 3 days.)

Fresh baby spinach ready for harvesting.

Farro Salad with Edamame and Arugula

Farro Salad with Edamame and Arugula

W E ALL KNOW THAT ADDING HEALTHY WHOLE GRAINS to our diet is important, but most of us fall short of the daily recommended three servings. If you're looking for something enticing in the grain category, farro may become your new favorite. This ancient grain is easy to cook and has a wonderful nutty flavor and an appealing chewy texture. Here we've paired it with edamame (Japanese green soybeans), which are rich in vitamins, minerals, protein, and omega-3 fatty acids, and with peppery, nutrient-rich arugula.

Serves 6 to 8

Salt

1¼ cups farro (see box, page 264)

1½ cups shelled fresh (1½ pounds unshelled) or frozen edamame (soybeans), thawed if frozen

2 cups lightly packed arugula, coarsely chopped

½ cup thinly sliced scallions (white part and 3 inches of green)

¾ cup Tomato Vinaigrette (recipe follows)

Freshly ground black pepper

1. Bring 6 cups of water to a boil in a large covered saucepan over high heat. Add 1 tablespoon salt and the farro, and return to a boil. Then reduce the heat to medium-low and cook, stirring occasionally, until the farro is puffed and slightly chewy, 20 to 30 minutes. (Do not overcook, or the farro will be mushy.) Drain the farro immediately, and rinse it under cold running water until it is cool. Drain again, and transfer it to a large bowl.

2. Bring a covered medium-size saucepan of water to a boil over high heat. Add the edamame and ½ teaspoon salt and cook until the edamame is crisp-tender, 3 to 5 minutes, or if frozen, according to the package directions.

3. Meanwhile, fill a medium-size bowl with ice water.

4. Drain the edamame and plunge it into the bowl of ice water. When the edamame is cool, drain it thoroughly and add it to the farro.

5. Add the arugula and scallions to the mixture, and toss to combine. Add ½ cup of the Tomato Vinaigrette and stir to combine. Taste, and add more dressing if desired. Season the salad with salt and pepper to taste, and serve at room temperature. (The salad can be refrigerated, covered, for up to 3 days.)

Tomato Vinaigrette

This fresh Tomato Vinaigrette adds a hint of sweetness to the farro salad—and if you have any dressing left over, it tastes great on leafy green salads, too.

—— Makes 1 cup

2 large tomatoes, peeled, seeded, and
   chopped (¾ cup; see sidebar, page 131)

2 tablespoons white wine vinegar

1½ tablespoons chopped fresh oregano,
   or 1½ teaspoons dried

½ teaspoon minced peeled garlic

1 teaspoon salt

¼ teaspoon freshly ground black pepper

¼ cup extra-virgin olive oil

1. Place the tomatoes, vinegar, oregano, garlic, salt, and pepper in a food processor or blender, and puree until smooth. With the machine running, add the olive oil in a slow, steady stream.

2. Use immediately, or transfer the dressing to a glass jar, seal the lid tightly, and refrigerate for up to 1 week. Let it return to room temperature and then shake vigorously before using.

THE BASICS

Farro

Farro (also known as "emmer wheat") is one of the first grains humans ate in Egypt and Mesopotamia—as early as 17,000 B.C., even before the development of domestic agriculture. It was valued for its hardiness as well as its heartiness— farro grows well in poor conditions, and its grain is packed with protein. It's said that farro sustained the Roman legions as they conquered the known world; its warm, nutty flavor is still especially prized by the Italians.

Today farro is returning to the limelight both for its delightful flavor and for its health benefits. Although it resembles a short-grain rice, it's actually a variety of wheat. Like barley and oats, farro is a cereal whose husk adheres to the grain, making it an excellent source of fiber. It's also a good source of the antioxidant vitamin E, which supports the body's immune system and its ability to heal an injury. When combined with legumes— as it is in many Tuscan recipes— farro forms a complete protein source, so it's a great choice for vegetarian diets.

With its chewy texture and delicious nutty flavor, farro is a healthy addition to soups, stews, and salads, and it can be used as a stand-in for Arborio rice in risottos. It's available in either whole-grain or a quick-cooking semi-pearled form (like rice, the more it's processed, the more nutrition it loses). Farro pastas are also gaining in popularity—they retain a nutty flavor but their tender texture is smooth, not grainy. Many people who are allergic to modern hybridized wheat find they can tolerate farro because it contains less gluten, and what it has is more easily digested. (People with severe allergies or celiac disease should check with their doctor before trying it, however.)

Panzanella Salad

PANZANELLA IS A TRADITIONAL ITALIAN BREAD SALAD that probably originated as a thrifty way to use up bread that was no longer fresh. Cubes of day-old (or older) bread are tossed with tomatoes, cucumbers, onions, and peppers. A zesty dressing made with sun-dried tomatoes adds another dimension and moistens the bread so that the ingredients meld into a very flavorful meal. This is a salad that lets you be creative: Capers, olives, or anchovies are also delicious additions. The bread can be toasted if you want more crunch. ⸺ *Serves 6*

12 ounces day-old country-style bread, with
crusts, cut into 1-inch cubes (8 cups)

4 large tomatoes, cored, seeded, and
chopped, juices reserved

1 large cucumber, peeled, seeded, and cut
into ½-inch dice

2 medium red, yellow, or green bell peppers,
stemmed, seeded, and cut into ¼-inch dice
(about 2 cups)

1 small red onion, cut into ¼-inch dice
(1 cup)

¾ to 1 cup Sun-Dried Tomato Vinaigrette
(recipe follows)

Salt and freshly ground black pepper

20 fresh basil leaves, cut into very thin
ribbons

1. Place the bread in a large bowl, and add the tomatoes, cucumber, bell peppers, and red onion.

2. Add ¾ cup of the Sun-Dried Tomato Vinaigrette to the mixture, and toss to coat all the ingredients evenly. Taste, and add more vinaigrette if the salad is dry.

3. Season the salad with salt and pepper to taste, and garnish with the basil. The salad should be served within an hour or two of making. If made too far in advance, the bread will soak up all the dressing and you will need to add more.

THE BASICS

Use that Stale Bread!

Bread that's a day or two old, and has gone a little stale, is even better than fresh for recipes like Panzanella Salad, Bonnie's Garlicky Croutons (page 56), and bread crumbs (the sidebar on page 179).

Sun-Dried Tomato Vinaigrette

Loaded with flavor, this vinaigrette is a perfect partner for our Panzanella Salad, but it's also terrific tossed with sturdy greens such as romaine. ⸺ *Makes about 2 cups*

⅓ cup sun-dried tomatoes, reconstituted in
hot water if not soft and pliable, chopped

½ teaspoon minced peeled garlic

½ cup red wine vinegar

¼ cup balsamic vinegar

½ cup canola oil

½ cup extra-virgin olive oil

Salt and freshly ground black pepper

Bulgur and Grilled Vegetable Salad

1. Place the sun-dried tomatoes, garlic, and both vinegars in a food processor or blender. Puree until smooth, scraping the sides of the bowl once during processing, about 1 minute.

2. With the machine running, add the canola and olive oils in a slow, steady stream. The dressing will be thick. Add salt and pepper to taste. (The vinaigrette can be refrigerated, covered, for up to 2 months. For the best flavor, serve at room temperature.)

Bulgur and Grilled Vegetable Salad

BULGUR WHEAT IS A QUICK-COOKING GRAIN that works well in salads because it's light and fluffy but still has a tender, chewy texture. Here I've added an assortment of colorful grilled vegetables, crumbles of briny feta cheese, and a zesty red wine vinaigrette to the bulgur, which soaks up the flavors in a delicious way. It is also makes a beautiful appetizer—simply top whole leaves of butter or romaine lettuce with about ¼ cup of the salad for each lettuce cup. The salad is meant to be served at room temperature, but I also like it served both cold and warm. It can be refrigerated, covered, for up to 5 days.

Serves 6 to 8

SALAD

2 cups bulgur wheat

3 cups cold water

Salt

3 medium zucchini, trimmed and cut lengthwise into ¼-inch-thick strips

1 large red onion, cut into ¼-inch-thick rounds

2 roasted red bell peppers (see page 411), cut into ½-inch pieces, or 2 raw red bell peppers, stemmed, seeded, and cut into large pieces

⅓ cup olive oil

Freshly ground black pepper

5 ounces feta cheese, crumbled (about 1 cup)

DRESSING

⅓ cup extra-virgin olive oil

2 tablespoons red wine vinegar

1½ tablespoons fresh lemon juice

1 tablespoon dried oregano

½ tablespoon minced peeled garlic

1 teaspoon salt

¼ teaspoon freshly ground black pepper

TO SERVE

Salt and freshly ground black pepper

THE BASICS

Bulgur

Bulgur is a staple food in the Middle East and North Africa. It is made by steaming whole wheat kernels, which are then hulled and dried. The kernels are either left whole or cracked into different sizes. This partial cooking transforms bulgur into a fast-cooking grain, which makes it easier to prepare than other grains. Bulgur can be purchased in coarse, medium, and fine grinds. It has a tender, chewy texture and is excellent in soups, pilafs, and salads—most familiar in tabbouleh, where it is the grain of choice.

THE BASICS

Peppers: First Green, then Red

All red bell peppers start out green, and then turn red over time, but certain varieties turn red more quickly and are more uniform. On average, it takes three additional weeks for a full-size green bell pepper to turn red on the vine.

1. Prepare the salad: Place the bulgur, cold water, and 1½ teaspoons salt in a large saucepan, cover, and bring to a boil over high heat. Reduce the heat to medium-low and cook until the bulgur is tender, 12 to 15 minutes. Drain off any excess water and transfer the bulgur to a large bowl, stirring to fluff the grains.

2. *If you intend to grill the vegetables,* place the zucchini, onion, and raw bell peppers, if using, in a bowl and toss with the olive oil, ½ teaspoon salt, and black pepper to taste. Grill over medium-high heat until the vegetables are tender, 3 to 8 minutes. (The zucchini will cook faster than the red peppers.) Set aside at room temperature.

If you are using a ridged grill pan or a cast-iron skillet for indoor cooking, heat the pan over medium-high heat. Add 2 tablespoons of the olive oil, and cook the zucchini until browned on one side, 2 to 3 minutes. Turn the strips over and cook on the other side until crisp-tender, another 1 or 2 minutes. Transfer the zucchini to a

cutting board and let cool. Repeat with the raw red peppers, if using, and the onion rounds, cooking each vegetable separately until crisp-tender, 4 to 6 minutes each, adding 2 tablespoons of oil to the skillet for each vegetable.

3. When the vegetables are cool enough to handle, cut them into ½-inch dice. Add the vegetables to the bulgur. (If you are using roasted red peppers, add them as well.) Add the feta, and toss to combine the ingredients.

4. Prepare the dressing: Place all the ingredients in a glass jar and seal the lid tightly. Shake the jar vigorously to combine. (The dressing can be refrigerated, covered, for up to 1 month. Let it return to room temperature and then shake vigorously before using.)

5. Add half of the dressing to the bulgur mixture, and toss to coat. Taste, and add more dressing if needed. Season the salad with salt and pepper to taste, and serve.

BAKING BREAD

Plus 8 more useful tips.

Nothing Beats Fresh-Baked Bread

THERE'S SOMETHING INTOXICATING ABOUT THE SMELL OF FRESH BREAD. ALL willpower melts like butter as warm loaves emerge from the oven, and baking is a sure-fire way to draw family and friends to the pleasures of your kitchen.

Homemade bread has an artisanal quality that's infinitely superior to most plastic-wrapped store-bought varieties. But it is, admittedly, a lot of work, and most towns of some size have several bakeries where you can pick up delicious breads fresh from the oven. So why make your own? First of all, going through the steps to make your own yeasty dough and bakery goods is intensely rewarding and satisfying. Even if you do it only once, you'll have a deeper appreciation for baked goods forever. Also, once you've nurtured and worked dough into bread, pita, pizza, or bagels, you develop a special relationship with it. There is a connection and a sense of pride because of the time you put into it and your intimate knowledge of every stage of its creation—akin to the difference between wearing a sweater you've knitted yourself and one you bought at a department store. Baking is also an adventure full of surprises. A recipe may turn out slightly different each time you make it because of variations in the weather, ingredients, your mood, and serendipity.

My memorable initiation into the pleasures of cooking was making bread for the first time. There was something magical and empowering about learning how to turn a few simple ingredients into incredibly delicious bread— a rite of passage of sorts. After that, I knew that if I put my mind to it, I could cook anything.

Myra's 100% Whole Wheat Bread is the first bread I learned to make, and it's the same simple recipe I have used since I was in college. It makes 2 loaves, so you can save one for later or give it as a gift. And you can use the same dough to make Whole Wheat Cinnamon Raisin Swirl for a deliciously sweet variation. You'll also find recipes here for other great breads: Rosemary Potato Bread, Kalamata Olive

Irresistible Mini Calzones (page 298)

Bread, Wickets Bistro Focaccia, and more.

I've included recipes to extend your baking experience to two foods not often made at home: bagels and pita bread. As former New Yorkers, Drew and I have high expectations when it comes to bagels. While they aren't exactly New York style, my Homemade Bagels taste great, and are made with healthy whole-grain flour. Also, trying out the different toppings is really fun. And I love our 100% Whole Wheat Pita Bread recipe. If you've never tasted a pita fresh from the oven, you're in for a treat. We experimented with many versions until we arrived at one that consistently puffs into pockets every time.

The pizza dough can serve as a springboard for several different recipes. You can make Whole Wheat Pizza with Heirloom Tomatoes, Fresh Mozzarella, and Pesto, which is something Drew and I taught ourselves to make in those early days of Earthbound Farm. But don't stop there. You'll also find recipes for using the dough to make Irresistible Mini Calzones, Focaccia-Style Flatbread, and Pesto Cheese Bread, a recipe my son invented

that's become a family favorite.

Even if you don't have the time to do it often, baking imparts a sense of accomplishment and takes you back to a time when cooking basic foods was literally in our own hands. Baking your own bread or making your own pizza dough is one of those activities that can take you out of the hurried pace

of modern life. It's a time to sink your hands into something as much an elemental part of life as rich sun-warmed soil in the garden—kneading dough on a floured board works out physical as well as mental kinks. Wonderfully relaxing and rewarding, bread baking is one of my favorite things to do.

Myra's 100% Whole Wheat Bread (page 273)

Myra's 100% Whole Wheat Bread

Myra's 100% Whole Wheat Bread

BAKING BREAD WAS WHAT MADE ME FALL IN LOVE with cooking. After my first year of college I rented a house for the summer in Burlington, Vermont, with a gang of friends, and one of them taught me this very simple recipe, which I still use decades later. The magic of bread rising, the smell of bread baking, the taste of a slice of freshly baked bread with butter melting into it—it was incredible. I'd never experienced anything like it.

Making bread really *is* magical: the simple alchemy of transforming flour, water, and yeast into a fragrant, great-tasting loaf. This is my basic whole wheat bread, one that I make over and over again, with consistently excellent results. I prefer using all whole wheat flour, but if you prefer a lighter loaf, use half bread flour and half whole wheat. The dough yields 2 loaves, so you can freeze one, or you might want to turn half of the dough into Whole Wheat Cinnamon Raisin Swirl (page 274). Just use half the filling ingredients specified in that recipe, which is meant for 2 loaves. ⁓⁓ *Makes 2 loaves*

2 packets active dry yeast

1 teaspoon sugar

1 cup warm water (105° to 115°F)

1¼ cups nonfat milk, warmed
   (105° to 115°F)

¼ cup honey

5 to 6 cups whole wheat flour, plus extra
   for kneading

2 teaspoons salt

1 tablespoon canola oil, for oiling
   the bowl

Unsalted butter, for the pans

1. Place the yeast and sugar in a large bowl and add the warm water. Cover the bowl with a clean kitchen towel and let the mixture sit until it is foamy, 5 to 10 minutes.

2. Add the warm milk, honey, 4 cups of the flour, and salt to the yeast mixture and stir until combined. Gradually add more flour until the dough is too stiff to stir, and then transfer the dough to a lightly floured work surface. Knead it, adding more flour as needed, until it is smooth and elastic, about 10 minutes. Form the dough into a ball.

3. Lightly oil a large bowl, add the dough, and roll it around so that it is coated with oil. Cover the bowl with a clean kitchen towel and let it sit in a warm, draft-free place until the dough has doubled in size, 1 to 1½ hours.

4. Gently punch down the dough to deflate it, and then cut it in half.

5. Butter two standard-size loaf pans (8½ x 4 inches). Form each piece of dough into a loaf and place them in the prepared pans. Cover the pans with a clean kitchen towel, set them in a warm, draft-free place, and let the dough rise until it has doubled in size, about 1 hour.

6. Position a rack in the center of the oven and preheat the oven to 350°F.

7. Bake until the loaves are golden brown and have pulled away from the sides of the pans, about 40 minutes. To test for doneness, turn the breads out of the loaf pans and tap the bottoms, listening for a hollow sound. If they seem soft or don't sound hollow, bake them a little longer and test again.

8. Transfer the pans to a wire rack, and turn out the loaves. Let them cool on the rack for 20 to 30 minutes before slicing.

Whole Wheat Cinnamon Raisin Swirl

START THIS BREAD WITH A BATCH of my whole wheat bread dough, flatten it into a rectangle, and work in honey, cinnamon, and raisins. Then I roll it up and bake it until it's golden brown, and my house smells of fresh bread, cinnamon, and raisins. When it's sliced, it has a beautiful swirl of color. My family loves this delectable bread toasted for breakfast or as a late-night snack. We usually devour a whole loaf fresh from the oven! ⌇⌇⌇⌇ *Makes 2 loaves*

TIP

For a lighter loaf: To make a delicious, lighter textured version of the Whole Wheat Cinnamon Raisin Swirl bread, prepare the dough using half whole wheat flour and half unbleached white flour.

Unsalted butter, for the pans
Whole wheat flour, for dusting
Dough for Myra's 100% Whole Wheat Bread (page 273), prepared through Step 4
⅔ cup honey
4 teaspoons ground cinnamon
1½ cups raisins

1. Butter two 8½ x 4-inch loaf pans and set them aside.

2. Lightly flour a work surface, and place the balls of dough on it. Pat one into a flat rectangle, roughly 8 x 16 inches. Spread ⅓ cup of the honey over the piece of dough, leaving a 1-inch border uncovered on all sides. Then evenly sprinkle 2 teaspoons of the cinnamon over the honey and rub it into the dough with your fingers. Sprinkle with

Whole Wheat Cinnamon Raisin Swirl

¾ cup of the raisins, lightly pressing them into the dough. Repeat with the remaining rectangle of dough and the remaining honey, cinnamon, and raisins.

3. Starting at a short end, tightly roll each piece of dough up to form a log, and pinch the ends to close the loaf. Place the loaves in the prepared loaf pans, and cover the pans with a clean kitchen towel. Set the pans in a warm, draft-free place and let the dough rise until it has doubled in size, 1 to 1½ hours.

4. Position a rack in the center of the oven and preheat the oven to 350°F.

5. Bake until the loaves are golden brown and have pulled away from the sides of the pans, about 40 minutes. To test for doneness, turn the breads out of the loaf pans and tap the bottoms, listening for a hollow sound. If they seem soft or don't sound hollow, bake them a little longer and test again.

6. Transfer the pans to a wire rack and turn out the loaves. Let them cool on the rack for 20 to 30 minutes before slicing.

Whole Wheat and Rye Bread

ALTHOUGH THIS DOUGH DOES NOT CONTAIN a large amount of rye flour, the fine-textured loaf has the distinctive aroma and delicious flavor of rye bread. It makes a particularly delicious sandwich bread when paired with ham and cheese or with roast beef. If you like, add a few teaspoons of caraway seed to enhance the rye flavor. Don't skimp on the kneading steps when making this bread; the dough needs to be well worked in order to develop a light texture. Also, be aware that rye flour will soak up lots of water, so add the mixture of flours little by little to ensure that your dough doesn't become too dense. —*— Makes one 10 x 5-inch loaf or two 8½ x 4-inch loaves*

2 packets active dry yeast

1 tablespoon sugar

1½ cups warm water (105° to 115°F)

¼ cup olive oil, plus extra for the pans

4 cups whole wheat flour

½ cup dark rye flour

½ cup unbleached all-purpose flour, plus extra for kneading

1 tablespoon salt

1. Place the yeast and sugar in a large bowl. Add ½ cup of the warm water and cover the bowl with a clean kitchen towel. Let the mixture sit at room temperature until it is foamy, 5 to 10 minutes. Then add the olive oil and the remaining 1 cup warm water.

2. In another large bowl, whisk together the whole wheat, rye, and all-purpose flours, and the salt. Add the flour mixture to the yeast mixture a little at a time, stirring to combine. If the mixture is very dry, add another tablespoon or two of warm water. The dough should be slightly tacky.

3. Transfer the dough to a floured work surface and knead it, adding more all-purpose flour as needed, until it is smooth and elastic, about 10 minutes. Form the dough into a ball.

4. Lightly oil a large bowl with olive oil, add the dough, and roll the dough in the bowl to coat it with oil. Cover the bowl with a clean kitchen towel. Let it sit in a warm, draft-free place until the dough has doubled in size, about 1½ hours.

5. Oil one large or two smaller loaf pans with olive oil.

6. Gently punch down the dough to deflate it, and then knead it for 5 minutes. Form the dough into 1 large or 2 small loaves, and transfer it to the prepared pan(s). Cover the pan(s) with a clean kitchen towel and set aside in a draft-free place until the dough has risen above the rim of the pan(s), 30 to 40 minutes.

7. Position a rack in the lower third of the oven and preheat the oven to 375°F.

8. Bake the bread for 20 minutes. Then reduce the oven temperature to 350°F and continue baking until the bread is golden brown and has pulled away from the sides of the pan, about 40 minutes for the smaller loaves and 1 hour for the larger one. To test for doneness, turn the bread out of the loaf pan and tap the bottom, listening for a hollow sound. If it seems soft or doesn't sound hollow, bake it a little longer and test again.

9. Transfer the bread to a wire rack, remove it from the pan(s), and let it cool on the rack before slicing.

THE BASICS

Rye

Rye is grown primarily in Eastern Europe, but also in the United States and many other countries. It's hardier than wheat, and grows well in poor soil and adverse climate conditions. While it's most commonly used for flour, it is also made into grits and flakes, and whole rye berries make delicious grain salads. Rye is a nutrient-dense, healthy grain. It's an excellent source of manganese, and a good source of dietary fiber, selenium, tryptophan, phosphorus, magnesium, and protein.

Bread-Baking Tips

Once you discover the pleasures of baking bread—enjoying the aroma that permeates your home; seeing that loaf emerge from the oven, golden crusted and perfectly risen; anticipating a still warm slice, butter melting into all the little spaces—you just might become hooked for life!

But as rewarding as bread baking can be, it can also be frustrating. A lot goes into determining the quality of bread, and it's truly an adventure each time you set out to make a loaf. With experience, you can learn to "read" the dough, anticipate problems, and recognize how to correct them. The principles of bread making revolve around a few basic techniques. Here are some bread baking tips to help ensure your success.

YEAST

The chemistry of home bread baking is quite simple. The yeast has to be active. Check the "use by" dates on dried and fresh yeasts and discard any product that is past its replacement date.

PROOFING

The activation of the yeast, by mixing it with a warm liquid, causes it to release gas, which in turn will make the dough rise. In many recipes sugar is added to the yeast/water mixture to activate the yeast, which feeds on the sugar. When the mixture bubbles and foams, this "proves" the yeast is still potent. Never add salt to the proofing mixture of yeast and water when using active dry yeast. Salt kills yeast when it comes into direct contact. Instead, add salt when the bulk of the flour is added to the dough.

MIXING AND MEASURING

Bread ingredients usually include flour, or a combination of flours and other grains, yeast, water or other liquid, sugar (or another sweetener), and salt. Mixing the ingredients means combining them in a large mixing bowl and stirring with a wooden spoon until a sticky dough is formed (you can also use your hands or a standing mixer fitted with the paddle attachment to mix the dough).

It is common for bread dough recipes to give a range of flour needed rather than an exact amount. This is because many factors determine what that amount will be. One is temperature and humidity; another is that different types of flour absorb different amounts of water, depending on where and when the wheat was grown.

The most accurate way to measure flour is to spoon it into a measuring cup and level it off with the back of a knife or spatula. Alternatively, if a recipe specifies weights, use a kitchen scale. The addition of too much flour is usually the reason why a loaf comes out too heavy and dense.

Learning to use the correct amount of flour takes practice. When preparing a dough, never add all of the flour specified until you are certain that the entire amount is needed. Moisture encourages fermentation, which improves the flavor and texture of the bread. Bread dough should be slightly tacky rather than dry or very sticky. Add flour in small amounts until the dough is no longer sticky. As you mix the dough, if you end up with lots of dough on the spoon, use a spatula or your fingers to remove the dough and incorporate it into the ball of dough. The dough should hold together before you take it out of the bowl and start to knead it.

KNEADING

Kneading is the process of working and stretching the dough by pressing down on it with your hands, and folding it over onto itself until it's nice and elastic. This is essential because it creates heat to stretch the gluten in the flour, which in turns creates a well-risen, light-textured loaf of bread. As strands of gluten warm and become more pliable, the dough will become elastic and springy. Inadequate kneading means the dough cannot hold tiny pockets of air, and the bread will collapse during baking, resulting in a heavy, dense loaf. Before you begin kneading, sprinkle flour over a clean work surface. Then, flour your hands, gather up the dough in the bowl, and place it on your floured surface. Don't be tempted to skimp on the kneading step. When the dough can be easily stretched without breaking, it is ready for the next step.

RISING

After kneading, the dough needs to rest. Oil a large bowl, add the dough, and roll it around to lightly coat all surfaces with the oil. This will prevent the dough from sticking. Keep the bowl covered with a clean kitchen towel during rising to prevent it from drying out. The ideal temperature for rising bread dough is 75° to 80°F, so avoid drafty areas or hot spots. At room temperature, the first rise should take 1½ to 2 hours—less if the temperature is warmer, more if the room is cool. Yeast loves warmth, but it also loves moisture. If it's a humid day, your bread will rise more rapidly.

The dough should rise until it doubles in bulk. If you are not sure that it's ready, gently insert a finger into the center of the dough. The dough should not immediately spring back. If it does, let it rise for a little longer. Remember that rapid rising does not guarantee developed flavor: The slower the rise, the more complex the flavor of the bread will be.

FORMING

After the dough has doubled in bulk for the first rise, use a gentle fist to deflate it (this is sometimes referred to as "punching down"). Then place it on a floured work surface and knead it lightly for 1 to 2 minutes. This redistributes the yeast and the gases formed by fermentation. Depending on the recipe, form the dough into a round or oval, or carefully divide the dough as specified.

There is more than one way to shape the dough to fit into a loaf pan, but the easiest is to form the dough roughly into a loaf, smoothing it in your hands so that the seams are on the bottom. Simply roll the dough into a log, tucking any stray bits of dough under with your fingertips, creating a seam under the log. Pinch the seams closed. Oil or butter the loaf pans, plump the loaf with your hands to shape it nicely, and place it, seam side down, in the pan.

After shaping the dough and placing it in the pan or on a baking sheet (don't oil it unless the recipe instructs you to), a second rise is required to develop a full-flavored, fine-textured loaf of bread. Cover the dough with a clean kitchen towel so that the surface does not dry out, and let it rise in a warm, draft-free spot until just doubled in bulk. This usually takes 45 minutes to 1½ hours. Do not let the dough over-rise, or the loaf may collapse in the oven.

BAKING

Preheating the oven is a very important step in bread baking. Also be sure that the oven rack is placed in the position specified in the recipe, with plenty of room above it so that the bread has space to rise. Bake the bread according to the recipe directions. Do not undercook bread, or it will be wet and soggy. To test, turn it out of the loaf pan (if it is in one) and tap the bottom, listening for a hollow sound. If it seems soft or does not sound hollow, bake it a little longer.

Turn the loaf out of the pan and let it cool on the rack. Bread needs to cool completely to cut smoothly, but it's hard to wait that long for a first taste!

Knead dough by pressing down on it with the heels of your hands.

Seeded Multigrain Bread

ROLLED OATS, WHOLE WHEAT FLOUR, AND FLAXSEEDS combine to make an earthy, nutritious bread with a wonderful taste and texture. The bread freezes well and is great to have on hand for sandwiches and toast. Try it in the morning, toasted and topped with butter, peanut butter, or a slice of sharp cheddar cheese. ⏤⏤ *Makes 2 loaves*

2 packets (4½ teaspoons) active dry yeast

1 tablespoon sugar

2½ cups warm water (105° to 115°F)

3½ to 4 cups bread flour, plus extra
   for kneading

1¼ cups old-fashioned rolled oats
   (see sidebar, page 307)

1¼ cups whole wheat flour

½ cup flaxseeds (see box, page 288)

1 tablespoon coarse (kosher) salt

3 tablespoons olive oil, for the bowl and pans

1. Place the yeast and sugar in a small bowl and add ½ cup of the warm water. Cover the bowl with a clean kitchen towel and let the mixture sit until it is foamy, 5 to 10 minutes.

2. Place 3½ cups of the bread flour, the rolled oats, whole wheat flour, flaxseeds, and salt in a large mixing bowl and whisk to combine.

3. Add the yeast mixture to the flour mixture, stirring to combine. Then slowly add the remaining 2 cups warm water, stirring to form a cohesive mass. The dough should come away cleanly from the sides of the bowl and should be slightly sticky.

4. Turn out the dough onto a lightly floured surface and knead it, adding more bread flour as necessary to prevent the dough from sticking, until it is smooth and elastic, about 5 minutes.

5. Lightly oil a large mixing bowl, add the dough, and roll it around so that it is lightly coated with oil. Cover the bowl with a clean kitchen towel and let it sit in a warm, draft-free place until the dough has doubled in size, 1¼ to 1½ hours.

6. Lightly oil two 9 x 5-inch loaf pans.

7. Gently punch down the dough to deflate it. Cut the dough in half, and roll each piece into a compact cylinder, squeezing the dough together with your fingers as you roll. Tuck the ends of the dough underneath, and transfer the dough to the prepared loaf pans, placing the pieces seam down. Cover the pans with a kitchen towel and let them sit in a warm, draft-free place until the dough has doubled in size, about 1 hour.

8. Position a rack in the middle of the oven and preheat the oven to 375°F.

9. Bake the loaves until they are golden brown and have pulled away from the sides of the pans, about 1 hour. To test for doneness, turn the breads out of the loaf pans and tap the bottoms, listening for a hollow sound. If they seem soft or don't sound hollow, bake them a little longer and test again.

10. Transfer the loaves to a wire rack and unmold them immediately so that the crusts do not get soggy. Cool for at least 30 minutes on the rack before slicing and serving.

Homemade Bagels, Three Ways

I GREW UP IN NEW YORK CITY, where great bagels are a way of life. Moving to California meant adjusting to the lack of New York-style bagels. Over the years, as I became more health-conscious, I tried to find organic or whole wheat bagels, and finally decided to learn how to make them myself. Many people assume that making bagels is difficult, but it's really fun and quite easy, and you'll be surprised at how gratifying it is to create your own. You have the freedom to devise your own toppings, and making bagels at home with friends and kids is a wonderful activity. I offer three different topping ideas here, but of course, experiment all you want. If there are any bagels left uneaten on the day I make them, I simply cut them and freeze them. They stay perfectly fresh for future eating—just pop them in the toaster and enjoy! ⎯⎯ *Makes 12 large bagels*

2 packets active dry yeast

2 tablespoons honey

2½ cups warm water (105° to 115°F)

2½ cups whole wheat flour

1½ tablespoons vegetable oil, plus extra for the baking sheets

Salt

3 cups bread flour, plus extra for kneading

Cornmeal, for the baking sheets

SINGLE SEED TOPPINGS

¼ cup poppy seeds

2½ tablespoons flaxseeds (see box, page 288)

2½ tablespoons sunflower seeds

MIXED SEEDS TOPPING

1½ tablespoons sesame seeds

1½ tablespoons poppy seeds

1½ tablespoons caraway seeds

2½ teaspoons sea salt or fleur de sel (see sidebar, page 358)

THE BASICS

Boiling Bagels

Boiling bagels prior to baking is the secret behind their signature dense, doughy, chewy texture. Immersing the dough in boiling water allows the starch in the flour to absorb moisture, resulting in a gelatinized coating. Once the bagel is baked, this starchy coating sets into a brown and shiny exterior crust.

1. Place the yeast and honey in a small bowl. Add 1 cup of the warm water and cover the bowl with a clean kitchen towel. Let the mixture sit until it is foamy, 5 to 10 minutes.

2. Place the whole wheat flour in a large bowl and make a well in the middle. Add the yeast mixture, the remaining 1½ cups warm water, the vegetable oil, and 2 teaspoons salt. Stir until the mixture is smooth. Then add the bread flour, 1 cup at a time, stirring until the dough is stiff. (You may not need to add all of the flour at this stage.) When the dough is too stiff to stir, turn it out onto a floured work surface.

3. Knead the dough, adding more bread flour as needed, until it is smooth and elastic, at least 10 minutes.

4. Line a baking sheet with parchment paper.

5. Form the dough into a round ball. Cut the dough in half; then cut each piece in half so that you now have 4 pieces. Cut each of the 4 pieces into thirds to create 12 equal pieces of dough. Form the pieces into round balls and place them on the prepared baking sheet. Cover it with a clean kitchen towel and let the dough rise in a warm, draft-free place for 30 minutes.

6. Form the bagels: Poke a hole in the middle of each ball of risen dough with your thumb. Using your fingers, gently press around both the inside and outside of the hole until you create an even circle, about 1 inch thick. The diameter of the bagel hole should be about 2 inches. (Alternatively, you can roll each piece of dough to form a 7-inch-long rope. Loop the rope to

Preparing Bagels

1. Knead the bagel dough on a well-floured work surface.

2. Form the bagel hole by poking a hole in the center of the dough and working it till it's about 2 inches in diameter.

3. Carefully lower the bagels into a pot of boiling water and cook for 2 minutes on each side.

form a circle, overlapping the ends by an inch. Gently press the dough together at the seam. Then, using your fingers, squeeze the dough to make an even circle with a 2-inch hole in the middle.)

7. Line two baking sheets with parchment paper and lightly oil the paper. Arrange 6 bagels on each of the sheets and cover them with clean kitchen towels. Let the bagels rest for 20 minutes.

8. Meanwhile, place a rack in the lower third of the oven and preheat the oven to 425°F. Lightly oil two rimmed baking sheets and sprinkle them with cornmeal. Set aside.

9. Bring 4 quarts of water to a boil in a large covered pot over high heat. Add 2 tablespoons salt to the water.

10. Spread the toppings of your choice in individual shallow bowls, and arrange the bowls near the stove.

11. Lower 2 or 3 bagels (depending on the size of your pot) into the boiling water, and boil for 2 minutes. Then turn the bagels over and cook for an additional 2 minutes. Remove the bagels with a slotted spoon or a slotted spatula, allowing excess water to drain off, and lightly press them facedown in the toppings. If you like a lot of topping, roll the bagels to coat the sides. Transfer the coated bagels to the cornmeal-dusted baking sheets, topping side up. Repeat with the remaining bagels, arranging 6 bagels on each baking sheet.

12. Bake the bagels until they are golden, 20 to 25 minutes. Transfer the bagels to a wire rack and let them cool for 20 minutes before slicing.

Even More Topping Suggestions

Besides the toppings suggested on page 281, you can also top your bagels with:

◆ Black sesame seeds (or a combination of black and white)

◆ Dehydrated garlic granules

◆ Dehydrated onion flakes

◆ Coarse salt

◆ A mixture of all of the above

4. After draining the boiled bagels, place them facedown on the toppings of choice and press gently to make sure the toppings stick.

5. Bagels, fresh out of the oven, with a heavy coating of toppings on them—the way I like them.

6. A mixture of flaxseeds and sunflower seeds top this ready-to-eat bagel.

reducing packaging and container waste

At home I'm diligent about reusing plastic bags, carrying reusable shopping bags, drinking water from reusable bottles, and storing food in glass containers to avoid overusing wraps and aluminum foil—yet every week my family still manages to fill two recycling bins with yogurt and salad containers, beverage bottles, and other packaging. And I feel bad about this.

According to a recent EPA report, Americans generate about 254 million tons of municipal solid waste annually—things like packaging, food scraps, grass clippings, old sofas, computers, tires, and refrigerators. The largest category of the nation's total waste—an estimated 31 percent—is containers and packaging. That's an estimated 78 million tons

of packaging waste—the approximate weight of 13 million adult male African elephants! I look at three factors when I consider how best to manage this kind of waste:

1. Can I reduce the amount of packaging I buy?
2. Can the packaging be recycled?
3. Am I supporting a viable market for those recycled materials by purchasing goods in containers that have been made from post-consumer recycled (PCR) content?

Reducing the amount of packaging we buy
Packaging, for many products, is a necessary evil. Even at our small farm stand in Carmel Valley, where we sell produce that is grown literally steps away, we often need packaging to protect the produce and keep it from spoiling too quickly. For example, our heirloom raspberries are very delicate—if we didn't put them in little plastic containers, they'd disintegrate before anyone could get them home. Packaging plays an important role in protecting products and preventing food waste, but it also uses a lot of resources and generates waste. So what are some good ways to cut down on the amount of packaging we use?

◆ Avoid single-serve, disposable containers when possible. Pack lunches and "on-the-go" water in your own reusable containers.

◆ Buy products in the largest size you can use before the expiration date. If you repackage these purchases at home, pack in reusable containers.

◆ If a product's packaging looks excessive, contact the manufacturer and express your concerns. Most companies will welcome your input and let you know why a certain packaging component really is necessary, or they'll be more motivated to reduce their packaging in order to keep people like you as customers.

Recycling packaging

I cover recycling in more detail on page 204, but when considering packaging, look for materials that can be recycled. Materials that are rarely recycled, such as polystyrene (Styrofoam), should be avoided. Then don't forget to recycle the recyclables. It saves both resources and energy. For example, every ton of paper-based food packaging that is recycled saves the energy equivalent of 185 gallons of gasoline, 17 fully grown trees, and 7,000 gallons of water. The 17 trees saved can absorb a total of 250 pounds of carbon dioxide from the air each year. Burning that same ton of paper would create 1,500 pounds of global-warming gas emissions!

Closing the loop: using post-consumer recycled (PCR) materials to make new containers

All the recycling in the world doesn't do any good if there's no end market for the recycled materials. That's why the PCR content in the products and packaging we use is the final, important step in reducing packaging waste. As an owner of a business that needs to use a lot of packaging to get its products to market, I can see how a change in packaging can benefit the environment.

At Earthbound Farm, we realized a longtime goal by switching to PCR plastic for all our clamshell salad packages, and switched to shipping cartons made from 99 percent post-consumer and 1 percent post-industrial recycled corrugate.

Compared to using virgin plastic, each year our switch to 100 percent PCR PET for our clamshell salad packages:

◆ saves 424,224 million BTUs (MMBTUs) of energy,
◆ avoids 16,191 tons of carbon dioxide emissions,
◆ saves 68,307 gallons of water, and
◆ keeps 1,308,623 pounds of solid waste out of the landfill.

Annually Earthbound Farm's switch to 99 percent PCR recycled shipping cartons (from our previous cartons that were 50 percent PCR) conserves:

◆ 106,594 trees,
◆ 2,382,603 gallons of oil,
◆ 18,811 cubic yards of landfill space,
◆ 25,081,030 kilowatts of energy, and
◆ 43,891,803 gallons of water.

Wheat Flours

Flour is one of the foundations of baking, and almost any grain, bean, or starchy food can be ground into flour. Wheat flour is the primary flour used throughout this cookbook, and it's available in several forms, each with its own virtues. Wheat is the world's largest cereal grass crop, and there are three major types: hard wheat, soft wheat, and durum wheat. Hard wheat is high in protein and yields a flour that's rich in gluten, making it the best choice for yeast breads. Soft wheat has less protein and gluten, and is best suited for tender baked goods, such as cakes, muffins, and pastries. Durum wheat has the highest protein content and is not suitable for baking; it's most often ground into a flour called semolina, which is the basis for high-quality pasta.

WHITE FLOUR

The vast majority of the wheat flour we eat in this country is white, or refined, flour, commonly referred to as all-purpose flour. All-purpose white flour is ground only from the starchy

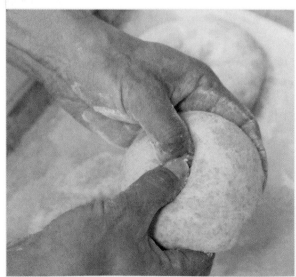

endosperm, the bran and germ having been stripped away. This process eliminates most of the flour's fiber and many of its nutrients as well. Ironically, most white flour is then "enriched" by adding back some vitamins and minerals, and occasionally fiber, so that the final product is not totally devoid of nutrients. In addition, some brands of white flour are also bleached because when freshly milled, flour is slightly yellow. Although the flour will gradually turn white as it ages, many manufacturers speed up the process by adding chemicals, such as benzoyl peroxide or acetone peroxide, to bleach it. To avoid this chemical process, I specify unbleached all-purpose flour in any recipe calling for white flour. All-purpose flour, as its name suggests, works in a wide range of recipes, including those for baked goods, noodles, quick breads, and yeast breads.

WHOLE WHEAT FLOUR

Whole wheat flour is unrefined, which means it's made from the entire wheat kernel. All of the fiber, vitamins, and minerals are retained, making whole wheat flour a much healthier choice than white. Because whole wheat flour contains the bran and germ, which are low in protein, this flour yields a denser finished product. It also has a more complex flavor and texture than refined white flour. However, whole wheat flour also contains natural oils causing it to turn rancid fairly quickly at room temperature, so keep an eye on the "best by" date. To increase its shelf life, you can refrigerate the flour in an airtight container for up to 8 months, or freeze it for up to 2 years.

WHITE WHOLE WHEAT FLOUR

A relative newcomer to supermarket shelves is unbleached white whole wheat flour. It performs in much the same way as whole wheat flour but is milled from hard white wheat berries instead of red wheat berries. It has a lighter, milder flavor but boasts the same nutritional advantages as traditional whole wheat flour.

WHOLE WHEAT PASTRY FLOUR

Because baked goods made from whole wheat flour are naturally heavier and denser than those made with white flour, I use whole wheat pastry flour in many of my recipes. Whole wheat pastry flour is made from soft wheat berries. The flour is very fine and powdery and contains less protein, and therefore less gluten, than regular whole wheat flour. It creates lighter-textured, finer-crumbed pastries and can often be substituted for white flour, in part or in whole.

BREAD FLOUR

For bread baking, bread flour is often specified. It's made entirely from hard wheat berries, which have more protein than soft wheat, and thus produces more gluten. Bread flour helps dough to rise higher by trapping air bubbles as the dough is mixed and kneaded. It is usually white and typically unbleached.

100% Whole Wheat Pita Bread

WHEN MY FIRST ATTEMPT TO MAKE PITA BREAD was successful, I couldn't stop telling all my friends how delicious it was. The process is surprisingly easy, and I just love the magical way the pitas puff up and form a pocket as they cook. During baking, heat causes the air trapped in the dough to expand. Because the pita forms a hard crust on both its top and bottom as it cooks, the trapped air inside the bread turns to steam and expands like a balloon, puffing the dough and forcing the crusts apart to form a pocket.

Pitas are perfect for stuffing with your favorite sandwich ingredients. They can also be served warm with soups or with dips such as Hummus (page 413). This version uses all whole wheat flour, a healthier option than white flour, and I like to add ground flaxseed for its nutty flavor and great nutritional value. If you've never had a fresh-baked pita, you don't know what you're missing. Commercial bagged pita breads just don't compare. ⟶ *Makes 8 breads*

1 packet active dry yeast

1 teaspoon sugar

1¼ cups warm water (105° to 115°F)

2 tablespoons honey

1 tablespoon olive oil, plus extra for
   the bowl and the baking sheet

2 cups whole wheat flour

1 cup whole wheat pastry flour, plus extra
   for kneading

1 tablespoon ground flaxseeds
   (see box, page 288; optional)

1 teaspoon salt

Cornmeal, for dusting

1. Place the yeast and sugar in a large bowl, and add the warm water. Cover the bowl with a clean kitchen towel and let the mixture sit until it is foamy, 5 to 10 minutes. Then stir in the honey and the olive oil.

2. Add both flours, the flaxseeds if using, and the salt to the yeast mixture, stirring to form a sticky dough. Turn the dough out onto a floured work surface and knead it for 5 minutes, adding more pastry flour as needed to form a soft, elastic dough. Form the dough into a ball.

3. Lightly oil a large bowl, place the dough in it, and roll the dough around to coat it with oil. Cover the bowl with a clean kitchen towel and let it sit in a warm, draft-free place until the dough has doubled in size, about 1 hour.

4. Lightly oil a baking sheet. Gently punch down the dough to deflate it. Divide the dough into 8 equal balls and place them on the prepared baking sheet. Cover loosely with a clean kitchen towel and let them rest for 20 minutes.

5. While the dough rests, position a rack on the lowest shelf of the oven. Place a pizza stone (see sidebar, page 295) or an inverted baking sheet or pizza pan on the oven rack, and preheat the oven to 500°F. Sprinkle a pizza peel or cookie sheet with cornmeal. Lightly dampen a kitchen towel and wring it out well; spread it out on the kitchen counter.

6. Flatten 1 ball of dough slightly, and then roll it out on a lightly floured work surface to form an 8-inch round, ⅛ to ¼ inch thick. Prepare as many rounds as will fit on your pizza peel or cookie sheet, usually 2 to 4. Transfer the rounds to the prepared pizza peel or cookie sheet, and slide them onto the pizza stone, baking sheet, or pizza pan. Bake until the pitas are completely puffed and filled with air and lightly browned, 4 to 6 minutes.

7. Transfer the pita breads to the damp kitchen towel (to keep them from getting crispy and dried out) and cover them loosely with a dry towel. Repeat with the remaining balls of dough.

THE BASICS

Flaxseeds

Flax is one of the oldest known cultivated plants dating back to 5000 B.C. Not only are the seeds edible, but the plant is used to produce linseed oil and cloth. Flaxseeds can be sprouted, pressed into oil, or ground into flour. This tiny seed is loaded with nutrients, including vitamin E, calcium, iron, and phosphorus. It supplies an essential fatty acid, alpha-linolenic acid (ALA), which studies show reduces inflammation and may prevent heart attacks. (ALA is converted by the body into omega-3 fatty acids, which are mainly found in fish.) Flaxseed also provides 800 times more cancer-fighting lignans than any other food (lignans are estrogen-like chemicals that act as antioxidants). Flaxseed is high in fiber, including a soluble fiber that helps to lower cholesterol levels. The insoluble fiber in flaxseeds keeps your digestive system running smoothly and helps prevent constipation. With their mild nutty flavor, whole or ground flaxseeds can be added to cereals, pancakes, baked goods, salads, stir-fries, and breads. Flaxseeds, ground flax, and flaxseed oil all have a high fat content and easily turn rancid. Store whole flaxseeds and flaxseed oil in an airtight container in the refrigerator for up to 1 year; store flax meal (flour) in the freezer for up to 6 months.

Kalamata Olive Bread

MAKING THIS BREAD IS A 2-DAY PROCESS, but it's definitely worth the wait. On the first day, you make a starter of flour, yeast, and water, which then sits at room temperature and ferments overnight. This is called the *biga,* the Italian word for "sponge." The sponge gives the bread a wonderful tangy flavor and a moist and chewy texture. I like to produce two differently shaped loaves with this recipe. Half of the dough is baked in a loaf pan, so that I can slice the bread for sandwiches. I make the other piece into a round loaf, in the rustic Italian style. Form the dough any way you like—the bread is delicious in any shape. ⎯⎯⎯ ***Makes 2 loaves***

FOR THE BIGA

1 packet active dry yeast

1 cup bread flour

⅛ teaspoon sugar

1 cup warm water (105° to 115°F)

FOR THE DOUGH

1 cup whole or 2% milk

2 teaspoons olive oil, plus 3 tablespoons for
   the bowl, baking sheet, and loaf pan

2½ cups whole wheat flour

2 cups whole wheat pastry flour

1 cup bread flour, plus extra for kneading

4 teaspoons salt

1 cup chopped pitted Kalamata olives

1. *Day 1:* Place the yeast, flour, and sugar in a large bowl and whisk to blend. Stir in the warm water, mixing to thoroughly combine. Cover the bowl with a clean kitchen towel or plastic wrap, and let it sit at room temperature overnight, or for at least 12 hours. The sponge should triple in size and then collapse.

2. *Day 2:* Add the milk and 2 teaspoons olive oil to the *biga,* stirring to combine. Then stir in the flours, salt, and olives.

3. Transfer the dough to a generously floured work surface and knead it vigorously for 5 minutes. Cover the dough with a kitchen towel and let it rest for 10 minutes. Then knead it again for 5 minutes, adding more bread flour as needed until it is smooth and elastic.

4. Lightly oil a large bowl with some of the olive oil. Dampen a clean kitchen towel and wring it out well.

5. Form the dough into a ball and transfer it to the prepared bowl. Turn the dough around in the bowl so that it is lightly coated with oil. Cover the bowl with the damp kitchen towel and let it sit in a warm, draft-free place until the dough has doubled in size, about 1½ hours.

Kalamata Olive Bread (page 289)

6. Lightly oil a baking sheet and a 9 x 5-inch loaf pan.

7. Transfer the dough to a lightly floured surface and divide it in half. Shape one piece of dough into a plump, round ball. Place the dough slightly near one end of the prepared baking sheet (you want to leave enough room on the baking sheet for the loaf pan). Cover the dough with a large bowl, preferably glass.

8. Form the remaining piece of dough into a loaf and place it in the prepared loaf pan seam side down. Cover it with a dry kitchen towel.

9. Let the two doughs rise in a warm, draft-free place until they have almost doubled in size, 30 to 45 minutes.

10. Position a rack in the lower third of the oven and preheat the oven to 425°F.

11. Remove the bowl, and cut 3 parallel slashes across the top of the round piece of dough. Then cut 3 more slashes at right angles to the first set.

12. Transfer the baking sheet, with the round loaf and the loaf pan on it, to the oven and bake until the loaves are golden, 25 to 35 minutes. To test for doneness, tap the bottom of the round bread, listening for a hollow sound. If it seems soft or doesn't sound hollow, bake it a little longer and test again. Both loaves should be done at the same time.

13. Unmold the rectangular loaf and transfer the breads to a wire rack. Let them cool completely before slicing.

choosing 100 percent post-consumer recycled (pcr) paper products

Buying products made from recycled paper helps reduce the need for virgin wood pulp, thus saving trees as well as substantial amounts of energy and water. Recycling paper and using post-consumer recycled products also keeps millions of tons of paper out of our landfills. When you can't use fabric dish towels or napkins, choose unbleached paper products with 100 percent PCR content if possible. The impact of switching is significant.

According to our research, if every household in the U.S. replaced just one . . .

◆ 500-count package of virgin-fiber paper napkins with napkins made from 100 percent PCR content, we could save 2.4 million trees; save enough energy to power 18,667 typical American homes for a year; save 451,600,000 gallons of water; prevent 566,533,333 pounds of greenhouse-gas emissions; and prevent 167,333,333 pounds of solid waste going into our landfills.

◆ 120-count roll of virgin-fiber paper towels with paper towels made from 100 percent PCR content, we could save 1 million trees; save enough energy to power 7,778 typical American homes for a year; save 188,166,667 gallons of water; prevent 236,055,556 pounds of greenhouse-gas emissions; and prevent 69,722,222 pounds of solid waste going into our landfills.

Rosemary Potato Bread

ADDING POTATOES TO BREAD DOUGH has a long history, notably in Ireland. Wherever wheat is scarce and expensive, potatoes have been used to stretch the flour, producing a nourishing bread. Here the potatoes are cooked in buttermilk, which adds flavor to the dough. The mashed potato produces a moist loaf with a springy texture, and as a bonus, the bread keeps for several days. With its golden crust and soft center, the rosemary-scented bread makes a great sandwich loaf and is a delicious accompaniment to a bowl of tomato-based or bean soup. ⎯⎯ *Makes 1 loaf*

8 ounces potatoes, such as russet,
    peeled and cut into small cubes
1 cup buttermilk
Salt
1 packet active dry yeast
1 teaspoon sugar
¾ cup warm water (105° to 115°F)
3 cups whole wheat flour
2 cups bread flour, plus extra for kneading
1½ tablespoons finely chopped fresh rosemary
1 tablespoon olive oil, for the bowl and
    the pan

1. Place the potato cubes in a medium-size saucepan and add the buttermilk, 1 cup water, and ½ teaspoon salt. Cover the pan and bring to a boil over medium heat. Then reduce the heat to medium-low and simmer until the potato is very soft, about 30 minutes. Drain well, and then mash the potato cubes in a bowl until they are smooth. Set aside to cool.

2. Place the yeast and sugar in a small bowl and add the warm water. Cover the bowl with a clean kitchen towel

and let the mixture sit until it is foamy, 5 to 10 minutes.

3. In a large bowl, whisk together the whole wheat and bread flours, 1½ teaspoons salt, and the rosemary. Make a well in the center and add the yeast mixture, stirring to combine. Stir in the cooled mashed potatoes.

4. Turn the dough out onto a floured work surface and knead it, adding more bread flour as needed, until it is smooth and elastic, about 10 minutes. Form the dough into a ball.

5. Lightly oil a large bowl with the olive oil, place the dough in the bowl, and roll it around to coat it with the oil. Cover the bowl with a clean kitchen towel and let it sit in a warm, draft-free place until the dough has doubled in size, about 1½ hours.

6. Generously oil a 9 x 5-inch loaf pan.

7. Gently punch down the dough to deflate it, and then form it into a loaf. Transfer the dough to the prepared loaf pan, cover it with a clean kitchen towel, set it in a warm, draft-free place, and let the dough rise until it has almost doubled in size, 30 to 45 minutes.

8. Position a rack in the lower third of the oven and preheat the oven to 375°F.

9. Bake until the bread is golden brown and has pulled away from the sides of the pan, about 45 minutes. Remove the loaf from the pan and insert an instant-read thermometer in the center of the bottom of the loaf. It should register 190°F. If it doesn't, return the loaf to the pan and bake it a few minutes longer.

10. Remove the bread from the pan and let it cool on a wire rack completely before slicing.

Wickets Bistro Focaccia

HOUSE-MADE FOCACCIA is a signature start to every meal at Wickets Bistro, located in the lovely Bernardus Lodge in Carmel Valley. Served warm, it is accompanied by shallow bowls of balsamic vinegar and extra-virgin olive oil for delicious dipping. Chef Cal Stamenov generously shared this recipe with us. In its simplest guise, focaccia is topped with just olive oil and sea salt, but for variety, you can sprinkle the dough with aromatic herbs, garlic, caramelized onions, grated cheese, olives, or sun-dried tomatoes. Although this recipe makes a large quantity of bread, the focaccia freezes beautifully. Cut the bread crosswise to make slices for sandwiches. Grill the sandwich, and you have a panini. One word of caution: For best results the dough needs to almost triple in size during its first rise, so don't rush this step. ⌁ *Makes one 12 x 17-inch loaf*

1½ tablespoons active dry yeast (slightly more than 1 packet)

½ tablespoon sugar

2 cups warm water (105° to 115°F)

About ⅔ cup extra-virgin olive oil

6 to 6½ cups bread flour, plus extra for kneading

1½ tablespoons salt

Sea salt, for the topping

1. Place the yeast and sugar in a large bowl. Add the warm water and cover the bowl with a clean kitchen towel. Let the mixture sit until it is foamy, 5 to 10 minutes. Then stir in a generous ⅓ cup of the olive oil.

2. Whisk 6 cups of the flour and the salt together in a large bowl. Add the flour mixture, a couple of cups at a time, to the yeast mixture, stirring to combine. The dough will be stiff and slightly sticky.

3. Transfer the dough to a generously floured work surface, and knead it, adding more flour as needed, until it is smooth and elastic, 8 to 10 minutes. Form the dough into a ball.

4. Add 1 to 2 tablespoons olive oil to a large, clean bowl, place the dough in the bowl, and roll it around so that it is coated with oil. Cover the bowl with a clean kitchen towel and let it sit in a warm, draft-free place until the dough has almost tripled in size, about 1½ hours.

5. Generously coat the sides and bottom of a 17 x 12-inch rimmed baking sheet with olive oil. Transfer the dough to the prepared baking sheet. Using your fingers and palms, press the dough to form an even layer, about ½ inch thick. Cover the baking sheet with a kitchen towel and let the dough rise in a warm, draft-free place until it has doubled in bulk, about 1 hour.

6. Position a rack in the middle of the oven and preheat the oven to 400°F.

7. Using your fingertips, gently poke the dough to make dimples over the entire surface. Drizzle about 3 tablespoons olive oil over the dough, and sprinkle with sea salt to taste.

8. Bake until the focaccia is golden brown and cooked through, 20 to 25 minutes. Transfer the baking sheet to a wire rack and let the focaccia cool. Cut it into squares to serve.

cooking with kids: tasty skills that last a lifetime

When my children were young, cooking was one of our most enjoyable activities.

Together, we'd look through cookbooks to decide what was most irresistible, check which ingredients we had on hand, and then get to work. From an early age, my kids knew where to find things in the kitchen—raisins, oats, flour, as well as mixing bowls and measuring cups and spoons. And while having fun, they learned some basic skills: counting, measuring, fractions, reading, and nutrition—what's healthy, what's not.

Of course the sweet things we baked were always appreciated treats, but my kids learned to love all sorts of foods by cooking with them. Vegetables were never a punishment—they were an exciting adventure in different shapes, colors, tastes, and textures. They learned how delicious fresh food tastes.

Now that my daughter is off on her own, cooking is one of her greatest joys, and I couldn't be more pleased. And whenever I babysit a friend's child, the first thing I ask is, "How about baking something special together?"

Whole Wheat Pizza Dough

MOST STORE-BOUGHT PIZZA DOUGH is made with white flour, and finding packaged organic dough can be a challenge. No problem: Making your own pizza dough is easy and fun. By using half whole wheat flour and half white, I've created a tasty pizza dough that is more nutritious than all-white versions. The dough is extremely easy to work with, and it freezes beautifully. This recipe makes enough dough for 3 large pizzas, but you're not limited to pizza: the dough is very versatile. I use it to make calzones (page 298), Pesto Cheese Bread (page 301), Piggies in a Blanket (see box, page 296), and Focaccia-Style Flatbread (page 302). The possibilities are limited only by your imagination. If you've never worked with yeast breads before, this dough is a great place to start.

Makes enough dough for three 16-inch pizzas

2 packets active dry yeast

2 tablespoons sugar

1¾ cups warm water (105° to 115°F)

3 tablespoons olive oil, plus 1 tablespoon for the bowl

1¾ cups whole wheat flour

1½ to 1¾ cups unbleached all-purpose flour, plus more for dusting

1 tablespoon salt

1. Place the yeast and sugar in a large bowl. Add the warm water and whisk to blend. Cover the bowl with a clean kitchen towel and let the mixture sit until it is foamy, about 5 minutes. Then add the 3 tablespoons olive oil and stir to combine.

2. Stir in the whole wheat and white flours in several increments—1 cup of whole wheat flour, then 1 cup of white flour—mixing until the dough is slightly sticky. You may not need all of the flour. Stir in the salt.

3. Transfer the dough to a lightly floured work surface and knead it until smooth and elastic, 5 minutes.

4. Dampen a kitchen towel and wring it out well.

5. Lightly oil a large bowl, place the dough in it, and turn the dough over so that it is lightly coated with oil. Cover the bowl with the damp kitchen towel and set it aside in a warm, draft-free place until the dough has doubled in size, about 1 hour.

6. Gently punch down the dough to deflate it, and then divide it into thirds. (Or, for smaller pizzas,

Recommended Pizza Tools

If you like to make pizzas at home, there are three tools worth buying:

◆ **PIZZA STONE**
A ceramic pizza stone is essential for creating crisp, golden crusts. The stone must be thoroughly preheated so that it absorbs the oven's heat.

◆ **PIZZA PEEL**
The best way to transfer your pizza to the oven is with a peel—a flat, smooth, shovel-like tool. The long handle protects you from the heat of the oven as you slide the pizza (or yeast bread) onto the baking stone. Pizza peels (or paddles) are made of metal or hardwood and can be found in gourmet specialty shops.

◆ **PIZZA CUTTER**
A pizza cutter (or pizza wheel) is a handy utensil for cutting pizzas. Because its round, rotating blade cuts vertically, pizza toppings are less likely to be dislodged than with the sawing motion of a knife.

divide the dough into quarters. The baking time will be the same whether you make large or small pizzas.) Keep the pieces you are not working with covered with the damp towel.

7. To form a piece of dough into a ball, flour your hands and then pull the opposite edges of a piece of dough toward the center. Pinch them together to form a seal.

Working around the circumference, continue pulling and pinching the dough until a smooth, tight ball forms. Repeat with the remaining pieces of dough. The dough is now ready to be used to make a pizza. Or, wrap the balls of dough individually in plastic wrap and refrigerate them for up to 24 hours or freeze them for up to 2 months (let the frozen dough thaw in the refrigerator overnight before using).

Piggies in a Blanket

I started making these for my son and his friends years ago, and the appeal of this snack hasn't diminished as they've all become teenagers (and I have a hard time resisting this yummy finger food as well). All-natural cocktail franks are the perfect size and shape for these tasty treats. You can also use full-size hot dogs, or precooked chicken or pork sausages, cut into smaller pieces; it's easy to adjust the size of the dough triangles to fit whatever you use. Top these "piggies" with melted butter and a sprinkling of Parmesan cheese or salt, serve them with a choice of spicy mustard, yellow mustard, and ketchup, and watch them disappear!

Makes 24

Dough for 1 pizza, homemade (page 295) or store-bought
Unbleached all-purpose flour, for dusting

24 small cocktail franks (or 6 hot dogs, cut in half widthwise, then lengthwise for 4 pieces each)
¼ cup (½ stick) butter, melted
Salt (optional)
Freshly grated Parmesan cheese (optional)

1. Position a rack in the middle of the oven, and preheat the oven to 450°F. Line a rimmed baking sheet with parchment paper (or oil a pizza pan and sprinkle it with cornmeal) and set it aside.

2. Cut the dough into 3 equal pieces. Lightly flour the work surface and a rolling pin. Working with 1 piece of dough at a time, roll the dough out to form a rectangle measuring approximately 12 x 3 inches.

3. Cut the dough into 4 squares, each 3 x 3 inches. Then cut each square on the diagonal to create 2 triangles. Repeat with

the remaining 2 pieces of dough, for a total of 24 triangles.

4. Place a cocktail frank in the center of a dough triangle, parallel to the long side. Roll the dough around the frank, starting from the long side of the triangle and working toward the pointed end, stretching the dough as you work so that it wraps around the frank. Transfer the wrapped "piggy" to the prepared baking sheet, placing it seam side down. Repeat with the remaining triangles and franks.

5. Brush the top of each "blanket" with some of the melted butter. Sprinkle the dough with salt or Parmesan cheese, if using.

6. Bake until the dough is puffed and golden, 8 to 12 minutes. Serve hot or warm.

Whole Wheat Pizza with Heirloom Tomatoes, Fresh Mozzarella, and Pesto

THIS HOMEMADE PIZZA was one of the first recipes Drew and I created together more than twenty-five years ago, and we're still making it today. It's perfect for the warm summer months when we look to take advantage of delicious in-season tomatoes and a bounty of fresh basil. Slices of ripe heirloom tomatoes in assorted colors and soft fresh mozzarella make a light and fresh-tasting topping. A liberal brushing of pesto and a scattering of Kalamata olives adds great flavor. If you love goat cheese, it makes a great substitute for the mozzarella: Just arrange the tomatoes in a single layer, top with pieces of goat cheese, and scatter olives over the top. Don't skimp on the pesto—it gets brushed onto the hot pizza just as it comes out of the oven and melts into the cheese and tomatoes. Beautiful!

~~~ Makes one 14-inch pizza

8 ounces fresh mozzarella cheese,
  cut into ¼-inch-thick slices
3 large red or yellow tomatoes (or a mixture),
  preferably heirloom, sliced ¼-inch thick
Unbleached all-purpose flour, for dusting
Dough for 1 pizza, homemade (page 295,
  thawed if frozen) or store-bought
Cornmeal, for dusting
Extra-virgin olive oil
½ cup Kalamata olives, pitted and halved
¼ cup Pesto (page 164), at room
  temperature

1. Position a rack at the lowest position in the oven, and if using a pizza stone, place it on the rack. Preheat the oven to 500°F for at least 30 minutes so that the stone will be hot.

2. Place the cheese and tomato slices on a clean kitchen towel, or on several layers of paper towels, to absorb any excess water. Let sit for 10 minutes, blotting any moisture that appears.

3. Lightly flour a work surface, and a rolling pin if using. Shape the dough by patting it into a flat, round disk. Then roll it out on the work surface to form a 14-inch round, ⅛- to ¼-inch thick. (Or use your hands to gently stretch the dough into shape, pressing outward from the center, rotating the dough occasionally to form a round.)

4. If using a pizza peel or pizza pan, generously dust it with

cornmeal. (Alternatively, turn a large baking sheet upside down and dust it with cornmeal.)

5. Transfer the dough to the prepared pizza peel, pizza pan, or baking sheet. Brush the dough lightly with olive oil, leaving a 1-inch border unoiled.

6. Arrange the tomatoes and cheese on the dough, alternating the slices and overlapping them slightly; leave the 1-inch border bare. Scatter the olives over the top.

7. Slide the pizza off the peel and onto the preheated stone, using a jerking motion to release it. (Alternatively, place the pizza pan or baking sheet in the oven.) Bake until the crust is golden brown on the bottom and the toppings are sizzling hot, 5 to 10 minutes.

8. Remove the pizza from the oven by sliding the peel under it, or use tongs to slide the pizza off the stone onto a cutting board. While the pizza is hot, dot it all over with teaspoonfuls of pesto. Then spread the pesto over the toppings with a pastry brush or the back of a spoon. Using a pizza cutter or a large knife, cut the pizza into wedges, and serve hot.

Irresistible Mini Calzones

A CALZONE IS SORT OF A PIZZA TURNOVER, an idea that originated in Naples, Italy. A regular calzone is often a full-size pizza folded in half, but because ours are made from 8-inch rounds of dough, the finished size is much more manageable. Bubbling with cheese and sauce, these mini calzones make a perfect one-person serving. I fill them with prosciutto, Kalamata olives, Parmesan and mozzarella cheeses, and tomato sauce for lots of great flavor. They're baked until they're puffed and golden, and served with extra tomato sauce for dipping. Delicious and irresistible. ⚋⚋ *Makes 4*

Unbleached all-purpose flour, for dusting
Dough for 1 pizza, homemade (page 295, thawed if frozen) or store-bought
Cornmeal, for the peel
Extra-virgin olive oil

1½ cups Myra's Heirloom Tomato Sauce (page 416), Quick Tomato Sauce (page 417), or store-bought marinara sauce
6 slices prosciutto, torn into small strips
1 cup shredded mozzarella cheese
1 cup freshly grated Parmesan cheese
⅓ cup pitted and sliced Kalamata olives

Irresistible Mini Calzones

YOUR GREEN KITCHEN

Post-Consumer Recycled Aluminum Foil

At long last, manufacturers of aluminum foil have begun to offer 100 percent recycled foil made from post-consumer and post-industrial aluminum (such as from auto bodies, cookware, and aluminum siding). It is very energy-intensive to make foil from aluminum's base material, bauxite. There are also serious environmental issues related to mining the ore, so recycling is important. Making recycled aluminum foil is estimated to use 80 percent less energy than foil made from virgin material, and the process creates fewer greenhouse-gas emissions. Because the vast majority of aluminum foil is not reused or recycled, choosing a recycled brand is an important step to making this a more eco-friendly option.

1. Position a rack at the lowest position in the oven, and if using a pizza stone, place it on the rack. Preheat the oven to 500°F for at least 30 minutes so that the stone will be hot.

2. Lightly flour a work surface, and a rolling pin if using. Divide the dough into 4 equal portions. Shape each ball of dough by patting it into a flat, round disk and then rolling it out on the work surface to form an 8-inch round, ⅛- to ¼-inch thick. (Or use your hands to gently stretch the dough into shape, pressing outward from the center, rotating the dough occasionally to form a round.)

3. If using a pizza peel, dust it generously with cornmeal. If not, turn a large baking sheet upside down and dust it with cornmeal.

4. Transfer the rounds of dough to the prepared pizza peel or baking sheet. Brush the dough lightly with olive oil.

5. Brush half of each round of dough with some of the tomato sauce. Divide the prosciutto among the 4 calzones, arranging the strips on top of the sauce. Top with the mozzarella. Then sprinkle each calzone with 3 tablespoons of the Parmesan cheese. Scatter the olives over the cheese, and then fold the unadorned half of the dough over the filling. Pinch the edges together to make a half-moon-shaped pie.

6. Lightly brush the top of the calzones with olive oil, and sprinkle with the remaining ¼ cup Parmesan cheese.

7. Slide the calzones off the peel and onto the preheated stone, using a jerking motion to release them. (Alternatively, place the baking sheet in the oven.) Bake until the calzones are puffed and golden brown, 10 to 12 minutes.

8. Meanwhile, pour the remaining tomato sauce into a saucepan and warm it over medium-low heat. (Alternatively, heat the sauce in the microwave.)

9. Serve the calzones hot, with warm Myra's Heirloom Tomato Sauce on the side for dipping.

Pesto Cheese Bread

M Y SON, JEFFREY, CREATED THIS DELICIOUS FLATBREAD one day when we were making pizzas together. He simply rolled out the dough, brushed it with pesto, and scattered a generous amount of Asiago cheese on top. He then folded the dough in half and rolled it out into a free-form shape. After topping it with more pesto and cheese, he slid the dough onto a hot pizza stone—and *voilà*, the result was a scrumptious flatbread. I'd never seen anything like it, but the recipe is now a family favorite. It takes only a few minutes to assemble, and the result is terrific—lots of flavor and a great chewy texture. A word to the wise, though: One might not be enough.

Makes one 10-inch flatbread

Unbleached all-purpose flour, for dusting
Dough for 1 pizza, homemade (page 295, thawed if frozen) or store-bought
½ cup pesto, homemade (page 164) or store-bought
1½ cups grated Asiago or Parmesan cheese
Cornmeal, for the pan

1. Position a rack at the lowest position in the oven, and if using a pizza stone, place it on the rack. Preheat the oven to 500°F for at least 30 minutes so that the stone will be hot.

2. Lightly flour a work surface, and a rolling pin if using. Shape the dough by patting it into a flat, round disk, then rolling it out on the work surface to form a 12-inch round, about ¼-inch thick. (Or use your hands to gently stretch the dough into shape, pressing outward from the center, rotating the dough occasionally to form a round.)

3. Brush the dough with ¼ cup of the pesto. Spread ¾ cup of the Asiago cheese on one half of the dough. Fold the dough in half, covering the cheese. Gently roll the dough into a free-form shape, about ⅓ inch thick. Brush the top of the dough with the remaining ¼ cup pesto, and sprinkle with the remaining ¾ cup Asiago.

4. If using a pizza peel or pizza pan, generously dust it with cornmeal. If not, turn a large baking sheet upside down and dust it with cornmeal.

5. Transfer the dough to the prepared pizza peel, pizza pan, or baking sheet.

6. Slide the bread off the peel and onto the preheated stone, using a jerking motion to release it. (Alternatively, place the pizza pan or baking sheet in the oven.)

7. Bake until the bread is golden brown on the bottom and the cheese and pesto are sizzling hot, about 10 minutes. Remove the bread from the oven by sliding the peel under it, or use tongs to slide the pizza off the stone onto a cutting board. Using a large knife, cut the bread into wedges, and serve hot.

Focaccia-Style Flatbread

I LOVE THE VERSATILITY OF MY PIZZA DOUGH RECIPE. Instead of making three pizzas, I sometimes just pat some of the dough into a baking pan to create a simple bread that's a cross between focaccia and flatbread. It's very easy and quick to make. I usually add a sprinkling of fresh rosemary and sea salt on top, but feel free to improvise and create your own toppings with any herb (fresh or dried), olives, cheese, or seeds. Cut into squares or triangles, this flatbread makes a terrific appetizer. It's great to dip in Hummus (page 413), or warm Myra's Heirloom Tomato Sauce (page 416), and it's perfect served alongside soups and pastas. ⟶ *Serves 4 (2 pieces each)*

Unbleached all-purpose flour, for dusting
Dough for 1 pizza, homemade (page 295, thawed if frozen) or store-bought
2 tablespoons olive oil, plus extra for the pan
1 tablespoon chopped fresh rosemary
Coarse sea salt or kosher salt, to taste

1. Position a rack in the middle of the oven and preheat the oven to 375°F. Generously oil a 9 x 13-inch glass baking dish.

2. Lightly flour the work surface, and pat the dough into a rough rectangle. Transfer the dough to the prepared baking dish, and using your fingers, push it into the corners of the dish. If the dough keeps shrinking back, let it relax for 5 minutes, then press again.

Continue in this manner until the dough is even and reaches the sides and corners of the pan. Cover the baking dish with a clean kitchen towel, and let the dough rise in a warm, draft-free place for 20 minutes.

3. Drizzle the olive oil over the dough. Then, using your fingers, lightly rub the oil all over the dough. Scatter the rosemary and salt over the surface. Press your fingertips down into the dough to make indentations all over the surface.

4. Bake until the focaccia is golden brown and sounds hollow when tapped, 20 to 25 minutes. Transfer the baking dish to a wire rack and let cool for 10 minutes before slicing.

CHAPTER 9

DESSERTS

Always Room for Dessert

DESSERTS ARE PURE PLEASURE. WHEN YOU'VE TAKEN THE TIME TO PREPARE this sweet conclusion to a meal, the pace usually slows a bit, and conversation is frequently punctuated with sighs of pleasure and contentment as each bite is held a bit longer in the mouth to savor all the flavor.

The dessert recipes in this chapter include a little bit of everything—simple, healthy, decadent, elegant, and in between. There are standard favorites that take full advantage of fresh fruits in season, like our All-American Apple Pie and Fresh Blueberry Pie. A scoop of delicious homemade Vanilla Bean Ice Cream is perfect as a topping for pie or as a fun dessert like our Ice Cream Sundaes. And of course I've included a tempting selection of cookies to fill your house with that heavenly fresh-baked cookie smell that everyone remembers from childhood.

If you want to keep dessert on the healthier side, you'll love the Baked Apples, Three Ways and Healthy Apple Crisp. And our simple-to-make Honey Frozen Yogurt is one of my favorites: all the notable health benefits of yogurt magically transformed into a creamy frozen treat. If you're in the mood for something a bit more elegant but still on the light side, try the Italian-Style Poached Peaches. Inspired by a memorable dish I discovered in Italy, these sun-ripened peaches are gently simmered in vanilla-and-lemon-scented white wine—a refreshing finish for almost any summer meal. I'm especially proud of the light Raspberry Yogurt Panna Cotta, topped with Rhubarb-Raspberry Sauce for a light touch of tangy sweetness. We cut the calories, not the flavor, in this creamy classic dessert. In fact, all these desserts have many nutritional benefits and not too many calories, so they make your body as happy as your taste buds!

Chocolate Pecan Cake with Chocolate Ganache Icing (page 317)

But if your goal is pure indulgence, try our Chocolate Soufflé Cake with Vanilla Whipped Cream. As a true chocolate lover, I would vote for this dessert to win the "Most Decadent" award. To help you make sure your chocolate is eco-friendly, you can read up on some of the socially responsible eco-labels found on chocolate and coffee (page 327).

I also hope you'll discover some new ingredients you may not have cooked with before, especially fruits that visit for only a short time each year. Our Quince Tarte Tatin makes use of the distinctive tart flavor of fall quinces to create a traditional French "upside-down" tart. And the Passion Fruit Semifreddo Soufflé Pie is a unique frozen dessert with a flavor reminiscent of the tropics with the clean fresh taste of citrus.

I don't believe desserts are meant to follow only well-balanced meals. Sweet treats can be very relaxing and restorative any time of the day. Put your feet up (mentally if not physically) and take a conscious break from the hectic pace of your busy schedule for ten minutes or so. I often make a ritual of spending a few minutes in the afternoon to slow down and enjoy every single bite of a favorite treat—perhaps an Earthbound Farm Oatmeal Raisin Cookie or a piece of Chunky Cherry-Nut Bark with a cup of tea or freshly brewed coffee.

Regardless of when you enjoy them—after a meal or as a delicious snack—desserts are an instant passport to a land of sweetness and delight. I wish you happy travels.

Cranberry-Walnut Baked Apple (page 348)

Earthbound Farm Oatmeal Raisin Cookies

Earthbound Farm Oatmeal Raisin Cookies

WHO CAN RESIST HOMEMADE COOKIES WARM FROM THE OVEN? Certainly not me! Oatmeal raisin cookies are a classic American tradition, and I think our Farm Stand version is one of the best. Although the original recipe used all white flour, we've found that a combination of whole wheat and white flours is even better tasting. For the best results, refrigerate the dough for at least 2 hours before baking the cookies. We recommend rolled oats, not quick oats, for this recipe, although either variety will work. Because rolled oats are thicker and have been processed less, they result in a chewier, oaty-flavored cookie. Not a raisin fan? Dried cranberries make a great substitution. *Makes about twenty-four 2½-inch cookies*

8 tablespoons (1 stick) unsalted butter, at room temperature, plus extra for greasing the pan

½ cup firmly packed light brown sugar

6 tablespoons granulated sugar

1 large egg

6 tablespoons whole wheat pastry flour

6 tablespoons unbleached all-purpose flour

¾ teaspoon salt

½ teaspoon baking soda

⅛ teaspoon ground nutmeg

1½ cups (5¼ ounces) old-fashioned rolled oats (see sidebar, this page)

¾ cup raisins

1. Place the butter, brown sugar, and granulated sugar in the bowl of an electric mixer fitted with the paddle attachment. Beat on medium-high speed, scraping down the sides of the bowl once or twice, until the mixture is light and fluffy, about 3 minutes. Then beat in the egg.

2. Whisk the flours, salt, baking soda, and nutmeg together in a small bowl.

3. With the mixer on low speed, add the flour mixture to the butter mixture and beat until the dough is smooth. Add the oats and raisins, and mix on low speed just until combined.

4. Press a piece of parchment paper firmly against the dough in the bowl to seal the surface, and refrigerate the dough until it is cold, at least 2 hours.

5. Position a rack in the middle of the oven and preheat the oven to 350°F. Butter several rimmed baking sheets, or line them with parchment paper.

6. Roll pieces of the dough between your palms to form 1-inch balls. Arrange the dough balls on the prepared baking sheets, spacing

THE BASICS

Oats Primer

Steel-cut oats, sometimes referred to as "Irish" oats, are whole oats (called groats) that have been hulled, steamed, and often roasted to enhance their flavor. They are then cut with large steel blades into smaller pieces. The texture of these oats is hard and firm. Steel-cut oats require a long cook time and are rarely used in baking.

Rolled oats, sometimes labeled "old-fashioned" or "regular" oats, are groats that have been steamed and then rolled into flat flakes between heavy industrial rollers. When these same oats are pressed very thin and fragmented into smaller flakes, they are called "quick" oats because they cook so much faster than steel-cut or old-fashioned oats.

Instant oatmeal is made from precooked oats and is not recommended for any of our recipes calling for oats.

them 1½ inches apart. Bake until the cookies are just set and lightly golden, 16 to 18 minutes.

7. Place the baking sheets on a wire rack to cool for 5 minutes. Then, using a spatula, transfer the cookies to the racks to finish cooling. (The cookies can be stored in an airtight container at room temperature for up to 2 weeks.)

Oatmeal Jammy Squares

THESE CHEWY SQUARES are easy to make and have just five ingredients. They are especially delicious and so versatile, they can be served for an elegant tea or packed in a lunch box. Rolled oats and whole wheat pastry flour form the tasty crust, which makes these bars a more nutritious treat than many. A layer of jam is sandwiched in the middle for a hint of fruity sweetness. This dessert needs to cool for at least 4 hours to cut into firm squares. Eaten warm, they'll be soft, but scrumptious. ⟶ *Makes 9 squares or 18 bars*

12 tablespoons (1½ sticks) cold unsalted
 butter, cut into small pieces, plus extra
 for greasing the pan
2 cups old-fashioned rolled oats
 (see sidebar, page 307)
1¼ cups whole wheat pastry flour
1 cup packed light brown sugar
1 cup Fresh Strawberry Jam (page 424)

1. Position a rack in the center of the oven and preheat the oven to 350°F. Butter the sides and bottom of an 8-inch-square baking dish and set it aside.

2. Place the oats, pastry flour, and brown sugar in a large bowl, and stir to blend. Add the butter, and using a pastry blender, two knives, or your fingers, blend it into the mixture until it is crumbly and well combined.

3. Transfer half of the oat mixture to the prepared baking dish, pressing it firmly to form an even layer.

4. Spread the strawberry jam over the oat layer, leaving ½ inch uncovered around the edges. Top with the remaining oat mixture, pressing it lightly to form an even layer.

5. Bake until the edges are golden brown, 30 to 40 minutes.

6. Cool in the pan on a wire rack for at least 4 hours; then cut into squares or bars.

Oatmeal Jammy Squares

Chunky Chocolate Raisin Cookies

CHUNKY CANDY BARS—those thick squares of raisin-and-nut-studded chocolate that come wrapped in distinctive silver foil—are the inspiration for these chunky cookies. With their rich chocolate flavor, toasted pecans, and plump, sweet raisins, these delectable treats have something to entice everyone. If someone at your house doesn't like pecans or raisins, you can substitute other nuts or dried cherries. ⁓ *Makes about twenty-four 2½-inch cookies*

8 tablespoons (1 stick) unsalted butter

2 cups semisweet chocolate chips

¼ cup unsweetened cocoa powder

3 large eggs

½ cup sugar

2 teaspoons pure vanilla extract

½ cup whole wheat pastry flour or
   unbleached all-purpose flour

1 teaspoon baking powder
   (see sidebar, this page)

¼ teaspoon salt

¾ cup pecans, toasted (see box, page 31)
   and chopped

1 cup raisins

1. Position a rack in the middle of the oven and preheat the oven to 325°F. Butter one or two rimmed baking sheets, or line them with parchment paper, and set aside.

2. Combine the butter, 1 cup of the chocolate chips, and the cocoa powder in a medium-size saucepan and place it over medium-low heat. Cook, stirring occasionally, until the butter and chocolate melt. Remove from the heat and let cool slightly.

3. Place the eggs, sugar, and vanilla in a large bowl and whisk to combine. Stir in the chocolate mixture.

4. Combine the flour, baking powder, and salt in a small bowl, and whisk to blend. Add the flour mixture to the chocolate batter and stir until just combined. Do not overbeat.

5. Gently stir in the remaining 1 cup chocolate chips, the pecans, and the raisins.

6. Drop heaping tablespoons of the batter onto the prepared baking sheets, spacing them an inch apart. Bake until the cookies have just set and look shiny, 14 to 16 minutes. Do not overbake.

7. Let the cookies cool on the baking sheet for 10 minutes. Then transfer them to a wire rack to finish cooling. (The cookies can be stored, tightly covered, in a cool, dry place for up to 3 days.)

THE BASICS

Baking Powder

Baking powder produces carbon dioxide when it is mixed with a liquid. In a batter, the reaction of the carbon dioxide produces tiny air bubbles, allowing the cookies or cake to rise and become spongy. It's important to work fast when using baking powder because the carbon dioxide escapes quickly, and if the mixed batter is allowed to sit too long, the baked product will not rise as expected. The effectiveness of baking powder deteriorates with time, so for the best results, replace your container of baking powder every 6 to 8 months.

Farm Stand Peanut Butter Cookies

IF YOU LIKE PEANUTS AND PEANUT BUTTER, this Earthbound Farm recipe may become one of your favorite cookies. They are very buttery, with the crunch of peanuts and a pronounced nutty flavor. The recipe works well with either all-purpose white flour or whole wheat pastry flour. Cookies made with whole wheat flour have a crisp and crunchy texture. Other folks prefer the cookies made with white flour because they bake up a bit thicker and are chewier. It's a matter of personal preference, but the health benefits of using whole wheat flour might convince you to give it a try (see box, page 286). ⟶ *Makes about 30 cookies*

½ cup crunchy peanut butter, preferably natural

12 tablespoons (1½ sticks) unsalted butter, at room temperature

1 cup firmly packed light brown sugar

½ cup unsalted raw peanuts, roughly chopped

2 tablespoons pure maple syrup

1 large egg

1½ cups (5 ounces) whole wheat pastry flour or unbleached all-purpose flour

¾ teaspoon baking soda

1 teaspoon salt

1. Place the peanut butter, butter, and brown sugar in the bowl of an electric mixer fitted with the paddle attachment. Beat at medium-high speed, scraping down the sides of the bowl once or twice, until the mixture is light and fluffy, about 3 minutes. Then beat in the peanuts, maple syrup, and egg.

2. Whisk the flour, baking soda, and salt together in a small bowl.

3. With the mixer on low speed, add the flour mixture to the peanut butter mixture, and beat just until the dough is smooth. Do not overmix, or the cookies will be tough.

4. Press a piece of parchment paper firmly against the dough in the bowl to seal the surface, and refrigerate the dough until it is cold, at least 2 hours.

5. Position a rack in the middle of the oven and preheat the oven to 325°F. Butter several rimmed baking sheets, or line them with parchment paper.

6. Roll pieces of the dough between your palms to form 1-inch balls. Arrange the dough balls on the prepared baking sheets, spacing

THE BASICS

Parchment Paper

Parchment paper is a nonstick cooking paper that can tolerate oven temperatures up to 450°F. It makes a great pan liner because it does not require greasing and allows for easy cleanup. Parchment is also used to cook en papillote (in a paper pouch). Look for it— preferably unbleached—in major supermarkets and at specialty cookware shops.

them 1½ inches apart. Bake until the cookies are just set and lightly golden, 15 to 18 minutes.

7. Place the baking sheets on wire racks to cool for 5 minutes. Then, using a spatula, transfer the cookies to the rack to finish cooling. (The cookies can be stored in an airtight container at room temperature for up to 2 weeks.)

Coconut and Macadamia Macaroons

LIGHT AND CRISPY, these macaroons are studded with macadamia nuts, adding texture and tropical flavor to the cookies. At the Farm Stand, where these are always popular, we often substitute chocolate chips or raisins for the nuts. Create your own versions using this basic recipe.

Makes 18 cookies

4 large egg whites, at room temperature
1 teaspoon salt
1½ cups sugar
2 teaspoons pure vanilla extract
5 cups shredded unsweetened coconut
1 cup unsalted macadamia nuts, halved

1. Position a rack in the center of the oven and preheat the oven to 350°F. Line two rimmed baking sheets with parchment paper.

2. Place the egg whites and the salt in the bowl of an electric mixer and beat on medium speed until the whites form soft peaks. Slowly add the sugar, beating on high speed. Then add the vanilla on low speed, mixing until blended. Stir in the coconut and the macadamia nuts by hand. The mixture will be quite thick.

3. Using an ice cream scoop or a large spoon, drop the batter onto the prepared baking sheets, spacing the cookies about 2 inches apart. Bake until the macaroons are golden, 15 to 25 minutes.

4. Transfer the baking sheets to wire racks and let the macaroons cool completely before removing them with a spatula. (The macaroons can be stored in an airtight container at room temperature for up to 3 days.)

THE BASICS

Cooling Racks

Cooling cookies on a rack after they bake allows air to circulate under them, which prevents the cookies from becoming soggy.

Chocolate Soufflé Cake with Vanilla Whipped Cream

DECADENTLY RICH AND INTENSE, this moist, truffle-like cake is a chocolate lover's dream. Using just five ingredients (and no flour), the cake comes together quickly. Be sure to use quality chocolate, preferably in the range of 63 to 72 percent cocoa solids (see the sidebar, page 314). The addition of beaten egg whites is what makes the cake puff like a soufflé. It will crack as it settles, but a big dollop of lightly sweetened Vanilla Whipped Cream will camouflage any imperfections. Enjoy! ⎯⎯⎯ *Makes one 9-inch cake*

12 tablespoons (1½ sticks) unsalted butter, cut into ¼-inch pieces, plus more for greasing the baking pan

Unsweetened cocoa powder, for dusting the baking pan

1 pound dark chocolate (63% to 72% cocoa solids), broken into small pieces

6 large eggs, at room temperature, separated

1¼ cups sugar

Pinch of salt

Vanilla Whipped Cream (recipe follows)

1. Position a rack in the middle of the oven and preheat the oven to 350°F. Generously butter the bottom and sides of a 9-inch springform pan or a 9-inch cake pan with a removable bottom (see Note). Place a round of parchment paper on the bottom of the pan. Dust the sides of the pan with cocoa powder.

2. Pour water into a saucepan, or the bottom of a double boiler, to a depth of 1 inch, and bring it to a boil over high heat. Reduce the heat to low so that the water just barely simmers.

3. Place the chocolate and butter in a medium-size metal or heatproof glass mixing bowl, or in the top of the double boiler, and set it over the barely simmering water. Cook, stirring frequently, until the chocolate and butter melt. Remove the bowl from the heat.

4. Place the egg yolks and sugar in a large bowl and whisk until the mixture is thick and pale-colored. Add the chocolate mixture and whisk until combined.

5. Place the egg whites and salt in a medium-size bowl, and beat with an electric mixer on high speed until the whites form soft, shiny peaks, 2 to 3 minutes. Do not overbeat.

6. Stir one third of the egg whites into the chocolate batter. Then fold in the remaining egg whites.

7. Pour the filling into the prepared pan and bake until the cake pulls

Dark Chocolate

Artisanal chocolate is very popular these days, especially dark chocolate. With so many choices available, it's difficult to know which brand to select.

Chocolate is derived from cocoa beans, which have more than 300 identifiable naturally occurring flavors, ranging from berries to tropical fruit. It's worth choosing a good-quality chocolate for baking because it affects the overall taste, texture, and appearance of the dish.

For baking, dark chocolate should have at least 60 percent cocoa solids. The higher the percentage of cocoa, the more intense and pronounced the flavor will be, which is especially important if the chocolate will be cooked.

For information about fair trade chocolate, see page 327.

away from the sides of the pan and the top is beginning to crack, 35 to 45 minutes.

8. Transfer the pan to a wire rack and let the cake cool to room temperature. Remove the sides of the pan before serving. Cut the cake into slices, and serve with a dollop of Vanilla Whipped Cream.

Note: A springform pan is round and can range in diameter from 6 to 12 inches. It has high, straight sides that are held in place with the aid of a clamp. The sides can be removed when the clamp is released. This allows cakes that are difficult to remove from a pan to be easily detached from the pan's sides. If you don't have a springform pan, you can use a 9-inch baking dish for this recipe. The batter won't soufflé quite as much, and the cake will be more like brownies, but it will taste delicious nonetheless.

Vanilla Whipped Cream

Whipped cream adds a lavish touch to most sweet treats. The warm, rich notes of pure vanilla mellow the cream, and this simple yet elegant topping turns ordinary desserts into extraordinary ones. For the best texture, whipped cream should be used right away. If you have any left over, it can be refrigerated overnight, covered. ~~~ ***Makes about 2 cups***

1 cup heavy (whipping) cream, chilled
2 tablespoons confectioners' sugar
1 teaspoon pure vanilla extract

1. Chill mixer blades and a medium-size mixing bowl in the freezer for at least 20 minutes.

2. Pour the cream into the chilled bowl and beat with the chilled mixer blades, starting on low and increasing the speed as the cream begins to froth.

3. Gradually add the confectioners' sugar and the vanilla, and continue to beat until the cream holds soft peaks, 2 to 3 minutes. For the best texture, use the whipped cream immediately; or refrigerate it, covered, for up to 1 hour.

Vanilla

Vanilla beans are the seedpods of a tropical orchid vine that blooms for only one day per year. If you've ever wondered why vanilla beans are so expensive, consider that on commercial farms the blossoms must be hand-pollinated in order for the pods to form. The beans are harvested when they are ripe, at which point they are an unrecognizable yellow-green color. Only after curing and drying for months do they turn a rich, dark brown and develop their characteristic flavor and fragrance. Used primarily in baking, the beans contain a multitude of tiny edible seeds that are infused with an intoxicating flavor.

When buying vanilla beans, look for plump, pliable pods and avoid those that are brittle or shriveled. Wrapped in plastic and refrigerated in an airtight container, vanilla beans will hold their flavor and moisture for a year. Vanilla beans impart a distinctive flavor to desserts, and they can be used more than once if the seeds are not scraped out: After cooking with a whole vanilla bean, rinse the pod and dry it thoroughly. Wrap it in plastic, place it in an airtight container, and refrigerate it until the next use. If you are using both the pod and the seeds, halve the bean lengthwise and gently scrape the seeds from the interior, using the flat side of a small paring knife. After cooking, wash and dry the split pods and bury them in a container of sugar to create vanilla sugar, or grind pieces of the pods with coffee beans for vanilla coffee.

Pure vanilla extract and vanilla paste are made from the pods—unlike imitation vanilla extract, which is an artificial flavoring and not recommended. Vanilla paste is a handy substitute for vanilla beans or extract. It's made with ground vanilla beans (including the seeds), sugar, vanilla extract, water, and a gum thickener. Look for this convenient paste at specialty kitchenware stores or online. As a substitute for vanilla extract, use an equal amount of vanilla paste; 1 tablespoon of paste is the equivalent of half a vanilla bean.

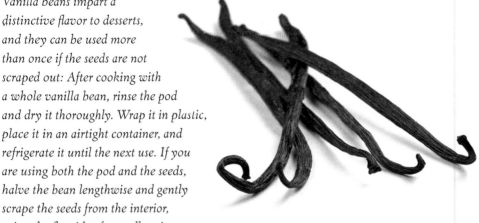

Chocolate Pecan Cake with Chocolate Ganache Icing

Chocolate Pecan Cake with Chocolate Ganache Icing

THIS DENSE, RICH CAKE IS EXTREMELY SATISFYING—a sure-fire hit with any chocolate lover. It has a very strong dark chocolate flavor, hints of orange, and added texture from ground pecans. The ganache icing makes it extra-decadent and delicious, and is surprisingly easy to make.
⸺ *Serves 10*

FOR THE CAKE

- **4 tablespoons (½ stick) unsalted butter**
- **13 ounces semisweet chocolate, broken into ¼- to ½-inch pieces, or 2 cups semisweet chocolate chips**
- **¼ cup frozen orange juice concentrate, thawed**
- **⅔ cup pecan pieces**
- **⅓ cup unbleached all-purpose flour**
- **⅓ cup sugar**
- **6 large eggs, separated**
- **Pinch of salt**

FOR THE ICING

- **⅔ cup heavy (whipping) cream**
- **⅔ cup semisweet chocolate chips**
- **¼ cup chopped pecans, for garnish**

1. Position a rack in the center of the oven, and preheat the oven to 350°F.

2. Line the bottom of a 9-inch round cake pan with a round of parchment paper or wax paper, and butter the paper and the sides of the pan.

3. Put the chopped chocolate or chocolate chips and the butter in a small heatproof bowl, and set it over a pan of simmering water. (Or put the chocolate and butter in the top of a double boiler set over simmering water.) Stir until melted and smooth. Stir in the orange juice concentrate, remove the bowl from the heat, and set it aside until it's warm, not hot.

4. Put the pecans, flour, and sugar in a food processor and pulse until the nuts are coarsely ground. Transfer the nut mixture to a mixing bowl and stir in the warm chocolate mixture. Add the egg yolks one at a time, whisking well after each addition. Set the mixture aside.

5. Combine the egg whites and the salt in a clean dry bowl, and whip until soft peaks form. Spoon half of the egg whites into the chocolate-nut mixture, and stir well. Fold in the remaining whites.

6. Spoon the batter into the prepared pan, and bake until the cake is firm to the touch, 40 minutes. Transfer the cake pan to a wire rack and let it cool for at least 45 minutes.

7. While the cake is cooling, prepare the icing: Heat the cream in a small saucepan until steaming (do not allow the cream to boil). Place the chocolate chips in a small heatproof bowl, and pour the hot cream over them; stir until the chips have melted. Let the icing cool for about 30 minutes. It should have thickened enough to coat a spoon.

8. Invert a platter over the cake pan, and holding the two together, turn them over to release the cake. Remove the parchment paper. Using a narrow spatula, spread the icing smoothly over the top of the cake, letting the excess drip down the sides. Garnish with the chopped pecans. Let the icing set for at least 1 hour, then serve. The cake can be refrigerated, covered, for up to 5 days.

food as a gift

These days many of us are questioning our overconsumption of "things," finding ways to tread more lightly on the planet, and trying to establish more personal ties to family, friends, and community. Giving food as gifts makes sense on all those levels, and it's economical, too.

Giving something that you've made yourself is almost always more meaningful, personal, and appreciated than buying something ready-made. I still have clear, sweet memories of the homemade butternut squash soup and freshly baked muffins my friend Trudy brought to the hospital after I had my first child—about two decades ago! The sight of her smile behind that beautiful tureen of golden soup, the muffins nestling in a lovely cloth napkin, and the delicious smells . . . There is no way a bunch of flowers or balloons would have made me feel so loved and nurtured after such a wonderful but exhausting experience.

Homemade food is always a gift from the heart. The gesture shows that you care enough to give someone a very precious commodity—your time and ingenuity. And be sure to make creative use of supplies you already have stowed away in a cupboard or closet to wrap or package food gifts. You can reuse baskets or tins; wrap baked goods in brown kraft paper for an organic look; pour a batch of homemade granola into a large, clean glass jar you've saved; salvage scraps of fabric, cut out rounds with pinking shears, and use them to cover jar lids by tying the fabric in place with raffia or a piece of ribbon.

Banana bread or whole wheat bread wrapped in a colorful organic-cotton tea towel is a gift that will smell and taste as good as it looks. Wait for the *oohs* and *aahs* when you present a jar of homemade Strawberry Jam or Quince and Pear Chutney as a hostess gift. Just tie on a bit of raffia (or use the fabric-covered-lid trick), and you're ready to arrive at the door with something very special. You can also give a gift certificate promising to prepare a special breakfast or candlelight dinner. There's nothing to end up in the landfill. And your gift is something your friends and family will literally "eat up," leaving nothing behind but smiles.

Sticky Toffee Pudding Cake

STICKY TOFFEE PUDDING IS A RENOWNED ENGLISH country dessert that in American terms is actually a cake, not a pudding—"pudding" being a generic British term for sweet desserts. Our chef Pam McKinstry first discovered this "pudding" almost forty years ago at the Sharrow Bay Hotel in England's Lake District. The cake is made with dates and is moderately sweet. The sauce is a rich, buttery caramel that soaks into the cake and delectably transforms it into the promised sticky toffee treat. The cake is excellent plain, or with just whipped cream and a drizzle of sauce. But if you love sweet desserts and want to experience the sticky toffee decadence, don't hold back on the sauce. We've added a twist to the original recipe to give it a little more kick: both ground and crystallized ginger, which add heat and spice to the moist, dense cake. —— *Serves 8*

FOR THE CAKE

4 tablespoons (½ stick) unsalted butter, at room temperature, plus extra for greasing the baking dish

1 cup packed dark brown sugar

2 large eggs, at room temperature

1 teaspoon pure vanilla extract

1½ cups (8 ounces) pitted dates

1 teaspoon baking soda

1 cup plus 2 tablespoons whole wheat pastry flour or unbleached all-purpose flour

⅓ cup finely minced crystallized ginger

2 teaspoons ground ginger

½ teaspoon baking powder

¼ teaspoon salt

FOR THE SAUCE

1½ cups heavy (whipping) cream

8 tablespoons (1 stick) unsalted butter

½ cup packed dark brown sugar

FOR GARNISH

Vanilla Whipped Cream (page 314)

1. Position a rack in the middle of the oven and preheat the oven to 350°F. Butter an 8-inch-square baking dish and set it aside.

2. Prepare the cake: Place the butter and the brown sugar in a food processor and process until the mixture is blended. Add the eggs and the vanilla, and run the machine for 1 minute to create a smooth batter. Transfer the batter to a medium-size bowl, and wash and dry the food processor bowl and blade in preparation for the next step.

3. Place the dates in the clean food processor bowl.

4. Combine 1 cup water and the baking soda in a small saucepan, and bring to a boil. With the food

THE BASICS

Dates

Dates thrive in hot desert climates, including Arizona and California. Although there are numerous varieties, the two most popular in the United States are Deglet Noor and Medjool. Deglet Noors (which represent about 95 percent of the commercial production in this country) are a semi-dry date with a light golden brown color. Medjools are generally sold as fresh fruit, and are often only available from September to early winter. Dried dates are sold year-round, packaged with or without pits. Store dried fruit in a cool, dark place for up to 6 months, or refrigerate for up to a year.

To chop or slice dates, snip with scissors or cut with a knife. If they are excessively sticky, freeze the dates for 45 minutes to firm them before preparing. Alternately, if chopped dates will be incorporated into a baked treat, you can dust them lightly with flour to help minimize sticking as you slice.

processor running, slowly add the hot mixture to the dates. Process to form a coarse puree. Add the date puree to the batter, and stir to blend.

5. Whisk the flour, crystallized ginger, ground ginger, baking powder, and salt together in a small bowl. Stir the flour mixture into the date batter until just combined. Pour the batter into the prepared baking dish, and bake until the cake is firm to the touch in the center and a toothpick inserted into the center comes out clean, 40 to 50 minutes.

6. Let the cake cool in the baking dish on a wire rack for about 10 minutes.

7. While the cake is cooling, prepare the sauce: Combine the cream, butter, and brown sugar in a medium-size saucepan and bring to a simmer over medium-high heat, stirring to melt the sugar. Reduce the heat to medium and simmer until the sauce thickens and turns toffee-colored, about 10 minutes.

8. Invert a plate over the baking dish, and holding the two together, invert to release the cake onto the plate.

9. To serve, cut the warm cake into squares and place them in shallow dessert bowls. Pour or ladle some of the hot sauce over each piece of cake. Garnish with whipped cream. (Both the cake and the sauce can be made a day or two ahead of time. Let them cool to room temperature, and then cover each item and refrigerate. Reheat the cake and the sauce separately in the microwave before serving.)

Baking Tips

When baking, it is usually important to be precise. Having the proper tools and equipment is essential, and never underestimate the importance of accurate measurements. To get you started, we've outlined a few simple guidelines to help you master the basics of successful baking.

◆ Use the proper measuring cups for the job: Measure liquids in glass or clear plastic liquid-measuring cups, and dry ingredients in dry-measuring cups that can be leveled off with a knife for exact measurements.

◆ Properly measure dry ingredients. When using measuring cups, be sure to lightly spoon the flour, not scoop it, into a dry-measuring cup, leveling off the excess with the flat side of a knife. Do not shake or tap the cup. Brown sugar is the exception: It should be firmly packed into the measuring cup.

◆ Measure baking pans and skillets across the top, not across the bottom.

◆ Invest in an oven thermometer. Oven calibration can vary by as much as 50 degrees from the temperature setting. Learn if you need to adjust your oven dial up or down to ensure that baked goods are cooked at the proper temperature.

Sorting Out Sweeteners

Sugar is a mainstay in the kitchen, and nowhere is it more elemental than in baking. While refined white sugar dominates the market, there are many other sweeteners readily available that offer a choice of intensity, texture, and flavor. Keep in mind that although some products might be perceived to be "healthier" choices than refined white sugar, all of these sweeteners have significant calories and, except for black strap molasses, no measurable nutritional benefits.

AGAVE NECTAR Agave nectar, like tequila, is traditionally derived from the boiled sap of the blue agave plant. This natural, unrefined liquid sweetener is a good alternative to table sugar, and because of its low glycemic index, it's a better choice for people with blood sugar issues. Amber-colored and raw agave syrups are unfiltered and have a slight maple flavor, while filtered light agave has a more neutral taste. Any of the three varieties can be substituted for honey in equal measure. Agave is more intensely sweet than table sugar, so when substituting agave for sugar, use only three-quarters of the amount called for.

HONEY Nature's natural sweetener, honey is made by bees from flower nectar. This all-purpose sweetener has a much more complex flavor than table sugar, depending on the source of the nectar. As a general rule, the darker the color of the honey, the stronger its flavor.

MOLASSES Molasses is used when a rich, earthy, and robustly flavored sweetener is desired. This thick brown syrup is the by-product of the sugar-making process and is available in light and dark forms. The color of molasses depends on which stage in the sugar-refining process it was produced, ranging from fancy, which is the lightest, to black strap, which is the darkest. Black strap molasses is a good source of iron, calcum, potassium, and magnesium. The darker the molasses, the more powerful the acidity and bitterness of its flavor.

WHITE SUGAR Made primarily from sugarcane, but also from sugar beets, this highly refined, free-flowing sugar is the type most of us know as table sugar. It's commonly sold in granulated form, but is also available as superfine or baker's sugar (fine grain) and confectioners' or powdered icing sugar (smooth, fine powder). Refined white sugars taste simply sweet. Unrefined white sugars, such as natural cane sugar, have a touch of natural color and a hint of molasses flavor. Organic granulated sugar is unbleached, less processed than conventional cane sugar, and is never made from genetically modified sugar beets

BROWN SUGAR All sugar is refined to some extent, but brown sugars are less processed, so the natural molasses goodness present in the plant has not been bleached and refined out of existence. It's sold in light and dark brown forms. Dark brown sugar, which is refined less than light brown, has a stronger flavor, deeper color, more moisture, and richer taste.

RAW SUGAR Raw sugar is less refined than white sugar, so it has a higher molasses content. The granules are large and crunchy with a rich, complex flavor. Two popular raw sugars are demerara and turbinado, often used to sweeten cups of coffee and tea.

MAPLE SYRUP Maple syrup is the concentrated sap of the sugar maple tree. Pure maple syrup imparts a deep, complex sweetness with caramel and vanilla overtones to everything from salad dressings to meats to desserts. It is a great all-round sweetener and comes in four grades, AA to C. AA (or Fancy) is the most expensive maple syrup and has the lightest color and flavor. With its dark amber color and robust flavors, Grade B is the best choice for baking.

CORN SYRUP Corn syrup is a thick sweet syrup that's often used in candy making, because it adds chewiness and prevents the crystallization of other sugars. It's sold in light and dark styles and is considered less sweet than granulated sugar. The difference in taste between the two forms is minimal. Light corn syrup has been clarified; caramel flavor and coloring have been added to dark corn syrup, giving it a slightly stronger flavor than the light version.

HIGH-FRUCTOSE CORN SYRUP (HFCS) is created by treating corn syrup with enzymes to produce a sweeter syrup with a higher level of fructose. Because HFCS is inexpensive and extends shelf life, it is a very common ingredient in processed foods.

Dried Cranberry and Pecan Tart

〰〰〰〰〰〰〰〰〰〰〰〰〰〰〰〰〰〰〰〰〰〰〰

BURSTING WITH FRUIT AND NUTS, THIS FESTIVE PIE is a real holiday favorite. Baked in a tart pan instead of a pie plate, the filling is densely packed with cranberries and pecans. The tart is very rich but not excessively sweet and doesn't really need any adornment. If you can't resist, add a dollop of whipped cream or a small scoop of Vanilla Bean Ice Cream.
〰 *Serves 8*

1 disk Sweet Pie Crust dough (page 425)

8 tablespoons (1 stick) unsalted butter, melted

½ cup packed dark brown sugar

½ cup light corn syrup, preferably not high-fructose

2 large eggs

1 teaspoon pure vanilla extract

Grated zest of 1 large lemon

1 tablespoon fresh lemon juice

1 teaspoon ground cinnamon

2 cups dried cranberries

½ cup chopped pecans

Vanilla Whipped Cream (page 314) or Vanilla Bean Ice Cream (page 352), for serving (optional)

1. Position a rack in the middle of the oven and preheat the oven to 400°F.

2. Roll out the pie crust dough to form a 12-inch round, and carefully fit it into a 9-inch tart pan with a removable bottom. Trim the dough with kitchen scissors, leaving a ½-inch overhang. Fold the overhang under to form a double-layer edge. Line the crust with aluminum foil, and fill it with pie weights or dried beans. Bake the crust for 20 minutes.

3. Remove the foil and weights, return the tart pan to the oven, and bake until the crust is lightly colored, 5 to 10 minutes.

4. Remove the crust from the oven and reduce the oven temperature to 375°F. If the crust has bubbled during baking, press it down gently with the back of a fork. Let the crust cool in the tart pan on a wire rack while you make the filling.

5. Place the butter, brown sugar, and corn syrup in a medium-size bowl and whisk to blend. Add the eggs, vanilla, lemon zest, lemon juice, and cinnamon, and whisk to combine. Stir in the cranberries and pecans.

6. Place the tart pan on a rimmed baking sheet, and pour the filling into the cooled crust. Bake until the tart is set in the center and golden brown, 30 to 40 minutes.

7. Transfer the tart pan to a wire rack and let the tart cool for at least 30 minutes before carefully removing the sides of the pan.

8. Cut the tart into wedges and serve it warm or at room temperature, with a dollop of whipped cream or a scoop of vanilla ice cream if desired. (The tart can be made a day in advance; store it, covered, at room temperature.)

Healthy Apple Crisp

MY FAMILY LOVES APPLE DESSERTS, and we especially love ones that are healthy as well as delicious. This crisp uses just a little canola oil instead of lots of butter, as well as whole wheat flour and nutritious nuts. It's a yummy, quick, and easy guilt-free pleasure. Great on its own, it's even better when served with a bit of our Honey Frozen Yogurt (page 351) or Vanilla Bean Ice Cream (page 352). ⟶ *Serves 6*

6 large Granny Smith or other tart apples

Juice of 1 lemon

1 cup old-fashioned rolled oats
   (see sidebar, page 307)

¾ cup chopped pecans or walnuts

½ cup packed light brown sugar

2 tablespoons whole wheat pastry flour

1 tablespoon ground cinnamon

¼ cup canola oil, plus more if needed

1. Position a rack in the middle of the oven and preheat the oven to 375°F.

2. Core and peel the apples, and cut them into ¼-inch-thick slices; you should have about 7 cups. Place the slices in a large bowl, add the lemon juice, and toss to coat them with the juice.

3. To make the topping, combine the oats, pecans, brown sugar, pastry flour, and cinnamon in a bowl, and stir to blend. Add the oil and stir again. If the mixture seems too dry (it should clump together when you squeeze it), add another teaspoon or two of oil.

4. Transfer the apples to a 9-inch-square baking dish. Add the topping, spreading it evenly over the apples; do not pack it down.

5. Bake until the apples are tender and the topping is golden, 45 to 50 minutes. Serve warm.

twelve important reasons to **choose organic**

I have spent my entire adult life devoted to organic farming, and I am passionate about sharing all the reasons why my commitment grows year after year. Here are twelve wonderful benefits of organic food and farming. I hope they convince you to make the organic choice whenever possible!

Choosing organic . . .

1. Keeps chemicals out of your body—and the environment.

Organic food is grown without toxic synthetic pesticides and fertilizers. Although you usually can't see or taste pesticides on your food, testing by government agencies shows that significant percentages of tested samples of some conventional produce have detectable pesticide residues. (For more information about lowering your exposure to pesticides in your diet, see page 57.)

In addition to entering our food supply, pesticides applied in the field drift from their target and contaminate our air, oceans, rivers, groundwater, and soil.

2. Eliminates the main source of dietary pesticide exposure for kids.

The average child in the United States is exposed to five pesticides every day in his or her food and drinking water. A study published in *Environmental Health Perspectives* in 2008 showed that switching to organic produce and juices for just five days virtually eliminates any sign of exposure to organophosphate insecticides in children who previously showed evidence of these chemicals in saliva or urine samples.

3. Protects farmworkers, wildlife, and nearby homes, schools, and businesses.

When conventional agricultural chemicals are used in farm fields, they affect the people who apply the chemicals as well as the environment nearby. A 2006 study published in the *Annals of Neurology* found that workers who handled pesticides had a 70 percent higher incidence of Parkinson's disease than those who did not. A 2009 follow-up to that study found that instances of Parkinson's were twice as high among people who lived near farms sprayed with certain types of pesticides, compared with people who weren't exposed.

4. Provides your family with highly nutritious produce.

According to The Organic Center's 2008 study titled "New Evidence Confirms the Nutritional Superiority of Plant-Based Organic Foods," average levels of 11 nutrients are 25 percent higher in organic foods than in conventional foods, based on 236 scientifically valid comparisons. Overall, organic produce is approximately 30 percent higher in antioxidants than conventional produce.

5. Protects our precious oceans.

Conventional fertilizers are a big contributor to the "dead zones" in our oceans, caused in large part by an excess of nitrogen from synthetic farm fertilizers that run off farmland into rivers and oceans. The excess nutrients lead to massive algal blooms, which consume most of the life-giving oxygen in the water as they decompose. The results are large areas in the ocean that can no longer support marine life. In the Gulf of Mexico, where one of the largest ocean dead zones has been created, the breakdown of nitrogen has been reported to be approximately 70 percent from fertilizers, 11 percent from municipal sewage, 12 percent from animal waste, and 6 percent from atmospheric deposition.

6. Reduces contaminants in our drinking water.

The U.S. Geological Survey's 2008 "Pesticide National Synthesis Project" found at least one pesticide in every stream tested. Pesticides found most frequently, and in the highest concentrations, were synthetic chemicals used in conventional agriculture.

7. Mitigates global warming.

The Rodale Institute, with more than 60 years of experience in studying soil health, has conducted 30 years of field research on the impacts of farming on soil health. They have looked at the levels of carbon in soil under conventional and organic management, and have shown that while conventional farming breaks down soil carbon, releasing it into the atmosphere in the form of CO_2, organic farming builds soil carbon levels by absorbing it from the atmosphere and can sequester up to 30 times more carbon than can conventionally managed soils.

If organic agriculture were practiced on the planet's 3.5 billion tillable acres, it could sequester nearly 40 percent of the world's current CO_2 emissions. And if all the 160 million acres of conventional corn and soybeans in the U.S. were converted to organic production, this would be the equivalent of taking 80 million cars off the road.

8. Assures you that you're not eating genetically modified or irradiated foods.

If you are concerned about consuming genetically modified organisms (GMOs), look for the USDA Organic Seal, which is currently your only assurance that the food you buy has not been genetically modified. The USDA's National Organic Program standards expressly prohibit the use of genetically modified ingredients and irradiation. There are no requirements for other types of food to be labeled as containing GMOs.

9. Avoids antibiotics and artificial growth hormones in meat and dairy.

Organically raised animals have been fed organic feed and grazed on organic pasture. They are raised in conditions that limit stress and promote health, and are never given antibiotics or synthetic growth hormones.

As an added benefit, the animals' all-organic diet supports farmland that does not pollute the environment with toxic synthetic pesticides and fertilizers.

10. Supports the farmers and other food producers who invest the extra care to produce food organically.

When you buy organic, you are supporting the farmers who believe that the extra cost and effort of growing food without toxic synthetic pesticides and fertilizers avoids serious—and ultimately more costly—long-term issues like groundwater pollution, soil erosion, loss of biodiversity, and human health problems caused by exposure to agricultural chemical residues.

11. Promotes healthy soils.

Ask organic farmers about the cornerstone of organic farming, and their answer will probably be the same: creating rich, healthy soil. Organic farmers know that agrichemicals kill more than pests—they wipe out beneficial microorganisms and earthworms in the soil that help create rich soil that holds nutrients and protects plants from diseases. The soil in chemically treated fields is less healthy and more vulnerable to erosion.

12. Preserves biodiversity.

Preserving a balanced ecosystem is essential for the long-term health of our environment. Organic farming encourages an abundance of species living in balanced, harmonious ecosystems because it works with natural processes, not against them.

Additional Resources:
www.foodnews.org
www.whatsonmyfood.org
www.rodale.com
water.usgs.gov/nawqa/pnsp/

All-American Apple Pie

EVERY COOK NEEDS AN APPLE PIE RECIPE in his or her repertoire. Loaded with juicy, tart apples, not too sweet, and with just a hint of spice, this apple pie is always a hit. You can prepare the pastry dough a day or two ahead of time or buy a good-quality ready-made pie crust. Enlist a helper to peel and slice the apples while you roll out the crusts. Variations on the classic apple pie can be interesting, so try adding raisins, dried cranberries, or crystallized ginger to the filling. I like to sprinkle cinnamon sugar on top of the crust before baking. ⎯⎯ *Makes one 9-inch double-crust pie*

2 disks Flaky Multigrain Pie Crust dough
   (page 426)
¾ cup sugar
1 teaspoon ground cinnamon
½ teaspoon ground nutmeg
1 tablespoon unbleached all-purpose flour
½ teaspoon salt
About 8 large (3 pounds) crisp apples,
   such as Fuji or Granny Smith
Juice of ½ lemon
2 tablespoons (¼ stick) unsalted butter,
   cut into small pieces
1 large egg, lightly whisked

1. Following the instructions on page 427, roll out the dough for the bottom crust to form an 11-inch round. Transfer the dough to a 9-inch pie plate, pressing it in firmly, and then trim the dough even with the edge of the plate. Refrigerate, uncovered, for 30 minutes.

2. Position a rack in the center of the oven. Place a rimmed baking sheet on the rack, and preheat the oven to 375°F.

3. Place the sugar, cinnamon, nutmeg, flour, and salt in a large mixing bowl, and stir to combine.

4. Peel, core, and slice the apples into ¼-inch-thick slices. Toss the apples with the lemon juice in a large bowl, and then add them to the sugar-spice mixture. Toss to coat.

5. Roll out the dough for the top crust to form an 11-inch round.

6. Transfer the apples to the chilled pie shell, mounding the fruit high. Dot with the pieces of butter and cover with the top crust. Trim the top crust, leaving a ¾-inch overhang. Fold the top crust under the edge of the bottom crust, and crimp or flute the edges together to make a decorative edge. Using a small knife, cut three or four slits in the center of the top crust to allow steam to vent as the pie bakes. Brush the top of the pie with the egg.

7. Place the pie on the baking sheet and bake for 15 minutes. Then reduce the oven heat to 350°F and continue baking until the crust is golden and the apple juices are bubbling up through the slits, 35 to 45 minutes. Let the pie cool on a wire rack. Serve it warm or at room temperature. (The pie can be refrigerated, covered, for 3 days. To rewarm it, bake it, uncovered, in a 325°F oven for 15 to 20 minutes.)

socially responsible eco-labels

It's nice to know when we are savoring a cup of coffee or nibbling on one of our favorite chocolate bars that they were produced in a way that didn't undermine ecological sustainability or fair and equitable business practices. Here are a few labels to look for so you can enjoy these products with peace of mind.

Fair Trade Certified

The internationally recognized Fair Trade Certified label ensures that farmers and workers who produce imported goods such as coffee, tea, some spices, chocolate, and flowers get their fair share of the profits.

"Fair Trade Certified" promotes fair prices, fair labor conditions, direct trade that eliminates unnecessary middlemen, and democratic and transparent organizations, community development, and environmental sustainability.

To learn more, visit the TransFair USA website: www.fairtradecertified.org.

USDA Organic Certified

An estimated 85 percent of fair trade coffee is organic. Fair Trade advisers help many small farmers become certified organic; those who are not certified are given information to help them resist the pressure of chemical companies promoting synthetic fertilizers and pesticides. Although products like coffee and chocolate generally have a relatively low instance of pesticide residue, there is a socially responsible reason for buying organic: It's safer for farmworkers, their families, and especially their young children. It also reduces soil, air, and groundwater contamination in their surrounding communities. (See page 47 for more information about organic certification.)

Rainforest Alliance Certified

The Rainforest Alliance Certified seal promotes and guarantees continual improvements in agriculture. The seal is awarded to farms that meet comprehensive standards, which protect the environment, wildlife, workers, and local communities. Products that feature the seal—including coffee, tea, and chocolate—contain ingredients from these sustainably managed farms. To learn more, visit www.rainforest-alliance.org.

Bird Friendly label

"Bird Friendly" coffee is a trademark of the shade-grown coffee program created by the Smithsonian Migratory Bird Center at the National Zoological Park. A traditional form of coffee production, shade-grown coffee is cultivated under a canopy of trees, which provides habitat for birds. In addition to birds, shaded coffee plantations provide habitat for myriad insects, orchids, mammals, reptiles, amphibians, and other less well-known denizens of tropical forests. Furthermore, the natural mulch from shade trees provides nutrients and suppresses weeds, thus reducing or eliminating the need for chemical fertilizers and herbicides and lowering farming costs.

To learn more, visit the Smithsonian Migratory Bird Center website: nationalzoo.si.edu/ConservationAndScience/MigratoryBirds/Coffee/.

Quince Tarte Tatin

Quince Tarte Tatin, ready to flip onto a platter.

TARTE TATIN IS A CLASSIC FRENCH APPLE TART with a crisp pastry crust and a sticky caramel topping. It is baked upside-down, with the crust on top, then flipped out of the pan to serve. Our version uses quinces instead of apples, which results in a beautiful and fragrant dessert. Quince has a distinctively tart flavor that is a wonderful contrast to the sweet intensity of the caramel topping. Smyrna quinces are sweeter than some other varieties and work best for this recipe. If quinces are impossible to find in your area, this recipe will work with apples or pears, or a combination of the two; reduce the sugar to ¾ cup, however—otherwise, the tart will be too sweet. Tarte Tatin is best the day it is made, as the crust quickly gets soggy from all the caramel. To save time, you can use a purchased pie crust. ⁓⁓⁓ ***Makes one 10- or 11-inch tart***

1¼ cups sugar

5 tablespoons unsalted butter,
   cut into 5 pieces, at room temperature

1 teaspoon ground star anise
   (see sidebar, page 385)

About 4 pounds (7 to 8) Smyrna quinces,
   peeled, cored, and cut into 1-inch-wide
   wedges

1 disk Sweet Pie Crust dough (page 425)

Vanilla Bean Ice Cream (page 352) or
   Crème Fraîche (page 415), for serving

1. Combine the sugar and ¼ cup water in a 10- or 11-inch ovenproof skillet (preferably cast-iron), and place it over medium heat. Stir until the sugar melts. Then raise the heat to medium-high and cook without stirring, occasionally brushing down the sides of the pan with a wet pastry brush to dissolve any sugar crystals, until the caramel turns a light brown, about 10 minutes. As the caramel begins to take on color, swirl the skillet to distribute the syrup so that it colors evenly.

2. Immediately remove the skillet from the heat. Add the butter and star anise, stirring until the mixture is thick and smooth.

3. Arrange the quince wedges in concentric circles on top of the caramel, placing them rounded side down. Fill in any gaps with small pieces of quince.

4. Position a rack in the center of the oven. Place a rimmed baking sheet on the rack, and preheat the oven to 400°F.

5. Following the instructions on page 426, roll the Sweet Pie Crust dough to form an 11- or 12-inch round (1 inch larger than the skillet).

Quince Tarte Tatin

Carefully transfer the dough to the skillet, placing it on top of the quinces. Tuck the edges of the dough down along the sides of the skillet. Using a sharp knife, cut several 2-inch slits in the pastry so that the steam can escape during baking.

6. Place the skillet on the baking sheet and bake the tart until the quinces are tender and the pastry is golden, 50 to 60 minutes.

7. Transfer the skillet to a wire rack and let the tart cool for 30 minutes, or until the pan is still warm but is cool enough to handle safely.

8. Run a small knife around the edges of the skillet. Invert a large flat platter over the skillet, and holding the platter and skillet together tightly, invert the tart onto the platter. If any pieces of fruit have remained in the skillet, carefully remove them and place them in the tart. Serve the Tarte Tatin warm, with a scoop of vanilla ice cream or a dollop of crème fraîche.

FARM   FRESH

Quince

The quince is an ancient fruit that despite its long and illustrious history in Asia and the Mediterranean region has gained little popularity in the U.S. This lack of interest may stem from the fact that quinces, unlike their apple cousins, are rarely eaten raw—their flesh is hard, dry, and somewhat tart. Quinces look like apples but have yellow skins; they taste like a cross between an apple and a pear. Their fragrance is unlike any other fruit, and although they are more difficult to prepare than apples, the extra effort is well rewarded.

Quinces are available in the market from October through early January. Look for fruits that are large, firm, and yellow, with little or no sign of green. At home, refrigerate them in a plastic bag for up to 2 months. They must be peeled and cored before using. The core of a quince is very large and rock-hard. To remove it, peel the quince, slice around the core to create 4 pieces of fruit, and then slice or dice these pieces. Like apples, the flesh discolors when exposed to air, but don't worry if there is some browning of the quinces as you prep them—this won't be apparent after cooking. Quinces have a very high pectin content, so they make excellent jam, jellies, and chutneys. Because of their tart flavor, they work well in both savory and sweet dishes.

Lemon Macaroon Pie

WHEN I SHARED THIS PIE WITH SOME OF MY COWORKERS, the reviews were unanimous: This is not a good pie . . . this is a *great* pie! The tartness of the lemon is perfectly balanced by the sweet coconut. The lemon filling is smooth and custardlike, contrasting nicely with the slight chewiness of the coconut, a combination that creates an exceptionally delicious dessert. ⟶ *Makes one 9-inch single-crust pie*

1 disk Sweet Pie Crust dough (page 425)

3 large eggs

3 large egg yolks

1¼ cups sugar

¼ teaspoon salt

1 cup shredded unsweetened coconut

¼ cup heavy (whipping) cream

⅓ cup fresh lemon juice

2 tablespoons (¼ stick) unsalted butter, melted

2 teaspoons grated lemon zest

½ teaspoon pure vanilla extract

¼ teaspoon pure almond extract

1. Following the instructions on page 426, roll out the dough to form an 11-inch round. Transfer the dough to a 9-inch pie plate, pressing it firmly into the plate. Trim the overhanging pastry to ½ inch, and turn it under. Flute the edge of the crust. Then refrigerate, uncovered, for 30 minutes.

2. Position a rack in the middle of the oven and preheat the oven to 350°F.

3. Place the eggs, egg yolks, sugar, and salt in a medium-size bowl and whisk to blend. Stir in the coconut and heavy cream.

4. Combine the lemon juice, melted butter, lemon zest, vanilla extract, and almond extract in a small bowl. Add this to the coconut mixture, and stir to blend.

5. Pour the filling into the chilled pie shell, and bake until the pie is golden brown and set in the middle, about 45 minutes.

6. Transfer the pie to a wire rack and let it cool completely before slicing and serving. (The pie can be refrigerated, covered, for up to 3 days.)

LIVING GREEN
Most white paper products—such as coffee filters, paper napkins, and paper towels—are bleached white by chlorine. The use of chlorine during the papermaking process produces dioxins, which persist in the environment for many years, and have been shown to be highly toxic. It's much better to purchase either unbleached products, or items that were whitened with hydrogen peroxide.

Fresh Blueberry Pie

NOTHING SAYS SUMMER LIKE A FRESH BLUEBERRY PIE. Either cultivated or wild blueberries can be used in this filling, which is quick and simple to prepare. If you have access to a good-quality frozen pastry crust, the pie will go together even faster. Blueberries make a very juicy pie, which needs a 2-hour rest after it comes out of the oven to allow the juices to thicken. Top this glorious creation with a scoop of our Vanilla Bean Ice Cream (page 352), and you have the perfect summer dessert. ⚊⚊ *Makes one 9-inch double-crust pie*

2 disks Sweet Pie Crust dough (page 425)

½ cup sugar

¼ cup cornstarch

¼ teaspoon ground nutmeg

⅛ teaspoon salt

Grated zest of 1 small lemon

6 cups fresh blueberries

1. Following the instructions on page 426, roll out the dough for the bottom crust to form an 11-inch round. Transfer it to a 9-inch pie plate, pressing the dough firmly into the plate. Trim the dough even with the edge of the pie plate. Refrigerate the pie shell, uncovered, for 30 minutes.

2. Position a rack in the lower third of the oven and place a rimmed baking sheet on the rack. Preheat the oven to 425°F.

3. Place the sugar, cornstarch, nutmeg, salt, and lemon zest in a large mixing bowl, and stir to combine. Add the blueberries and stir to combine.

4. Roll out the dough for the top crust to form an 11-inch round.

5. Spoon the blueberry mixture into the chilled pie shell, and cover it with the top crust. Trim the top crust, leaving a ¾-inch overhang. Then fold the top crust under the edge of the bottom crust, and crimp or flute the edges together to make a decorative edge. Using a small knife, cut two slits in the center of the top crust to allow steam to vent as the pie bakes.

6. Transfer the pie plate to the baking sheet and bake for 25 minutes. Then reduce the heat to 375°F and cook until the blueberry juices start to ooze out around the edges and bubble out of the steam cuts, 30 to 40 minutes more.

7. Let the pie cool on a wire rack for at least 2 hours before serving.

Fresh Blueberry Pie

Pumpkin and Winter Squash Pie

LOTS OF AROMATIC SPICES ADD FRAGRANCE AND FLAVOR to this festive seasonal pie. I like the combination of pumpkin and winter squash purees, but you can use all pumpkin or all squash if you prefer. For convenience, use canned purees—but it will taste extra fresh and delicious if you roast your own pumpkins or squash (see the sidebar). Serve the pie warm, with a scoop of Vanilla Bean Ice Cream (page 352) or a dollop of Vanilla Whipped Cream (page 314) or Crème Fraîche (page 415). —*mmm*— ***Makes one 9-inch single-crust pie***

How to Make Pumpkin and Squash Purees

Although you can't beat the convenience of canned squash and pumpkin purees, making your own is really quite simple and the taste is superior to anything you can buy. Roasting is the best method, as it brings out the natural sweetness of the flesh and intensifies its flavor without adding extra moisture.

1. Position a rack in the middle of the oven and preheat the oven to 400°F.

2. Cut the pumpkin or squash into several large pieces, all about the same size. Scrape out and discard the seeds and fibers (or save the seeds for roasting, see page 232).

3. Lightly butter a rimmed baking sheet. Place the pumpkin or squash pieces on the baking sheet, cover with aluminum foil, and bake until the pieces are soft when pierced with a fork, about 45 minutes.

4. Let the pumpkin cool in the foil wrapping. Then scoop out the flesh, discard the skins, and mash the pulp with a potato masher or a handheld stick blender or in a food processor until smooth. Refrigerate, covered, for up to 5 days.

1 disk Sweet Pie Crust dough (page 425) or Flaky Multigrain Pie Crust dough (page 426)

1 cup canned or homemade pure pumpkin puree (not pumpkin pie mix; see sidebar, this page)

1 cup canned or homemade butternut squash puree

¾ cup packed light brown sugar

3 large eggs, lightly beaten

¾ teaspoon ground cinnamon

¾ teaspoon ground ginger

¼ teaspoon ground nutmeg

¼ teaspoon ground cloves

¼ teaspoon salt

¾ cup heavy (whipping) cream

1. Following the instructions on page 426, roll out the dough to form an 11-inch round. Transfer the dough to a 9-inch pie plate, pressing it firmly into the plate. Trim the overhanging pastry to ½ inch, and turn it under. Flute the edge of the crust. Then refrigerate it, uncovered, for at least 30 minutes or up to 4 hours.

2. Position a rack in the middle of the oven and place a rimmed baking sheet on the rack. Preheat the oven to 350°F.

3. Place the pumpkin and squash purees in a large bowl and whisk to combine. Add the brown sugar, eggs, cinnamon, ginger, nutmeg, cloves, and salt, and whisk to combine. Add the cream and whisk again to blend.

4. Pour the filling into the chilled pie shell, place it on the rimmed baking sheet, and bake until the pie is set in the middle and golden brown, 40 to 50 minutes.

5. Let the pie cool on a wire rack for at least 30 minutes before serving. (The pie can be refrigerated, covered, for up to 3 days.)

Passion Fruit Semifreddo Soufflé Pie

SEMIFREDDO IS ITALIAN FOR "HALF COLD," and in culinary terms it refers to any dessert that is partially frozen. In this delectable pie, passion fruit custard is mixed with whipped egg whites and baked in a cookie-crumb crust until puffed and golden. The result is an ethereally light dessert that is a cross between a soufflé and a meringue pie. It can be served right out of the oven, but freezing the pie actually improves its texture and intensifies its flavor. Passion fruits are available year-round, but may be difficult to find in some areas. Frozen passion fruit puree can be purchased in some supermarkets, as well as in specialty markets and online. ⁓ **Serves 8**

FOR THE CRUST

Butter, for greasing the pan
1 cup gingersnap or graham cracker crumbs
4 tablespoons (½ stick) unsalted butter, melted
¼ cup sugar

FOR THE FILLING

4 large eggs, at room temperature, separated
½ cup sugar
¼ cup passion fruit puree, fresh (from about 12 passion fruits, seeds removed and reserved; see box, page 337) or frozen (thawed)
¼ teaspoon cream of tartar

FOR THE GARNISH

Vanilla Whipped Cream (page 314)
Passion fruit seeds (optional)

1. Position a rack in the middle of the oven and preheat the oven to 350°F. Lightly butter the bottom of an 8-inch pie plate or springform pan, and cut out a round of parchment to fit. Place the paper round in the bottom of the pie plate and set it aside.

2. Prepare the pie crust: Place the cookie crumbs, melted butter, and sugar in a small bowl and stir to combine. Press the crumbs over the bottom and sides of the prepared pie plate, and bake until golden, about 10 minutes. Let the crust cool on a wire rack while you prepare the filling.

3. Prepare the filling: Pour water into a saucepan or the bottom of a double boiler to a depth of 1 inch, and bring it to a boil over high heat. Reduce the heat to medium-low so that the water just barely simmers.

4. Place the egg yolks in a medium-size heatproof mixing bowl or in the top of the double boiler. Add ¼ cup of the sugar and the passion fruit puree,

Double Boiler

A double boiler is an arrangement of two interlocking pans, with one pan sitting partway inside the other. The lower pan holds simmering water which gently heats the contents of the upper pan. Double boilers are used for gentle cooking and to warm heat-sensitive foods such as chocolate, custards, and delicate egg-based sauces. A makeshift double boiler can be created by setting a heatproof metal or glass bowl over a pan of simmering water. The bottom of the bowl must not touch the water.

and whisk to combine. Set the bowl over the barely simmering water. Cook, stirring constantly with a wooden spoon or a whisk, until the mixture thickens and an instant-read thermometer registers 150°F, 5 to 10 minutes. Be careful not to let the mixture simmer, or the yolks will overheat and scramble. If you do not have a thermometer, you will know the custard is done when it coats the spoon so thickly that if you draw your finger across it, the mark holds.

5. Remove the custard from the heat and let it cool for 10 minutes. Then refrigerate it until it is lukewarm, about 15 minutes.

6. Position a rack in the middle of the oven and preheat the oven to 350°F.

7. Place the egg whites in a medium-size bowl and beat with an electric mixer on high speed until foamy, about 1 minute. Add the cream of tartar and beat for another minute. Gradually add the remaining ¼ cup sugar and continue to beat until the whites form soft yet distinctive shiny peaks, 2 to 3 minutes. Do not overbeat, or the whites will become grainy and dry.

8. Stir one-third of the egg whites into the passion fruit custard. Then carefully fold in the remaining whites. Pour the filling into the crust, and bake until the pie has puffed, the surface has turned lightly golden, and the filling has set, 15 to 20 minutes.

9. Let the pie cool on a wire rack for 1 hour.

10. Transfer the pie, uncovered, to the freezer and let it freeze for at least 6 hours. Once it is frozen, cover the pie tightly with plastic wrap.

11. To serve, warm a sharp knife blade under hot running water, wipe it dry, and then slice the pie with the hot knife, reheating the blade as needed as you cut more slices. Garnish each serving with Vanilla Whipped Cream and a scattering of passion fruit seeds if desired.

Lusciously ripe passion fruit.

Passion Fruit

Passion fruit: Just the name conjures up the tropics. Indeed, passion fruit is a warm-weather vine that thrives in hot and humid subtropical and tropical climates. Portuguese missionaries in southern Brazil, where it is native, called it "passion fruit" because the flowers have elements they believed depicted the crucifixion of Christ.

There are two common varieties: the abundant purple passion fruit and the less common, elongated yellow variety variously called "vanilla" or "banana" passion fruit. The purple variety grows in subtropical areas such as southern California and Florida, while the yellow form flourishes in true tropical regions such as Hawaii, parts of South Africa, and Indonesia.

Despite its alluring name, this intensely flavorful fruit is something of an ugly duckling. The common passion fruit is round to egg-shaped and between 1½ and 3 inches wide. Its smooth but tough, inedible rind becomes wrinkled, dimpled, and dented and fades to a brownish purple when the fruit is ripe. But inside that not-too-attractive package lies a seeded, jellylike pulp that is simply heavenly. Passion fruit has a distinctive, haunting flavor that is unlike any other fruit and for many defines the true taste of the tropics. The pulp of the purple variety is egg-yolk yellow and intensely aromatic, and the flavor ranges from sweet-tart to very tart. Yellow passion fruit has greenish pulp with larger seeds than the common variety, and yields twice as much pulp. Although the taste is similar, the flavor is less acidic and has hints of vanilla.

When buying either variety, select fruit that feels heavy and looks plump. Let your nose be your guide: Ripe passion fruit is richly fragrant. Wrinkled skin is also a sign of ripeness, not of spoilage. Avoid overly wrinkled, featherlight fruits as these are past their prime, or conversely, very hard specimens, which were picked before fully ripened. If the skin is still smooth, ripen the fruit at room temperature, turning it occasionally. Ripe passion fruit can be stored in the refrigerator for up to 2 weeks. If you have excess fruit (lucky you), simply cut the passion fruit in half, scoop out the pulp, and freeze it for future use. The seeds are completely edible and have a crunchy texture and consistency similar to pomegranate seeds.

As a general guide, 12 ripe passion fruits will yield about 1 cup of pulp and about ½ cup of strained juice. Straining out the seeds is purely a matter of personal preference, but they are a good source of fiber. Passion fruit is also an excellent source of vitamins C and A and a significant source of potassium, magnesium, and riboflavin.

THE BASICS

Almond Flour

Almond flour (also marketed as "almond meal") is simply ground-up almonds. Look for it at supermarkets and natural foods stores. You can also make it yourself in a blender or clean coffee grinder: Grind ½ cup of blanched almonds at a time until they become powdery; be sure to stop processing before the nuts turn into butter. If a very fine flour is desired (as fine as all-purpose flour), transfer the ground flour to a fine-mesh sieve and strain it to remove any residual nut pieces; the small pieces can be reground with the next ½ cup of almonds. A pound of nuts yields about 4 cups of flour.

Almond flour is an excellent substitute for regular flour. It's loaded with nutrients, vitamin E, and magnesium. Almond flour can be used in cakes, cookies, and brownies in combination with all-purpose flour.

Cherry Almond Clafouti

CLAFOUTI IS A RUSTIC COUNTRY DISH FROM FRANCE, characterized by a layer of fresh fruit topped with a batter. There are many versions of this dessert, which falls somewhere between a cake and a custard. Cherries are traditional, but other stone fruits are also delicious. In this recipe, we've married fresh sweet cherries with almond flour and almond extract. Beaten egg whites are folded into the batter to keep the cake light. The cherries are cooked until they are soft and juicy, and then used both in the cake and as a sauce.

—— *Serves 8 to 10*

3 tablespoons unsalted butter, plus extra
   for greasing the cake pan
⅓ cup plus 3 tablespoons sugar
Grated zest of 1 lemon
¼ teaspoon ground cinnamon
5 cups (about 1¾ pounds) fresh sweet
   cherries, stemmed and pitted
2 large eggs, separated
⅔ cup almond flour (see sidebar,
   this page)
Scant ½ cup whole wheat pastry flour or
   unbleached all-purpose flour
1 teaspoon pure almond extract
½ cup heavy (whipping) cream
Pinch of salt
1 tablespoon fresh lemon juice

1. Position a rack in the middle of the oven and preheat the oven to 400°F. Lightly butter a 9-inch round cake pan and set it aside.

2. Melt the butter in a medium-size saucepan over medium heat. Add the ⅓ cup sugar, the lemon zest, and the cinnamon, and cook, stirring, until the sugar melts. Then add the cherries and cook, stirring occasionally, until they are soft and the juices have thickened slightly, 10 to 15 minutes.

3. Remove the pan from the heat and use a slotted spoon to transfer two thirds of the cherries to the prepared cake pan, creating a single layer of fruit. Reserve the remaining cherries and the juices.

4. In a medium-size bowl, whisk the egg yolks with the remaining 3 tablespoons sugar until light and fluffy. Beat in the almond flour, pastry flour, almond extract, and cream.

5. Beat the egg whites with the pinch of salt in a small bowl until they form soft peaks. Whisk in one third of the whites to loosen the batter. Then fold in the remaining whites, taking care not to deflate the batter.

Pour the mixture over the cherries in the cake pan.

6. Bake the clafouti until the cake is set and golden and has pulled away from the sides of the pan, 20 to 25 minutes.

7. Transfer the pan to a wire rack and let the clafouti cool for at least 5 minutes before serving.

8. Just before serving, combine the reserved cherries and juices with the lemon juice in a small saucepan, and warm over medium-low heat. Cut the cake into wedges, and top each piece with some of the warm cherry sauce.

avoiding unwanted ingredients

For me, eating healthy means more than just eating fresh produce and whole grains; it also means staying away from chemical additives and unhealthy trans fats (also called partially hydrogenated oils). A great way to avoid unwanted ingredients is to cook from scratch, but that isn't always possible. So, when I do buy processed foods, I prefer to buy certified organic products, which are prohibited from containing any artificial preservatives, colors, trans fats, or GMOs (genetically modified organisms).

Even if you're an avid label reader, some label claims can be misleading. For example, foods marketed for retail sale are required to list trans fat in their nutritional information, but if the product contains a half gram of trans fat or less per serving, manufacturers are allowed to claim "0 grams of trans fat." Depending on how much you eat (remember, designated portions are often very small; you might wind up eating two or even three portions), you could wind up consuming a significant amount of trans fats in a "trans fat–free" product.

Most commercial cake mixes are good examples of a processed food with a long list of unhealthy ingredients. The time you save really isn't worth it when you look at what's in the box. Trans fats (which raise your bad cholesterol and lower your good) are high up on the list of ingredients for most cake mixes and pre-made frostings, and they often contain artificial colors (including red dye 40, which has been linked to hyperactivity in children), artificial flavors, and preservatives.

Compare a typical cake mix's list of unpronounceable ingredients to those in our easy-to-make Chocolate Pecan Cake with Chocolate Ganache Icing on page 317, and it really inspires you to bake from scratch. When I choose to splurge on a decadent dessert, I enjoy it much more knowing it's made with wholesome ingredients.

Banana–Chocolate Chip Crêpes

CREPES ARE ONE OF MY FAMILY'S FAVORITE DESSERTS, and this sliced banana-and-chocolate-chip combination is the one we make most often. In my household, we usually eat dessert crêpes after having savory crêpes for dinner, and this whole wheat batter works perfectly well for both types. (See page 175 for a savory recipe for Spinach, Mushroom, and Gruyère Crêpes using these crêpes.) I prefer to make and fill crêpes when it's time to eat them. Of course, you can also make crêpes ahead of time and then reheat them when you're ready to finish the dish (see the sidebar).

I encourage you to experiment with different flavor combinations. My son, Jeffrey, spreads a little butter and raspberry jam on his, folds it up, and then sprinkles confectioners' sugar and a few fresh raspberries on top. I love mine with just a little butter and brown sugar. Have fun finding your personal favorite! For best results, make the crêpe batter one to three hours ahead of time, so it has time to rest in the refrigerator before using.

—— *Makes about 8 crêpes*

WHOLE WHEAT CRÊPES

1 cup whole wheat pastry flour

⅛ teaspoon salt

1¼ cups whole milk

2 large eggs, lightly beaten

2 tablespoons unsalted butter, melted

FILLING AND ASSEMBLING

2 tablespoons unsalted butter

3 medium bananas, peeled and cut on a
    slight diagonal into ¼-inch-thick slices

¼ cup milk

1 cup semisweet chocolate chips,
    or 8 ounces semisweet chocolate,
    finely chopped

Confectioners' sugar, for garnish

1. Prepare the crêpes: Place the flour and salt in a medium-size bowl and whisk to combine. Add 1¼ cups of the milk and the eggs, whisk to combine, then add the 2 tablespoons of melted butter and whisk again until the batter is smooth. You can also make the batter in a blender or with an immersion blender if you prefer. Cover the bowl with a plate and refrigerate 1 to 3 hours.

2. Prepare the filling: Melt the butter in a skillet over medium heat, and add the banana slices. Cook the bananas until they are seared and golden brown, about 1 minute. Then turn them over and continue cooking until they have softened slightly, about 30 seconds. Transfer the bananas to a small bowl and cover to keep them warm.

3. If the crêpe batter is thick—it should have the consistency of thin pancake batter—add 2 tablespoons of the milk and whisk to combine.

4. Place a 12-inch cast-iron skillet or a crêpe pan over medium heat and when the pan is hot, brush with some of the melted butter. Pour or ladle ¼ cup of batter into the center of the the pan, lift the pan off the stove, and tilt and swirl the pan so that the batter spreads thinly across the bottom of the pan in a widening circle; don't worry if the crêpe is not a perfect circle. There may be some small holes, but again this is of no consequence as the crêpes are meant to be thin. If the holes are large, you can immediately dot a bit of batter on them to fill them. Cook until tiny bubbles begin to appear in the crëpe batter; depending on how hot the pan is, the crêpe will be ready to flip in 15 to 30 seconds. With a spatula, lift up one corner of the crêpe to check if the cooked surface is lightly golden around the edges, and if so, flip the crêpe.

5. To assemble: Sprinkle 2 tablespoons of chocolate into the middle of the crêpe. Arrange some of the banana slices on top of the chocolate. Using a spatula, fold all four sides of the crêpe in toward the center to enclose the filling. Cook until the chocolate begins to soften and melt, about 15 to 30 seconds, being careful not to let the crêpe get too dark. Flip the crêpe and cook another 15 seconds or so, then slide the crêpe onto a serving plate. Sprinkle with confectioners' sugar and serve hot. Alternatively, you can stack finished crêpes on a plate as you make them, and keep them warm in a 250°F oven while you make the remainder. Sprinkle with confectioners' sugar right before serving.

6. Repeat with the remaining crêpe batter, whisking the batter between making each crêpe and thinning the batter with the remaining milk if needed. Be sure to grease the crêpe pan lightly between each crêpe.

Tilt the pan to spread the crêpe batter.

Roasted Banana Cream

THIS DESSERT IS VERY SIMPLE AND SATISFYING, and a great way to use up a surplus of ripe bananas. Roasting bananas in their skins concentrates their sweetness and makes them tender and moist. When mixed with cream and rum, they are transformed into a light, silky mousse with intense banana flavor. ⎯ᴡᴡᴡ⎯ *Serves 6*

5 ripe bananas

⅓ cup sugar, or more to taste

2 tablespoons dark rum, or more to taste

½ teaspoon pure vanilla extract

Freshly grated nutmeg

1¼ cups heavy (whipping) cream

2 tablespoons chopped salted macadamia nuts, for garnish (optional)

1. Position a rack in the middle of the oven and preheat the oven to 425°F.

2. Set 4 bananas, in their skins, directly on the oven rack and bake until the fruit is very soft, about 15 minutes. Using tongs, transfer the bananas to a wire rack to cool.

3. When they are cool enough to handle, peel the bananas and discard the skins. Transfer the bananas to a food processor, and puree them. Then add the sugar, rum, vanilla, and a pinch or two of nutmeg, and process until the mixture is smooth. Add the cream and process for 1 minute.

4. Divide the mixture among six small ramekins. (If you are not serving the dessert immediately, refrigerate the ramekins, covered, for up to 1 day.)

5. To serve, slice the remaining (unroasted) banana into thin rounds. Arrange 2 or 3 rounds on top of each serving, sprinkle with the macadamia nuts if using, and top with a light dusting of nutmeg.

Italian-Style Poached Peaches

DURING MY TRAVELS IN TUSCANY, I fell in love with the simplicity and elegance of this dessert: sun-ripened peaches that are gently poached in white wine scented with vanilla and lemon. Served chilled in a pool of sweet, aromatic syrup, they make a wonderful light ending to a summer meal. *Serves 4*

3 cups fruity white wine, such as Riesling or
   Muscat

½ cup sugar

Zest of 1 lemon, removed in strips

1 tablespoon vanilla paste; or 1 vanilla bean,
   split lengthwise (see box, page 315)

4 large peaches, preferably freestone,
   just shy of perfectly ripe, unpeeled

⅓ cup, plus 2 tablespoons if needed,
   peach liqueur or peach schnapps

4 fresh mint sprigs, for garnish (optional)

1. Combine the wine, sugar, lemon zest, vanilla paste or vanilla bean, and 1 cup water in a saucepan that is just large enough to hold the peaches. (The liquid should barely cover the peaches when they are added.) Bring the mixture to a boil over medium-high heat, stirring to dissolve the sugar. Then reduce the heat to low, and add the peaches and the ⅓ cup peach liqueur. Cover the pan and cook at a very low simmer until the peaches are tender when pierced with the tip of a small knife, 10 to 15 minutes.

2. Using a slotted spoon, remove the peaches from the poaching liquid and transfer them to a plate. Set them aside to cool at room temperature.

3. Meanwhile, remove the lemon zest and vanilla bean, if used, from the poaching liquid. Reheat the liquid over high heat and cook until it reduces to about 1 cup, about 15 minutes (this concentrates the flavors of the syrup). Remove the pan from the heat and let the syrup cool to room temperature.

4. Cover and refrigerate the peaches. Taste the syrup, and add the remaining 2 tablespoons peach liqueur if it is not sweet enough. Cover and refrigerate the syrup for at least 1 hour. Chill both peaches and syrup. (The peaches can be stored, covered, in the refrigerator for up to 3 days. The syrup will keep for up to 1 week.)

5. To serve, cut the peaches in half lengthwise and remove the pits. Carefully pull or peel off the skins, and discard them. For each serving, place 2 peach halves in a small bowl, and pour some of the syrup over them. Garnish each with a mint sprig, if desired.

Italian-Style Poached Peaches

Raspberry Yogurt Panna Cotta

Raspberry Yogurt Panna Cotta

SIMPLE TO MAKE AND LOW IN CALORIES, this is a dessert you can feel good about serving to family and friends. *Panna cotta* means "cooked cream," but I've substituted yogurt for some of the cream to create a lighter, less fat-laden custard. I also added a puree of raspberries, which contributes a fresh berry flavor and a beautiful color. Although I've specified a rhubarb-raspberry sauce to accompany the panna cotta, the sauce can be made with just raspberries if rhubarb is not in season. Because this is a gelatin-based dessert, be sure to allow at least 6 hours for the panna cotta to set up in the refrigerator before serving it. ⎯⎯ *Serves 4*

Canola oil, for the ramekins

1½ cups fresh raspberries

½ cup sugar

2 tablespoons plus ½ cup heavy (whipping) cream

1¼ teaspoons unflavored powdered gelatin (less than 1 packet)

¾ cup plain nonfat or low-fat yogurt

Rhubarb-Raspberry Sauce (recipe follows) or lightly mashed fresh raspberries

1. Lightly oil four ½-cup ramekins, and set them aside. If you wish, you can use small goblets or bowls if you prefer not to unmold the dessert.

2. Place the raspberries and the sugar in a small saucepan and bring to a boil over medium-high heat, stirring until the sugar dissolves and the raspberries liquefy, about 5 minutes.

3. Meanwhile, place the 2 tablespoons heavy cream in a small cup, and sprinkle the gelatin over the cream. Let the gelatin soften, about 4 minutes.

4. Set a fine-mesh sieve over a medium-size saucepan, and strain the raspberry mixture into it; discard the seeds. Add the remaining ½ cup cream, and place the pan over medium heat. Add the gelatin mixture and cook, stirring constantly, until the gelatin completely dissolves and the mixture begins to simmer, 2 to 3 minutes.

5. Remove the pan from the heat and whisk in the yogurt. Divide the custard among the ramekins and chill, uncovered, until the panna cottas are firm, at least 6 hours.

6. To serve, run a knife around the edges of the ramekins and invert each panna cotta onto a chilled plate. (If you're using pretty dessert dishes, you don't need to unmold the panna cottas.) Garnish each serving with some of the Rhubarb-Raspberry Sauce or fresh raspberries.

Rhubarb

Rhubarb has a distinctive tart and fruity flavor. There are two basic types: hothouse (or strawberry rhubarb) and field-grown (also called cherry rhubarb). Field rhubarb is generally available across the country from April to October, and hothouse rhubarb is usually grown from December through March.

Look for glossy stalks that are firm, crisp, and unblemished with a deep red hue, with some leaves still attached. Slender stalks, less than an inch wide, are preferable. Thicker stalks can be stringy and tough. Rhubarb dries out quickly. Store your stalks, unwashed, in a plastic bag in the refrigerator for up to 1 week. Rhubarb freezes exceptionally well. The leaves are inedible, so trim them well, then wash and slice the stalks, and store in a freezer bag or an airtight container for up to 6 months.

Rhubarb-Raspberry Sauce

Rhubarb and raspberries are a terrific combination, as good as the familiar strawberry-rhubarb team. This quick and easy sauce is a favorite. Use it to flavor plain yogurt, to mix into smoothies, or as a sauce for ice cream and cakes. It can be varied by using orange juice instead of water, and ginger has a natural affinity for these fruits. If you want the sauce to be more elegant, pass it through a fine-mesh sieve before serving it. ⟿ *Makes 1½ cups*

½ cup sugar

2 cups sliced rhubarb (¼-inch-thick slices)

1 cup fresh raspberries

1 tablespoon fresh lemon juice

1. Combine the sugar and ½ cup water in a medium-size saucepan and cook over high heat, stirring frequently, until the sugar has dissolved. Then reduce the heat to low and add the rhubarb. Cook, stirring occasionally, until the rhubarb is tender and soft, about 5 minutes.

2. Add the raspberries and cook for 1 minute, mashing them lightly with a spoon. (The berries will fall apart as soon as they are heated.) Remove the pan from the heat, stir in the lemon juice, and let the sauce cool to room temperature; serve it at room temperature or chilled with the Raspberry Yogurt Panna Cotta. (The sauce can be refrigerated, covered, for up to 5 days. It can be served warm with other desserts.)

Gratinéed Nectarines with Sabayon

I N THIS ELEGANT YET EASY SUMMER DESSERT, wedges of juicy ripe nectarines are cloaked in a delicate sabayon sauce and briefly gratinéed under the broiler. Sabayon is the French equivalent of *zabaglione,* an ethereal Italian dessert sauce composed of eggs, sugar, and sweet wine, usually Marsala. Although sabayon is typically made just before it is served, in our version the custard base is prepared ahead of time and chilled; then, prior to assembling the dessert, softly whipped cream is folded into the sauce. We recommend using yellow nectarines because their firm texture holds up during cooking and their tangy flavor balances the rich sweetness of the sauce. The sabayon is also sensational with other stone fruits, berries, and fresh figs. ⟿ *Serves 6*

3 large egg yolks

⅓ cup sugar

½ cup sweet white dessert wine, such as Sauternes or Late Harvest Riesling

2 tablespoons (¼ stick) unsalted butter

3 pounds (about 6 large) yellow nectarines, peeled, pitted, and cut into ½-inch-thick slices

½ cup heavy (whipping) cream

Fresh mint sprigs, for garnish

1. Combine the egg yolks, sugar, and wine in a heavy-bottomed saucepan, and place it over medium-high heat. Cook, whisking constantly. The mixture will foam, but continue to whisk vigorously until it thickens into a custard, 3 to 5 minutes. Do not overcook, or the eggs will scramble. (If you are faint of heart, this step can be done in the top of a double boiler set over simmering water, although it will take longer to thicken.) Remove the pan from the heat and transfer the sauce to a clean bowl. Let the mixture cool for 15 minutes, and then cover and refrigerate until it is completely cold. (This step can be done 1 day in advance.)

2. Place a mixer bowl and beaters in the freezer to chill.

3. Melt the butter in a large skillet, preferably nonstick, over medium-high heat. Add the nectarines and cook until they are lightly browned on one side, 1 to 2 minutes. Turn the fruit over and cook on the other side for no more than 1 minute. You want to soften the nectarines slightly but not cook them so much that they turn to mush. Using a spatula, transfer the fruit to a platter, and set it aside at room temperature.

4. Set a rack 4 inches below the broiler element and preheat the broiler on high.

5. Divide the nectarines among six shallow gratin dishes or shallow ovenproof bowls.

6. Place the heavy cream in the chilled bowl and, using a mixer with chilled blades, whip until it just holds soft peaks. Whisk one third of the cream into the chilled sabayon base; then fold in the remainder with a rubber spatula.

7. Spoon the sauce over the nectarines, and place the dishes under the broiler. Cook until the sauce browns, about 1 minute, watching carefully to avoid burning. Serve the dessert hot or warm, garnished with mint sprigs.

THE BASICS

Gratin

A gratinée, or gratin, is a dish that is topped with a sauce, cheese, or buttery breadcrumbs and then heated in the oven or under a broiler until it is golden brown.

Baked Apples, Three Ways

WHEN I WANT A DESSERT THAT IS SWEET AND SATISFYING but not loaded with calories, a baked apple is one of my top choices. They are quick, easy, and versatile—as these three recipes demonstrate. The stuffing can be adapted to whatever suits your fancy. Baked apples taste great either warm or cold, and can also be served as a side dish with roast chicken or pork.

Cranberry-Walnut Baked Apples

Dried fruits and nuts partner beautifully with apples, and none more so than cranberries and walnuts. The cranberries add a sweet tang and the walnuts contribute a nice textural contrast to the baked apples. Moistened with apple juice and maple syrup, the ingredients meld together to create a sweet, simple sauce. ⚬⚬⚬ *Makes 4*

4 crisp apples, such as Gala, pippin, or Fuji

3 tablespoons chopped walnuts

2 tablespoons dried cranberries

1½ tablespoons light brown sugar

1 teaspoon ground cinnamon

⅓ cup apple juice

2 teaspoons pure maple syrup

2 teaspoons unsalted butter

1. Position a rack in the middle of the oven and preheat the oven to 350°F.

2. Starting at the top (stem) end of each apple, remove the core, making sure to leave enough of the apple intact at the bottom to form a pocket for the stuffing. Discard the cores and arrange the apples in a small baking pan.

3. Place the walnuts, cranberries, brown sugar, and cinnamon in a small bowl and stir to combine.

4. Combine the apple juice, maple syrup, and butter in a small saucepan, and heat over medium heat until the butter melts. Add the hot liquid to the walnut mixture, and stir to blend. Divide the mixture among the apples, filling the hollowed-out cores. Drizzle any extra liquid over the apples.

5. Cover the pan with aluminum foil, preferably recycled, and bake until the apples are just soft, 35 to 45 minutes. Drizzle the apples with the pan juices, and serve warm or cold.

Baked Apples, Three Ways

Honey-Raisin Baked Apples

Warm baked apples are a classic comfort food, and these are a lovely variation. Honey-sweet and studded with raisins and almonds, they make a rich yet healthy treat that's satisfying any time of the day. ⁓ *Makes 4*

4 crisp apples, such as Gala, pippin, or Fuji
3 tablespoons raisins
1½ tablespoons chopped or slivered blanched almonds
1 teaspoon ground cinnamon
3 tablespoons honey
1½ tablespoons unsalted butter

1. Position a rack in the middle of the oven and preheat the oven to 350°F.

2. Starting at the top (stem) end of each apple, remove the core, making sure to leave enough of the apple intact at the bottom to form a pocket for the stuffing. Discard the cores and arrange the apples in a small baking pan.

3. Place the raisins, almonds, and cinnamon in a small bowl, and stir to combine.

4. Combine the honey and butter in a small saucepan, and heat over medium heat until the butter has melted. Add the hot liquid to the raisin mixture, and stir to blend. Divide the mixture among the apples, filling the hollowed-out cores. Drizzle any extra liquid over the apples.

5. Cover the baking pan with aluminum foil, preferably recycled, and bake until the apples are just soft, 35 to 45 minutes. Drizzle the apples with the pan juices, and serve warm or cold.

Classic Baked Apples

Plain and simple, but ever so delicious, these are baked apples in their purest form. We've added just a hint of sugar and spice, and a drizzle of lemon and vanilla to flavor and baste the apples as they cook. ⁓ *Makes 4*

4 crisp apples, such as Gala, pippin, or Fuji
¼ cup packed light brown sugar
½ teaspoon ground cinnamon
⅛ teaspoon ground nutmeg
¼ cup apple juice
1 tablespoon fresh lemon juice
1 tablespoon unsalted butter
½ teaspoon pure vanilla extract

1. Position a rack in the middle of the oven and preheat the oven to 350°F.

2. Starting at the top (stem) end of each apple, remove the core, making sure to leave enough of the apple intact at the bottom to form a pocket for the stuffing. Discard the cores and arrange the apples in a small baking pan.

3. Place the brown sugar, cinnamon, and nutmeg in a small bowl, and stir to combine.

4. Combine the apple juice, lemon juice, and butter in a small saucepan, and heat over medium heat until the butter has melted. Add the hot liquid to the brown sugar mixture, and stir to blend. Stir in the vanilla. Divide the mixture among the apples, filling the hollowed-out cores. Drizzle any extra liquid over the apples.

5. Cover the baking pan with aluminum foil, preferably recycled, and bake until the apples are just soft, 35 to 45 minutes. Drizzle the apples with the pan juices, and serve warm or cold.

Honey Frozen Yogurt

FROZEN YOGURT IS MUCH HEALTHIER AND LIGHTER than ice cream, and I find it just as delicious. This super-fast dessert is sweetened and flavored only with honey. My family likes frozen yogurt when it's the consistency of soft-serve ice cream, so we eat it right out of the ice cream maker because it gets hard quickly in the freezer. Topped with fresh fruit or our Very Berry Sauce (page 356), this makes a terrific treat any time of the year.
Makes about 1 quart

4 cups (32 ounces) nonfat plain yogurt
⅔ cup honey
1 cup whole milk

1. Place the yogurt and honey in a bowl and whisk to combine. Add the milk and whisk until smooth.

2. Transfer the yogurt mixture to the bowl of an ice cream maker, and churn following the manufacturer's

instructions until it is softly frozen. Serve immediately.

Vanilla Bean Ice Cream

NOTHING TOPS VANILLA ICE CREAM for versatility, and it's still America's favorite flavor (surprise, chocolate lovers!). With a wide array of inexpensive ice cream makers available in kitchenware stores, making homemade ice cream is easy and fun. You can't beat this version, with its rich, dense texture and smooth creaminess. Flecks of vanilla seeds imbue the ice cream with an exotic fragrance and flavor that surpasses that of vanilla extract alone. — *Makes about 1 quart*

2 vanilla beans, split in half lengthwise
   (see box, page 315)
2 cups whole milk
4 large egg yolks
⅔ cup sugar
1 cup heavy (whipping) cream
2 teaspoons pure vanilla extract

1. Using a small knife, scrape the seeds from the vanilla pods, and place both seeds and pods in the top of a double boiler (or in a heatproof bowl). Add the milk, stir, and set the pan or bowl over a pan of gently simmering water. Cook until the milk is hot but not boiling.

2. Meanwhile, fill a large bowl with cold water and ice.

3. Combine the egg yolks and sugar in a small bowl, and whisk to blend. Whisk in about half of the hot milk mixture to temper the yolks, and then pour the yolk mixture back into the top of the double boiler or heatproof bowl. Cook, stirring frequently, until the custard thickens and coats the back of a spoon, about 10 minutes.

4. Immediately transfer the top of the double boiler or bowl to the prepared ice bath, and stir the custard occasionally until it cools to room temperature.

5. Stir in the heavy cream and vanilla extract, and transfer the ice cream base to a clean container. Cover and refrigerate until the mixture is thoroughly chilled, at least 3 hours, or overnight.

6. When you are ready to freeze the ice cream, remove the vanilla bean pods. (They can be washed, dried, and reserved for another use.)

7. Freeze the ice cream in an ice cream maker according to the manufacturer's instructions. Transfer it to a container, press a piece of plastic wrap directly against the surface of the ice cream, cover, and freeze until firm, about 2 hours.

LIVING GREEN
When making recipes that call for just the yolks of eggs, don't waste those precious whites. They will keep for 3 days covered in your refrigerator, and you can use them to make the delicious macaroons on page 312, or an egg white omelet or fried egg whites. Egg whites are high in protein and low in calories and cholesterol, making them a very healthy food choice.

Ice Cream Sundaes

ANY GOOD ICE CREAM SUNDAE IS ALL ABOUT THE TOPPINGS— the more, the better. Start with our homemade Vanilla Bean Ice Cream, perfect to make with the kids on a hot day. Then mix and match from our selection of sauces for the ultimate summer treat. If you're looking for a festive, do-it-yourself dessert, set up a sundae bar with an array of ice creams, sauces, and toppings. Let the fun begin!

Hot Fudge Sauce

This is the classic ice cream topper—dark and rich, and not too sweet. The sauce goes together in a flash. ━━ *Makes 2 cups*

⅔ cup heavy (whipping) cream
½ cup light corn syrup
⅓ cup packed light brown sugar
3 tablespoons unsweetened cocoa powder
¼ teaspoon salt
⅔ cup bittersweet (60% cocoa) chocolate chips
2 tablespoons (¼ stick) unsalted butter
1 teaspoon pure vanilla extract

1. Place the cream, corn syrup, brown sugar, cocoa powder, salt, and ⅓ cup of the chocolate chips in a heavy saucepan and bring to a boil over medium heat, stirring frequently until the chocolate has melted. Reduce the heat to maintain a simmer, and cook the sauce, stirring occasionally, for 5 minutes.

2. Remove the pan from the heat, and add the butter, the remaining ⅓ cup chocolate chips, and the vanilla. Stir until the sauce is smooth and thick. Let it cool slightly before using as a topping for ice cream. (The sauce can be cooled to room temperature and then refrigerated, covered, for up to 2 weeks. Reheat it in a microwave or over low heat before using.)

Ice Cream Sundaes

Butterscotch Sauce

Butterscotch has been edged out by caramel sauce in recent years, but we love its old-fashioned, pure buttery flavor. It's lighter than caramel in both texture and taste, and kids love it. You do need a candy thermometer to make the sauce, but this handy gadget will last a lifetime and is worth the small investment if you like to cook. —*mm*— *Makes about 2 cups*

8 tablespoons (1 stick) unsalted butter

2 tablespoons light corn syrup

¾ cup granulated sugar

¼ cup packed light brown sugar

⅓ cup heavy (whipping) cream

2 teaspoons dark rum

1 teaspoon pure vanilla extract

¼ teaspoon salt

1. Place the butter, corn syrup, and ¼ cup water in a small saucepan and cook over medium heat, stirring frequently, until the butter melts. Add the granulated and brown sugars and raise the heat to high. Stir the mixture just until the sugars melt, washing down the sides of the pan with a wet pastry brush to ensure there are no sugar crystals. Then let the sauce boil without stirring until it is thick and golden brown and a candy thermometer reads 245°F, about 10 minutes.

2. Remove the pan from the heat and add the cream, rum, vanilla, and salt. Stir until the sauce is smooth. Let it cool slightly before using it as a topping for ice cream. (The sauce can be cooled to room temperature, then refrigerated, covered, for up to 2 weeks. Reheat it in a microwave or over low heat before using.)

Caramel Chocolate Sauce

This is a foolproof caramel sauce, and it is delicious on its own without the addition of chocolate. However, if you want to simplify your sundae making, this sauce provides both hot fudge and caramel flavors all in one. —*mm*— *Makes about 2½ cups*

1 cup sugar

¼ cup light corn syrup

1 cup heavy (whipping) cream

2 tablespoons (¼ stick) unsalted butter

1 teaspoon pure vanilla extract

½ teaspoon fleur de sel (see sidebar, page 358) or sea salt

4 ounces bittersweet (60% cocoa) chocolate, chopped (¾ cup)

1. Combine the sugar, corn syrup, and ¼ cup water in a medium-size heavy-bottomed saucepan over medium heat, and stir until the sugar dissolves. Raise the heat to medium-high and cook without stirring, occasionally brushing down the sides of the pan with a wet pastry brush to ensure there are no sugar crystals, until the syrup turns a medium amber color, about 10 minutes.

2. Immediately remove the pan from the heat and add the cream and butter, stirring to combine. When it is smooth, add the vanilla, *fleur de sel,* and chocolate, and stir until the salt is dissolved and the chocolate is melted. Serve warm. (The sauce can be refrigerated, covered, for up to 10 days. Reheat it in a microwave or over low heat before using.)

Very Berry Sauce

Sun-ripened strawberries and blueberries team up in this fresh-tasting, summer-sweet sauce. When partnered with Vanilla Bean Ice Cream, this is a simple and perfect dessert. It's also delicious served with pancakes, crêpes, pound cake, or yogurt. ⟶ *Makes about 2 cups*

½ cup sugar
1½ cups fresh blueberries
1½ cups fresh strawberries, hulled and
    quartered
1 tablespoon fresh lime juice

1. Combine the sugar and 2 tablespoons water in a medium-size saucepan and cook over medium heat, stirring occasionally, until the sugar dissolves. Add the blueberries and strawberries and cook, stirring frequently, until the berries have softened and the sauce has thickened, about 10 minutes.

2. Remove the pan from the heat and stir in the lime juice. Serve warm or at room temperature. (The sauce can be refrigerated, covered, for up to 5 days. Reheat it in a microwave or over low heat before using.)

White Chocolate, Cranberry, and Pistachio Bark

TART DRIED CRANBERRIES AND HOT-SPICY CRYSTALLIZED GINGER offset the super-sweetness of white chocolate. The ruby red cranberries, green pistachios, and orange ginger look wonderfully festive against the white chocolate base. This should be stored in the refrigerator. ⌁⌁⌁ *Makes about 1 pound*

11 ounces (about 1¾ cups) white chocolate chips

1 teaspoon canola oil

½ cup shelled unsalted pistachio nuts

½ cup dried cranberries

2 tablespoons finely minced crystallized ginger (optional)

1. Line a baking sheet with a piece of parchment paper, and set it aside.

2. Place the white chocolate chips in a heatproof bowl, or in the top of a double boiler, set over a pan of barely simmering water. The water should not touch the bottom of the bowl. Stir the chocolate until it has melted. Then add the canola oil and stir until the mixture is smooth.

3. Add the pistachios and cranberries to the chocolate mixture, and stir to combine. Pour the mixture onto the prepared baking sheet, spreading it out with an offset spatula. Sprinkle the bark with the crystallized ginger, if using.

4. Place the baking sheet in the refrigerator and chill until the chocolate is firm, at least 30 minutes.

5. When the chocolate has hardened, peel off the parchment and break or cut the bark into pieces. Transfer the pieces to an airtight container and refrigerate, covered, until serving time. (It will keep, tightly covered, in the refrigerator for up to 2 weeks.)

Applying a little pressure on the back of the knife makes for a clean cut through the bark.

THE BASICS

Fleur de Sel

Fleur de sel, *which means "flower of salt" in French, is a hand-harvested salt that is gathered from the very top layer of sea salt beds, in a process much like skimming cream from milk. The natural crystals crackle like lace and are bright as snow. Fleur de sel is delicate and expensive, and is prized for its complex flavor. It should never be added during cooking, but saved instead for sprinkling on food just before serving, or as a garnish for chocolate and caramel desserts.*

Chunky Cherry-Nut Bark

A HANDMADE GIFT FROM THE KITCHEN IS ALWAYS APPRECIATED, especially during the holidays. Packed in a pretty tin lined with colored foil or acetate, fruit-and-nut-filled chocolate bark makes an ideal gift for friends with a sweet tooth. Think of these recipes as a guideline and substitute your favorite dried fruits or nuts, or if you like a more intense chocolate flavor, substitute bittersweet for the semisweet chocolate. Because our recipe, unlike one for commercial candies, does not contain stabilizers or gums, the bark needs to be kept lightly chilled to prevent melting. ⁓ ***Makes about 1 pound***

2 cups semisweet chocolate chips
⅓ cup dried tart cherries
⅓ cup raisins
⅓ cup salted cocktail peanuts
⅓ cup roasted cashews, salted or unsalted
⅛ teaspoon fleur de sel
   (optional; see sidebar, this page)

1. Line a baking sheet with a piece of parchment paper, and set it aside.

2. Place the chocolate chips in a heatproof bowl, or in the top of a double boiler and set over a pan of barely simmering water. The water should not touch the bottom of the bowl. Stir the chocolate until it is melted and smooth.

3. Add the dried fruits and the nuts to the chocolate, and stir to combine. Pour the mixture onto the prepared baking sheet, spreading it out with an offset spatula. Sprinkle the bark with the *fleur de sel,* if using.

4. Place the baking sheet in the refrigerator and chill until the chocolate is firm, at least 30 minutes.

5. When the chocolate has hardened, peel off the parchment and break or cut the bark into pieces. Transfer the pieces to an airtight container and refrigerate, covered, until serving time. (It will keep, tightly covered, in the refrigerator for up to 2 weeks.)

Cranberry-Walnut Granola Clusters

IF YOU'RE A GRANOLA FAN, you're sure to enjoy these snack-size granola clusters. Studded with walnuts and cranberries and enlivened with a hint of citrus and ginger, these treats are addictively good. Add the clusters to yogurt, use them as a topping for fresh fruit or ice cream, or eat them as a snack when you are on the go. They can be stored in an airtight container for up to 3 weeks . . . if they last that long! ~~~ *Makes about 5 cups*

2 cups (7 ounces) old-fashioned rolled
  oats (see sidebar, page 307)
1 cup (4 ounces) shredded unsweetened
  coconut
1 cup chopped walnuts
⅔ cup dried cranberries
⅔ cup (4 ounces) finely chopped
  crystallized ginger
Grated zest of 1 large orange
¾ cup sweetened condensed milk

1. Position a rack in the middle of the oven and preheat the oven to 275°F. Line a rimmed baking sheet with parchment paper and set it aside.

2. Place the oats, coconut, walnuts, cranberries, ginger, and orange zest in a large bowl and stir to combine. Add the condensed milk and stir thoroughly to coat all the ingredients.

3. Transfer the mixture to the prepared baking sheet and spread it out into an even layer. Bake until the granola is lightly browned, 45 to 55 minutes.

4. Let the granola cool completely on the baking sheet on a wire rack. Then break it into pieces or cut it into bars.

Four-Seed Granola Clusters

THESE DELICIOUS CLUSTERS incorporate flax, sunflower, sesame, and pumpkin seeds. Dried apricots add a sweet tang to the clusters, but feel free to experiment and customize with your own combinations of fruits and nuts.

Makes about 8 cups

**2 cups old-fashioned rolled oats
   (see sidebar, page 307)
1 cup shredded unsweetened coconut
1 cup chopped dried apricots
1 cup unsalted shelled sunflower seeds
1 cup unsalted shelled pumpkin seeds
½ cup flaxseeds
½ cup white sesame seeds
1 cup sweetened condensed milk**

1. Position a rack in the middle of the oven and preheat the oven to 275°F. Line a rimmed baking sheet with parchment paper and set it aside.

2. Place the oats, coconut, apricots, and sunflower, pumpkin, flax, and sesame seeds in a large bowl, and stir to combine. Add the condensed milk and stir thoroughly to coat all the ingredients.

3. Transfer the mixture to the prepared baking sheet and spread it out into an even layer. Bake until the granola is lightly browned, 45 to 55 minutes.

4. Let the granola cool completely on the baking sheet on a wire rack. Then break it into pieces or cut it into bars. (Stored in an airtight container at room temperature, the granola will keep for 3 weeks.)

Sunflower seeds

CHAPTER 10

BREAKFAST AND BRUNCH

A Brand New Day

EVERYTHING FEELS FRESH FIRST THING IN THE MORNING. BREAKFAST is a symphony of new beginnings—the sounds and smells of making fresh coffee, the sizzle of bacon on a cast-iron skillet, and the heavenly aroma of just-baked muffins.

What I eat for breakfast sets the tone for how energized I feel all day long, so choosing something tasty and healthy reaps rewards long past morning. I'm one of those people who wake up hungry, ready to eat. But I believe even those of you who are not big breakfast eaters will be tempted by the recipes in this chapter. There are delicious new options that you can fit into any morning schedule—from a leisurely breakfast or brunch to things that are ready to grab when you're running out the door.

One of my favorites is the Oatmeal, Carrot, and Apple Breakfast Squares. They're sweet, but contain lots of healthy ingredients like whole grains, grated carrots and apples, flaxseeds, and walnuts. The squares stay fresh, moist, and delicious for days, and the recipe feeds a lot of people.

I love great muffins, and there are two outstanding recipes here: Honey Bran Muffins with oats and raisins, which bake up with a wonderfully crispy top, and Buttermilk Blueberry Muffins— light, moist, and absolutely irresistible.

We've also shared two of our most popular Farm Stand breakfast breads: Zucchini and Sweet Potato Bread and Farm Stand Banana Bread. Our customers enjoy these delicious baked goods any time of the day, and they are especially popular with the after-school snack crowd.

For those days when you have time to prepare a hot breakfast, we have some special recipes to try. Potatoes Rösti combines the taste and texture of crispy hash browns with creamy Gruyère cheese and onions. Great for breakfast, this dish also works well for lunch or dinner. Adding the simple but delicious topping of sautéed mushrooms and spinach with an over-easy egg turns this dish into a complete meal with veggies, protein, and lots of flavor. The Ham and Gruyère Frittata makes a great savory breakfast, and

Honey Bran Muffins (page 372)

if you're planning a brunch, it makes a perfect buffet dish: Beautiful on the table, it's delicious fresh from the oven or at room temperature. For an alternative to eggs, the Tofu Scramble is a tasty and filling dish that starts your day with a generous serving of vegetables and protein. Both the Tofu Scramble and the Frittata are great recipes to get creative with: Take advantage of leftovers in your fridge or experiment with other ingredients that spark your imagination.

I've fallen in love with two new hot cereal recipes: Oats, Quinoa, and Raisin Bran Hot Cereal and Four-Grain Hot Cereal with Blueberries. A warm breakfast is so nurturing, especially when it's full of chewy, healthy whole grains. Homemade cereals are more original and fresher-tasting than instant varieties in packets or cups, plus they don't involve all that packaging.

On the lighter side, our Warm Citrus Compote enhances the bright flavors of citrus with some wonderful accents that may not have made it to your breakfast table yet: lemongrass, star anise, and cardamom. The compote is perfect for Sunday brunch or a light dessert. And if you've never tasted an Indian *lassi*, you're in for

a refreshing treat. This icy yogurt-based drink is thirst-quenching and full of all the calcium and healthy probiotics of yogurt. It complements many different foods, from sweet baked goods to anything spicy. I've included five versions for you to try: Mango, Orange Cream, Passion Fruit and Banana, Pineapple Mint, and Raspberry.

Foods that smell and taste delicious boost your sense of optimism for the new day ahead. So add some new flavor to your morning routine. Rise and shine!

Look! There's More

Don't miss these delicious homemade breads and bagels in the breads chapter—they are terrific for breakfast and brunch:

- Myra's 100% Whole Wheat Bread, page 273
- Whole Wheat Cinnamon Raisin Swirl, page 274
- Whole Wheat and Rye Bread, page 276
- Seeded Multigrain Bread, page 280
- Homemade Bagels, page 281
- Kalamata Olive Bread, page 289
- Rosemary Potato Bread, page 292
- Wickets Bistro Focaccia, page 293

Warm Citrus Compote (page 385)

Whole Wheat Pecan Pancakes with Pecan Maple Syrup

M Y KIDS AND THEIR FRIENDS look forward to weekend mornings when I cook a big batch of delicious pancakes. This version, with whole wheat flour and pecans, is always a big hit, especially with Pecan Maple Syrup. My family thinks they are even tastier when I add sliced bananas to the pancakes. It's easy to do—simply pour the batter into the hot skillet and add about 4 thin slices of banana to each pancake. Cook until set, and then flip to finish on the other side. Be inventive and try your own combinations. Thin slices of apples and berries work well, too, and walnuts are a great variation on the pecans.

Makes eighteen to twenty 4-inch pancakes

1¼ cups whole wheat flour

¾ cup unbleached all-purpose flour

¼ cup chopped pecans

3 tablespoons packed light brown sugar

4 teaspoons baking powder

¾ teaspoon salt

2 cups reduced-fat (2%) milk

2 large eggs

¼ cup canola oil, plus extra for cooking

1 teaspoon pure vanilla extract

Pecan Maple Syrup (recipe follows)

1. Place the whole wheat and all-purpose flours, pecans, brown sugar, baking powder, and salt in a large bowl and whisk to combine.

2. In a small bowl, whisk together the milk, eggs, oil, and vanilla. Pour the milk mixture into the dry ingredients and stir just until combined. If the batter is very thick, it can be thinned with a bit of milk if desired.

3. Heat a large cast-iron skillet or griddle pan over medium heat. Brush the skillet with canola oil, stir the pancake batter to ensure an even distribution of pecans in the mix, and spoon some of the batter onto the skillet to form pancakes that are about 4 inches in diameter. Cook until the pancakes are golden brown on the bottom and tiny holes appear on the top surface, about 2 minutes. Turn them over and cook on the other side until golden, about 1 minute.

4. Repeat with the remaining batter, making sure to stir the batter before scooping it.

5. Serve the pancakes hot, with warm Pecan Maple Syrup.

Whole Wheat Pecan Pancakes with Pecan Maple Syrup

Pecan Maple Syrup

Heating pure maple syrup with nuts is a simple way to infuse flavor and add an element of crunch at the same time. This easy-to-make pecan-based syrup goes well with our Whole Wheat Pecan Pancakes, reinforcing their nutty flavor and texture, but chopped walnuts, almonds, or hazelnuts work equally well. Be sure to serve the maple syrup piping hot so your pancakes stay nice and warm. —⁓ *Makes about 1½ cups*

1½ cups pure maple syrup
   (see box, page 321)
¾ cup chopped, toasted pecans (see box,
   page 31)

Pour the maple syrup into a small saucepan and bring it to a simmer over low heat. Add the pecans and simmer until they are warmed through, about 3 minutes. Serve hot.

Farm Stand Banana Bread

THERE IS SOMETHING IRRESISTIBLE about the smell of fresh-baked banana bread. It's great with coffee in the morning, and a thin slice topped with peanut butter is one of my favorite snacks. Our Farm Stand recipe is especially good: Loaded with bananas and walnuts, it's incredibly moist and tender. This is one of the bestselling bakery items we offer, and it's so delicious we recommend you bake the two loaves this recipe makes. You'll use your oven more efficiently, and having a loaf in the freezer is very handy, especially since it can be frozen for up to 3 months without any loss of quality. —⁓ *Makes two 8 x 4½-inch loaves*

Butter, for greasing the pans
2¼ cups unbleached all-purpose flour
1 cup whole wheat pastry flour
2 teaspoons baking soda
1 teaspoon ground cinnamon
½ teaspoon salt
4 large eggs
2⅓ cups sugar
1 cup canola oil

3 cups coarsely mashed ripe bananas
   (about 6 large bananas)
¼ cup sour cream
2 teaspoons pure vanilla extract
1⅓ cups chopped walnuts

1. Position a rack in the middle of the oven and preheat the oven to 325°F. Butter two 8 x 4½-inch loaf pans and set them aside.

2. Place the all-purpose flour, pastry flour, baking soda, cinnamon, and salt in a medium-size bowl and whisk to blend.

3. In a large bowl, whisk the eggs with the sugar until thick and light-colored, about 3 minutes (or use an electric mixer if you prefer). Add the canola oil and whisk again to combine. Stir in the bananas, sour cream, and vanilla, and blend completely.

4. Add the flour mixture and the walnuts to the banana batter, and stir just until combined. Do not overbeat.

5. Divide the batter between the prepared pans and bake until the bread is set and golden brown, and a toothpick inserted into the center comes out clean, about 1¼ hours.

6. Let the bread cool in the pans on a wire rack for 5 minutes. Then remove the loaves from the pans and let them cool further on the wire rack. Slice the bread with a serrated knife, and serve warm or at room temperature. (The bread stays fresh, tightly wrapped, for up to 5 days. It can be frozen for up to 3 months. Thaw it overnight before serving.)

the usda organic seal and organic labeling rules

The USDA Organic seal signifies that a product was produced and handled according to strict standards outlined in the National Organic Program (NOP) of the United States Department of Agriculture.

When a product carries the USDA Organic seal, it means that all ingredients, processing activities, and even the label compliance have been closely scrutinized to ensure that organic integrity has been preserved and verified. The USDA Organic seal can be displayed only on products meeting the following two criteria:

◆ **100% ORGANIC** means all ingredients are grown and processed organically.

◆ **ORGANIC** means that at least 95 percent of ingredients are grown and processed organically. The remaining 5 percent must be made from ingredients specified in the NOP regulations, for which an organic alternative is not available. These ingredients must not be produced by prohibited practices.

Products with less than 95 percent organic ingredients may not bear the seal, but are covered in Organic Labeling Rules:

◆ **MADE WITH ORGANIC INGREDIENTS** on the front of a product's package means that at least 70 percent of ingredients were grown and processed organically.

◆ If a product contains less than 70 percent organic ingredients, the ingredient list may state which products are organic, but there can be no organic claim on the front of the package.

Zucchini and Sweet Potato Bread

Sweet Potatoes or "Yams"?

The nomenclature and marketing of sweet potatoes and yams can be confusing. In this country, orange-fleshed sweet potatoes are marketed as "yams" to distinguish them from the dry-textured yellow or white sweet potatoes harvested in the northern states. They are not true yams, however, which are grown in Africa and Asia and rarely appear in domestic markets. Look for colorful varieties of "yams" such as Beauregard, Garnet, or Jewel, as these have excellent flavor and a moist, sweet flesh loaded with fiber, potassium, and beta-carotene, a potent antioxidant.

TWO GARDEN STAPLES TEAM UP to create a delicious and unique breakfast bread that's a perennial Farm Stand favorite. Zucchini and sweet potatoes both have a high water content, which in tandem with their natural sweetness contributes to a moist bread that is great for breakfast, brunch, or just about anytime. It could even be an easy way to sneak some vegetables into a picky eater's diet. To grate the zucchini and sweet potato, use the medium shredding disk of a food processor or the coarse side of a box grater. —— ***Makes one 9 x 5-inch loaf***

Butter, for greasing the loaf pan

2 cups (14 ounces) sugar

¾ cup canola oil

3 large eggs

1 teaspoon pure vanilla extract

1 cup lightly packed (about 8 ounces) grated zucchini

1 cup lightly packed (8 ounces) grated peeled orange-fleshed sweet potato or yam (see sidebar, this page)

1 cup chopped walnuts, toasted (see box, page 31)

2 cups (6¾ ounces) whole wheat pastry flour

2 teaspoons ground cinnamon

1 teaspoon baking soda

¼ teaspoon baking powder

¼ teaspoon salt

1. Position a rack in the center of the oven and preheat the oven to 325°F. Generously butter a 9 x 5-inch loaf pan, and set it aside.

2. Place the sugar, oil, eggs, and vanilla in a large mixing bowl and whisk to combine. Add the zucchini, sweet potato, and walnuts, and stir to blend.

3. In another large bowl, combine the pastry flour, cinnamon, baking soda, baking powder, and salt and whisk to blend. Add the zucchini mixture and stir to combine. Do not overmix, or the bread will be tough. Pour the batter into the prepared loaf pan.

4. Bake the bread until a toothpick inserted in the center comes out clean, 1 hour and 15 minutes to 1 hour and 25 minutes.

5. Let the bread cool in the pan on a wire rack for 15 minutes. Then remove the bread from the pan and return it to the rack to finish cooling. Serve it warm or at room temperature. (The bread stays fresh tightly wrapped for up to 5 days. It can be frozen for up to 3 months. Thaw it overnight before serving.)

the benefits of choosing organic **dairy products**

Raising cows to produce milk, yogurt, butter, and cheese uses a lot of resources and has a larger environmental footprint than food products that are lower on the food chain. But switching to organic dairy products can take us a long way toward lightening their environmental load.

To bear the USDA Organic seal (see page 367), dairy products must be produced according to the following practices:

◆ Animals must be provided with 100 percent certified organic feed (for organic farming and handling guidelines, see page 78).

◆ Animals may not be given synthetic hormones to increase milk production, antibiotics, GMOs (genetically modified organisms), plastic feed pellets for roughage, or animal by-products. If antibiotics are required because of serious illness, the animal must be treated, then removed permanently from the organic herd.

◆ Organic dairy farmers must follow humane practices: giving animals access to adequate room, pasture, fresh air, and a high standard of care. Organic dairy farmers use natural methods—without antibiotics—to ensure the health of their herds. They avoid overcrowding and provide healthy living environments. They also allow cows to produce a volume of milk in accord with their natural cycles, without the use of growth hormones or high-energy feed rations designed to push cows to produce beyond their natural physiological limits.

Organic dairy farming helps remove potentially dangerous amounts of antibiotics from our food chain and our environment. The Union of Concerned Scientists estimates that the use of antibiotics in livestock agriculture accounts for 84 percent of total use in the U.S., far outweighing the amount used on humans. Also, as much as 80 to 90 percent of all the antibiotics given to humans and animals is not fully digested or broken down in the body, so these drugs eventually enter the environment, where they may encounter new bacteria and create antibiotic-resistant disease strains. The rise of antibiotic-resistant bacteria is a public health crisis, and infections from resistant bacteria are becoming more difficult and expensive to treat.

Environmental Benefits of Organic Dairy
If you consider the pesticides and synthetic fertilizers used to grow all the nonorganic feed to support conventional dairy cows, the impacts to the environment are staggering. In their 2009 report *Shades of Green,* the Organic Center calculated some of the positive impacts of organic dairy production (about 120,000 cows) in 2008:

• Approximately 40 million pounds of synthetic nitrogen were not applied.

• Over 785,000 pounds of pesticides were not sprayed on crop fields.

• Cows were administered 1,776,000 fewer treatments (usually injections) of hormones and antibiotics.

These impacts are significant despite the fact that only 1.5 percent of the total U.S. dairy herd of 8.5 million cows is organic. When you choose organic dairy products, you are supporting an entire organic agro-ecosystem with wide ripples that benefit human health and the health of the planet. You are not only supporting organic dairy farmers, you are also supporting the organic farmers who grow feed for the cows. They, in turn, help to nurture the land and reduce the amount of synthetic fertilizers and toxic pesticides entering our air, water, land, and food supply.

Buttermilk Blueberry Muffins and Honey Bran Muffins (page 372)

Buttermilk Blueberry Muffins

THESE TENDER, LIGHT MUFFINS are the outstanding creation of Pam McKinstry, who developed them many years ago for her Nantucket restaurants. The secret to their delicate texture lies in the buttermilk, which creates a light and moist crumb. They taste as if they're made with butter, but heart-healthy canola oil is used instead. The batter is a basic template that you can vary by using other fruits, such as cranberries or blackberries, in the same quantity. Either fresh or frozen (unthawed) blueberries will work in this recipe, which means you can make these fabulous muffins all year long.

—— *Makes 18 muffins*

Butter, for greasing the muffin cups
    (optional)
3¼ cups unbleached all-purpose flour
1½ cups sugar
4 teaspoons baking powder
1 teaspoon baking soda
1 teaspoon salt
2 cups buttermilk (see sidebar, this page)
½ cup canola oil
2 large eggs
Grated zest of 1 lemon
1 cup fresh or frozen blueberries (do not
    thaw)

1. Position a rack in the middle of the oven and preheat the oven to 375°F. Butter 18 standard-size muffin cups or line them with cupcake liners.

2. Place the flour, sugar, baking powder, baking soda, and salt in a large bowl and whisk to combine.

3. In a medium-size bowl, whisk together the buttermilk, oil, eggs, and lemon zest until smooth.

4. Add the buttermilk mixture to the flour mixture and stir just until the batter is almost blended. Add the blueberries and stir gently just until combined. Do not beat the batter or the muffins will not be tender.

5. Spoon the batter into the prepared muffin cups, filling them two-thirds full.

6. Bake the muffins until they are firm to the touch and golden brown, and a toothpick inserted into the center of one comes out clean, 20 to 30 minutes.

7. Transfer the muffin pans to a wire rack and let the muffins cool for 10 minutes. Then remove the muffins from the pans and let them finish cooling on the rack. (The muffins taste best the day they are made. If necessary, you can store them in an airtight container for up to 3 days and then reheat them in a microwave for 10 seconds or in a preheated 375°F oven for 5 minutes. They don't freeze well.)

THE BASICS

Buttermilk

Cultured buttermilk is widely available in the refrigerated dairy case of most supermarkets. It is made commercially from skim or low-fat milk that is heat-fermented and then cultured to make it thick, tangy, and smooth. Old-fashioned buttermilk, which is rarely found outside a working dairy, is the liquid that is left over after churning cream into butter— hence the name. Buttermilk is widely used in baking because it adds a tangy, moist richness that is not found in other dairy products. It is also available in a powdered form in the baking section of many markets.

THE BASICS

Make-Ahead Muffin Batter

Our bran muffins are made with only baking soda (no baking powder), so the batter doesn't need to be cooked right away. Unlike many other muffins, you can store the batter in the refrigerator for up to three days, which makes it quick and easy to bake fresh muffins in the morning. The batter also freezes well. Thaw it for 24 hours in the refrigerator, and it's ready to use.

Honey Bran Muffins

MUFFINS, ESPECIALLY BRAN MUFFINS, satisfy my desire for a healthy and sweet (but not too sweet) bakery treat. Honey and buttermilk make these muffins tender and moist, while rolled oats and plump, nutritious raisins contribute great texture. We worked to make these perfectly delicious with as little oil as possible (there's only ¼ cup oil for 10 muffins), but because the fat content is so low, the muffins are best the day they are made. If they dry out over time, revive them by heating them for 15 seconds in the microwave or by toasting them. Once they have cooled completely, I usually freeze the muffins I don't eat that day. After defrosting, the muffins are perfectly fresh and moist. That also keeps me from eating the whole batch at once! ⁓⁓⁓ *Makes 10 muffins*

Butter, for greasing the muffin cups (optional)

2 cups wheat bran

½ cup plus 2 tablespoons old-fashioned rolled oats (see sidebar, page 307)

1 cup low-fat buttermilk (see sidebar, page 371)

½ cup raisins

½ cup sugar

¼ cup canola oil

¼ cup honey

1 large egg

½ cup plus 2 tablespoons whole wheat pastry flour

1½ teaspoons baking soda

1. Position a rack in the middle of the oven and preheat the oven to 350°F. Butter 10 standard-size muffin cups or line them with cupcake liners.

2. Place the wheat bran, oats, buttermilk, and raisins in a medium-size bowl and stir to combine. The mixture will be stiff.

3. In a large bowl, whisk together the sugar, oil, honey, and egg until smooth.

4. Place the pastry flour and baking soda in a small bowl and whisk to combine.

5. Add the bran-oat mixture to the sugar-honey mixture, and stir to combine. Then add the flour mixture and stir again to combine.

6. Spoon the batter into the prepared muffin cups, filling them to the brim.

7. Bake the muffins until they are firm to the touch and a toothpick inserted into the center of one comes out clean, 25 to 30 minutes.

8. Place the muffin pan on a wire rack and let the muffins cool for 10 minutes. Then remove the muffins from the pan and serve warm or at room temperature. (These muffins taste best the day they are made. If necessary, you can store them in an airtight container for up to 3 days; reheat them in a microwave oven for 15 seconds or in a preheated 375°F oven for 5 minutes. The muffins can be frozen in an airtight container for up to 3 months.)

Note: Use the same measuring cup for the oil and the honey. If you measure the oil first, followed by the honey, the honey will plop right out of the cup without any assistance from you.

Apricot and Oat Scones

ROLLED OATS AND WHOLE WHEAT PASTRY FLOUR give these scones a better nutritional profile than pastries made with all white flour. To counter the heavier nature of these grains, we use buttermilk, a great tenderizer, to lighten the texture. Loaded with bits of dried apricots, and not too sweet, these scones make a wonderful breakfast, brunch, or afternoon tea-time treat. You can use this basic recipe to create your own variations with other dried fruits and nuts, such as cranberry-ginger, cherry-almond, or pineapple-mango. Unbaked scones freeze beautifully, so you might want to make a double batch. ⟶ *Makes 8 scones*

Butter, for greasing the baking sheet (optional)

1 cup (4¼ ounces) unbleached all-purpose flour, plus extra for dusting the work surface

1 cup (3½ ounces) old-fashioned rolled oats (see sidebar, page 307)

½ cup (1⅝ ounces) whole wheat pastry flour

½ cup (3¾ ounces) firmly packed light brown sugar

1¼ teaspoons baking powder

½ teaspoon plus ⅛ teaspoon salt

½ teaspoon plus ⅛ teaspoon baking soda

½ cup (about 3 ounces) diced dried apricots

10 tablespoons (1¼ sticks) cold unsalted butter, cut into bits

⅓ cup low-fat buttermilk (see sidebar, page 371)

Turbinado sugar, for dusting (see box, page 321, optional)

1. Position a rack in the middle of the oven and preheat the oven to 400°F. Lightly butter a baking sheet or line it with parchment paper.

2. Place the all-purpose flour, oats, pastry flour, brown sugar, baking

The Secret to Perfect Scones

♦ Always use very cold butter to ensure a flaky texture.

♦ Light hands and a light touch make for fluffier scones. Don't overwork the dough.

♦ To avoid overworking the gluten in the flours, use a pastry blender to mix in the butter. A pastry blender, also called a pastry cutter, is a useful and inexpensive tool if you like to make biscuits, pastry crusts, and scones. It consists of several U-shaped wire strands connected to a straight handle. The wires do a good job of cutting the butter into the flour. Unlike working with your hands, the pastry blender stays cool, so the butter doesn't melt and stays at the optimum temperature.

♦ Use a sharp knife to cut the dough into scones. If the knife is blunt, the twisting motion used in cutting the scones will result in lopsided pastries that will rise unevenly.

♦ Place the scones fairly close together on the baking sheet— about 2 inches apart. They will stay soft on the sides and achieve a nice crisp top.

Freezing Scones

If you want to bake just a few of the scones, arrange the extras (after cutting them into wedges but before sugaring the tops), on a baking sheet lined with parchment or wax paper and place it in the freezer. When they are frozen solid, transfer the scones to a plastic bag or an airtight container. They can be thawed overnight in the refrigerator or baked frozen. Sprinkle them with the sugar, if using, just before popping them into a 375°F oven, and bake as described in the recipe; add 5 to 10 minutes for frozen scones.

powder, salt, baking soda, and apricots in a large bowl and stir to combine. Add the cold butter. Using a pastry blender, two knives, or your fingers, blend the butter into the mixture until it is crumbly and well combined.

3. Stir in the buttermilk and mix until the dough starts to form a ball. Turn the dough out onto a lightly floured work surface and pat it into a 6-inch disk about 1½ inches thick. Use a knife to cut the dough into 8 wedges, and place them on the prepared baking sheet, spacing them 2 inches apart. Sprinkle the tops with turbinado sugar, if desired.

4. Bake the scones until they are golden brown and firm to the touch, 15 to 20 minutes.

5. Transfer the baking sheet to a wire rack and let the scones cool for about 10 minutes. Serve the scones warm or at room temperature. (The scones taste best the day they are made, but if necessary they can be stored in an airtight container for up to 2 days. Reheat them in a microwave oven for about 10 seconds or in a preheated 350°F oven for 5 to 10 minutes.)

Ham and Gruyère Frittata

FRITTATAS ARE BASICALLY OPEN-FACE OMELETS, and they can be served hot or warm. They are easier to make than omelets because they don't need to be folded. In this recipe, the frittata is finished under the broiler rather than on the stovetop. A classic pairing of ham and Gruyère cheese, this is really only a starting point. Use whatever odds and ends you have in your refrigerator to create your own one-dish breakfasts. Leftover cooked pasta or potatoes can be added to make a heartier frittata, and just about any vegetable goes well with eggs. ~~~ *Serves 2 to 4*

1 tablespoon olive oil

¼ cup finely diced red onion

About 3 ounces ham, cut into ¼-inch dice (½ cup)

½ teaspoon dried tarragon

Salt and freshly ground black pepper

6 large eggs

⅓ cup whole or low-fat milk

1 cup (4 ounces) grated Gruyère cheese

1. Heat the oil in an 8-inch nonstick, ovenproof skillet (preferably cast-iron) over low heat. Add the onion and cook slowly, stirring frequently, until soft, about 8 minutes. Stir in the ham and tarragon, and cook for another minute. Then season with salt and pepper to taste, and set the skillet aside, off the heat.

2. Position a rack about 5 inches below the broiler, and preheat the broiler on high.

3. Place the eggs and milk in a medium-size bowl and whisk to combine. Add ½ cup of the cheese and stir to blend.

4. Add the egg mixture to the skillet, return it to medium-low heat, and cook without stirring until the bottom and sides have set, about 4 minutes. The top of the frittata will still be wet.

5. Sprinkle the remaining ½ cup cheese over the frittata and place the skillet under the broiler. Cook until the top puffs and turns golden brown, about 5 minutes. Remove the frittata from the broiler and let it rest for 3 minutes to finish cooking.

6. Run a heatproof rubber spatula or a small knife around the edge of the frittata to release it from the skillet. Slide the frittata onto a warmed serving plate. Cut it into wedges, and serve hot or warm.

Ham and Gruyère Frittata

egg label claims: what are they talking about?

There is very little regulation of the claims on egg cartons, and truth in labeling can be woefully lacking. Without oversight and regulation, producers are able to make a wide range of claims in their own self-interest, using terms such as "farm fresh," "healthy," "animal-friendly," or "naturally raised," even if the eggs come from birds that are confined inside tiny wire cages and are fed the cheapest food. So, which label claims can you really trust?

Animal Welfare Approved: This is a free program, which audits and certifies family farmers who raise their animals on pasture or range with high animal welfare standards. Chickens must be able to move freely, forage, dust-bathe, spread their wings, and engage in other natural behaviors.

Certified Humane: The birds may be kept indoors but are not allowed to be caged. Living conditions must allow natural behaviors such as nesting, perching, and dust-bathing, and hens must be raised with access to shelter, resting areas, and sufficient space. Humane Farm Animal Care, a leading nonprofit organization, certifies producers and conducts third-party audits to verify compliance.

Certified Organic: The USDA National Organic Program sets standards and requires annual third-party audits to verify compliance. Hens are uncaged and are required to have outdoor access. In addition, they must be fed a 100 percent organic all-vegetarian diet made from crops grown without chemical pesticides, fertilizers, irradiation, genetic engineering, or sewage sludge. The birds can never receive antibiotics or growth hormones.

Cage Free: This simply means that the hens are not confined to cages, but there are no standards, regulations, or auditing mechanisms to substantiate the claim.

Free Range: There are no standards for free-range egg production as of this writing. The Humane Society of the United States (HSUS) states that "typically, free-range egg-laying hens are uncaged inside barns or warehouses and have outdoor access. They can engage in many natural behaviors such as nesting and foraging." This said, there is no third-party auditing and the USDA has no inspection system in place to verify that farms claiming to be free range actually are.

Pasture Raised: Although there is no regulation or oversight on the use of this term, the USDA does define it in their *Trade Descriptions for Poultry* standard. The pasture-raised standard requires that birds are raised outdoors using movable enclosures located on grass. They can be fed a traditional high-protein diet, can be fed an organic diet, and/or can be raised without antibiotics. Some people believe that eggs from pasture-raised hens, who are allowed to eat a natural diet of plants and grubs, are tastier. A handful of small studies also suggest that eggs from genuine foraging hens may have better nutritional profiles—containing less cholesterol, less total and saturated fat, and more omega-3s, vitamins, and nutrients. Adherence to the USDA Trade Description standards is strictly voluntary. Producers may conform, but there is no certification process to verify compliance.

Omega-3: Omega-3 eggs contain extra omega-3 fatty acids, which are believed to have numerous health benefits. Hens are fed diets that are fortified with good sources of omega-3s, like algae or flaxseed. Producers in the USDA egg grading program are audited to ensure that the hens' diets have been fortified and that omega-enriched eggs do not get swapped out for cheaper ones.

Fertile: The term is unregulated but implies that the eggs came from hens that lived with roosters, which presumes they most likely were uncaged. Some consumers purchase fertile eggs because they believe they're more nutritious (although there is no data to substantiate that belief) or because they approve of the more natural living conditions that this term implies.

Pasteurized: This term is regulated by the FDA and refers to raw whole-shell eggs that are heated to temperatures just below the coagulation point to destroy harmful bacteria such as salmonella. Pasteurized shell eggs behave and taste just like regular eggs, but they are safer, since the risk of disease has been eliminated, or at least greatly reduced. Eggs that have been pasteurized before sale are commonly marked with a special stamp so they're very easy to recognize and identify. These eggs are recommended for recipes that call for raw eggs and for people who are especially susceptible to illness.

Vegetarian Fed: For eggs that bear a USDA grade shield, the term "vegetarian-fed" means the eggs were produced by hens raised on all-vegetarian feed.

United Egg Producers Certified: Presented by the United Egg Producers (UEP), America's leading trade association for egg farms, this voluntary certification program sets guidelines for caged and cage-free layers. One of the organization's stated commitments is to provide "the most economical eggs in the world." The overwhelming majority of the U.S. egg industry complies with this voluntary program. The caged hens can be confined in restrictive, barren cages and cannot perform many of their natural behaviors, including perching, nesting, foraging, or even spreading their wings.

Tofu Scramble

WHEN YOU'RE IN THE MOOD TO MIX IT UP, this tofu scramble is a great alternative to eggs that will give you energy and a nutritious start to the day. Tofu goes well with all types of vegetables, herbs, and spices, and is very filling and satisfying. In this scramble, tofu marries well with a flavorful and tasty assortment of fresh herbs, spinach, tomatoes, and shiitake mushrooms. I like to finish the sauté with a sprinkling of cheese, but this is optional. For extra flavor, serve the tofu scramble with a side of salsa. —— *Serves 4*

1 tablespoon olive oil

1 bunch (about 8) scallions, green and white parts chopped separately

5 ounces (3 packed cups) spinach leaves, well rinsed and patted dry if not prewashed, coarsely chopped

2 packed cups (about 7 ounces) thinly sliced shiitake mushroom caps

1 pound firm tofu, drained and crumbled

1 large tomato, cut into ¼-inch dice (about 1 cup)

2 teaspoons chopped fresh oregano

2 teaspoons chopped fresh thyme

Salt and freshly ground black pepper

1 cup grated mozzarella, cheddar, or other cheese (optional)

1. Heat the olive oil in a large skillet (preferably cast-iron) over medium heat. Add the white part of the scallions and cook, stirring frequently, for 1 minute. Add 1 tablespoon water, the spinach, and the mushrooms, and stir to blend. Cover the skillet and cook, stirring once or twice, until the mushrooms are soft and the spinach has wilted, about 4 minutes.

2. Add the tofu, tomato, oregano, thyme, and scallion greens and cook, uncovered, stirring occasionally to prevent sticking, until the mixture is hot, 3 to 5 minutes. Season with salt and pepper to taste.

3. If you are using the cheese, reduce the heat to low, sprinkle the cheese over the scramble, cover the skillet, and cook until the cheese melts, 1 to 2 minutes.

4. Serve immediately.

LIVING GREEN
A great alternative to commercial spray cans of oil is a reusable oil mister. You fill it with your own oil, and refill it when it runs low. It's the perfect kitchen gadget, and it pays for itself quickly. Commercial spray cans of cooking oil come with a high monetary and environmental price. Not only is the extra packaging costly, the amount of oil the cans hold is relatively small because so much room is needed for the propellant. The oil usually costs 50 percent more per ounce than if you were to buy it in a regular big bottle.

Primer on Cooking Eggs

Eggs are a chef's best friend: Incredibly versatile and inexpensive, they're a great source of protein. Here we've outlined the basic techniques and cooking times for 2 large eggs.

BOILING

Hard-cooked: Ideally, remove the eggs from the refrigerator about 30 minutes in advance of cooking. Very cold eggs may crack when immersed in hot water. Fill a small saucepan two-thirds full of water and bring it to a boil over high heat. Place the eggs in a slotted spoon and lower them into the boiling water. Reduce the heat to a low boil and set a timer for 10 minutes. When the time is up, use the slotted spoon to transfer the eggs to a bowl of ice water, and let them cool completely.

Soft-boiled: Ideally, remove the eggs from the refrigerator about 30 minutes in advance of cooking. Fill a small saucepan two-thirds full of water and bring it to a boil over high heat. Place the eggs, in their shells, in a slotted spoon and lower them into the water. Set a timer for 3 to 5 minutes, depending on how runny you like your yolks. When the time is up, use the slotted spoon to transfer the eggs to an egg cup. Gently tap around the top of the egg with a knife. Then slice across the top to remove a small portion. Use a teaspoon to eat the egg directly from its shell.

FRYING

Place 2 tablespoons olive oil (or a combination of half butter and half oil; if using butter, make sure it melts before adding the eggs) in a small skillet (preferably cast-iron) over medium heat. One at a time, crack the eggs into a small bowl or cup, and remove any pieces of shell with the tip of a spoon. Slide the egg from the bowl into the hot skillet.

For sunny-side-up eggs, spoon the fat over the yolks to help them cook, 3 to 4 minutes. To ensure the egg is cooked, cover the pan and remove it from the heat to finish cooking, 1 to 2 minutes. Lift the eggs out with a slotted spatula and let the fat drain back into the pan. For eggs over easy, once the whites start to firm, gently turn the eggs over with the spatula and continue cooking for 1 minute before removing them from the pan.

Season fried eggs with salt and pepper to taste and serve immediately.

POACHING

Place 6 cups water in a saucepan and bring to a boil over high heat. Reduce the heat to maintain a slow simmer, and add 1 tablespoon distilled white vinegar (this helps to solidify the white). Crack each egg into a small bowl or cup, removing any pieces of shell with the tip of a spoon. Slide the egg from the bowl into the water. Poach, uncovered, until the white is just set, about 3 minutes. Remove the eggs with a slotted spoon, letting the excess water drain off. For an attractive presentation, trim off any flyaway strands of egg white with a knife or kitchen scissors.

SCRAMBLING

For 1 serving, place 2 eggs, 1 tablespoon cold water, and a pinch of salt and freshly ground pepper to taste in a small bowl. Whisk until the mixture is completely combined and no clear egg white is visible. Melt 1 tablespoon butter in a small skillet (preferably cast-iron) over low heat. Add the egg mixture and cook, stirring gently with a wooden spoon or spatula, until the eggs reach the desired consistency. The more you stir, the finer the curd will be. Keep the heat low so that the eggs do not become rubbery or dry. Properly cooked, scrambled eggs will be moist and shiny.

Potatoes Rösti

Potatoes Rösti

M Y DAUGHTER, MAREA, DISCOVERED THIS DELICIOUS DISH on a trip to Switzerland. *Rösti* (which is variously pronounced RAW-stee, ROOSH-tee, RO-sti, or REU-shti, depending on the source) means "crisp and golden," and in culinary parlance usually refers to fried shredded potatoes. It originated as a Swiss breakfast dish, but is now popular as a main course for lunch or cut into wedges and served as a side dish for roasts. Rösti is similar to latkes and hash browns, but in our version Gruyère cheese is added to finely shredded potatoes and onions to make it meltingly delicious. Marea likes it served with a sauté of vegetables and an over-easy egg on top, so I've included her recipe for the topping. There are numerous regional variations of rösti, so feel free to incorporate other ingredients into the potatoes, such as cooked bacon, fresh herbs, or ribbons of ham. If you have a food processor, use the shredding disk to grate the potatoes and onions; otherwise use the coarse side of a box grater. A heavy 12-inch skillet, preferably cast-iron, is essential to ensure that the potatoes cook slowly and get very brown and crisp. Although rösti is best eaten when it's first cooked, you can reheat the potatoes on a baking sheet in a 475°F oven until hot. *Serves 2*

1 to 1¼ pounds russet or Yukon Gold potatoes, peeled and shredded (about 3 cups)

½ medium onion, shredded (about ½ cup)

1 cup (4 ounces) grated Gruyère or Comté cheese

2 tablespoons unbleached all-purpose flour

½ teaspoon salt

Freshly ground black pepper

1 tablespoon unsalted butter

1 tablespoon olive oil

Marea's Vegetable Sauté (optional; recipe follows)

1. Place the shredded potatoes and onion in a bowl of cold water and let them soak for 5 minutes. Then drain them in a colander, and rinse thoroughly with cold water to remove the starch. Drain them well again. Place the potato-onion mixture in a clean kitchen towel and wrap it tightly. Twist and wring the towel over the sink to extract as much moisture as possible. This is a key step that will ensure that the finished rösti is crisp.

2. Transfer the mixture to a clean, dry bowl and add the cheese. Using your hands, toss to combine. Add the flour, salt, and pepper to taste, and toss again to combine.

3. If you're making Marea's Vegetable Sauté to go with the rösti, begin

Does Egg Shell Color Matter?

There is no difference in taste or nutrition between white and brown eggs. The color of the egg is determined by the breed of the hen: White eggs come from hens with white feathers and earlobes; brown eggs are produced by hens with red feathers and red earlobes. Although the only difference between brown and white eggs is cosmetic, brown eggs do tend to be more expensive than white. Among the breeds that lay brown eggs are the Rhode Island Red, the New Hampshire, and the Plymouth Rock—all larger birds that require more food.

that recipe at Step 1 now, so that you can cook both components simultaneously.

4. Place a heavy 12-inch skillet (preferably cast-iron) over medium heat, and when the pan is hot, melt the butter in the oil. Spread the potato mixture in the pan, pressing it into an even layer with the back of a fork. Cover the skillet and cook the mixture for 6 minutes.

5. Uncover the skillet and continue cooking until the underside is brown and crisp, 5 to 7 minutes. If you have another 12-inch skillet, slide the rösti onto a flat plate, and then flip it back into the skillet. Return the skillet to medium heat and cook until the other side is brown and crisp, 8 to 10 minutes.

6. Transfer the rösti to a warmed serving plate and serve with Marea's Vegetable Sauté if desired.

Marea's Vegetable Sauté

A quick sauté of fresh vegetables served atop the crispy rösti makes a hearty start to the day. Marea tops this with an over-easy egg to provide a bit of protein and because she likes the way the runny yolk binds the various components. The vegetable sauté (without the egg) is also terrific folded into an omelet or served on its own as a side dish alongside fish or meat. In Switzerland, rösti is made as a single-serving portion, but we think it's enough to share, cooking two eggs instead of one. ⟋⟍ *Serves 1 or 2*

1 tablespoon olive oil

½ small yellow onion, cut into ¼-inch dice (about ½ cup)

1 cup (about 2 ounces) small brown or white mushrooms, sliced ¼ inch thick

Salt and freshly ground black pepper

5 ounces (3 packed cups) baby spinach, well rinsed and patted dry if not prewashed

1 tomato, seeded (see sidebar, page 131) and cut into ¼-inch dice

1 tablespoon butter

1 large egg (or 2 if sharing)

1. Heat the olive oil in a medium-size skillet over medium heat. Add the onion and cook, stirring frequently, until it begins to soften, about 6 minutes. Add the mushrooms and raise the heat to medium-high. Season the mixture with salt and pepper to taste, and cook, stirring frequently, until the mushrooms exude their liquid and begin to soften, about 8 minutes.

2. Stir in the spinach and cook until it wilts, about 2 minutes.

3. When the spinach has wilted, add the tomato, cook for 1 minute to heat through, and then remove the skillet from the heat.

4. Melt the butter in a small skillet over medium heat. When the butter is hot, crack the egg and add it to the skillet. Cook until the white has set.

Then carefully flip the egg over and continue cooking on the other side until the yolk is done to your liking.

5. Scatter the hot vegetables over the hot rösti, and top with the egg. Serve immediately.

Potatoes Rösti with Marea's Vegetable Sauté

Warm Citrus Compote

Warm Citrus Compote

FRESH CITRUS BRIGHTENS THE SHORT DAYS OF WINTER and is sweetly refreshing, bright, and colorful. Our dazzling combination of jewel-toned citrus segments makes a gorgeous and healthy fruit salad for a Sunday brunch or a light dessert. A fragrant syrup infused with exotic spices—lemongrass, star anise, cardamom, and vanilla—mellows the natural tartness and acidity of the citrus. If you're feeling creative, you can garnish the compote with slivers of crystallized ginger, a chiffonade of fresh mint, some toasted shredded coconut, or diced candied orange peel. For an artful presentation, carefully section the fruits or slice them crosswise into thin rounds. A combination of segments and slices is also pretty. ～～ **Serves 4**

2 ruby red or pink grapefruits

4 blood oranges

3 Cara Cara or navel oranges

2 cups sweet dessert wine, such as Muscat de Beaumes-de-Venise or Sauternes

½ cup sugar

2 lemongrass stalks, outer leaves discarded, bottom 4 inches finely chopped (see sidebar, page 19)

1 star anise pod (see sidebar, this page)

16 cardamom pods, lightly crushed

1 tablespoon vanilla paste, or seeds from 1 vanilla bean (see box, page 315)

1 cup thinly sliced kumquats

¼ cup fresh orange or tangerine juice

1 tablespoon fresh lime juice

1. Using a small sharp knife, cut the peel and white pith from the grapefruits and oranges. Working over a shallow bowl, slice down either side of each membrane, releasing the citrus segments into the bowl. (Alternatively, slice the fruit crosswise into ¼-inch-thick rounds.) Remove any seeds and pour off the accumulated citrus juices. Measure out and reserve ½ cup.

2. Place ¼ cup water and the wine, sugar, lemongrass, star anise, and cardamom pods, and vanilla paste in a medium-size saucepan and bring to a simmer over medium heat, stirring to dissolve the sugar. Simmer the syrup for 5 minutes to allow the flavors and aromas to develop. Then remove the pan from the heat, cover it, and let the syrup cool to room temperature.

3. Strain the syrup through a fine-mesh sieve into a bowl, and discard the solids. Return the syrup to the saucepan and bring it to a simmer over medium heat. Add the kumquats and poach until they are tender, about 10 minutes.

4. Use a slotted spoon to transfer the kumquats to the bowl containing the grapefruit and oranges.

THE BASICS
Star Anise

The eight-pointed, star-shaped seedpod of an evergreen tree native to China, star anise is supremely fragrant and is surely one of the world's most extraordinary spices. Each of its eight segments contains a pea-size seed whose licorice-like perfume and flavor are similar to, but more pronounced than, that of anise seed. Star anise is one of the most important spices in Chinese cuisine and is the dominant flavor in Chinese five-spice powder. In Western dishes, it is mostly associated with desserts and baked goods. It can be found in whole pods at most supermarkets, and sometimes also in its ground form. You can easily grind your own in a small spice or coffee grinder.

5. Return the syrup to the heat and add the orange and lime juices, plus the reserved collected citrus juices. Simmer the mixture over medium heat until the syrup reduces and thickens slightly, about 5 minutes.

6. Pour the warm syrup over the fruit in the bowl, and let the mixture macerate for 10 to 15 minutes before serving.

LIVING GREEN
In 2006, Americans used and threw away an estimated 16 billion disposable coffee cups. Production of these cups consumed 6.5 million trees, created 253 million pounds of solid waste, sucked up 4 billion gallons of water, and used more than 4.8 billion BTUs of energy—enough to power 53,000 homes for a year. So its's always a better choice to use your own cup when you can!

Tropical Granola

CRISPY, GOLDEN, AND NOT TOO SWEET, this granola is studded with the iconic fruits of the tropics: coconut, mango, pineapple, banana, and cashews. Sprinkle a handful over yogurt and fresh fruit, or just add milk for a sweet start to your day. ⟶ *Makes about 8 cups*

3 cups thick-cut old-fashioned rolled oats (see sidebar, page 307)

2 cups shredded unsweetened coconut

1 cup raw cashew pieces

⅓ cup canola oil

⅓ cup honey

¼ cup packed light brown sugar

2 tablespoons boiling water

1 teaspoon pure vanilla extract

½ teaspoon ground ginger

½ cup diced dried pineapple

½ cup diced dried mango

½ cup diced banana chips

1. Position a rack in the middle of the oven and preheat the oven to 325°F.

2. Place the oats, coconut, and cashews in a large mixing bowl and stir to combine.

3. In a medium-size bowl, whisk together the oil, honey, brown sugar, boiling water, vanilla, and ginger. Add this to the oat mixture and stir to combine.

4. Transfer the granola to a rimmed baking sheet, spread it out, and bake until it is golden brown, 45 to 50 minutes, stirring several times during the last 20 minutes of cooking so that the mixture cooks evenly. Cool the granola completely on the baking sheet on a wire rack. The granola will crisp as it cools.

5. Transfer the granola to a large bowl and add the pineapple, mango, and banana, tossing to evenly distribute the fruit. Store it in an airtight container at room temperature for up to 4 weeks, or freeze it for up to 6 months.

A Guide to Citrus Fruits

Blood Orange
A thin-skinned variety with deep magenta to blood red–colored flesh. The flavor is complex with hints of wine and berries.

Cara Cara Orange
This variety of navel orange has salmony-pink flesh. It is low in acidity, and its sweet flavor has floral overtones.

Honey Tangerine
Thin-skinned and easily peeled, honey tangerines are full of juice and low in acid.

Kumquats These olive-size fruits have sweet skins and tart flesh—a reverse of the expected. The entire fruit is edible.

Tangelo A hybrid of a tangerine and a pomelo (a large, sweet grapefruitlike fruit), these baseball-size fruits have a sweet tangerine taste and loose skin that makes them easy to peel. A protruding knob at the top of the fruit is characteristic.

Meyer Lemon
A hybridized lemon with smooth skin and tart juice that is slightly sweeter than other types of lemons.

Pink Grapefruit
A sweet variety with meaty, pink flesh and a pleasantly acidic flavor.

Yuzu A Japanese citrus fruit with tart juice distinguished by notes of lime, tangerine, and pine. The rind is also extremely fragrant.

Really Healthy Granola

M Y DAUGHTER, MAREA, AND I BOTH LOVE GRANOLA, but we're not enthusiastic about all the oil and sweeteners used in most versions. Looking for a lower-fat option, we developed this recipe, which uses apple juice concentrate instead of oil to moisten the cereal. Full of healthy seeds and nuts, and lightly sweetened with juice, molasses, and a little honey instead of refined white sugar, this is a nutritious and delicious granola with a flavorful, less sweet taste. —— *Makes 12 cups*

4 cups old-fashioned rolled oats
   (see sidebar, page 307)
1 cup shredded unsweetened coconut
1 cup unsalted sunflower seeds
1 cup raw pumpkin seeds
1½ cups chopped almonds (skin on)
½ cup flaxseeds (see box, page 288)
½ cup white sesame seeds
1½ tablespoons ground cinnamon
1½ cups (one 12-ounce can) apple juice
   concentrate, thawed
⅓ cup unsulfured molasses
¼ cup honey
1½ cups raisins

1. Position a rack in the top third of the oven and another rack about 2 inches below it. Preheat the oven to 325°F.

2. Place the oats, coconut, sunflower seeds, pumpkin seeds, almonds, flaxseeds, sesame seeds, and ground cinnamon in a large bowl and stir to combine.

3. In a small bowl, combine the apple juice concentrate, molasses, and honey, and whisk until the molasses and honey dissolve. Pour this mixture over the oat mixture and stir until the oats are coated.

4. Divide the granola between two rimmed baking sheets, spreading it out on the sheets. Bake, stirring the granola and switching the positions of the baking sheets several times, until it is brown, dry, and fragrant, 35 to 45 minutes. Watch carefully during the final stages of cooking as the granola can burn easily.

5. Stir in the raisins while the granola is still hot. Then let it cool completely on the baking sheets. Store it in an airtight container at room temperature for up to 4 weeks, or freeze it for up to 6 months.

Really Healthy Granola

Four-Grain Hot Cereal with Blueberries

BARLEY, OATS, BROWN RICE, AND BRAN FLAKES are slowly simmered until just tender, creating a nutritious whole-grain cereal that has a great chewy texture and lots of flavor. Blueberries and applesauce add a hint of sweetness, and the grains are fragrant with cinnamon. Delicious on its own, this cereal is even tastier with the addition of our Sweet Cinnamon-Almond Topping. Alternatively, you can mix in any chopped nut or sliced fruit, and add maple syrup, honey, or brown sugar if you like it sweetened. Serve the cereal hot, with or without milk. It takes only about half an hour to make, and it reheats beautifully in the microwave (see the sidebar, this page). *Serves 6*

½ cup pearled barley

½ cup short-grain brown rice

1 teaspoon salt

1 cup old-fashioned rolled oats
    (see sidebar, page 307)

¼ cup wheat bran

1 cup fresh or frozen (unthawed) blueberries

½ cup applesauce

1½ teaspoons ground cinnamon

Sweet Cinnamon-Almond Topping
    (facing page, optional)

1. Pour 4 cups of water into a large saucepan and add the barley, brown rice, and salt. Cover the pan and bring the mixture to the start of a boil over medium-high heat. Reduce the heat to low and simmer for 10 minutes.

2. Add the oats and wheat bran and cook, covered, until most of the liquid has evaporated, about 10 minutes.

3. Stir in the blueberries, applesauce, and cinnamon. Remove the pan from the heat and let the cereal sit, covered, for 5 to 10 minutes before serving.

4. Divide the cereal among six bowls, and sprinkle each serving with some of the Sweet Cinnamon-Almond Topping if desired. (Let any leftover cereal cool slightly; then refrigerate it, covered, for up to 5 days. It reheats well in the microwave.)

Oats, Quinoa, and Raisin Bran Hot Cereal

I LIKE TO START MY DAY with a healthy bowl of delicious hot cereal. It not only has great taste and nutritional value, but it's also very filling and keeps me satisfied for hours. Here rolled oats, quinoa, and bran flakes combine in a nutty-flavored hot cereal. Raisins are a terrific addition, but you could also add other dried fruits such as chopped dates or cranberries. We suggest trying it with a drizzle (or sprinkle) of your favorite sweetener and some chopped nuts, or with our Sweet Cinnamon-Almond Topping for a touch of sweetness and crunch. —*mm*— *Serves 4*

1 cup old-fashioned rolled oats
  (see sidebar, page 307)

½ cup quinoa, rinsed

½ teaspoon salt

½ cup wheat bran

½ cup raisins

1 teaspoon ground cinnamon

Sweet Cinnamon-Almond Topping (optional;
  recipe follows)

1. Pour 4 cups of water into a medium-size saucepan and add the oats, quinoa, and salt. Cover the pan and bring the mixture to the start of a boil over medium-high heat. Reduce the heat to low and simmer for 10 minutes.

2. Add the wheat bran and cook, covered, until most of the liquid has evaporated, 8 to 10 minutes.

3. Stir in the raisins and cinnamon. Remove the pan from the heat and let the cereal sit, covered, for 5 to 10 minutes.

4. Divide the cereal among four bowls, and sprinkle each serving with some of the Sweet Cinnamon-Almond Topping if desired. Serve hot. (The cereal can be refrigerated, covered, for up to 5 days and reheated in the microwave.)

Sweet Cinnamon-Almond Topping

—*mm*— *Makes about ⅔ cup*

⅓ cup packed light or dark brown sugar

¼ cup chopped toasted whole (skin-on)
  almonds

½ teaspoon ground cinnamon

Combine the sugar, almonds, and cinnamon in a small bowl, and stir to blend. (The topping can be frozen for up to 3 months.)

Oatmeal, Carrot, and Apple Breakfast Squares

SARAH LACASSE AND I WORKED ON THIS RECIPE FOR WEEKS, testing version after version until the result was a perfect breakfast square. Packed into every sweet and wholesome square are 8 grams of protein, 20 percent of your daily requirement for fiber, 10 percent of your calcium, and over 100 percent of your vitamin A. Buttermilk keeps the cake tender, carrots and apples add moisture, and walnuts and coconut combine for a crunchy topping. This recipe makes enough to feed a dozen, and the squares stay fresh and delicious for days. And although we call these "breakfast squares," you may like them best as an afternoon or late-night snack. ⎯⎯ *Makes 12 squares*

Butter, for greasing the baking dish
1¾ cups old-fashioned rolled oats
   (see sidebar, page 307)
1½ cups (5 ounces) whole wheat
   pastry flour
¼ cup ground flaxseeds
   (see box, page 288)
1 tablespoon baking soda
1 teaspoon baking powder
2 teaspoons ground cinnamon
¼ teaspoon salt
1¼ cups (11¼ ounces) packed light
   brown sugar
⅔ cup canola oil
2 large eggs
1½ cups low-fat buttermilk
   (see sidebar, page 371)
1½ cups grated peeled carrots
   (about 4 medium carrots)
1 cup grated peeled apples
   (2 medium apples)

TOPPING

2 cups walnut pieces
½ cup (2 ounces) unsweetened shredded
   coconut
¼ cup (scant 2 ounces) packed light brown
   sugar
1 teaspoon ground cinnamon

1. Position a rack in the center of the oven and preheat the oven to 350°F. Generously butter the bottom and sides of a 13 x 9-inch baking dish.

2. Place the oats, flour, flaxseeds, baking soda, baking powder, cinnamon, and salt in a medium-size mixing bowl and stir to combine.

3. In a large bowl, whisk together the brown sugar and the oil. Add the eggs, one at a time, beating well after each addition. Stir in the buttermilk.

Oatmeal, Carrot, and Apple Breakfast Squares

4. Add the oat mixture to the buttermilk mixture, and stir to combine. Add the carrots and apples, and stir just until blended. Transfer the batter to the prepared baking dish.

5. Place the walnuts, coconut, brown sugar, and cinnamon in a small bowl. Stir to blend, and sprinkle the topping mixture evenly over the batter.

6. Bake the squares until the batter has set and a toothpick inserted in the center of the cake comes out clean, about 45 minutes. Let cool on a wire rack for 1 hour. Then cut into 12 pieces. (The squares can be stored in an airtight container at room temperature for up to 4 days.)

bubbling over with enthusiasm for my electric teakettle

Boiling water is probably the most basic kitchen skill there is, and I've found a better way to do it—faster, more energy efficient, and quieter. So even though I hesitate to recommend buying another kitchen gadget, I believe an electric teakettle is a worthwhile exception. According to TreeHugger.com, electric kettles convert a full 80 percent of energy into heat that actually boils the water, whereas a microwave is approximately 55 percent efficient, and a stovetop kettle is only about 40 percent efficient.

This higher efficiency also means water boils faster, which I really appreciate, especially in the morning when I'm eager for caffeine. I actually set up a race between my electric and stovetop kettles, each filled with exactly six cups of cold water. My electric kettle boiled its water in 4½ minutes; the one on my stove took 7¾ minutes.

Not only is the electric kettle faster, I don't need to turn on my stove's ventilation hood, which saves additional energy, and the electric kettle shuts off automatically as soon as water boils, avoiding non-productive boiling time. I also appreciate the kettle's gentle "click" when the water is ready instead of the screaming train whistle of my stovetop model. And not having a kettle "stored" on a stove burner avoids playing musical pots when I'm cooking, and keeps the kettle from getting splattered with grease.

I bought my first electric kettle years ago, and the energy-efficient little workhorse quickly became one of my favorite appliances.

Five Lassis

LASSI IS A TRADITIONAL YOGURT-BASED DRINK that is sold by street vendors and in restaurants all over India. Lassis come in just about every imaginable flavor, both sweet and savory, often blended with Indian spices, saffron, or even salt and pepper, depending on the region. Our variations on the lassi theme are blends of fresh fruit, yogurt, spices, and ice. They are very refreshing, filling, and energizing. Fruit smoothies are similar but usually rely on frozen fruit and juice as their base. Lassis are meant to be served very cold, so if you use room-temperature fruit, it's best to refrigerate the mixture after blending until it's chilled. Lassis can be refrigerated for up to 5 hours.

Mango Lassi

Sweet and juicy mango combined with cardamom, honey, and yogurt makes a delightful breakfast or any-time-of-day energy drink. If you have a choice of mango varieties, choose Ataulfo (also called Champagne mangos), as they are sweet and stringless. *Serves 2*

1 cup cubed fresh mango (1 large or 2 small mangos, peeled; see Note)

1 cup plain yogurt, preferably Greek-style

¼ teaspoon ground cardamom, or to taste

8 ice cubes, cracked into small pieces (about 1 cup)

Honey to taste (depending on the sweetness of the mango)

2 thin mango wedges, for garnish (optional)

Place the mango, yogurt, cardamom, and ice in a blender and run the machine until the mixture is completely smooth. Add honey to taste, and process again for 1 minute. Divide the lassi between two glasses and serve immediately, or refrigerate it for up to 5 hours. Garnish with the mango wedges, if using.

Note: All mangos have a large, flat central seed that clings to the flesh. To cut a mango, place it on one of its ends. With a sharp knife cut from the top down, keeping the knife blade parallel to, and as close to one side of, the seed as possible. Repeat on the other side of the seed. With a small paring knife, score the flesh of each cheek in parallel cuts, then cut crosswise to make small squares, taking care not to cut through the skin. Push against the outside of the mango skin to flip the fruit inside-out, and carefully undercut the squares with a small knife.

THE BASICS

Mangos

You may be surprised to learn that mangos are the most widely eaten fruit in the world. A good source of fiber, vitamins A, B, C, E and potassium and an excellent source of beta-carotene and other antioxidants, mangos come in a variety of shapes and colors. Although all are green when unripe, some stay green even when they are ripe, while others turn yellow, gold, or bright red. Look for mangos with an intense floral fragrance, plump flesh at the stem end that yields slightly when pressed gently, and fruit that's heavy for its size, with firm, unblemished skin. Fruit that's past its prime will have loose, shriveled skin or an "off" smell.

If your mangos aren't ripe yet, leave them at a cool room temperature for a few days, or place in a paper bag to speed ripening. Once ripened, enjoy your mangos immediately or refrigerate them for a day or two—otherwise, they'll ferment and spoil rapidly due to their high sugar content.

Three Lassis: Pineapple Mint, Raspberry, and Mango

Orange Cream Lassi

Lots of people remember Creamsicles, a frozen treat on a stick that coated vanilla ice cream with orange sherbet. That yummy combination inspired this lassi, which combines fresh-squeezed orange juice and vanilla yogurt with the merest hint of nutmeg. Refreshing and satisfying, this is the perfect way to start your day. —— *Serves 1 or 2*

1 cup vanilla yogurt

¾ cup fresh orange juice

1 tablespoon agave nectar or honey, or more
to taste (see box, page 321)

6 ice cubes, cracked into small pieces
(about ⅔ cup)

Freshly grated nutmeg, for garnish (optional)

Place the yogurt, orange juice, agave syrup, and ice in a blender and run the machine until the mixture is completely smooth. Pour the lassi into one or two tall glasses, and garnish with a grating of nutmeg, if desired. Serve immediately, or refrigerate it for up to 5 hours.

Passion Fruit and Banana Lassi

The tartness of passion fruit balances the sweet banana in this tropical lassi. If you're using fresh passion fruit, add the seeds to the blender then strain them out of the pureed mixture—they add flavor, but they're also very hard and crunchy. —— *Serves 2*

1 cup plain yogurt, preferably Greek style

1 small banana, cut into 6 pieces

2 tablespoons passion fruit puree
(see box, page 337), or pulp from 8
passion fruit

1 tablespoon agave nectar or honey, or
more to taste (see box, page 321)

¼ teaspoon vanilla paste (see box,
page 315; optional)

8 ice cubes, cracked into small pieces
(about 1 cup)

1. Place the yogurt, banana, passion fruit, agave syrup, and vanilla paste, if using, in a blender and run the machine until the mixture is completely smooth. If you have used fresh passion fruit pulp with seeds, strain the mixture through a fine-mesh sieve into a bowl, and discard the seeds; return the mixture to the blender.

2. Add the ice cubes and process until smooth.

3. Divide the lassi between two glasses and serve immediately, or refrigerate it for up to 5 hours.

Probiotics in Yogurt

Probiotics (from pro *and* biota, *meaning "for life") are live microorganisms (in most cases, bacteria) that are similar to the beneficial microorganisms found in the human gut. They are also called "friendly bacteria" or "good bacteria." The live active cultures in some yogurt make it a probiotic, a source of friendly bacteria. Studies suggest that probiotic bacteria in yogurt may have many health benefits, including aiding digestive health and bolstering the immune system. The good bacteria in yogurt can help restore imbalances in the intestinal system that might occur after a course of antibiotic medication.*

Probiotics can also be found in fermented and unfermented milk, miso, some juices and soy drinks, and in supplement form.

Pineapple Mint Lassi

Fresh mint is the key element of this lassi, adding a bright and refreshing note to balance the sweetness of the pineapple. Fresh pineapple is best, but canned pineapple packed in water will also work. ⟶ *Serves 2*

**1 cup honey yogurt or plain yogurt,
  preferably Greek-style**
1 cup pineapple chunks
**1 tablespoon agave nectar or honey,
  or more to taste (see box, page 321)**
**8 ice cubes, cracked into small pieces
  (about 1 cup)**
8 to 10 fresh mint leaves

Combine all the ingredients in a blender and run the machine until the mixture is very smooth. Divide the lassi between two glasses and serve immediately, or refrigerate it for up to 5 hours.

Raspberry Lassi

Sweet raspberries are combined with a squeeze of lime and a pinch of star anise for a refreshing, not-too-sweet breakfast drink. The seeds are good for you, but if you prefer, strain them out before serving the lassi. Frozen raspberries can also be used, but when they're in season, fresh berries have the best flavor. ⟶ *Serves 2*

1 cup plain yogurt, preferably Greek-style
6 ounces (about 1⅓ cups) fresh raspberries
**2 tablespoons agave nectar or honey, or more
  to taste (see box, page 321)**
**8 ice cubes, cracked into small pieces
  (about 1 cup)**
1 teaspoon fresh lime juice, or more to taste
½ teaspoon ground star anise

Place the yogurt, raspberries, agave syrup, and ice in a blender and run the machine until the mixture is completely smooth. Add the lime juice and star anise and process again for 30 seconds. Strain the mixture through a fine-mesh sieve to remove the seeds, if desired. Divide the lassi between two glasses and serve immediately, or refrigerate it for up to 5 hours.

Harvesting delicate raspberries by hand.

PANTRY BASICS

Plus 17 more useful tips.

Stocks, Sauces, Dips, and More

Homemade stocks, sauces, and toppings can raise a meal up a notch—from simply good to spectacular. Great examples are the Coconut Chile Sauce spooned over our amazing Coconut-Crusted Salmon, or the Quince and Pear Chutney alongside slices of Herbed Rib Roast of Pork. Our Seared Salmon topped with Grilled Corn Salsa captures the sweet fresh tastes of summer. And our Hummus beautifully complements my latest passion: baking homemade whole-wheat pita bread.

Spending time over the weekend to make a special sauce, stock, or condiment gives me a head start preparing certain dishes during a busy workweek. When tomatoes are ripe—just begging to be picked and enjoyed—I try to make a big batch of Farm Stand Pico de Gallo. I reap the reward when I come home famished after a long day at work, and can cook up cheese quesadillas in just a few minutes. The fresh tomato salsa elevates this quick meal from just ordinary to extra-delicious and very nutritious.

There are other recipes here that are well worth the time to make yourself. They also make good eco-sense: preserving bumper crops in season, or using up foods that ordinarily go to waste, such as bones, Parmesan rinds, shellfish shells, and older vegetables. For Fresh Strawberry Jam, I buy organic strawberries at the peak of their season, when they're red, sweet, plentiful, and least expensive—usually July and August. My jam recipe is a bit less sweet than most versions, so the fresh strawberry taste really shines through—long into winter, when we enjoy it spread on our morning toast. It brings back memories of summer sunshine and the feel of warm earth on bare feet.

Stock—meat, vegetable, seafood—is the flavor foundation for many recipes, so I've given you all the basics here. I admit that I don't often have time to make my own stock, but when I do put in the effort, I realize just how much better my soups taste. And I don't have to worry about cans or cartons winding up in landfills. Making your own stock also allows you to control all the ingredients,

Fresh Strawberry Jam (page 424)

avoiding the undesirable additives often present in commercial brands.

I like the idea of not wasting anything when I make my own stock. I simmer all the nutrients and flavor out of the bones from roasted meat or poultry, clean out the leftover vegetables in the fridge, add my own herbs and spices—and *voilà*, I have a flavorful foundation for soup that rivals anything you'd find in a great restaurant.

Top-quality ingredients separate the flavor of homemade basics from their commercial counterparts. And you can save money, too. Gourmet components like crème fraîche or chutney can be very expensive to buy ready-made, but with a bit of time and simple know-how, you can make your own for a fraction of the cost. You can also turn some of the recipes into wonderful gifts. Who wouldn't appreciate a jar of our Fresh Strawberry Jam or Quince and Pear Chutney, or a little tin of the Savory Nut Mix?

Many of the recipes in this chapter are for foods that are readily available in the grocery store; we don't *have* to make them. So when you have the opportunity to make your own, I hope the extra time and effort you spend in your kitchen brings you a special joy and satisfaction.

Pantry Staples

Stock your pantry so that basic staples are always on hand. This will save you from running to the store, and you'll never go hungry!

Basic Staples:

Pasta in assorted shapes and grains

Rice (such as jasmine, brown, Arborio, and wild)

Grains (such as quinoa, barley, farro, bulgur, and couscous)

Chicken broth

Vegetable broth

Dried and canned beans

Diced tomatoes

Tomato paste

Unsweetened coconut milk

Peanut butter

Tahini

Extra-virgin olive oil

Canola oil

Sesame oils (plain and toasted)

Specialty oils (such as walnut, hazelnut, and truffle)

Vinegars (such as balsamic, red and white wine, rice wine)

Salt (table, kosher, sea, specialty)

Black peppercorns

Spices (such as cumin, cayenne pepper, and curry, onion, and garlic powders)

Dried herbs (such as oregano, basil, thyme, parsley, tarragon, and bay leaves)

Bread crumbs

Ketchup

Mayonnaise

Dijon mustard

Soy sauce

Olives

Capers

Anchovies

Baking Staples:

Flour (all purpose, whole wheat pastry, whole wheat)

Old-fashioned rolled oats

Cornmeal

Baking soda

Baking powder

Sugar (white, brown, confectioners')

Honey

Agave nectar (syrup)

Pure maple syrup

Molasses

Corn syrup

Cornstarch

Pure vanilla and almond extracts

Yeast

Chocolate chips

Unsweetened cocoa powder

Raisins and other dried fruits

Dried coconut

Spices (such as cinnamon, nutmeg, cloves, and ginger)

Nuts (such as walnuts, pecans, almonds, and hazelnuts)

Seeds (such as sunflower, pumpkin, sesame, and flax)

Basic Beef Stock

Deglazing

Deglazing is a culinary technique whereby liquid is poured into a hot pan to dissolve and capture the flavorful residue left in the pan after browning or roasting meat or vegetables. Generally the liquid used is wine, stock, or water, and deglazing is done by stirring to loosen the browned and caramelized bits of food on the bottom of the pan as the liquid simmers. The deglazed mixture is then added to stocks, pan sauces, and gravies for a richer flavor.

RICH AND FLAVORFUL, HOMEMADE BEEF STOCK is the foundation of many soups and sauces, adding a clean, bright flavor. It takes all day to slowly simmer a really flavorful beef stock, but it's worth it to make your own rather than purchase commercial stock. Accumulate meaty scraps and vegetables in the freezer so that when you have a little extra kitchen time, you can cook up a batch. Adding red wine boosts the flavor and complexity of the stock, but is not required. If you plan on freezing your stock and your freezer space is at a premium, you can reduce the stock to a manageable quantity by simmering it longer. The greater the reduction, the stronger the concentration of flavor will be. You'll be glad to have it on hand. ⎯⎯ ***Makes about 3 quarts***

10 pounds beef or veal bones,
  preferably with some meat attached
2 tablespoons olive oil
2 large yellow onions, unpeeled,
  cut into wedges
4 large carrots, unpeeled, cut into
  2-inch pieces
4 celery ribs with leaves, cut into
  2-inch pieces
1 bottle (750 milliliters) dry red wine
1 pound brown (cremini) or white
  mushrooms, cut in half
1 can (28 ounces) crushed Italian plum
  tomatoes, with their juices
¼ cup tomato paste
1 teaspoon whole black peppercorns
½ bunch (about 4 ounces) fresh flat-leaf
  parsley
8 fresh thyme sprigs

1. Position a rack in the lower third of the oven and preheat the oven to 450°F.

2. Place the meat bones in a single layer in a large roasting pan, and rub

the olive oil over them. (If necessary, arrange the bones in two pans to avoid crowding, which could slow down the browning process.) Roast the bones until they begin to brown, about 1 hour.

3. Reduce the heat to 400°F and add the onions, carrots, and celery. Continue roasting, stirring occasionally, until the bones are deep brown and the vegetables have begun to caramelize, 45 to 60 minutes.

4. Transfer the bones and vegetables to a very large soup pot, or divide them between two pots if necessary. Add the wine to the roasting pan and deglaze it by scraping any brown bits from the bottom of the pan. Pour this into the soup pot and add enough cool water to cover the bones, about 12 cups.

5. Bring the liquid to the start of a boil over high heat. Then reduce the heat to medium-low to maintain a simmer.

Using a large spoon, skim off any foam that accumulates on the surface.

6. Add the mushrooms, tomatoes, tomato paste, peppercorns, parsley, and thyme. Simmer gently, uncovered, adding more water as needed to keep the bones barely covered with liquid, for at least 6 hours or up to 12 hours.

7. Remove and discard the bones. Strain the stock through a fine-mesh sieve into a large, clean pot and discard the solids. If the stock lacks flavor, bring it to a simmer over medium heat and cook, uncovered, until reduced by a third to intensify the flavor, 30 to 45 minutes.

8. If you are using the stock at this time, let the fat rise to the surface, then skim it off with a metal spoon or ladle. If it's not for immediate use, let the stock come to room temperature using the quick cooling method (see sidebar, page 405). Refrigerate the stock, covered, until the fat has solidified on the surface; discard the fat. The stock can be refrigerated, covered, for up to 3 days or frozen for up to 6 months.

Chicken Wing Stock

THE FLAVOR AND NUTRITION OF HOMEMADE CHICKEN STOCK cannot be overstated, and once you realize how easy it is to make, you may become a convert. The technique is very basic: Oven-roast chicken wings with aromatic vegetables until they are golden brown, cover with water, add herbs, and cook until the liquid is reduced and flavorful. Chicken wings are one of the least expensive cuts of meat, but they are full of flavor and collagen, which makes them perfect for stock. If you're pressed for time, skip the roasting step. The resulting stock will be lighter and less full-bodied, but still far superior to canned or boxed versions. —*Makes about 8 cups*

5 pounds chicken wings

Coarse (kosher) salt and freshly ground
    black pepper

2 large yellow onions, unpeeled,
    cut into 8 wedges each

4 large carrots, unpeeled, cut into
    2-inch pieces

2 celery ribs, cut into 2-inch pieces

4 cups very hot water

About 16 cups cold water

2 dried bay leaves

20 fresh parsley stems (or whole sprigs;
    see sidebar, page 404)

1 teaspoon whole black peppercorns

1. Position a rack in the middle of the oven and preheat the oven to 400°F.

TIP

If you own a large stockpot with a pasta insert, it can do double duty for stock making. Place the insert in the stockpot, add all of the ingredients, and cook. When finished cooking, simply lift out the insert and discard the bones and vegetables. This eliminates the messy job of having to pour the contents of the stockpot into a colander.

Parsley Stems

Parsley stems have even more flavor than the leaves and are typically used in stocks, with the leaves reserved for another use. However, there's no reason not to use the whole sprig—stem with leaves—if you like.

2. Season the chicken wings with salt and pepper and arrange them in a single layer in a large roasting pan (use two pans if necessary). Roast until the wings turn golden, 30 to 40 minutes.

3. Stir the wings, add the onions, carrots, and celery to the pan, and continue to cook until the vegetables start to soften, 20 to 30 minutes.

4. Transfer the wings and vegetables to a large stockpot. Add the hot water to the roasting pan and scrape the pan to loosen the bits that have browned and hardened (which is where much of the flavor resides). Add this combination of water and pan drippings to the stockpot.

5. Add the 16 cups cold water to the stockpot—or enough cold water to cover the wings by 2 inches. Bring the stock to the start of a simmer over medium-high heat. Reduce the heat to medium-low and simmer for 15 minutes, using a large spoon to skim off any foam that rises to the top. Add the bay leaf, parsley stems, and peppercorns, and cook the stock at a slow simmer, uncovered, for 5 hours. Do not let the stock boil or it will be cloudy.

6. Place a colander or sieve over a clean pot and strain the stock into it, discarding the solids. Return the stock to the stove and reduce over medium heat until the flavor has concentrated and you have approximately 8 cups of liquid.

7. If you are using the stock at this time, let the fat rise to the surface, then skim it off with a metal spoon or ladle. If it's not for immediate use, let the stock come to room temperature using the quick cooling method (see sidebar, facing page). Refrigerate the stock, covered, until the fat has solidified on the surface; then discard the fat. The stock can be refrigerated, covered, for up to 3 days or frozen for up to 6 months.

Duck Stock

DUCK STOCK CAN BE VERY DIFFICULT TO FIND, so it's great to know how to make it yourself. The technique is similar to our Chicken Wing Stock: Vegetables and bones are roasted to maximize flavor, then a long slow simmer extracts all the rich flavors and aromas. Using duck stock really adds dimension and complexity to sauces, as in our Braised Duck with Quince and Apples (page 121) and Duck Breasts with Dried Cherry Sauce (page 119). ⸺ ***Makes about 6 cups***

2 duck carcasses with wings, necks,
and giblets

Coarse (kosher) salt and freshly ground
black pepper

1 large yellow onion, unpeeled,
cut into wedges

2 large carrots, unpeeled, cut into
1-inch pieces

2 celery ribs with leaves, cut into
1-inch pieces

1 cup dry white wine

1 dried bay leaf

1 teaspoon whole black peppercorns

8 fresh flat-leaf parsley sprigs

4 fresh thyme sprigs

2 large tomatoes, cut into ½-inch dice

1. Position a rack in the lower third of the oven and preheat the oven to 425°F.

2. Remove the wings from the duck carcasses and place the wings in a roasting pan. Add the necks and carcasses, and season the duck with salt and pepper. Roast the duck bones until they begin to brown, about 45 minutes.

3. Add the onion, carrots, and celery, and continue roasting, stirring occasionally, until the bones are brown and the vegetables have softened and begun to caramelize, about 30 minutes.

4. Transfer the bones and vegetables to a large stockpot. Add the wine to the roasting pan and deglaze it, scraping with a wooden spoon to

release the caramelized brown bits that have stuck to the bottom of the pan. Pour this into the stockpot and add just enough cool water to cover the bones (about 12 cups).

5. Bring the liquid to the start of a boil over high heat. Then reduce the heat to low to maintain a simmer. Cook for 30 minutes, using a large spoon to skim off any foam that accumulates on the surface during that time. Then add the bay leaf, peppercorns, parsley, thyme, and tomatoes. Simmer the stock, uncovered, until it has reduced by half, 3 to 4 hours.

6. Let the stock cool slightly. Then strain it through a fine-mesh sieve set over a clean pot, and discard the solids. If the stock lacks flavor, bring it to a simmer over medium heat and cook until reduced by a third to intensify the flavor, about 30 minutes.

7. If you are using the stock at this time, let it the fat rise to the surface, then skim it off with a metal spoon or ladle. If it's not for immediate use, let the stock come to room temperature using the quick cooling method (see sidebar, this page). Refrigerate the stock, covered, until the fat has solidified on the surface; then discard the fat. The stock can be refrigerated, covered, for up to 3 days or frozen for up to 6 months.

Quick Cooling Method for Stock

To prevent harmful bacteria from developing, it's important to cool stocks or meat sauces that you are not using immediately as quickly as possible, before refrigerating or freezing them. If you have a large quantity, divide the stock into several small containers so it will reach room temperature more quickly. Or even better, use an ice bath to rapidly cool down the liquid: Place the strained stock in a clean pot and immerse the pot in a pan filled with ice and water. Stir the stock occasionally to speed the cooling process. Never put hot stock directly in the refrigerator as the heat from the liquid could raise the temperature inside the refrigerator to an unsafe level.

cleaning green

It feels as if I am always cleaning my kitchen—wiping counters, loading the dishwasher, scrubbing pots, washing dish towels, rearranging food and cleaning up spills in an overcrowded refrigerator. To get all this done, I rely on quite a few cleaning products. Over time I've learned how important it is to use non-toxic, biodegradable cleaners that don't harm me or my family when we handle them, or adversely affect our waterways and wildlife when they go down the drain. In the past few years, I've been very happy to see more and more "green" cleaning products popping up in almost every store I go to.

Lately, though, I've been opting to make many of my own cleaners from common ingredients used in cooking—it's ecological and inexpensive. One part distilled white vinegar, diluted with two parts water, makes a perfect glass and counter cleaner. I find that the vinegar odor fades quickly, but if you prefer, you can temper the smell by adding a splash of lemon juice. You can also use pure vinegar to sanitize wooden cutting boards. A gallon of white vinegar is inexpensive and lasts for months. Also, keeping your homemade mixture in a reused plastic bottle instead of buying a new one saves energy and resources.

Baking soda is another green-cleaning staple.

Keep counters clean by sprinkling them with baking soda, then scrubbing with a damp cloth or sponge. If you have stains, make a paste of baking soda and a little water. Place it on the stain and let it sit for a while before you wipe it up. This method also works great for stainless steel sinks, cutting boards, containers, refrigerators, oven tops, and more. I feel good knowing that I'm preparing food on—and often eating right off of—surfaces cleaned with just vinegar or baking soda instead of harsh chemicals.

Label Claims to Look for in Cleaners That You Buy:

- Made from natural ingredients, from renewable and/or abundant natural resources
- Non-toxic, non-irritating, and non-hazardous
- 100% biodegradable
- Free of formaldehyde, petrochemicals, phosphates, chlorine, and ammonia

Ingredients to Avoid

Many chemicals used in cleaning products are harmful to our environment. Check the labels and try to avoid the ones listed below.

Phosphates

Phosphates are minerals that act as water softeners, but once released into waterways, they also act as fertilizers and are known to promote algae growth that in turn suffocates aquatic life in rivers, lakes, estuaries, or oceans. Some states have banned phosphates in laundry detergents, but automatic dishwasher detergents are usually exempt from phosphate restrictions, and most major brands still contain them. Look for phosphate-free alternatives, which are becoming more readily available.

Common pantry ingredients, like baking soda, make ecologically sound cleansers.

Chlorine

Chlorine bleach, or sodium hypochlorite, is hazardous because it's a lung and eye irritant. Products containing chlorine bleach also usually contain trace amounts of organochlorines, which cause cancer in animals and are suspected of also doing so in humans. After disappearing down drains, chlorine reacts with environmental organic matter, creating harmful organochlorines such as dioxin.

Petrochemicals

The key ingredients in most cleansers are called surfactants. Most surfactants are made from petroleum, a limited resource whose extraction and refining process pollutes the environment. Petroleum-based synthetic dyes, fragrances, and other chemicals are often added to detergents for aesthetic appeal, and these synthetic fragrances may contain hormone-disrupting phthalates, which prevent the scent from dissipating but also provoke asthma and other respiratory problems.

APEs (alkylphenol ethoxylates)

You probably won't see "APEs" on a product label, but if "surfactants" are mentioned, chances are the product contains these commonly used chemicals. A study of contaminants in stream water samples across the country by the U.S. Geological Survey found evidence of detergent and disinfectant chemicals in 69 percent of streams tested. These contaminants were members of a class of chemicals called alkylphenol ethoxylates (APEs). APEs are surfactants, or "surface active agents" that are added to some laundry detergents, disinfectants, laundry stain removers, and citrus cleaner/degreasers to make them more effective. APEs have been shown to mimic the hormone estrogen, and their presence in water may be harming the reproduction and survival of salmon and other fish.

For more information:

Washington Toxics Coalition:
ww.watoxics.org/files/cleaningproducts.pdf

The National Geographic Green Guide:
www.thegreenguide.com

Healthy Child Healthy World:
www.healthychild.org

Parmesan Stock

AT THE ASTRONOMICAL PRICE PER POUND you have to pay for quality Italian Parmesan cheese (Parmigiano-Reggiano), it's plain good sense to use the hard rinds. Tightly wrap the heels and ends of your cheese in plastic wrap, place them in a zip-lock bag, and freeze until you have at least half a pound of rinds. Then cook them to make a flavorful stock that's a wonderful addition to soups, pasta sauces, and vegetable braises. ⟶ ***Makes about 1 quart***

½ tablespoon olive oil

½ cup thinly sliced yellow onions or leeks

1 cup white wine

8 ounces Parmesan rinds

1 small dried bay leaf

10 whole black peppercorns

6 cups cold water

1. Heat the oil in a large stockpot over medium-high heat until it is hot, and then add the onions. Reduce the heat to low, place a round of parchment or wax paper directly on top of the onions, and sweat the onions (see sidebar, this page), stirring them occasionally, until they have softened, about 15 minutes.

2. Discard the paper and add the wine to the pot. Raise the heat to high and bring to the start of a simmer. Add the Parmesan rinds, bay leaf, peppercorns, and water, and bring the mixture to a boil. Reduce the heat to maintain a slow simmer, and cook the stock, uncovered, for 2 hours, or until the liquid has reduced by about half.

3. Let the stock sit at room temperature until it is lukewarm. Strain it through a fine-mesh sieve into a container, and discard the solids. If it's not for immediate use, refrigerate the stock until it is cold; then cover and freeze for up to 3 months.

THE BASICS

Sweating

In culinary parlance, sweating is a common preliminary step in vegetable cooking, particularly for onions and leeks. The vegetables are cooked in a small amount of butter or oil over low heat, with a piece of parchment paper pressed directly onto the vegetables. (The parchment traps the heat so the vegetables soften without browning and cook in their own juices.) Sweating vegetables usually results in tender, sometimes translucent, pieces and is used further in various culinary preparations.

Shrimp Stock

A STOCK MADE OF SHRIMP (OR ANY SHELLFISH) SHELLS makes a flavorful base for soups, chowders, risottos, and pasta dishes. This quick version utilizes raw shrimp shells, an item that is usually discarded. Rather than waste them, simmer the shells with a few aromatic vegetables (whatever you have on hand will suffice) to make a quick stock that adds a briny depth of flavor to dishes such as our Shrimp and Corn Chowder (page 14). Shrimp shells can be saved and frozen for several months, so if you like, store them in an airtight container until you have about a pound; then, when you have time, make a larger quantity of this stock, doubling all of the ingredients for a yield of 8 cups. ~~~

Makes about 4 cups

Reserved shrimp shells and tail pieces, or
   other shellfish shells (at least 2 cups)
1 small carrot, chopped
1 medium leek, white and light green parts
   only, rinsed and chopped
1 small onion, quartered
2 celery ribs with leaves, chopped
6 whole black peppercorns
1 dried bay leaf
12 fresh flat-leaf parsley sprigs
   (see sidebar, page 404)
6 cups cold water

1. Combine all the ingredients in a medium-size saucepan. Bring to the start of a simmer over medium-high heat, skimming off any foam that rises to the surface. Reduce the heat to maintain a simmer, and cook, uncovered, for 45 minutes.

2. Strain the stock through a fine-mesh sieve, discarding the solids. Store, covered, for up to 2 days in the refrigerator, or in the freezer for up to 2 months.

Vegetable Stock

MAKING STOCK IS A GREAT WAY TO USE UP THOSE ODDS AND ENDS lurking in your refrigerator. To make this stock as flavorful as possible, we've loaded up on the vegetables. There is no hard-and-fast rule about what vegetables or herbs to use, although strong-flavored items (such as cabbage, broccoli, peppers, and rosemary) and deeply colored vegetables (beets, red bell peppers) should be used only in small quantities so as not to dominate or overwhelm the flavor of the stock. Experiment with different vegetables and herbs to create your own personalized vegetable stock. —— *Makes 6 cups*

3 cups (about 4) diced fresh tomatoes (see Note)

2 large carrots, unpeeled, thinly sliced

2 celery ribs with leaves, thinly sliced

1 medium yellow onion, cut into chunks

1 cup cauliflower florets

1 cup corn kernels (fresh or frozen)

1 cup (2½ ounces) cremini or shiitake mushrooms, stems and caps chopped

1 fennel bulb, trimmed and thinly sliced

6 garlic cloves, unpeeled

1 teaspoon whole black peppercorns

1 dried bay leaf

9 cups cold water

12 fresh flat-leaf parsley stems (see sidebar, page 404)

4 fresh thyme sprigs

1. Place the tomatoes, carrots, celery, onion, cauliflower, corn, mushrooms, fennel, garlic, peppercorns, and bay leaf in a large stockpot. Add the water and bring to a simmer over medium-high heat. Reduce the heat to low and simmer, uncovered, until the flavor develops, about 1 hour.

2. Add the parsley stems and thyme sprigs and let simmer until the herbs release their flavor, about 15 minutes.

3. Remove the pot from the heat and let the stock cool slightly. Then strain the stock through a fine-mesh sieve into a large bowl or pot, and discard the solids. If you are not planning on using the stock at this time, let it come to room temperature using the quick cooling method on page 405. The stock can be refrigerated, covered, for up to 5 days or frozen for up to 6 months.

Note: Fresh tomatoes are specified here because the canned variety will tint your stock a rosy-red hue. If this is not a concern, canned tomatoes can be used in place of fresh tomatoes.

Roasted Bell Peppers

THE RICH, PURE FLAVOR of home-roasted bell peppers is a world removed from the jarred variety. Roasted peppers are a terrific item to have in your pantry. They add a touch of color and distinction to sautéed or steamed vegetables, sweet flavor to sandwiches and crostini, and punch to pasta and bean salads, like our cumin-scented French Lentil Salad (page 143). Store roasted peppers in the refrigerator for up to a week, where they'll come in handy for leafy green salads, grain salads, egg dishes, appetizers, pizza, casseroles, and more.

Bell peppers of any color, preferably a mix of red, yellow, and orange

Extra-virgin olive oil

1. Place a rack 4 inches from the broiler element, and preheat the broiler. Brush a rimmed baking sheet lightly with oil.

2. Place the whole peppers on the baking sheet so that they do not touch each other. Broil, turning them frequently with tongs, until the skin is blistered and charred all over, 10 to 20 minutes. Have patience and turn the peppers frequently so that the skin chars but the flesh itself does not burn. Take care not to pierce the peppers with the tongs, or you will lose the delicious juices.

3. As the peppers become charred, transfer them to a bowl or a paper bag. Cover the bowl or seal the bag, and allow the peppers to steam for 5 to 10 minutes to loosen the skins.

4. When the peppers are cool enough to handle, slit them over a medium bowl to catch the juices. Scrape or peel off and discard the skins. Cut the peppers in half and remove and discard the seeds, stems, and membranes. If you wish, cut the pepper halves into wide strips.

5. Transfer the peppers to a container and drizzle olive oil over them. Covered tightly, they can be refrigerated for up to 7 days. For the best flavor, serve at room temperature.

Baba Ghanouj

A MIDDLE EASTERN SPECIALTY, BABA GHANOUJ (or Baba Ghanoush) is traditionally served as a dip or spread for pita or flatbreads. There are numerous versions, some of which feature pomegranate seeds, tahini, pistachios, or mint. Our version is all about the eggplant, which is cooked to a silky softness, then simply flavored with sesame oil, lemon, and garlic. Baba Ghanouj makes a delicious accompaniment to our Greek-Style Lamb Chops (page 103) or Maklube (page 104). ⸻ *Makes about 2½ cups*

3 pounds eggplant

2 tablespoons toasted sesame oil (see sidebar, page 25)

2 tablespoons fresh lemon juice

1 garlic clove, peeled and minced

Salt

Cayenne pepper, to taste

¼ cup chopped fresh flat-leaf parsley

1. Position a rack 8 inches from the broiler element, and preheat the broiler.

2. Wash and dry the eggplants. Transfer the whole eggplants to a rimmed baking sheet. Broil, turning the eggplants once or twice, until they are soft and tender, 15 to 20 minutes.

3. Remove the baking sheet from the oven and let the eggplants cool

for 10 minutes. Then peel them, discarding the stems and skins, and coarsely chop.

4. Combine the sesame oil, lemon juice, garlic, and 2 teaspoons salt in a small bowl and whisk to blend.

5. Place the eggplant in a medium-size bowl, and beat with an electric mixer or an immersion blender until smooth. Gradually beat in the oil-lemon mixture. Season with additional salt to taste. Transfer the Baba Ghanouj to a pretty bowl and serve at room temperature sprinkled with the cayenne pepper and parsley. It can be stored, covered, in the refrigerator for up to 5 days. Let come to room temperature before serving.

Hummus

MAKING HOMEMADE HUMMUS IS SUPER-EASY, and it puts you in control of the garlic. This is a classic version with garlic, sesame oil, and tahini, and with a splash of fresh lemon juice to brighten and enliven the flavors. It makes a terrific sandwich spread or dip for raw vegetables. Or serve it with the whole wheat pita bread on page 287. ⁓ *Makes about 1½ cups*

LIVING GREEN
Homemade chickpeas taste fresher and have better texture than canned. So if you have the time, avoiding those cans is a delicious way to go.

1¾ cup cooked chickpeas (garbanzo beans), rinsed and drained if canned (or see page 422 to cook your own)

3 tablespoons toasted sesame oil (see sidebar, page 25)

¼ cup fresh lemon juice

2 tablespoons sesame tahini

1 garlic clove, peeled and minced

1 teaspoon salt

½ teaspoon freshly ground black pepper

¼ cup chopped fresh flat-leaf parsley

1. Place the chickpeas, sesame oil, lemon juice, and 3 tablespoons water in a food processor or blender and puree until smooth. Add the tahini, garlic, salt, and pepper and puree until smooth.

2. Transfer the hummus to a pretty bowl and sprinkle the parsley around the edges. The hummus can be refrigerated, covered, for up to 1 week. Serve chilled or at room temperature.

Hummus

Garlic Confit

SLOW-COOKING WHOLE CLOVES OF PEELED GARLIC in extra-virgin olive oil results in a fragrant garlic oil as well as garlic that literally melts in your mouth. This easy-to-prepare condiment is one of the most useful staples to have on hand in your kitchen. Need garlic for a pasta dish? Mash a few cloves of garlic confit into your sauce and *voilà*—that distinctive rich and mellow flavor is at your fingertips, without the worry of burning or bitterness, which can often be the case when cooking raw garlic. You'll find that both the oil and the garlic are useful additions to your pantry, ideal for flavoring everything from mayonnaise to mashed potatoes. ⁓ ***Makes about 2 cups oil and 30 cloves of garlic confit***

2 whole garlic bulbs, cloves separated, peeled, and trimmed
2 to 3 cups extra-virgin olive oil

1. Place the peeled garlic in a small pan and cover with the oil. The garlic must be completely submerged, so if your pan is large, you will need to add more oil.

2. Place the pan over medium-low to low heat and cook until the garlic is very tender, about 45 minutes. Do not allow the oil to simmer. You want a very gentle, slow cooking temperature. Remove the pan from the heat and let the garlic cool in the oil at room temperature.

3. Transfer the garlic and oil to a clean, dry container. Seal tightly and refrigerate for up to 6 weeks. Before using, let the oil and garlic sit at room temperature until the oil softens enough to remove the cloves with a spoon.

Fresh Horseradish Sauce

SO MUCH BETTER THAN PREPARED HORSERADISH sold in jars, this homemade version is fresh-tasting and zesty without any added preservatives. It just takes a few minutes to make, and once you've had a taste, we think you'll be convinced that homemade is superior to anything you can buy. ⁓ ***Makes 1½ cups***

1 cup sour cream

⅓ cup mayonnaise

3 tablespoons finely grated fresh peeled
    horseradish (see Note)

1 teaspoon fresh lemon juice

1 teaspoon salt

Place all the ingredients in a small
bowl and whisk to blend. Refrigerate,
covered, for at least 30 minutes before
serving, to allow flavors to infuse.
The sauce can be stored, covered,
in the refrigerator for up to 5 days.

Note: Fresh horseradish is very
pungent. When grating, be aware
that, like onions, horseradish may
cause your eyes to burn and water.

Crème Fraîche

CREME FRAICHE IS THICKENED CREAM with a slightly tangy, nutty
flavor. Generally available at specialty food shops, it's expensive to buy.
Crème fraîche is a convenient item to have in your pantry. It makes a
delicious substitute for sour cream, especially in soups or sauces because it can
be heated to a boil without curdling. Crème fraîche can also be used in place of
whipped cream. To serve it with fresh fruit, crisps, or pies, stir in a little honey
or sugar for a touch of sweetness. ⎯⎯ *Makes about 2¼ cups*

2 cups heavy (whipping) cream

2 tablespoons sour cream or buttermilk

Place the heavy cream in a small
container and add the sour cream.
Whisk to combine. Cover the
container with a lid and let it sit at
room temperature (about 70°F) until
thick, 12 to 18 hours (the sour cream
or buttermilk protects the cream from
developing harmful bacteria while it
is thickening). Once thickened, the
crème fraîche can be refrigerated,
covered, for up to 1 week.

Coconut Chile Sauce

JUST FOUR INGREDIENTS COMBINE TO FORM A TASTY, MELLOW sauce that has intriguing hints of sweetness and spice. For a change of pace, substitute ½ tablespoon Thai red curry paste for the chile paste. This velvety sauce partners beautifully with our Coconut-Crusted Salmon (page 134), with Thai-Style Salmon Cakes (page 138), and with grilled fish or scallops.
—— *Makes about ¾ cup*

1 cup unsweetened coconut milk
1 tablespoon fresh lime juice
1 tablespoon honey
½ tablespoon Thai chile paste
Salt

Combine the coconut milk, lime juice, honey, and chile paste in a small saucepan and cook over medium-high heat until the sauce reduces and thickens slightly, about 4 minutes. Season the sauce with salt to taste. The sauce can be refrigerated, covered, for up to 5 days.

THE BASICS

Coconut Milk

Coconut milk is derived from the white flesh of mature coconuts. It is not the watery drinkable liquid that fills the center of a coconut. Coconut milk is thick, rich, and sweet, and high in natural oil and sugar. Used in the cuisines of Thailand and other Southeast Asian countries, it is a common addition to soups, curries, sauces, and bakery sweets. Besides the recipe for Coconut Chile Sauce, check out the Coconut Rice on page 11.

Myra's Heirloom Tomato Sauce

I CAN'T THINK OF MANY THINGS THAT taste better than heirloom tomatoes that have ripened on the vine in the warm sunshine. When the season is upon us, I take full advantage of summer's bounty to make my favorite tomato sauce in huge batches, which I then put away in the freezer to use all winter long. If I'm setting aside some time to make a large quantity, I generally peel the tomatoes first. But if I'm just making enough sauce for one meal, I skip that step and just pick out the skins with tongs—much faster! I generally don't seed the tomatoes unless they are particularly "seedy." I like to combine a mix of heirlooms—any color—and usually add some Romas too, because they have fewer seeds and are very meaty. —— *Makes about 3 quarts*

2 tablespoons extra-virgin olive oil

1 large yellow onion, cut into ½-inch dice

3 large garlic cloves, peeled and chopped

12 pounds assorted vine-ripened tomatoes, peeled (see sidebar, page 131) and cut into large chunks

½ cup tomato paste

Salt and freshly ground black pepper

1 cup fresh basil leaves, roughly chopped

1. Heat the olive oil in a large, heavy pot over medium heat. Add the onion and cook, stirring frequently, until soft but not browned, about 6 minutes. Add the garlic and cook until fragrant, about 2 minutes.

2. Add the tomatoes and any accumulated juices to the pot. Raise the heat to medium-high, cover the pot, and cook until the tomatoes slump and are very soft, 10 to 15 minutes.

3. Using a potato masher, smash the tomatoes, right in the pot, into a coarse puree. Use tongs to pick out any missed pieces of skin.

4. Add the tomato paste and simmer the sauce, uncovered, stirring frequently, until it thickens to the desired consistency and the flavors are concentrated, 30 to 45 minutes.

5. Season with salt and pepper to taste. Stir in the basil, and cook for 2 minutes to release the flavors. Remove the pan from the heat. If you are not planning to use the sauce immediately, let it cool to room temperature. It can be refrigerated, covered, for up to 1 week or frozen for up to 6 months.

LIVING GREEN
I like to use plastic produce bags, both for when I shop and for storing fruits and vegetables in the refrigerator, but I don't take fresh ones every time I go to the store. They are sturdy enough to reuse multiple times. Most are still pretty clean once the original produce has been used up. If they're a little dirty, I rinse them with cold water and let them air dry completely before I use them again. When they look tired or start to rip, I make sure to recycle them.

Quick Tomato Sauce

WE LOVE THIS LIGHT, FRESH-TASTING SAUCE, which is a handy addition to your repertoire when ripe, sun-kissed tomatoes are not in season. Because there are so few ingredients, the quality of the canned tomatoes is paramount. The very best variety is San Marzano, which originated in the volcanic fields near Mount Vesuvius. These are acclaimed as one of the best cooking tomatoes in the world, so look for "San Marzano" on can labels. Garlic confit is great in this sauce because the mellow, rich taste of the garlic, slow-cooked in oil, adds depth of flavor to the sauce without a strident note. To preserve its fresh, bright taste, stir in the basil only after the sauce is cooked.
Makes about 3 cups

Chipotles in Adobo Sauce

Canned chipotles are packed in adobo sauce, which is made from ground chiles, herbs, and vinegar. Generally a recipe will call for only a few chipotles, which means you have the better part of the can left over. Rather than discard them, portion them out by the teaspoon or tablespoonful on a baking sheet, and freeze. Once they are frozen, transfer the chiles to a container or zip-lock bag and store them in the freezer until you need them. One tablespoon roughly equals 1 chipotle chile.

1 can (28 ounces) crushed Italian plum tomatoes, preferably San Marzano
¾ teaspoon dried oregano
3 cloves Garlic Confit (page 414), mashed, or 3 fresh garlic cloves, peeled and minced
2 tablespoons extra-virgin olive oil
2 tablespoons finely minced yellow or white onion
1 teaspoon sugar, or to taste
Salt and freshly ground black pepper, to taste
6 fresh basil leaves, coarsely torn

1. Place the tomatoes, oregano, garlic confit (if using), and 1 tablespoon of the oil in a medium-size saucepan and bring to the start of a simmer over medium heat, stirring occasionally.

2. Meanwhile, place a small skillet over medium-high heat, and when the pan is hot, add the remaining 1 tablespoon oil. Reduce the heat to medium and cook the minced onion, stirring frequently, until it is soft, about 5 minutes. If you are using minced garlic (not garlic confit), add the garlic to the skillet and cook, stirring frequently, until the garlic is fragrant, about 2 minutes. Add the onion-garlic mixture to the tomato sauce.

3. Simmer the sauce over medium-low heat, stirring frequently, until it has thickened slightly, about 15 minutes. Taste the sauce, and if it is too acidic, add the teaspoon of sugar, or more or less to taste. Season with salt and pepper and stir in the basil leaves. Remove the sauce from the heat and cool to room temperature. The sauce can be refrigerated, covered, for up to 5 days or frozen for up to 3 months.

Roasted Tomatillo Salsa

SALSA IS SO SIMPLE TO MAKE, and homemade is much fresher-tasting than store-bought versions. Best of all, you control the amount of garlic and the heat, so it's a custom blend of your favorite flavors. Our version balances the sweet-tangy edge of roasted tomatillos, the complexity and richness of roasted garlic, and the smoky heat and spice of both jalapeño and chipotle chiles. Serve the salsa with grilled meats or chicken, add it to soup, mix it with sour cream for a vegetable dip, or use it as a condiment with Fish Tacos (page 139). This is a necessary accompaniment to our Chicken and Green Olive Enchiladas (page 109). ⟿ **Makes about 1¼ cups**

1 pound (about 8 large) tomatillos, husked
   and rinsed (see sidebar, page 98)

6 large garlic cloves, peeled

½ medium yellow or white onion, cut into
   6 chunks

1 jalapeño chile, cut in half and seeded

1 tablespoon olive oil

1 teaspoon salt, or to taste

1 canned chipotle chile in adobo sauce
   (see sidebar, facing page), or more to taste

¾ cup (loosely packed) fresh cilantro leaves

1. Position a rack in the middle of the oven and preheat the oven to 375°F.

2. Place the tomatillos, garlic, onion, jalapeño, oil, and salt in a glass baking dish and toss or stir to coat the vegetables. Roast until the vegetables are very soft, about 1 hour.

3. Transfer the mixture to a food processor, and add the chipotle chile and cilantro. Pulse until coarsely pureed. Pour the salsa into a clean bowl, and let it cool. Serve chilled or at room temperature.

Grilled Corn Salsa

SWEET AND SMOKY FROM A BRIEF STINT ON THE GRILL, fresh corn really makes this pretty salsa sing. It's not fiery hot, but you can certainly increase the heat by adding chile peppers. If you prefer not to turn on the grill, use a cast-iron skillet to brown the corn. We like this salsa served as a condiment with our Fish Tacos (page 139) and with Seared Salmon with Chipotle-Lime Butter (page 136). ⌇⌇⌇ *Makes about 5½ cups*

4 ears fresh corn, shucked, silk removed

2 teaspoons canola oil

Salt and freshly ground black pepper

1½ cups diced tomatoes (¼-inch dice;
   about 3 small tomatoes)

¼ cup finely diced red onion

3 tablespoons chopped fresh cilantro

1 tablespoon fresh lemon juice

1 tablespoon thinly sliced scallion,
   green part only

1. Set up a barbecue grill and preheat it to high. (Alternatively, heat a cast-iron skillet over high heat.)

2. Rub the ears of corn with the canola oil, and season with salt and pepper. Grill the corn (or cook in the skillet), turning it frequently, until lightly browned all over, 3 to 4 minutes on each side.

Cilantro

Cilantro is an herb that plays an important role in the culinary traditions of China, India, and Latin America. It looks similar to Italian (flat-leaf) parsley, and is sometimes referred to as "Chinese parsley." Coriander, a popular spice, is the seed of mature cilantro plants.

Not many foods have as many adamant fans and foes as cilantro— people seem to love it or hate it. There are even some controversial theories that there is a gene some people have that makes cilantro taste like soap on their tongues!

When buying cilantro, choose bunches that have firm, bright green leaves, avoiding ones that are yellowing or spotty. Cilantro can be stored in the refrigerator for up to a week if it is fresh. It loses its flavor quickly when heated, so it's best to add it to a dish after it's been cooked, or use it raw as a garnish.

3. Transfer the corn to a bowl, cover, and let steam until the kernels are tender, 5 to 10 minutes. When the corn is cool enough to handle, cut the kernels off the cobs (you should have about 4 cups).

4. Place the kernels in a medium-size bowl and add the tomatoes, onion, cilantro, lemon juice, and scallions. Stir to combine, and let the salsa rest at room temperature for 30 minutes to develop the flavors before serving. Season with salt and pepper to taste. The salsa can be refrigerated, covered, for up to 2 days.

Black Bean and Corn Salsa

THIS IS A VARIATION ON OUR LIGHT AND FRESH-TASTING Grilled Corn Salsa. We've added black beans to make it more substantial. A touch of cumin contributes a subtle dimension to the salsa, enhancing the mild flavor of the beans. We encourage you to cook your own beans, but if time is short, you can substitute a 15-ounce can. Just be sure to rinse and drain the beans before adding them to the salsa. —*mm*— *Makes about 7½ cups*

4 ears fresh corn, shucked, silk removed

2 teaspoons canola oil

Salt and freshly ground black pepper

**2 cups cooked black beans
   (see box, page 422)**

**1½ cups diced tomatoes (¼-inch dice;
   about 3 small tomatoes)**

¼ cup finely diced red onion

3 tablespoons chopped fresh cilantro

1 tablespoon fresh lime juice

**1 tablespoon thinly sliced scallion,
   green part only**

1 tablespoon ground cumin

1. Set up a barbecue grill and preheat it to high. (Alternatively, heat a cast-iron skillet over high heat.)

2. Rub the ears of corn with the canola oil, and season with salt and pepper. Grill the corn (or cook it in the skillet), turning it frequently, until lightly browned all over, 3 to 4 minutes on each side.

3. Transfer the corn to a bowl, cover, and let steam until the kernels are tender, 5 to 10 minutes. When the corn is cool enough to handle, cut the kernels off the cobs (you should have about 4 cups).

4. Place the kernels in a medium-size bowl and add the black beans, tomatoes, onion, cilantro, lime juice, scallion, and cumin. Stir to combine, and let the salsa rest at room temperature for 30 minutes to develop the flavors before serving. Season with salt and pepper to taste. The salsa can be refrigerated, covered, for up to 2 days.

Farm Stand Pico de Gallo

P*ICO DE GALLO* (SPANISH FOR "ROOSTER'S BEAK") is a fresh salsa typically served as a condiment with tacos, fish, eggs, meat, and poultry dishes. It's easy to make and adds a terrific zestiness to just about everything. We like it with our Fish Tacos (page 139) or Tofu Scramble (page 378), and it even makes a great dip for chips. This salsa is especially good made with heirloom tomatoes when they're in season. ⎯⎯ *Makes about 2⅓ cups*

2 cups diced fresh tomatoes (¼-inch dice;
    about 3 medium tomatoes)
½ cup finely minced red onion
½ jalapeño pepper, seeded and finely
    minced
⅓ cup chopped fresh cilantro
1½ teaspoons fresh lemon juice
Salt and freshly ground black pepper

Combine the tomatoes, red onion, jalapeño, cilantro, and lemon juice in a small bowl and stir to combine. Season with salt and pepper to taste. Let sit at room temperature for 30 minutes before serving, to allow the flavors to develop. If making in advance, refrigerate, covered, for up to 5 days.

Farm Stand Pico de Gallo and Grilled Corn Salsa (page 419)

How to Cook Dried Beans

When you cook your own beans, you save both money and natural resources. Dried beans are a nutritional powerhouse of protein, fiber, and iron and a valuable component of every pantry. There are numerous ways to cook dried beans, and several methods involve presoaking, which will shorten the cooking time. To presoak dried beans, place them in a large pot with cold water to cover. If you have the time, presoak small beans for 4 hours; large beans for 8 hours or overnight. If you're short on time, quick-soak the beans by boiling them in water to cover for 1 minute. Then remove from the heat, cover the pot, and let sit for an hour. With either method, drain the beans and cover them with fresh water or other liquid for cooking. One pound of beans will yield 5 to 6 cups when cooked.

1 pound dried beans

Cold water

Salt and freshly ground black pepper

1. Pick through the beans, removing any pebbles or clumps of dirt. Rinse them thoroughly.
2. Place the beans in a large pot and add cold water to cover by 2 to 3 inches. Bring the water to a boil over high heat; then reduce the heat to maintain a slow simmer. Partially cover the pot and cook, stirring occasionally, until the beans are close to tender. The cooking time can range from 30 minutes to 4 hours, depending on the variety and age of the beans (see box for approximate times), and whether or not you presoaked them. Sample them frequently to gauge doneness, adding more water as necessary to keep the beans covered.
3. When the beans are tender, add salt and pepper to taste. Continue to simmer until they are cooked to the texture you prefer. Let the beans cool in their liquid, and then refrigerate, tightly covered, for up to 5 days.

Tips on Cooking Dried Beans

◆ Always cook beans in plenty of water and at a very slow simmer (the water should barely bubble) so that they will remain intact and have room to expand.

◆ Add salt during the last 15 minutes of cooking, when the beans are nearly ready. Adding salt too early causes the skin of the bean to seize and resist absorption of water, which results in tough beans.

◆ Add a few sprigs of fresh herbs, a crushed garlic clove, and one or two large pieces of aromatic vegetables (such as onion, carrot, celery, or leek) to your pot of beans to flavor the cooking water. You can also use chicken stock or a combination of stock and water.

◆ Squeeze gently to test if a bean is tender—it should feel soft through to the center.

◆ Store cooked beans, tightly covered, in the refrigerator for up to 5 days.

◆ Cooked beans can be frozen for up to 3 months. Spread the drained beans in a single layer on a baking sheet and freeze. Then transfer the frozen beans to an airtight container.

◆ Ideally, buy dried beans that have been harvested and dried within the past year. Because this can be difficult or impossible to determine, purchase beans at a store that has a large selection and quick turnover. Those that are old take longer to cook and are more difficult to rehydrate and prepare.

◆ Store dried beans in a dark cupboard; some of their nutrients deteriorate quickly when exposed to light.

Cooking Times for Dried Beans

Cooking times are affected by the age and type of beans you use, so this chart is a very rough approximation, not a precise guide. Average times are given for both the presoak (8 hours or overnight) and no-soak methods.

Variety	No-Soak Cook Time	Presoak Cook Time
Black beans	1¼ hours	1 hour
Black-eyed peas	1 hour	40 minutes
Borlotti, cranberry, and pinto	1¼ hours	1 hour
Cannellini	1¾ hours	1¼ hours
Chickpeas	2 hours	1¼ hours
Great Northern	1¼ hours	1 hour
Kidney	1¼ hours	30 minutes

Quince and Pear Chutney

I F YOU'VE NEVER COOKED WITH QUINCE BEFORE, you're in for a pleasant surprise. Although they closely resemble apples, this heirloom fruit is refreshingly distinctive (see box, page 330). With sticky skins, a large proportion of seeds and core, and tart flesh, quinces are more obstinate to prepare than apples, but the extra bit of effort involved is rewarded by their haunting fragrance and flavor. Here we've created a sweet-spicy condiment that makes a delicious accompaniment to roast pork, chicken, or turkey. Quince pairs beautifully with other autumn fruits, and juicy pears make an exceptional partner. Ginger, in both fresh and crystallized forms, enlivens the mixture and adds a counterpoint of spice and heat to the chutney. Verjus is the juice of unripe grapes and is nonalcoholic; look for it at specialty stores. ⎯⎯ *Makes about 4 cups*

1½ cups verjus or fruity white wine,
     such as Riesling or Viognier

1 cup sugar, or more to taste

1 star anise pod

1 cinnamon stick (3 inches), broken in half

¼ cup finely grated peeled fresh ginger

2 cups diced peeled quince (½-inch dice;
     about 3 medium quinces)

3 large firm pears, cored, peeled, and
     cut into ½-inch dice (about 3 cups)

½ cup golden raisins

¼ cup finely diced crystallized ginger

1. Combine the verjus or wine, sugar, star anise, cinnamon stick, and grated fresh ginger in a medium-size saucepan. Bring to a boil over medium-high heat, stirring frequently until the sugar dissolves. Reduce the heat to medium and cook, uncovered, for 10 minutes. Add the quince and cook for 5 minutes. Then add the pears and raisins. Reduce the heat to low and simmer the mixture until the quince and pears are tender but not mushy, 15 to 20 minutes.

2. Remove the pan from the heat and skim off any foam. Stir in the crystallized ginger.

3. Spoon or ladle the hot chutney into clean glass jars, cover tightly, and let sit at room temperature until cool. The chutney can be refrigerated for up to 6 months. Discard the cinnamon stick and star anise pod before serving.

Fresh Strawberry Jam

W HEN STRAWBERRIES ARE AT THEIR PEAK AND PRICES have fallen to a seasonal low, set aside an hour to make a batch of homemade jam. Making jam is an age-old pastime: one that connects us with the land and the rhythm of the seasons. Best of all is the vibrant flavor. There is nothing mysterious about jam making. This recipe requires just four ingredients and no special tools. Our version is less sweet than traditional jams and sets to a slightly looser consistency, but we like its true fruit flavor. If you want to improvise on this basic recipe, get creative and add spices, liqueurs, or candied ginger. Long after summer-sweet berries have disappeared, it will be a pleasure to pull a jar of jam out of your pantry to share with family and friends—a treat that will be welcomed by all. ⸻ *Makes about 4 half-pints*

Fresh Strawberry Jam

3 pounds fresh strawberries, hulled and finely chopped or coarsely mashed (to make 6 cups)
1 cup sugar
3 tablespoons fresh lemon juice

1. Combine the strawberries and sugar in a heavy-bottomed 6- or 8-quart saucepan. Cover and bring the mixture to a full rolling boil, and then reduce the heat to maintain a simmer. Cook, stirring frequently, until the jam is thick, 30 to 40 minutes. In the latter stages of cooking, watch carefully so that the jam does not scorch.

2. Remove the pan from the heat and skim off any foam. Stir in the lemon juice.

3. Spoon or ladle the hot jam into clean glass or sterilized canning jars, filling them to within ⅛ inch of the top. Seal them following the manufacturer's directions. (You will need four half-pint jars.) If you are not using sealed canning jars, allow the jam to cool completely and then transfer it to clean containers with tight-fitting lids. The regular containers of jam will keep, covered and refrigerated, for up to 2 months.

Sweet Pie Crust

THIS RICH, BUTTERY PASTRY CRUST IS LIGHT AND TENDER, perfect for fruit pies and tarts. I find the food processor technique the quickest and least messy method for making pie dough. It's almost foolproof—just be sure not to overwork the dough in the machine or the pastry will be tough. For directions on making pastry by hand, see sidebar, this page. *Makes enough for 2 single-crust pies or 1 double-crust pie, 9 to 10 inches in diameter*

2½ cups unbleached all-purpose flour, plus extra for rolling out the dough

2 tablespoons sugar

¼ teaspoon salt

1 cup (2 sticks) cold unsalted butter, cut into ½-inch pieces

¼ cup ice water, or more as needed

1. Place the flour, sugar, and salt in a food processor and process to blend. Add the butter and pulse until the mixture looks like coarse meal.

2. With the machine running, add the ice water and process just until the dough holds together loosely in a ball, 5 to 8 seconds. Do not allow the dough to form a solid mass or it will be overworked. Test the dough by pinching a small amount between your fingers. If the dough is not moist enough to form a cohesive mass, add an additional tablespoon of ice water, process briefly, and test again.

3. Turn the dough out onto a large piece of parchment paper and divide it in half. Form each half into a flat disk. Wrap a piece of parchment paper around each piece of dough to cover it, and refrigerate until chilled, 20 to 30 minutes. (If you intend to chill the dough overnight or freeze it, tightly wrap the pieces in plastic wrap. The wrapped dough can be frozen for up to 3 months. Let the frozen dough thaw overnight in the refrigerator before rolling out.)

Making Pie Crusts by Hand

If you don't own a food processor, here is the technique for making pastry by hand:

1. Place the flour, sugar, and salt in a large bowl and whisk to blend.

2. Add the butter and cut it into the flour with your fingertips until it resembles coarse meal.

3. Add the water and mix it into the dough with a rubber spatula, using a folding motion to moisten all of the dough. Press the dough into a rough ball against the side of the bowl with the broad side of the spatula.

4. Continue with the Sweet Pie Crust recipe at Step 3.

4. Remove the dough from the refrigerator (for a single-crust pie you'll need one disk of dough; for a double-crust pie you'll need both disks), and open the parchment paper to a flat rectangle. If it was refrigerated for more than 1 hour, let it sit at room temperature for 10 to 20 minutes to soften slightly. (If the dough is too cold or firm, it will crack when you try to roll it out.) Lightly dust a work surface and rolling pin with flour. Roll the dough into a round about ⅛ inch thick and 2 inches larger than your pie plate.

5. Fold the dough in half or drape it over the rolling pin, and transfer it to the pie plate. Press the dough firmly into the pie plate, and brush off any excess flour with a pastry brush. If there are holes or cracks, press the dough back together or patch them with small bits of the overhanging dough.

6. *For a single-crust pie,* trim the dough with a pair of kitchen scissors, leaving a ¾-inch overhang. Fold the edge under to form a double layer, and crimp or flute it.

For a double-crust pie, fit the dough for the bottom crust into the pie plate and trim the dough even with the rim. Roll out the second disk of dough. Place the filling in the bottom crust and place the dough for the second crust on top. Trim the top crust with scissors, leaving a ½-inch overhang. Fold the top crust under the edge of the bottom crust, and crimp or flute it to seal.

7. Cut three slits in the center of the top crust with a sharp knife to allow steam to vent as the pie bakes.

Flaky Multigrain Pie Crust

AT OUR FARM STAND we use whole wheat pastry flour and rolled oats in lieu of refined white flour whenever possible in our recipes. Creating a delicious-tasting, light, and workable pastry crust was a challenge, but we think the result is spectacular. This pie dough is extremely easy to make, and as an added bonus, it's also very easy to handle. The result is a light, flaky crust with a pronounced nutty, buttery flavor. The recipe can be doubled and the dough refrigerated for up to 3 days or frozen for up to 3 months. Let the frozen dough thaw overnight in the refrigerator before rolling it out. ⎯⎯ ***Makes enough for 2 single-crust pies or 1 double-crust pie, 8 to 9 inches in diameter***

1¼ cups unbleached all-purpose flour,
   plus extra for rolling out the dough
½ cup whole wheat pastry flour
½ cup old-fashioned rolled oats
   (see sidebar, page 307)
1 tablespoon sugar
¼ teaspoon salt
12 tablespoons (1½ sticks) cold unsalted
   butter, cut into ½-inch pieces
2 tablespoons ice water, or more as
   needed

1. Place the white and whole wheat flours, rolled oats, sugar, and salt in a food processor and process until the mixture is combined and the oats have been pulverized to a flourlike meal. Add the butter and pulse until the mixture looks like coarse meal.

2. With the machine running, add the ice water and process just until the dough holds together loosely in a ball, 5 to 8 seconds. Do not allow the dough to form a solid mass or it will be overworked. Test the dough by pinching a small amount between your fingers. If the dough sticks together, it is ready. If the dough is not moist enough to form a cohesive mass, add an additional ½ tablespoon ice water, process briefly, and test again.

3. Turn the dough out onto a large piece of parchment paper and divide it in half. Form each half into a flat disk. Wrap a piece of parchment paper around each piece

of dough to cover it, and refrigerate until chilled, 20 to 30 minutes. (If you intend to chill the dough overnight or freeze it, wrap the pieces tightly in plastic wrap. The wrapped dough can be frozen for up to 3 months. Let the frozen dough thaw overnight in the refrigerator before rolling out.)

4. Remove the dough from the refrigerator (for a single-crust pie you'll need one disk of dough; for a double-crust pie you'll need both disks), and open the parchment paper to a flat rectangle. If it was refrigerated for more than an hour, let it sit at room temperature for 10 to 20 minutes to soften slightly. (If the dough is too cold or firm, it will crack when you try to roll it out.) Lightly dust a work surface and rolling pin with all-purpose flour. Roll the dough into a round about ⅛ inch thick and 2 inches larger than your pie plate.

5. Fold the dough in half or drape it over the rolling pin and transfer it to the pie plate. Press the dough firmly into the pie plate and brush off any excess flour with a pastry brush. If there are holes or cracks, press the dough back together or patch them with small bits of the overhanging dough.

6. *For a single-crust pie,* trim the dough with a pair of kitchen scissors, leaving a ¾-inch overhang. Fold the edge under to form a double layer, and crimp or flute it.

LIVING GREEN
Most natural foods stores have self-serve bulk bins of dozens of foods, including beans, grains, cereals, nuts, seeds, and spices. Buying in bulk (especially if you bring your own reused plastic bag) cuts down on packaging and also avoids food waste. It allows you to buy only as much as you need, so you're less likely to have extra food around that has passed its expiration date. I like to save my spice bottles when they're empty, and then buy the spices in bulk to refill the jars. Buying in bulk not only saves natural resources, it saves money, too, because packaging adds a significant cost to food products.

For a double-crust pie, fit the dough for the bottom crust into the pie plate and trim the dough even with the rim. Roll out the second disk of dough. Place the filling in the bottom crust and place the dough for the second crust on top. Trim the top crust with scissors, leaving a ½-inch overhang. Fold the top crust under the edge of the bottom crust, and crimp or flute to seal.

7. Cut three slits in the center of the top crust with a sharp knife to allow steam to vent as the pie bakes.

YOUR GREEN KITCHEN

Freezing Fresh Produce

When there's a seasonal bounty of fresh fruits and vegetables, it makes good sense to preserve some of it for later use. Here are some guidelines to help you get the best results:

VEGETABLES

Firm vegetables such as fresh beans, carrots, parsnips, broccoli, cauliflower, peas, and favas can be frozen with very good results. High water content vegetables like tomatoes, summer squash, and eggplant do not freeze well. This type of vegetable should be cooked first, cooled completely, and then frozen.

Select vegetables at their peak of quality and freshness.

Vegetables need to be blanched to prevent deterioration. Bring at least 4 quarts of water to a full boil and add 2 tablespoons of salt. Parboil the vegetables 1 to 3 minutes (1 minute for soft items such as peas and favas; 2 minutes for medium-textured vegetables like broccoli and beans; 3 minutes for woody produce such as carrots). Drain, and plunge them into an ice-water bath to stop the cooking process. When cool, drain again, and dry them thoroughly. Spread vegetables in a single layer without touching on parchment-lined baking sheets and freeze until solid. Once frozen, transfer produce to freezer bags, removing as much air as possible.

Use frozen vegetables without thawing; cooking times will be about 50 percent faster than with fresh vegetables.

FRUITS

Berries, stone fruits, apples, pears, pineapple, mango, figs, and rhubarb all freeze successfully. Citrus fruits do not, although you can juice them, and freeze the juice.

Choose fruits that are in good condition and not over-ripe, soft, or bruised.

Wash and dry fruits and berries before freezing. Spread fruit slices or berries in a single layer without touching on parchment-lined baking sheets and freeze until solid. Once frozen, transfer produce to freezer bags, removing as much air as possible to avoid freezer burn. Air shortens shelf life and negatively affects food color, flavor, and texture. Label packages or containers with the item name and the date. Frozen produce has a 3- to 6-month shelf life.

Use frozen fruit without thawing in recipes, or defrost in the refrigerator. After freezing, the texture of thawed fruit will be softer than that of fresh fruit.

Buckwheat Crêpes

BUCKWHEAT CREPES ARE STURDIER than ones made with white flour, and thus better suited to an array of hearty fillings such as eggs, mushrooms, creamed spinach, or ham and cheese. We think they taste delicious and work perfectly with sweet fillings as well; see the recipe for Banana–Chocolate Chip Crêpes on page 340.

The key to the perfect crêpe lies in technique. Once the batter hits the hot pan, you must quickly tilt and swirl the pan so the batter spreads into a thin round. The old adage "practice makes perfect" is especially true for the art of crêpe making. The proper pan is also important. French steel crêpe pans, with shallow sloping sides, are available at good cookware stores, but I think that a cast-iron skillet is the best choice because it retains the heat exceptionally well. Crêpes can be made a day or two ahead of serving. Simply stack them neatly on a piece of parchment paper as you make them, and when they are cool, wrap the stack tightly in plastic wrap and refrigerate. ⬗⬗⬗ ***Makes about fifteen 10-inch crêpes***

⅔ cup buckwheat flour (see sidebars,
    this page and page 430)
⅓ cup unbleached all-purpose flour
¼ teaspoon salt
2 cups low-fat (2%) milk, or more if needed
2 large eggs
About ¼ cup (½ stick) unsalted butter

1. Place both flours and the salt in a medium-size bowl and whisk to combine. Add 1½ cups of the milk and whisk to combine. Add the eggs and whisk until the batter is smooth. (You can also make the batter in a blender or with an immersion blender if you prefer.) Transfer the batter to a large measuring cup with a spout or to a pitcher. The batter can be used immediately, or you can cover it with plastic wrap and refrigerate it overnight.

2. Before cooking the crêpes, add ¼ to ½ cup of the remaining milk to the batter, depending on how thick it has become while resting, and whisk to combine. The batter should resemble fairly thin pancake batter and should be whisked before making each crêpe.

3. Melt the butter in a small saucepan and keep it warm.

4. Place a 12-inch skillet, preferably cast-iron, over medium heat, and when the skillet is hot, brush it with some of the melted butter. Pour or ladle a scant ¼ cup of the batter into the center of the skillet, lift the skillet off the heat, and tilt and swirl the skillet so that the batter spreads thinly in a widening circle across the bottom. Don't worry

THE BASICS

Buckwheat

Buckwheat, despite its name, is not related to wheat. In fact, it's not a true grain at all but is a flowering plant, related to sorrel and rhubarb, that is native to Central Asia. The triangular seeds, called groats, can be milled into a nutritious flour that is gluten-free and high in protein, fiber, iron, and magnesium. Buckwheat flour has a distinctive, assertive flavor. It's a common ingredient in pancake mixes and soba noodles, and is most famously associated with blinis, the thick Russian pancakes traditionally served with caviar. Buckwheat flour is also no stranger to the French, who use it in making savory crêpes, sometimes called galettes.

Buckwheat Flour

To make your own buckwheat flour, process whole buckwheat groats in a blender or food processor until very fine and powdery.

if the crêpe is not a perfect round. If there are some small holes in the crêpe, simply dot some of the crêpe batter on the holes and they will fill in quickly. Return the skillet to the heat and cook until tiny bubbles begin to appear in the crêpe batter; depending on how hot the pan is, the crêpe will be ready to flip in 15 to 30 seconds. Using a spatula, lift up one corner of the crêpe to check if the cooked surface is golden around the edges. If it is, flip the crêpe over, using the spatula.

5. Cook the crêpe on the second side until it is lightly golden, 15 to 30 seconds. Then transfer the crêpe to a parchment-lined plate, cover it loosely with a towel, and repeat with the remaining batter, stacking the crêpes as you go. Make sure to brush the crêpe pan with butter before cooking each crêpe. The batter will thicken as it rests, so thin it with a tablespoon or two of milk as needed, and whisk it before making each crêpe. For thin, lacy crêpes you need a fairly thin batter.

creating a sustainable future

A simple definition of environmental sustainability is "to use the resources we have inherited in ways that protect and preserve them for our children, their children, and their children's children." This means not using our resources faster than they can regenerate themselves, or creating waste that far outlasts the products we produce.

Taking the health of our planet for granted has led us down a dangerous path, but I believe we can find a way to live in balance if we always remember that this Earth is our only home—we have no other. We are all truly earthbound—wholly *dependent* on our planet for fresh air, healthy food, and clean water—and not *independent* of its natural limitations.

Today, we face an additional challenge to living sustainably: Not only must we find ongoing ways to live within our planet's means, we also need to repair existing environmental damage. Our oceans and rivers are polluted; our planet is warming; we're over-reliant on fossil fuels; and we've created mountains of waste.

These problems can feel overwhelming, but we all hold the power to make small changes in our daily lives that have significant, positive impacts. The choices we make about the foods we eat are powerful and far-reaching. In my kitchen I am often keenly aware of the delicious and miraculous abundance of this Earth, and I feel grateful and protective. In preparing food for the family I cherish, I am inspired to take meaningful steps to safeguard this bounty for generations to come.

Savory Nut Mix

A WORD OF WARNING: THESE NUTS ARE ADDICTIVE. Lightly coated with a mixture of pure maple syrup, oregano, and thyme, with a subtle kick of cayenne, they make an irresistible cocktail nibble. We suggest these nuts as a crunchy topping for our Curried Garnet Yam Soup (page 21) and like them with salads, too, such as Chopped Autumn Salad (page 62) or Escarole with Walnuts, Dates, and Bacon (page 59). They make a delicious, nutritious snack and a perfect hostess gift. The nuts will keep, tightly covered, at room temperature for up to 3 weeks. ⎯⎯ *Makes 6 cups*

½ cup pure maple syrup

3 tablespoons olive oil

1 teaspoon salt

1 teaspoon cayenne pepper

1½ teaspoons dried oregano

1½ teaspoons dried thyme

1½ cups whole almonds (skin on)

1½ cups walnut halves and pieces

1½ cups blanched hazelnuts

1½ cups pecan halves

1. Position a rack in the middle of the oven, and preheat the oven to 300°F. Line a rimmed baking sheet with parchment paper or aluminum foil, preferably recycled.

2. Combine the maple syrup, olive oil, salt, cayenne, oregano, and thyme in a medium-size bowl and whisk to blend. Add all the nuts and stir to thoroughly coat.

3. Pour the nut mixture onto the prepared baking sheet, and spread the nuts into a single layer. Bake, stirring several times, until the nuts are fragrant and lightly browned, 35 to 45 minutes. Cool completely before storing at room temperature in an airtight container for up to 3 weeks.

Garam Masala

GARAM MASALA IS A BLEND OF GROUND DRY-ROASTED SPICES that is traditionally used in regional Indian cuisine. There may be as many recipes for this spice blend as there are cooks in India. Although you can buy it prepared, it's fun and easy to make your own, and it will usually be fresher than anything you find in the market. Try it in the Curried Garnet Yam Soup (page 21). Don't be tempted to skip the dry-roasting step, as this is what contributes the depth of flavor to the spices. The spices can be ground in a mortar with a pestle, if you don't have a spice (coffee) grinder.

Makes about ½ cup

**1 cinnamon stick (3 inches),
   broken into 3 pieces**

1 teaspoon whole black peppercorns

1 tablespoon cumin seeds

1 teaspoon fennel seeds

1 tablespoon coriander seeds

1 teaspoon black mustard seeds

1 teaspoon ground fenugreek

1 teaspoon ground allspice

1 tablespoon chili powder

1 tablespoon ground turmeric

1½ tablespoons ground ginger

1. Combine the cinnamon stick, the peppercorns, and the cumin, fennel, coriander, and mustard seeds in a small skillet and toast over medium heat until the mixture is hot to the touch and fragrant, 4 to 8 minutes. Do not allow the pan to smoke. Remove the pan from the heat and let cool completely.

2. Transfer the toasted spices to a spice grinder and grind to a fine powder. Transfer the mixture to a small bowl and add the ground fenugreek, allspice, chili powder, turmeric, and ginger, whisking to blend.

3. Store the Garam Masala in an airtight bottle for up to 6 months, keeping it away from heat and light.

APPENDIX

green kitchen design

When I wanted to research green kitchen design for this book, I contacted April Sheldon, a San Francisco interior designer, whom I've worked with for over a dozen years. She has a long history with green design and a passion for creating beautiful, eco-friendly living spaces. I asked her to give us some tips.

The goal of green design is to make the kitchen healthy for both people and the planet. April explains that even though the initial cost of green design is sometimes a bit more, future household expenses for energy and water will be reduced.

There are many green design choices for the kitchen, and April broke them down into four basic categories: (1) energy-efficient appliances; (2) energy-efficient lighting; (3) water-conserving appliances and plumbing fixtures; and (4) nontoxic, sustainably produced building and decorating materials. You certainly don't have to completely remodel your kitchen to go green, but if a construction project or a new appliance is in your future, here are some things to consider.

1. Energy-Efficient Appliances

Look for appliances with an Energy Star label.

◆ The Energy Star label is given by the U.S. Environmental Protection Agency (EPA) and the Department of Energy (DOE) to appliances and products that exceed federal energy efficiency standards. One of the main goals of the Energy Star program is to develop performance-based specifications that determine the most efficient products in a particular category.

◆ Look for the Energy Star label on cooktops, ovens, dishwashers, and refrigerators. Study the Energy Star rating to find the kilowatt use of an appliance.

Remember, a larger appliance will probably use more energy, so don't buy a larger one than you need.

Some tips for choosing an energy-efficient refrigerator:

◆ Models with the freezer on top use the least amount of energy. Bottom-freezer models use more. Side-by-side models use the most.

◆ Water dispensers in the refrigerator door and ice makers can increase energy consumption by as much as 14 to 20 percent.

2. Energy-Efficient Lighting

◆ Whenever possible, use natural lighting.

◆ Use CFL (compact fluorescent lighting) bulbs instead of incandescent bulbs. CFLs are four times more efficient and last up to ten times longer than incandescent bulbs.

Replacing a single incandescent bulb with a CFL will keep a half-ton of carbon dioxide (CO_2) emissions out of the atmosphere over the life of the bulb. If everyone in the U.S. used energy-efficient lighting, we could retire ninety average-size power plants.

◆ Consider using LED (light-emitting diode) lights: small, solid light bulbs, which are extremely energy-efficient. New LED bulbs are grouped in clusters with diffuser lenses that have broadened the applications for LED use in the home. These are wonderful for under-counter lighting.

LEDs last up to ten times longer than CFLs and far longer than typical incandescent bulbs, making them cost efficient in the long run. They do not cause heat buildup, producing 3.4 BTUs per hour compared to 85 for incandescent bulbs. LEDs are mercury-free and efficient, using one-third the energy of incandescent bulbs and one-thirtieth of CFLs.

3. Water-Conserving Appliances and Fixtures

◆ Most Energy Star dishwashers also conserve water. In the future, kitchen faucets will probably carry the EPA's Water Sense Label as well (this label is currently on selected bathroom plumbing fixtures only and verifies water efficiency and performance, backed by independent testing and certification).

◆ Install water aerators in faucets if they are not already built into your model.

4. Nontoxic, Sustainable Building and Decorating Materials

FSC Certified Woods

Look for the FSC (Forest Stewardship Council) seal for all new woods. FSC-certified woods are harvested from responsibly managed forests. This means that the wood is grown in a manner that replenishes the forest, and that biodiversity as well as air and water quality are preserved. FSC certification ensures environmental responsibility, social equity, and economic viability. FSC certification is applicable for reclaimed and salvaged wood as well as virgin material.

Recycled materials

Consider building materials that contain recycled materials. Look for a high percentage of post-consumer recycled content (PCR).

Nontoxic paints, glues, and laminated products

Look for a low- or no-VOC (volatile organic compounds) rating on glues, paints, and laminated products. VOCs are chemicals that become a gas at room temperature. This is called off-gassing. Breathing in high concentrations of many of these chemicals can cause health and environmental problems, so look for the VOC content on the label or in the product literature. Usually listed in grams per liter, VOC content can range from 5 to 200. Using a product with the lowest VOC content will yield the lowest overall health risk. Ask the manufacturer if the product has been manufactured with VOCs, such as formaldehyde or other toxic chemicals.

Nontoxic maintenance

Consider a material's maintenance. Will it require future treatments with toxic sealants or cleaners? For example, stone countertops are often factory-sealed with products that contain toxic petroleum distillates with high levels of VOCs. Ask the manufacturer about this and inquire about safer water-based options.

Responsible suppliers

When purchasing some materials, such as stone, there are no regulations or environmental certifications to show that your material has been responsibly produced or quarried, avoiding damage to the earth, air, and waterways. The best course is to find a trusted supplier or fabricator who is able to answer your questions and explain how the materials were produced.

Shipping miles

Take into account how far the materials were shipped. A material may be eco-friendly, but if it's shipped from overseas, that adds a lot to its carbon footprint—especially if the material is heavy, like stone.

pros and cons of some building materials

◆ **Bamboo (floors, butcher-block countertops, cabinets)**

Pros: Fast growing, renewable, and commonly grown without pesticides and fertilizers.

Cons: Often shipped from Asia, which adds to its carbon footprint.

Green: Look for bamboo material that has been manufactured without formaldehyde glues.

◆ **Cork (floors)**

Pros: Rapidly renewable, made from the bark of the cork tree.

Cons: May have been shipped from Europe, which adds to its carbon footprint.

Green: Use low- or no-VOC adhesives and sealants.

◆ **Cement Concrete (floors, countertops)**

Pros: Made from natural minerals, often · hardened with recycled fly ash (residue scraped out of coal smokestacks).

Cons: Often finished with noxious stains, so the finishing process can be toxic, although it is inert when dry.

Green: Use high volume of fly ash, the noncombustible mineral portions of coal, which makes concrete harder; its use avoids the need to put it in landfill. Use water-based or low-VOC sealants.

◆ **Linoleum (floors)**

Pros: Made from linseed oil and recycled wood parts. It's biodegradable.

Cons: Often shipped from Europe, which adds to its carbon footprint. Slight odor from linseed oil.

Green: Install with low-VOC adhesives. Do not confuse with sheet vinyl flooring, which is actually polyvinyl chloride.

◆ **Natural stone (floors, countertops)**

Pros: Healthy inert material that lasts for generations. It can often be found in local quarries.

Cons: Not a renewable resource. Stone is heavy, with high energy cost to transport.

Green: Choose local or salvaged stone that you finish with low- or no-VOC sealant.

◆ **Ceramic, porcelain, or glass tile (floors, countertops)**

Pros: Ceramic and porcelain tiles are made with clay, a natural and abundant material. Some tile contains recycled content. Glass tile is often made with recycled content.

Cons: Manufacturing porcelain and ceramic tile is energy-intensive.

Green: Look for tiles with recycled content. Use low- or no-VOC sealants.

◆ **Wood (floors, countertops, cabinets)**

Pros: FSC certification ensures harvesting from well-managed forests and plantations. Some woods are salvaged from old buildings. Some woods are harvested from plantation trees (Durapalm, for example, is made from plantation palm trees that no longer produce coconuts).

Cons: Certified or reclaimed woods may be more expensive.

Green: Avoid engineered floors made with formaldehyde binders.

◆ **Terrazzo tiles and precast slabs (floors, countertops)**

Pros: Terrazzo is made with chips of marble, glass, granite, or other aggregate in a cement binder. Often contains recycled content.

Cons: Traditionally made terrazzo has a cement binder, but some terrazzo materials use an epoxy or resin binder instead of cement. While some of these products are green, you need to ask your supplier to find out if the resin is petroleum-based or contains other compounds that are not eco-friendly.

Green: Look for terrazzo with a high recycled content.

◆ **Paper-based "stone" (countertops)**

Pros: Material is made from post-consumer recycled paper. It's very durable.

Cons: May be hard to find or contractors may be unfamiliar with installation. Manufacturers include PaperStone, ShetkaSTONE, and Richlite.

Green: Make sure that the product is made with petroleum-free resins.

◆ **Polymer sheets made from post-consumer recycled plastic (countertops)**

Pros: Material uses a high percentage of post-consumer recycled plastic.

Cons: Contractors may not be familiar with installation.

Green: Look for a high percentage of recycled content. 3form manufactures a product called 100 Percent, which is made from 100% post-consumer recycled high-density polyethylene, such as detergent bottles.

◆ **Agrifiber (cabinets)**

Pros: Material is made from reclaimed agricultural by-products, such as sorghum straw, coconut shells, wheat stalks.

Cons: May not be available locally.

Green: Make sure that products use nontoxic adhesives. Manufacturers include Kirei and PrimeBoard.

Some Green Materials Certification Programs

Energy Star
Energy-efficient appliances
www.energystar.gov

Forest Stewardship Council (FSC)
Wood from sustainably managed
forestry operations
www.fsc.org

Green Seal
Low-VOC-emitting paints and coatings,
and nontoxic cleaning products
www.greenseal.org

Rediscovered Wood
Products that use reclaimed, recycled,
or salvaged wood
www.rainforest-alliance.org

Scientific Certification Systems
Verification that a product is produced
from recycled content, is biodegradable,
or conforms to other single-attribute
environmental claims.
www.scscertified.com

U.S. Green Building Council
Provides certification, education,
and resources for green buildings
www.usgbc.org

Conversion Tables

approximate equivalents

1 STICK BUTTER = 8 tbs = 4 oz = ½ cup

1 CUP ALL-PURPOSE PRESIFTED FLOUR
OR DRIED BREAD CRUMBS = 5 oz

1 CUP GRANULATED SUGAR = 8 oz

1 CUP (PACKED) BROWN SUGAR = 6 oz

1 CUP CONFECTIONERS' SUGAR = 4½ oz

1 CUP HONEY OR SYRUP = 12 oz

1 CUP GRATED CHEESE = 4 oz

1 CUP DRIED BEANS = 6 oz

1 LARGE EGG = about 2 oz or about 3 tbs

1 EGG YOLK = about 1 tbs

1 EGG WHITE = about 2 tbs

Please note that all conversions are approximate but close enough to be useful when converting from one system to another.

weight conversions

US/UK	METRIC	US/UK	METRIC
½ oz	15 g	7 oz	200 g
1 oz	30 g	8 oz	250 g
1½ oz	45 g	9 oz	275 g
2 oz	60 g	10 oz	300 g
2½ oz	75 g	11 oz	325 g
3 oz	90 g	12 oz	350 g
3½ oz	100 g	13 oz	375 g
4 oz	125 g	14 oz	400 g
5 oz	150 g	15 oz	450 g
6 oz	175 g	1 lb	500 g

liquid conversions

U.S.	IMPERIAL	METRIC
2 tbs	1 fl oz	30 ml
3 tbs	1½ fl oz	45 ml
¼ cup	2 fl oz	60 ml
⅓ cup	2½ fl oz	75 ml
⅓ cup + 1 tbs	3 fl oz	90 ml
⅓ cup + 2 tbs	3½ fl oz	100 ml
½ cup	4 fl oz	125 ml
⅔ cup	5 fl oz	150 ml
¾ cup	6 fl oz	175 ml
¾ cup + 2 tbs	7 fl oz	200 ml
1 cup	8 fl oz	250 ml
1 cup + 2 tbs	9 fl oz	275 ml
1¼ cups	10 fl oz	300 ml
1⅓ cups	11 fl oz	325 ml
1½ cups	12 fl oz	350 ml
1⅔ cups	13 fl oz	375 ml
1¾ cups	14 fl oz	400 ml
1¾ cups + 2 tbs	15 fl oz	450 ml
2 cups (1 pint)	16 fl oz	500 ml
2½ cups	20 fl oz (1 pint)	600 ml
3¾ cups	1½ pints	900 ml
4 cups	1¾ pints	1 liter

oven temperatures

°F	GAS MARK	°C °	F	GAS MARK	°C
250	½	120	400	6	200
275	1	140	425	7	220
300	2	150	450	8	230
325	3	160	475	9	240
350	4	180	500	10	260
375	5	190			

Note: Reduce the temperature by 20°C (68°F) for fan-assisted ovens.

INDEX

Photography Credits

Cover: Author portrait by Scott Campbell; farm photo by Greig Cranna.

Back cover: Recipe photos by Miki Duisterhof; Farm Stand photo by Alli Pura.

Original photography by Miki Duisterhof pgs. xi (top), 3, 10, 15, 24, 29, 61, 75, 90, 91, 93, 111, 118, 125, 135, 139, 140, 142, 149, 167, 181, 184, 194, 199, 202, 207, 214, 223, 231, 237, 243, 250, 259, 262, 299, 304, 305, 306, 316, 333, 344, 349, 354, 362, 365, 370, 375, 396, 421.

Original photography by Patrick Tregenza pgs. ix (right), xvi, 5, 35, 36, 42, 49, 52, 54, 69, 100, 106, 130, 152, 161, 170, 176 (all), 177, 178, 187, 229 (all), 233, 238, 266, 270, 271, 272, 275, 277, 290, 309, 328, 329, 341, 359, 363, 380, 383, 384, 389, 393, 400, 413, 424.

Original photography by Greig Cranna pgs. x (top), xiii, xiv, xvii, 2, 7, 14, 30, 37 (all), 41, 53, 57 (all), 64, 67, 70, 72, 83 (top), 127, 150, 183, 196, 198, 203, 209, 213, 219, 224, 236, 244, 248, 260, 261, 346, 356, 398.

Original photography by Alli Pura pgs. i, viii, 21, 32, 38, 44 (red and green butter lettuces, escarole, frisée, green leaf lettuce, Little Gem), 45 (bottom right), 47(top), 48, 68, 77, 81, 82 (all), 83 (bottom row), 84 (all), 97, 98, 103, 105 (all), 109, 148, 158, 168, 169, 171, 201, 234, 257 (all), 264, 268, 282 (all), 283 (all), 286, 297, 343, 357, 387 (all except bottom right), 402, 410, 418, 431.

Original photography by Scott Campbell p. xii, p. 461.

Original photography by Tom O' Neal p. xv.

Original photography by Batista Moon Studio pgs. 44 (arugula, wild arugula, chard, belgian endive, red endive, red leaf lettuce, entire bottom row), 45 (all except bottom right), 146, 216.

Additional photography from Taurus/ age fotostock america, inc. p. 122; Fotolia: Monika Adamczyk p. 120, Agphotographer p. 432, arnowssr pgs. xi (bottom), 66, Marilyn Barbone p. 255, Joseph Becker p. 16, Miroslav Beneda, p. 128, Ionescu Bogdan p. 288, Silvia Bogdanski p. 330, Yuriy Borysenko p. 172, Pierre Brillot p. 407, Maria Brzostowska p. 210, Alessio Cola p. 23, Marc Dietrich pgs. 94, 414, dinostock p. 387 (bottom right), Le Do p. 19, Elenathewise pgs. 228, 416, 462, ExQuisine p. 249, eyewave p. 193, Flashon Studio p. 411, Joy Fera pgs. 62, 326, Foodlovers pgs. 114, 420, fotogal p. 218, Ekaterina Fribus p. 315, Ieva Geneviciene p. 284, GoodMood photo p. 285, Mau Horng pgs. 58, 246, Ovidiu Iordachi p. 351, Irochka p. 51, Denis Istomin p. 192, iTake Images p. x (bottom) Joss pgs. 188, 419, Juice Images p. 342, kix p. 153, Ivan Kmit p. 293, Artyom Komelknov p. 8, KT89 p. 336, Lamax p. 217 (bottom), Olga Lyubkina p. 423, Marek p. 50, Alix Marina p. 377, mirrormere p. 408, Elena Moiseeva p. 133,

Noam p. 240, pegasosart p. 217 (top), Uros Petrovic p. 360, quayside p. 205, Laurent Renault p. 220, rimglow p. 154, robynmac pgs. ix (left), 39, 409, Yves Roland p. 60, Elzbieta Sekowska p. 254, L.Shat p. 230, Alex Starosltsev p. 11, Bojan Stepancic p. 78, Stocksnapper p. 337, surabhi25 p. 162, thierryH p. 204, Unclesam p. 46, Simone van den Berg p. 379, Viktor p. 406, Vitas p. 17, volff p. 59, Martine Wagner p. 104, Yassonya p. 395; Getty Images: Clive Champion-Champion Photography Ltd. p. 279, Eric Futran-Chefshots p. 160; istockphoto p. 345.

Logos Courtesy American Grassfed Association p.112 (top right); Courtesy American Humane Association p.113; Courtesy Animal Welfare Institute p. 376 (top left); Courtesy EPA and U.S. Department of Energy p. 434; Courtesy Transfair USA p. 327 (left); Courtesy Forest Stewardship Council p. 435; Courtesy Humane Farm Animal Care pgs.112 (bottom right), 376 (bottom left); Courtesy Marine Stewardship Council p. 144; Courtesy Rainforest Alliance p. 327 (middle bottom); Courtesy Smithsonian Migratory Bird Center p. 327 (right); Courtesy United States Department of Agriculture pgs. 47 (bottom), 112 (left), 327 (middle top), 367, 376 (top right).

Meet the Author and Her Team

Myra Goodman cofounded Earthbound Farm in 1984 with her husband, Drew. The company has become the largest grower of organic produce in the country, and has received numerous awards for their sustainability initiatives. Myra's cooking has always been inspired by fresh organic produce, and she is the author of the popular cookbook *Food to Live By*. Myra started Earthbound Farm's farm stand in 1992, and opened its certified organic café in 2003.

Pamela McKinstry ran three restaurants on Nantucket Island and served as an organizer, guide, and chef for safaris in the African bush. Currently Pam is a consulting chef for Earthbound Farm and an inspector for California Certified Organic Farmers (CCOF). She collaborated with Myra Goodman on Myra's first cookbook, *Food to Live By*.

Sarah LaCasse has worked as a restaurant chef, private chef, and caterer. Currently the Executive Chef for Earthbound Farm, some of Sarah's recipes also appear in *Food to Live By*.

Ronni Sweet is a California writer who has worked on many projects (including the introduction to *Food to Live By*) with Myra Goodman and Earthbound Farm since 1999.

From left to right: Sarah, Ronni, Myra, and Pamela.